PAUL C. BRAGG N.D., Ph.D.

Life Extension Specialist • W
Lecturer and Advisor to Olympic A

Originator of Health Food Sto

For almost a Century, Livi...
"Health and Fitness Way of Life" Works Wonders!

Paul C Bragg is the Father of the Health Movement in America. This dynamic Crusader for worldwide health and fitness is responsible for more "firsts" in the history of Health than any other individual. Here are a few of his incredible health pioneering achievements that the world now enjoys:

★ Bragg originated, named and opened the first "Health Food Store" in America.

★ Bragg Crusades pioneered the first Health Lectures throughout America, inspiring followers to open health stores in cities across the land and now world-wide.

★ Bragg introduced pineapple juice and tomato juice to the American public.

★ He was the first to introduce and distribute honey nationwide.

★ He introduced Juice Therapy in America by importing the first hand-juicers.

★ Bragg pioneered Radio Health Programs from Hollywood three times daily.

★ Paul and Patricia pioneered a Health TV show from Hollywood to spread Health and Happiness . . . the name of the show! It included exercises, health recipes, visual demonstrations, and guest appearances of famous. health-minded people.

★ He created the first health foods and products and made them available nationwide: herb teas, health beverages, seven-grain cereals and crackers, health cosmetics, health candies, vitamin and mineral supplements, wheat germ, digestive enzymes from papaya, kelp & herb seasonings, amino acids from soybeans. He inspired others to follow and now thousands of health items are available worldwide.

★ He opened the first health restaurants and the first health spas in America.

Crippled by TB as a teenager, Bragg developed his own eating, breathing. and exercising program to rebuild his body into an ageless, tireless, painfree citadel of glowing, radiant health. He excelled in running, swimming, biking. progressive weight training, and mountain climbing. He made an early pledge to God, in return for his renewed health, to spend the rest of his life showing others the road to health... Paul Bragg made good his pledge!

A living legend and beloved counselor to millions, Bragg was the inspiration and personal advisor on diet and fitness to top Olympic Stars from 4-time swimming Gold Medalist Murray Rose to 3-time track Gold Medalist Betty Cuthbert of Australia, his relative Don Bragg (pole-vaulting Gold Medalist). and countless others. Jack LaLanne, "the original TV's King or Fitness," says. "Bragg saved my life at age 14 when I attended the Bragg Crusade in Oakland. California." From the earliest days. Bragg was advisor to the greatest Hollywood Stars, and to giants of American Business. Gloria Swanson, J.C Penney, Del E. Webb, and Conrad Hilton are just a few that he inspired to long, successful, healthy. active lives!

Dr. Bragg changed the lives or millions worldwide in all walks of life... through his Health Crusades, Books, Tapes, and Radio, TV, and personal appearances.

Health Science - Box 7, Santa Barbara, California 93102 U.S.A.

PAUL C. BRAGG, N.D., Ph.D.
LIFE EXTENSION SPECIALIST
JOIN THE FUN AT THE BRAGG "LONGER LIFE, HEALTH & HAPPINESS CLUB" WHEN YOU VISIT HAWAII – IT'S FREE!

Paul C. Bragg, daughter Patricia and their wonderful healthy members of the Bragg "Longer Life, Health and Happiness Club" exercise daily at the beautiful Fort DeRussy lawn, at the world famous Waikiki Beach in Honolulu, Hawaii. Membership is free and open to everyone who wishes to attend any morning – Monday through Saturday, from 9:00 to 10:30 a.m. for deep breathing, exercising, meditation, group singing. And on Saturday, after the class – health lectures on how to live a long, healthy life! The group averages 75 to 125 per day, according to the seasons. From December to March it can go up to 200. When away lecturing, their dedicated leaders carry on until their return. Thousands have visited the club from around the world and then carry the message of health and fitness to friends and relatives back home. Patricia extends an invitation to you and your friends to join the club for wholesome, healthy fellowship . . . when you visit Honolulu, Hawaii. Be sure also to visit the outer Hawaiian Islands (Maui, Kauai, Hawaii, Molakai) for a fulfilling, healthy vacation.

To maintain good health the body must be exercised properly (walking, jogging, running, biking, swimming, deep breathing, good posture, etc.) and nourished wisely (natural foods), so as to provide and increase the good life of radiant health, joy and happiness.   *- Paul C. Bragg*

BRAGG
GOURMET
HEALTH
RECIPES

For Life Extension & Vital, Healthy Living to 120!

By
PAUL C. BRAGG, ND., PH.D.
LIFE EXTENSION SPECIALIST
and
PATRICIA BRAGG, ND., PH.D.
LIFE EXTENSION NUTRITIONIST

Health   *Peace*

Happiness   *Youthfulness*

Love   *Joy*

Praise   *Patience*

Vitality   *Fortitude*

Strength   *Charity*

Faith

<u>JOIN</u>

The Bragg Crusades for a 100% Healthy, Better World for All!

HEALTH SCIENCE
Box 7, Santa Barbara, California 93102 U.S.A.

Bragg
GOURMET HEALTH RECIPES

**For Life Extension & Vital,
Healthy Living to 120!**

Genesis 6:3

By
PAUL C. BRAGG, N.D., Ph.D.
LIFE EXTENSION SPECIALIST
and
PATRICIA BRAGG, N.D., Ph.D.
LIFE EXTENSION NUTRITIONIST

- REVISED -
Copyright © Health Science

Eighteenth printing MCMXCII
ISBN: 0-87790-031-0

Published in the United States by
HEALTH SCIENCE - Box 7, Santa Barbara, Calif. 93102, USA

Paul C. Bragg and daughter Patricia

LIFE'S GREATEST TREASURE IS RADIANT HEALTH

Paul C. Bragg and daughter Patricia say, "There is no substitute for Health! Those who possess it are richer than kings."

WHY WE WROTE THIS BOOK

My father, Paul C. Bragg, and I have lived exclusively on Natural Foods . . . scientifically and tastefully prepared, as shown in this Health Food Cook Book. Many of these recipes have been in our family for four generations . . . many more have been gathered during our research travels and lecture tours throughout the world.

Because we want you to share the Superior State of Radiant Health . . . with an Abundance of Vitality and Energy . . . that we have always enjoyed, we have compiled this book for you.

Remember, whoever prepares the family's meals . . . holds the health . . . and therefore most of the happiness . . . of all members of the family in his/her hands. Careful selection of the ingredients . . . correct preparation . . . delicate blending of flavors . . . serving with eye appeal as well as aroma and taste . . . all of these are equally important in leading you and your loved ones on the Glorious Road to Health!

Here is your guide. Follow it! Eat well and stay well! You and yours will look and feel younger than your calendar years.

Remember, when you are Healthy . . . you are Happy.

Paul C. Bragg　　　*Patricia Bragg*

BRAGG CRUSADES 1990s
Teaching People World-Wide To Live
Healthier, Stronger Lives For A Better World

We love sharing, teaching & giving and you can share this love by being part of Bragg Crusades World-Wide Outreach. Bragg Crusades is dedicated to helping others. We feel blessed when your life improves from our teachings in the Bragg Books & Crusades. It makes our years of service so worthwhile!

The Miracle of Fasting book has been the No. 1 book for 8 years now in underground Russia. Why? Because we show them how to live a good, wholesome life ... easy to understand and so easy to follow and it costs less money. Most healthful lifestyle habits are free. We are continuing with all our teachings, lectures, Crusades, radio, TV and video outreaches.

My joy & priorities come from God & healthy living. I'm excited about spreading health world-wide, it's needed more than ever. My father and I were TV Health Pioneers, with our program "Health & Happiness" filmed in Hollywood. It's thrilling to be a Health Crusader & you will enjoy it also.

By reading the Bragg Self-Health Books you can also gain a new confidence that you are helping yourself, family & friends to Healthy Principles of Living! Please call your local health store & book store & ask for the Bragg Books. We hope to have all the stores stock the Bragg Books so they will be available to all.

I have visions of Health Retreats where people can find radiant health, joy & rebirth! They will be **Recharging - Physically, Mentally, Emotionally & Spiritually.** I was reared on Retreats ... holidays & vacations were at Retreat Camp for precious weeks of growth & recharge. You'll love them, too!

We are planning Bragg Recharge Retreats for the 1990s and are just waiting for the right locations and funding. We can accept all gifts, monetary and land (appraised value), and we can give a receipt for tax deductions. We could develop seldom-used ranches, farms and old estates into Recharge Centers for everyone to rejuvenate their mind, body and soul, and then spread health worldwide. Those who would like to be part of Bragg Health Crusades, please write to me.

We are not new to Retreats ... my Dad pioneered the first health spa (MacFadden's Deauville) years ago in Miami Beach & others in Highland Springs, California & Danville, New York.

I expend all my energy & funds helping others to help themselves! Genuine love seeks ways to express itself! I thank you for your love & support. For with your help we can achieve our goals for the 1990s. I know God will bless you. Your needed help will be a blessing to the Bragg Crusades. Our 1990s budget is for a mighty worthwhile cause. I know you, your family & friends will enjoy and benefit from the teachings & retreats.

With a Loving, Grateful Heart,

Patricia Bragg

BRAGG CRUSADES, America's Health Pioneers
Over 75 continuous years spreading health and fitness worlwide
7340 Hollister Ave., Santa Barbara, CA 93117 U.S.A.
A non-profit charitable organization. Gifts are tax deductible

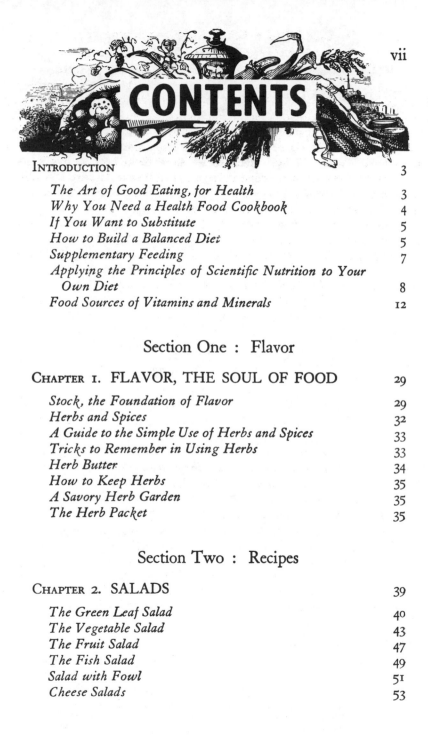

CONTENTS

◇◇◇

◇◇

Section Three : Special-Purpose Diets

Slow Me Down, Lord

Slow me down, Lord

Ease the pounding of my heart by the quieting of my mind.

Steady my hurried pace with a vision of the eternal reach of time.

Give me, amid the confusion of the day, the calmness of the everlasting hills.

Break the tensions of my nerves and muscles with the soothing music of the singing streams that live in my memory. Help me to know the magical, restoring power of sleep.

Teach me the art of taking minute vacations—of slowing down to look at a flower, to chat with a friend, to pat a dog, to read a few lines from a good book.

Slow me down, Lord, and inspire me to send my roots deep into the soil of lifes enduring values that I may grow toward the stars of my greater destiny.

Your Daily Habits Form Your Future

Habits can be right or wrong, good or bad, healthy or unhealthy, rewarding or unrewarding, powerful for good, or powerful for bad. The right or wrong habits, decisions, actions, words and deeds . . . are up to you! Wisely choose your habits, as they can make or break you!

I love sharing our nuggets of wisdom with you - Patricia Bragg

Jack LaLanne, Patricia Bragg, Elaine LaLanne & Paul Bragg

Jack says, "Bragg saved my life at age 14 when I attended the Bragg Health & Fitness Lecture in Oakland, California." From that day on, Jack has lived the health life and teaches Health & Fitness to millions.

FOOD FOR THOUGHT

Now good digestion waits on appetite, and health on both. — Shakespeare

We live not upon what we eat, but upon what we digest. — Abernethy

Almost every human malady is connected, either by highway or byway, with the stomach. — Sir Francis Head

It is a well-established fact that a leg of mutton caused a revolution in the affairs of Europe. Just before the battle of Leipsic, Napoleon the Great insisted on dining on boiled mutton, although his physicians warned him that it would disagree with him. The emperor's brain resented the liberty taken with its colleague, the stomach; the monarch's equilibrium was overturned, the battle lost, and a new page opened in history.

The kitchen [that is, your stomach] being out of order, the garret [the head] cannot be right, and every room in the house becomes affected. Remedy the evil in the kitchen, and all will be right in parlor and chamber. If you put improper food into the stomach, you play the mischief with it, and with the whole machine besides. — Abernethy

Cattle know when to go home from grazing, but a foolish man never knows his stomach's measures. — Scandinavian Probert

Simplicity of diet is the characteristic of the dwellers in the Orient. According to Niebuhr, the sheik of the desert wants only a dish of pillau, or boiled rice, which he eats without fork or spoon. Notwithstanding their frugal fare, these sons of the desert are among the most hardy and enduring of all members of the human family. A traveler tells of seeing one of them run up to the top of the tallest pyramid and back in six minutes.

One fourth of what we eat keeps us, and the other three fourths we keep at the peril of our lives. — Abernethy

Bad cooking diminishes happiness and shortens life. — Wisdom of Ages

Says Mrs. Partington: "Many a fair home has been desiccated by poor cooking, and a man's table has been the rock on which his happiness has split."

Introduction

The Art of
Good Eating, for Health

for the whole family

THE person you are today, the person you will be tomorrow, next week, next month, ten years from now—depends on what you eat. You are the sum total of the food you consume. How you look, how you feel, how you carry your years, all depend on what you eat.

Every part of your body is made from food—the hair on top of your head, your eyes, teeth, bone, blood, and flesh. Even your expression is formed from what you eat, because the healthy man is a well-fed, happy man.

Today, because of economic necessity, our markets are surfeited with dead, soft, demineralized foods. We have milled the life out of our grains, the vitamins and minerals out of many of our foods; and processing and preservatives have killed off some of our most valuable food factors.

If you do not put the basic minerals and vitamins into your body, some day you are going to face a serious deficiency disease. You cannot get away from it: it is the law of biochemistry. And yet for many years the so-called "Health foods" have been looked upon as unappetizing, tasteless, uninteresting dishes. If properly prepared, "Health foods" are the most delicious in all the world. They are the true essence of fine cooking.

Our foods should mean physical restoration, sensual enjoyment tempered with intelligence, and the keen enjoyment of true mental relaxation. It is not what we eat that feeds the body; it is what we digest. And digestion depends in a great measure on enjoyment.

Flavoring must be discreet, must present itself subtly while the appreciative eater is unaware. The intangible sense of pleased discovery and the enjoyment of unexpected, harmonious blending of subdued flavors add much to the rhythmic functioning of the physical processes of the body. Food that announces its presence with impressive blasts of flavor may be nutritionally good, but still not good cookery. Both are important.

Basically, your food must contrive to fill your physical needs, but it cannot do so completely unless it gives stimulation to the appetite and delight in eating, and leaves a feeling of contented satisfaction that makes for better digestion. Remember food is your body's fuel!

Moderation is intimately tied to the art of good eating. Excesses dull the appetite and appreciation. No food remains a "good" food when overindulgence governs the appetite, making you sluggish!

Nutritional Science alone is not enough. It must be blended with inspiration, art, and imagination. For those who have never learned to blend science and art in their everyday eating, this book is written with the hope that it will guide them firmly onto the path of good living with healthy food . . . for a long, healthy, happy, fulfilled life!

Why You Need a Health Food Cookbook

In Health Food Cookery white flour and white sugar are not used, nor processed, devitalized, degerminated, demineralized foods. We use the whole grain, containing all the life element, and the natural sweetenings instead of the over-refined white sugar. That is why cooking with whole natural foods requires special proportions, ingredients and directions.

On the whole you will find cooking with natural whole-grain flours and natural sweetenings well worth the trouble; and bringing out the "soul" of foods with natural herbs and spices is a tremendous thrill and adventure for the uninitiated.

Most of the good, wholesome natural foods you need for these recipes can be found in Health Food Stores and Wholefood Supermarkets. Many of these stores have everything from organically grown fruits and vegetables, organic meats, poultry, fertile eggs to 100% whole-grains, their flours, pastas and cereals, vitamin and mineral supplements, natural sweeteners, fresh juices and delicious natural beverages; unsulphured, sun-dried fruit and thousands of other health products. My father, Paul C. Bragg originated Health Food Stores and today they are playing a major part in American's Health!

Almost any recipe prepared with dead, demineralized, devitaminized ingredients can be made 100% better with healthful, wholesome foods. As you learn to prepare foods the Bragg Healthy Lifestyle way you may begin adjusting these recipes to your individual taste. Following are some healthy, wholesome substitutions.

HEALTHY RECIPE SUBSTITUTES

The best food is natural, unprocessed and when preparing these recipes you can adjust the amount of natural sweetening, seasonings, proportions, etc., up or down to your own tastes! Not all the foods listed for substitution are "bad" foods.

BAKING POWDER , SODA & YEAST: Use Health Food Store, non-aluminum baking powders only: Rumford, Featherweight and Cellu. Try quick rise dry yeast instead of compressed yeast cakes.

CHOCOLATE: Carob is a perfect nutritious substitute.

CORNSTARCH: (for thickening): Arrowroot, instant Tapioca, Agar Agar for baking & desserts. Potato flour for gravies, soups, stews, etc.

COFFEE, CHINA TEA: Herbal & Grain Coffee Substitutes, Ovaltine, Herbal Teas, Unsweetened Fruit Juices—fresh are best.

COW'S MILK: Soy Milks (variety available), Nut Milks (almond, etc.) If Dairy: Raw Certified Cows & Goat Milk products are best, salt-free Raw Butter, Kefirs, Yogurts, etc. Over-processed milk is dead!

MEAT: Soybeans, Tofu (soybean curd), Tempeh, Beans, Cereals, Fertile Eggs, Natural Cheeses, Sprouts, Raw Nuts & Seeds, etc. See back pages to order our Gourmet Vegetarian Recipe Book.

SALT: Herbs, Garlic, Kelp, Brewer's Yeast Flakes, Bragg Liquid Aminos (from sodium rich soybeans) are delicious seasonings.

SHORTENING: Never use hardened lards or commercial oils. Use un-refined natural, cold-pressed (expeller) oils (olive, safflower, sunflower, soy, canola, sesame, etc.). In baking I often use salt-free butter.

VINEGAR: Use only Apple Cider Vinegar—raw is best when available. You may use fresh lemon or lime juice as substitute. Read Bragg Apple Cider Vinegar Book for more info—see back pages for ordering.

WHITE FLOURS: Use only 100% Whole Grain and their Pastry Flour for Pastries. Use 20% more moisture with Whole-Grain Flours due to Bran & Wheat Germ. Use 10% less shortening (butter, oil).

WHITE SUGAR: Adjust all natural sweeteners to your taste. When preparing recipes Raw Honey is best. For every cup of sugar, substitute 1/2 cup honey. After Honey, use Barley Malt or Brown Rice Syrups-2tsp. to 1 cup honey. Concentrated Fruit Juices, 100% Maple Syrup, Molasses, Date or Raw Brown Sugars. As you live the "Bragg Healthy Lifestyle" you will enjoy fresh fruits instead of sweets.

How to Build a Balanced Diet

In planning meals . . . check off these items on the fingers of your hand to see if you are eating a well-balanced combination nutritionally. Healthy food is your key to health and longevity!

1. One fifth of your diet should be vegetarian or animal protein, one of the most important food elements. Proteins are available in animal forms — meat, fish, fowl, milk, cheese and eggs — and non-animal forms — beans, raw nuts & seeds, cereals and sprouts are very high in protein. Our favorite is healthy vegetarian protein. Protein is your

—flesh, muscle, blood, heart, bones, skin, hair, and components of the body, all are essentially composed of protein. You are literally *built* of protein. The basic function of your entire body, that of converting food into living tissue, is one of the miracles of life itself. Your life processes, the factors that help you resist disease— all are composed of protein, of amino acids.

Every time you move a muscle, every time you breathe, you consume protein—amino acids. Without them you would be a

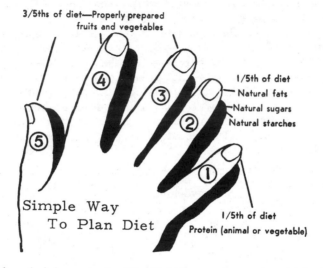

3/5ths of diet—Properly prepared
fruits and vegetables

1/5th of diet
Natural fats
Natural sugars
Natural starches

④ ③ ② ⑤ ①

Simple Way
To Plan Diet

1/5th of diet
Protein (animal or vegetable)

hopeless, helpless cripple. The link between protein and body tissue is the amino acids. When the aminos enter the blood stream, they are carried to every part of the body, where they set to work repairing, rebuilding, and maintaining body tissue, building up rich red blood, and "conditioning" the various body organs.

2. One fifth of your diet should be split three ways among fats, starches, and sugars. Fat is a source of energy in the diet. It has more than twice the energy value of the same amount of carbohydrates (sugars and starches) or protein, so it follows that those who wish to reduce should reduce the fat content of their diet, and those who wish to gain should increase it. But even if you are on a reducing diet, there should always be some fat in the menu because it plays an important part in the body.

Stored in the body, fat provides a source of heat and energy, and the accumulation of a certain amount of fat around the vital organs, such as the kidneys, gives great protection against cold and injury. Fat also has a function in the body cells, and certain kinds of fat, which are called unsaturated fatty acids, are needed in small amounts in the diet. Without them there is a roughness or scaliness of the skin. Fats have another all-important function: they carry the fat-soluble vitamins A, D, E, and K in the body.

Starches and Sugars. Starches and sugars come under one classification in the diet—carbohydrates. They also furnish energy. They are the preferred food for muscular work and physical activity. In addition to their energy value, carbohydrates appear to regulate the internal secretion of the glands.

3, 4, and *5.* Vegetables and fruits, both raw in salads and properly cooked, are among the protective foods and should represent three fifths of the diet. These foods not only contribute vitamins and minerals to the diet but add bulk required for proper body functioning. They also help maintain the alkaline reserve of the body. They add variety, color, flavor, and texture to the diet.

Supplementary Feeding

If we were living strictly according to nature's plan, we should not need supplementary vitamins, minerals, or amino acids. If we were able to get meat from animals that had been fed on highly mineralized and vitaminized feed or foraged in rich, fertile pastures, if we were able to obtain vegetables and fruits fresh from highly mineralized and vitaminized virgin soil, our problems would be simple. But today, through means of mass distribution, we get our foods after they have been long in storage. Many of them have lost their high vitamin and mineral content. Many of them have never had a high vitamin and mineral content to lose because they were not grown in rich virgin soil or fed on foods that came from this rich soil. Thus our eggs, our milk, our grains, and other foods are not always what they should be, even though we get them in sufficient quantities and prepare them properly. For that reason, supplementary feeding has come into great prominence.

You can obtain fine vitamin and mineral supplements at your Health food store. You can make sure you are getting your standardized amounts of vitamins A, B, C, D, E, calcium, iodine, phosphorus, and iron. These supplementary foods are no substitute for an adequate diet, but they are one way of making certain that your diet is supplemented adequately so that you do not fall prey to vitamin or mineral deficiencies.

The Principles of Scientific Nutrition

It is only in recent years that the practice of dietetics has been guided by the modern science of nutrition. Many diet kitchens and diet lists are still dominated by traditions and fads. Many so-called "special diets" are needlessly complex, unscientific and often, if continued over a long time, positively dangerous because of a nutritional unbalance that brings about deficiency conditions. Too often they tend toward the correction of only one particular difficulty and completely ignore the interrelation of ample quantities of essential foods for normal nutrition of the entire body. Common sense must be used in treating special conditions.

The Alkaline or Acid Effect of Food

Foods, such as meat and eggs, that are rich in proteins tend to exert an acid effect in the body, because when they are" burned" in the body a number of the normal" end products" are acidic, such as uric acid, sulfuric acid and phosphoric acid. But these acids are rendered harmless when they are balanced with alkaline material from the body, as they then form neutral salts. The neutral salts are eliminated normally by the kidneys.

Fruits and vegetables usually exert an alkaline effect because they contain the alkaline salts, such as calcium and neutralize the acid products in the body. When we do eat the fruits and vegetables with free acids such as citric (in lemons), malic (in apples), tartaric (in grapes) and lactic (in sauerkraut), the body "burns" them up and converts them to carbonic acid, which is easily eliminated in the breath. The body is protected by "buffers" in the blood so it is not subject to sudden changes in its normally slight alkaline reaction.

It is hard for the body to "burn" up oxalic acid such as is present in rhubarb, chard, kale and cocoa (chocolate), so when these foods are eaten a liberal supply of natural calcium from other sources, such as mustard greens, asparagus, cabbage, tofu, figs and prunes should be provided.

A normal healthy body is equipped to utilize efficiently the healthy foods eaten regardless of its alkaline or acid property. Especially when you add Apple Cider Vinegar to your salads and green vegetables. This makes for a healthy alkaline - acid balance.

"The use of Apple Cider Vinegar is a wonderful aid, and the #1 food I recommend in helping to maintain the acid-alkaline balance in the vegetarian and raw food diet. Everyone should read the Bragg *'Apple Cider Vinegar'* book."
  -Gabriel Cousens, M.D. Author of *"Conscious Eating"* & *"Spiritual Nutrition"*

How to Maintain the Mineral
and Vitamin Content

Avoid storage of perishable vegetables, particularly greens. Store vegetables, when necessary, in an atmosphere as cool as possible. Stored vegetables, even those not wilted, may have lost a large part of their vitamin C content.

Avoid trimming or paring vegetables or fruit before cooking, if possible, but if they must be handled in this manner, cook them as quickly as possible after exposing their surfaces.

Avoid blanching or boiling in excessive amounts of water that must be discarded later or concentrated. Minerals are indestructible, but like the water-soluble vitamins they are lost where cooking water is discarded. Use only a small amount of cooking water.

Never add baking soda to non-acid vegetables. It destroys the vitamin B_1 and vitamin C content.

Do not overcook. Most foods are easily digestible and of better color and flavor if cooked moderately tender. Heat is destructive to vitamin B_1.

Avoid cooking too large quantities at one time; reheating leftovers causes further vitamin loss. Serve all hot foods promptly.

Plunge foods into boiling water quickly whenever possible in the boiling process, rather than starting them in cold water. This avoids oxidation and conserves vitamins A and C.

Effect of Cooking Processes

Boiling. If the food is added to a small volume of actively boiling water and the water all retained, and overcooking avoided, the vitamins may be well conserved. . . .With slow heating from cold water, discarding of cooking waters containing soluble nutrients, boiling dry or nearly dry with air exposure, and unnecessarily long boiling, the vitamin losses . . . . particularly of ascorbic acid, may be high. (*Steaming* . . . is the most desirable process of cooking for vitamin retention.)

Baking or Roasting. The effect of these methods of cooking varies with the food. For best vitamin conservation, the baking or roasting should be stopped as soon as the food is well cooked; they are especially good for vegetables in the jackets. On the other hand, long roasting of meats, such as is necessary with pork, may cause a large loss of vitamin B_1.

Frying. Frying is a generally destructive process for vitamins sensitive to oxidation.

Broiling. The retention of vitamin and mineral content of foods is good during broiling, particularly if the operation is brief; it is superior to frying and is comparable to light roasting. But if the food is cut thin, permitting a large surface exposure, the vitamin loss may be comparatively high.

Steaming. Theoretically this is the most desirable process of cooking for vitamin retention.

Pressure Cooking. Carefully timed pressure cooking with a good atmosphere of steam is satisfactory, but if too much air remains at the start of cooking or if heating is prolonged, there may be heavy losses of both vitamins B_1 and C.

WE THANK THEE

For flowers that bloom about our feet;
　　For song of bird and hum of bee;
For all things fair we hear or see,
　　Father in heaven we thank Thee!
For blue of stream and blue of sky;
　　For pleasant shade of branches high;
For fragrant air and cooling breeze;
　　For beauty of the blooming trees,
Father in heaven, we thank Thee!
　　For mother-love and father-care,
For brothers strong and sisters fair;
　　For love at home and here each day;
For guidance lest we go astray,
　　Father in heaven, we thank Thee!
For this new morning with its light;
　　For rest and shelter of the night;
For health and food, for love and friends;
　　For every thing His goodness sends,
Father in heaven, we thank Thee!
　　　　　　　　　- *Ralph Waldo Emerson*

Food Sources of Vitamins and Minerals

Life cannot be maintained unless life be taken in, and this is best done by making at least 60 percent of your diet raw and cooked vegetables, with a plentiful supply of fresh juicy fruits.
— **Patricia Bragg**

*Food Sources of

	Vitamin A	Vitamin B₁	Vitamin B₂	Niacin
VEGETABLES				
Artichokes (globe)	fair	fair	fair	——
Asparagus	fair	fair	fair	——
Bamboo shoots	——	——	——	——
Beans, baked	——	fair	fair	——
Beans, dried	——	excellent	excellent	fair
Beans, green	fair	——	fair	——
Beans, dried lima	——	excellent	excellent	fair
Beans, green lima	fair	good	good	——
Beans, green kidney	fair	good	——	——
Beans, soy, dried	fair	excellent	excellent	fair
Beans, soy, green	fair	good	good	——
Beans, soy, sprouts	——	fair	fair	——
Beets	——	——	——	——
Beet greens	excellent	fair	good	——
Broccoli	excellent	fair	good	——
Brussels sprouts	fair	fair	——	——
Cabbage	——	fair	——	——
Carrots	excellent	——	——	——
Cauliflower	——	fair	fair	——
Celeriac (celery root)	——	——	——	——
Celery	——	——	——	——
Chard, leaves	excellent	——	fair	——
Chives	fair	fair	——	——
Collards	excellent	good	good	——
Corn, canned (yellow)	——	——	——	——
Corn, fresh (yellow)	fair	fair	fair	——
Cucumbers	——	——	——	——
Dandelion greens	excellent	good	good	——
Eggplant	——	——	——	——
Endive	excellent	fair	good	——
Escarole (chicory)	excellent	——	good	——
Garlic	——	fair	——	——
Horseradish	——	——	——	——

* Spaces left blank are either totally lacking, not determined, or very low in potency.

Vitamins and Minerals

	Vitamin C	Calcium	Phos-phorus	Iron	Copper
(continued)					
artichokes (globe)	good	——	fair	——	good
asparagus	excellent	——	fair	——	fair
bamboo shoots	fair	——	——	good	fair
beans, baked	——	fair	good	excellent	fair
beans, dried	excellent	good	excellent	——	excellent
beans, green	——	fair	——	excellent	fair
beans, dried lima	excellent	fair	excellent	fair	excellent
beans, green lima	excellent	fair	good	——	excellent
beans, green kidney	excellent	——	fair	excellent	excellent
beans, soy, dried	good	excellent	excellent	good	excellent
beans, soy, green	fair	fair	excellent	fair	——
beans, soy, sprouts	good	——	fair	——	——
beets	fair	——	——	good	fair
beet greens	excellent	fair	——	fair	——
broccoli	excellent	good	fair	fair	fair
brussels sprouts	excellent	——	good	——	fair
cabbage	excellent	——	——	——	——
carrots	——	fair	——	——	——
cauliflower	excellent	——	fair	——	fair
celeriac (celery root)	——	——	fair	——	fair
celery	fair	fair	——	——	——
chard, leaves	excellent	good	——	excellent	fair
chives	excellent	——	fair	fair	——
collards	excellent	excellent	fair	fair	——
corn, canned (yellow)	fair	——	fair	——	fair
corn, fresh (yellow)	good	——	good	——	——
cucumbers	good	——	——	——	——
dandelion greens	excellent	good	fair	good	fair
eggplant	good	——	——	——	fair
endive	good	good	——	fair	——
escarole (chicory)	fair	——	——	fair	fair
garlic	good	good	good	fair	good
horseradish	excellent	good	fair	fair	fair

The book that will benefit most is the one that inspires men to think and to act for themselves. —Elbert Hubbard

Food Sources of Vitamins

	Vitamin A	Vitamin B₁	Vitamin B₂	Niacin

	Vitamin A	Vitamin B_1	Vitamin B_2	Niacin
VEGETABLES				
Kale	excellent	fair	excellent	——
Kohlrabi	good	——	——	——
Lambs-quarters	excellent	——	——	——
Leeks	fair	fair	——	——
Lentils, dried	——	excellent	good	fair
Lettuce	fair	——	——	——
Marrow, vegetable	——	——	——	——
Mushrooms	——	fair	excellent	excellent
Mustard greens	excellent	fair	good	——
Okra	fair	fair	fair	——
Onions	——	——	——	——
Parsley	excellent	——	good	——
Parsnips	——	fair	——	——
Peas, dried	excellent	excellent	good	——
Peas, green	good	good	fair	fair
Peppers, green	excellent	——	fair	——
Potatoes, sweet	excellent	fair	——	——
Potatoes, white	——	fair	——	——
Pumpkins	good	——	——	——
Radishes	——	——	——	——
Rhubarb	——	——	——	——
Rutabagas	——	——	——	——
Salsify (oyster plant)	——	——	fair	——
Sauerkraut	——	——	——	——
Spinach	excellent	fair	——	——
Squash, summer	fair	——	good	——
Squash, winter	excellent	——	——	——
Tomatoes	good	——	——	——
Turnips	——	——	——	——
Turnip greens	excellent	good	good	——
Watercress	excellent	fair	good	——
Yams	——	——	——	——
FRUITS				
Apples	——	——	——	——
Apricots	excellent	——	——	——

and Minerals (*continued*)

	Vitamin C	Calcium	Phos-phorus	Iron	Copper
(*continued*)					
kale	excellent	good	fair	fair	excellent
kohlrabi	excellent	good	fair	——	fair
lambs-quarters	excellent	——	——	——	——
leeks	——	fair	fair	——	excellent
lentils, dried	good	good	excellent	excellent	excellent
lettuce	good	——	——	——	——
marrow, vegetable	good	——	——	——	——
mushrooms	fair	——	good	fair	excellent
mustard greens	excellent	excellent	——	fair	good
okra	excellent	fair	fair	——	fair
onions	good	——	——	——	——
parsley	excellent	——	——	good	fair
parsnips	excellent	fair	fair	——	fair
peas, dried	——	fair	excellent	excellent	excellent
peas, green	excellent	——	good	fair	fair
peppers, green	excellent	——	——	——	fair
potatoes, sweet	excellent	——	——	——	fair
potatoes, white	excellent	——	fair	——	fair
pumpkins	fair	——	fair	——	——
radishes	excellent	——	——	——	fair
rhubarb	good	——	——	——	——
rutabagas	excellent	fair	fair	——	fair
salsify (oyster plant)	fair	fair	fair	fair	fair
sauerkraut	fair	——	——	——	——
spinach	excellent	fair	fair	fair	fair
squash, summer	excellent	——	——	——	——
squash, winter	fair	——	——	——	——
tomatoes	excellent	——	——	——	——
turnips	excellent	fair	——	——	——
turnip greens	excellent	excellent	fair	good	——
watercress	excellent	good	——	good	——
yams	——	——	fair	fair	——
(*continued*)					
apples	fair	——	——	——	fair
apricots	good	——	——	good	fair

Food Sources of Vitamins

	Vitamin A	Vitamin B_1	Vitamin B_2	Niacin
FRUITS				
Avocados	——	fair	fair	——
Bananas	fair	——	——	——
Blackberries	——	——	——	——
Blueberries (huckleberries)	——	——	——	——
Cantaloupes	fair	——	——	——
Cherries	——	——	——	——
Cranberries	——	——	——	——
Currants	fair	——	fair	——
Dates, dried	——	——	fair	fair
Figs, dried	——	fair	fair	fair
Gooseberries	fair	fair	——	——
Grapefruit	——	——	——	——
Grapes	——	——	——	——
Guavas	——	fair	——	——
Honeydew melons	——	——	——	——
Lemons	——	——	——	——
Limes	——	——	——	——
Loganberries	——	——	——	——
Mangoes	fair	——	fair	——
Muskmelons	good	——	——	——
Nectarines	excellent	——	——	——
Olives, green	fair	——	——	——
Oranges	——	——	——	——
Papayas	excellent	——	fair	——
Peaches, yellow	fair	——	——	——
Pears	——	——	——	——
Persimmons	good	——	——	——
Pineapples	——	——	——	——
Plums	fair	fair	——	——
Pomegranates	——	——	fair	——
Prunes, dried	fair	fair	fair	——
Quinces	——	——	——	fair
Raisins	——	fair	fair	——
Raspberries, black	——	——	——	——
Raspberries, red	——	——	——	——

and Minerals (*continued*)

	Vitamin C	Calcium	Phos-phorus	Iron	Copper
(*continued*)					
avocados	good	——	——	——	fair
bananas	excellent	——	——	——	fair
blackberries	fair	——	——	——	fair
blueberries (huckleberries)	good	——	——	——	fair
cantaloupes	excellent	——	——	——	——
cherries	good	——	——	——	fair
cranberries	good	——	——	——	——
currants	excellent	fair	——	——	excellent
dates, dried	——	fair	fair	good	good
figs, dried	——	good	good	fair	good
gooseberries	excellent	——	fair	——	——
grapefruit	excellent	——	——	——	——
grapes	fair	——	——	——	——
guavas	excellent	——	——	——	——
honeydew melons	excellent	——	——	——	——
lemons	excellent	——	——	——	——
limes	excellent	fair	——	——	excellent
loganberries	excellent	——	——	fair	fair
mangoes	excellent	——	——	——	——
muskmelons	excellent	——	——	——	——
nectarines	excellent	——	——	——	——
olives, green	——	good	——	——	fair
oranges	excellent	——	——	——	——
papayas	excellent	——	——	——	——
peaches, yellow	fair	——	——	——	——
pears	fair	——	——	——	fair
persimmons	excellent	——	——	——	——
pineapples	excellent	——	——	——	——
plums	fair	——	——	——	fair
pomegranates	fair	——	good	——	——
prunes, dried	——	fair	good	fair	excellent
quinces	fair	——	——	fair	fair
raisins	——	fair	good	excellent	fair
raspberries, black	excellent	——	fair	——	fair
raspberries, red	excellent	——	——	——	fair

Food Sources of Vitamins

	Vitamin A	Vitamin B₁	Vitamin B₂	Niacin
FRUITS				
Strawberries	——	——	——	——
Tangerines	fair	fair	——	——
Watermelons	fair	——	——	——
CEREALS				
Bread, rye	——	good	——	fair
Bread, white	——	——	——	——
Bread, whole-wheat	——	good	fair	good
Cookies (average)	——	——	——	——
Cornmeal, yellow	fair	good	fair	fair
Flour, buckwheat	——	good	——	fair
Flour, rye	——	good	——	——
Flour, soybean	——	excellent	good	fair
Flour, white	——	——	——	——
Flour, whole-wheat	——	excellent	good	excellent
Noodles, egg	——	fair	fair	fair
Oatmeal (rolled oats)	——	excellent	fair	——
Popcorn, popped	fair	——	——	——
Rice, brown	——	good	——	good
Rice, white	——	——	——	——
Wheat bran	——	excellent	good	excellent
Wheat germ	——	excellent	excellent	excellent
Wheat, whole	——	excellent	good	excellent
MEAT, FISH, & POULTRY				
Beef brains	——	fair	good	good
Beef, chuck	——	——	good	good
Beef heart (lean)	fair	excellent	excellent	excellent
Beef kidney	fair	good	excellent	excellent
Beef liver	excellent	good	excellent	excellent
Beef, loin	——	good	good	excellent
Beefsteak	——	good	good	excellent
Beef sweetbreads	——	excellent	excellent	fair
Beef tongue	——	good	good	excellent
Bluefish	——	——	good	fair

and Minerals (*continued*)

	Vitamin C	*Calcium*	*Phosphorus*	*Iron*	*Copper*
(*continued*)					
strawberries	excellent	——	——	——	——
tangerines	excellent	——	——	——	——
watermelons	fair	——	——	——	——
(*continued*)					
bread, rye	——	——	good	fair	fair
bread, white	——	fair	fair	——	fair
bread, whole-wheat	——	fair	excellent	good	excellent
cookies (average)	——	fair	fair	fair	——
cornmeal, yellow	——	——	excellent	fair	fair
flour, buckwheat	——	——	good	fair	excellent
flour, rye	——	——	excellent	fair	excellent
flour, soybean	——	excellent	excellent	excellent	excellent
flour, white	——	——	fair	——	——
flour, whole-wheat	——	——	excellent	good	excellent
noodles, egg	——	——	good	fair	——
oatmeal (rolled oats)	——	fair	excellent	good	excellent
popcorn, popped	——	——	——	fair	——
rice, brown	——	——	excellent	excellent	good
rice, white	——	——	fair	——	——
wheat bran	——	good	excellent	excellent	excellent
wheat germ	——	fair	excellent	excellent	excellent
wheat, whole	——	fair	excellent	excellent	excellent
(*continued*)					
beef brains	good	——	excellent	excellent	fair
beef, chuck	——	——	excellent	good	fair
beef heart (lean)	——	——	excellent	good	——
beef kidney	fair	——	good	excellent	fair
beef liver	excellent	——	excellent	excellent	excellent
beef, loin	——	——	excellent	good	fair
beefsteak	——	——	excellent	good	fair
beef sweetbreads	good	——	excellent	fair	——
beef tongue	good	——	excellent	excellent	——
bluefish	——	——	excellent	——	fair

Food Sources of Vitamins

	Vitamin A	Vitamin B₁	Vitamin B₂	Niacin
MEAT, FISH, & POULTRY				
Chicken	——	fair	fair	excellent
Clams	——	——	fair	——
Codfish	——	——	——	fair
Crabs	——	fair	good	fair
Duck	——	good	good	fair
Egg whites	——	——	good	——
Egg yolks	excellent	good	good	——
Eggs	fair	fair	good	——
Gelatin, dried	——	——	——	——
Goose	——	fair	——	fair
Haddock	——	fair	fair	——
Halibut	——	fair	fair	fair
Lamb chops	——	good	good	excellent
Lamb, leg	——	good	good	excellent
Lobster	——	fair	fair	——
Mackerel	——	fair	excellent	excellent
Oysters	——	good	good	——
Pork chops	——	excellent	good	excellent
Rabbit	——	——	——	excellent
Salmon	——	fair	good	excellent
Sardines in oil	——	——	good	good
Scallops	——	——	——	——
Shrimp	——	——	fair	——
Tripe	——	——	fair	fair
Tuna in oil	——	——	good	excellent
Turkey	——	fair	good	excellent
Veal chops	——	good	good	excellent
Veal cutlets	——	fair	good	excellent
Whitefish	——	——	——	——
NUTS				
Almonds	——	good	excellent	good
Brazil nuts	——	excellent	——	——
Butternuts	——	——	——	——
Cashews	——	fair	fair	——

and Minerals (*continued*)

	Vitamin C	Calcium	Phos-phorus	Iron	Copper
(*continued*)					
chicken	fair	——	excellent	good	good
clams	excellent	good	fair	excellent	——
codfish	——	——	good	——	excellent
crabs	good	——	good	excellent	excellent
duck	fair	——	excellent	fair	excellent
egg whites	——	——	——	——	——
egg yolks	——	——	excellent	excellent	excellent
eggs	——	fair	excellent	good	fair
gelatin, dried	——	excellent	excellent	——	——
goose	good	——	good	fair	good
haddock	——	——	good	——	fair
halibut	——	——	excellent	fair	fair
lamb chops	——	——	good	fair	excellent
lamb, leg	——	——	good	fair	excellent
lobster	fair	——	good	——	excellent
mackerel	——	——	excellent	fair	good
oysters	——	fair	good	excellent	excellent
pork chops	——	——	good	fair	good
rabbit	——	——	good	——	fair
salmon	fair	——	excellent	fair	fair
sardines in oil	——	excellent	excellent	fair	——
scallops	——	good	excellent	good	fair
shrimp	——	fair	excellent	fair	excellent
tripe	——	good	good	fair	——
tuna in oil	——	——	excellent	fair	excellent
turkey	——	——	excellent	excellent	fair
veal chops	——	——	excellent	good	fair
veal cutlets	——	——	excellent	good	fair
whitefish	——	——	excellent	——	fair
(*continued*)					
almonds	——	excellent	excellent	excellent	excellent
brazil nuts	——	good	excellent	excellent	excellent
butternuts	——	——	——	excellent	excellent
cashews	——	——	excellent	——	excellent

Food Sources of Vitamins

	Vitamin A	Vitamin B_1	Vitamin B_2	Niacin
NUTS				
Chestnuts, fresh	——	good	——	——
Coconut, dried	——	——	fair	——
Hazelnuts (filberts)	fair	excellent	——	——
Hickory	——	excellent	——	——
Peanuts	fair	good	excellent	excellent
Peanut butter	fair	good	good	excellent
Pecans	fair	excellent	good	——
Pistachios	——	——	——	——
Walnuts, black	——	good	——	——
Walnuts, English	——	good	good	——
BEVERAGES				
Apple juice	——	——	——	——
Cocoa, with milk	fair	——	good	——
Grape juice	——	——	——	——
Grapefruit juice	——	——	——	——
Lemonade, plain	——	——	——	——
Orange juice	——	——	——	——
Pineapple juice	——	——	——	——
Prune juice	fair	——	——	——
Raspberry juice	——	——	——	——
Sauerkraut juice	——	fair	——	——
Tomato juice	fair	——	——	——
DAIRY PRODUCTS				
Butter	good	fair	——	——
Buttermilk	——	——	fair	——
Cheese, American	good	——	good	——
Cheese, Cheddar	good	——	excellent	——
Cheese, cottage	——	——	good	——
Cheese, cream	good	——	fair	——
Cheese, Roquefort	excellent	——	good	——
Cheese, Swiss	excellent	——	good	——
Cream, sour	good	——	good	——
Cream, sweet	fair	——	good	——
Ice cream, vanilla	fair	——	fair	——

and Minerals (*continued*)

	Vitamin C	Calcium	Phos-phorus	Iron	Copper
(*continued*)					
chestnuts, fresh	fair	——	fair	excellent	excellent
coconut, dried	——	——	good	good	excellent
hazelnuts (filberts)	——	excellent	excellent	excellent	excellent
hickory	——	——	——	fair	excellent
peanuts	——	fair	excellent	fair	excellent
peanut butter	——	fair	excellent	fair	excellent
pecans	——	fair	excellent	fair	excellent
pistachios	——	——	——	excellent	excellent
walnuts, black	——	——	——	excellent	excellent
walnuts, English	——	fair	excellent	fair	excellent
(*continued*)					
apple juice	——	——	——	——	——
cocoa, with milk	——	good	good	——	fair
grape juice	fair	——	——	——	——
grapefruit juice	excellent	——	——	——	——
lemonade, plain	fair	——	——	——	fair
orange juice	excellent	——	——	——	——
pineapple juice	excellent	——	——	——	——
prune juice	fair	——	——	——	——
raspberry juice	good	——	——	——	——
sauerkraut juice	fair	——	——	——	——
tomato juice	excellent	——	——	——	——
(*continued*)					
butter	——	——	——	——	——
buttermilk	——	good	fair	——	——
cheese, American	——	excellent	excellent	fair	fair
cheese, Cheddar	——	excellent	excellent	fair	——
cheese, cottage	——	fair	excellent	——	——
cheese, cream	——	excellent	excellent	fair	——
cheese, Roquefort	——	excellent	excellent	——	——
cheese, Swiss	——	excellent	excellent	fair	fair
cream, sour	——	fair	fair	——	fair
cream, sweet	——	fair	fair	——	fair
ice cream, vanilla	——	good	good	——	——

Food Sources of Vitamins

	Vitamin A	Vitamin B₁	Vitamin B₂	Niacin
DAIRY PRODUCTS				
Milk, condensed (sweetened)	——	——	good	——
Milk, dried skim (defatted milk solids)	——	good	excellent	——
Milk, dried whole	good	good	excellent	——
Milk, evaporated	excellent	——	good	——
Milk, goat	good	——	——	——
Milk, human	excellent	——	——	——
Milk, skim	——	——	fair	——
Milk, whole (pasteurized)	fair	——	fair	——
Whey, dried	——	excellent	excellent	excellent
MISCELLANEOUS FOODS				
Cod-liver oil	excellent	——	——	——
Corn oil	——	——	——	——
Corn syrup	——	——	——	——
Honey	——	——	——	——
Maple syrup	——	——	——	——
Marmalade, orange	——	——	——	——
Molasses	——	——	fair	good
Olive oil	——	——	——	——
Sugar, brown	——	——	——	——
Yeast, fresh	——	excellent	excellent	excellent
Yeast, dried brewer's	——	excellent	excellent	excellent

Let food be your medicine, and medicine be your food. — **Hippocrates**

The more natural the food you eat, the more radiant health you will enjoy and you will be better able to promote the higher life of love and brotherhood.
— **Patricia Bragg**

and Minerals (*continued*)

	Vitamin C	Calcium	Phos-phorus	Iron	Copper
(*continued*)					
milk, condensed (sweetened)	——	excellent	excellent	——	——
milk, dried skim (de-fatted milk solids)	fair	excellent	excellent	good	excellent
milk, dried whole	fair	excellent	excellent	——	fair
milk, evaporated	——	excellent	excellent	——	fair
milk, goat	——	good	good	——	——
milk, human	fair	——	——	——	——
milk, skim	——	good	fair	——	——
milk, whole (pasteurized)	——	good	fair	——	——
whey, dried	——	excellent	excellent	——	——
(*continued*)					
cod-liver oil	——	——	——	excellent	——
corn oil	——	——	——	——	——
corn syrup	——	——	——	fair	——
honey	fair	——	——	——	fair
maple syrup	——	——	——	good	——
marmalade, orange	fair	——	——	——	fair
molasses	——	excellent	——	excellent	excellent
olive oil	——	——	——	——	——
sugar, brown	——	fair	——	fair	——
yeast, fresh	——	——	excellent	excellent	——
yeast, dried brewer's	——	good	excellent	excellent	excellent

God sends the food, man by refining and processing foods destroys its nutritional value. Eat only God's natural foods.—**Patricia Bragg**

"*To preserve health is a moral and religious duty, for health is the basis for all social virtues. We can no longer be useful when not well.*"
— **Dr. Samuel Johnson, Father of Dictionaries**

AVOID THESE PROCESSED, REFINED, HARMFUL FOODS

Once you realize the irreparable harm caused to your body by refined, chemicalized, deficient foods, it is not difficult to eat correctly. Simply eliminate these "killer" foods from your diet...and follow an eating plan which provides the basic, essential nourishment your body needs.

- Refined sugar or refined sugar products such as jams, jellies, preserves, marmalades, yogurts, ice cream, sherberts, Jello, cake, candy, cookies, chewing gum, soft drinks, pies, pastries, tapioca puddings, sugared fruit juices & fruits canned in sugar syrup.

- Salted foods, such as corn chips, salted crackers, salted nuts

- Catsup & mustard w/salt-sugar, Worchestershire sauce, pickles, olives

- White rice & pearled barley   • Fried & greasy foods

- Commercial, highly processed dry cereals such as corn flakes, etc.

- Saturated fats & hydrogenated oils...(heart enemies that clog bloodstream)

- Food which contains palm & cottonseed oil. Products labeled vegetable oil...find out what kind, before you use it.

- Oleo & margarines...(saturated fats & hydrogenated oils)

- Peanut butter that contains hydrogenated, hardened oils

- Coffee, decaffeinated coffee, China black tea & all alcoholic beverages

- Fresh pork & pork products   • Fried, fatty & greasy meats

- Smoked meats, such as ham, bacon & sausage, smoked fish

- Luncheon meats, such as hot dogs, salami, bologna, corned beef, pastrami & any packaged meats containing dangerous sodium nitrate or nitrite

- Dried fruits containing sulphur dioxide - a preservative

- Do not eat chickens that have been injected with stilbestrol, or fed with chicken feed that contains any drug

- Canned soups - read labels for sugar, starch, white, wheat flour & preservatives

- Food that contains benzoate of soda, salt, sugar, cream of tartar...& any additives, drugs or preservatives

- White flour products such as white bread, wheat-white bread, enriched flours, rye bread that has wheat-white flour in it, dumplings, biscuits, buns, gravy, noodles, pancakes, waffles, soda crackers, macaroni, spaghetti, pizza, ravioli, pies, pastries, cakes, cookies , prepared and commercial puddings, and ready-mix bakery products. (Health Stores have a huge variety of 100% whole grain products.)

- Day-old, cooked vegetables & potatoes, & pre-mixed old salads

FOOD AND PRODUCT SUMMARY

Today many of our foods are highly processed or refined, thus robbing them of essential nutrients, vitamins, minerals, and enzymes; many contain harmful and dangerous chemicals.

The research, findings, and experience of top nutritionists, physicians and dentists have led them to discover that devitalized foods are a major cause of poor health, illness, cancer and premature death. The enormous increase in the last seventy years in degenerative diseases such as heart disease, arthritis, and dental decay, would seem to substantiate this belief. Scientific research has shown most of these afflictions may be prevented; and others, when once established, may be arrested or in some cases even reversed through nutritional methods.

THESE STEPS ARE FOR SUPER HEALTH THROUGH HEALTHY, WHOLESOME, NATURAL FOOD

1. Serve foods in raw, original state, organically grown when possible – fresh fruits, vegetables, wholegrains, brown rice, beans, raw nuts & seeds.

2. PROTEIN

    a. Animal meat, including the variety meats — liver, kidney, brain, heart — poultry and sea food, suggest using sparingly. Cook meat as little as possible (bake, roast, wok, or broil) because protein is injured by prolonged high heat. (My Dad and I prefer a vegetarian diet.)

    b. Dairy products, eggs (fertile), unprocessed hard cheese, and certified raw milk. (Personally we do not use milk and only occasionally low-fat dairy by-products).

    c. The legumes, soy and all other beans . . . these are our favorites.

    d. Nuts and seeds, raw and unsalted.

3. Use FRUITS and VEGETABLES (organically grown without the use of poisonous chemical sprays and fertilizers, when possible). Ask your market to stock organic produce. Steam, bake, saute or wok vegetables with a minimum of distilled water, at low heat, for as short a time as possible. Use the vegetable liquid.

4. Use 100% WHOLEGRAIN CEREALS, BREADS, & FLOURS, they contain important B complex vitamins, vitamin E, minerals, & the important unsaturated fatty acids.

5. Use COLD-PROCESSED VEGETABLE OILS, OLIVE OIL, CANOLA and SESAME OIL, etc.... These are an excellent source of the healthy essential unsaturated fatty acids, but still use sparingly.

4 BRAGG BOOKS FOR PLANNING HEALTHY MEALS

These Books are a must reading for planning your Bragg Health Building Program. They are: • *Healthful Eating Without Confusion* • *Bragg's Health Gourmet Recipes For Vital Healthy Living* (448 pages) • *Bragg Vegetarian Health Gourmet Recipes* (sugar free, salt free, low fat) and the • *Bragg Health Sauerkraut (raw, salt free) Recipe Book* ... Learn why and how to make your own delicious sauerkraut – it's so healthy for you. See back pages for ordering.

BRAGG LIQUID AMINOS
ADDS DELICIOUS FLAVOR TO MANY OF THESE BRAGG RECIPES
Bragg liquid Aminos are used by these best-selling health authors:

• The Diamonds • John Robbins • Dr. McDougall M.D. • Dr. Klaper M.D.
• Ann Wigmore • Lindsay Wagner • Victor Kulvinskas

TASTE YOU'LL LOVE — NUTRITION YOU NEED!

Pure Soybeans and Pure Water Only:

- No Added Sodium
- No Coloring Agents
- No Preservatives
- Not Fermented
- No Chemicals
- No Additives
- No MSG

Dash or Spray BRAGG AMINOS For New Taste Delights On:

- Salads & Dressings   • Soups
- Veggies   • Rice & Beans
- Tofu   • Tempeh   • Meats
- Wok & Stir-frys   • Casseroles
- Potatoes   • Gravies & Sauces
- Macrobiotics   • Poultry
- Fish   • Popcorn

HOLLYWOOD GOURMETS USE
BRAGG AMINOS ON 2 NETWORK TV SHOWS

"The Home Show" guest Olivia Newton-John, actress and singer, uses Bragg's daily and showed recipes using it. Lindsay Wagner, actress and health advocate appearing on the "Regis and Kathie Lee Show," showed delicious gourmet recipes using Bragg Aminos.

Most Health Food Stores stock Bragg Liquid Aminos ... if they do not stock this wonderful product, ask the store manager to order it from their distributor for you. If there are no Health Stores in your area and Bragg Liquid Aminos are impossible to obtain, you may send for them directly from:

Live Food Products, Inc.
Box 7, Santa Barbara, CA 93102

For Bragg Liquid Aminos (16 oz) send $3.95 plus $3 shipping. For more ordering information, see order form on back pages.

Chapter 1

Flavor,
Soul of Food

ORDINARILY, Cook Books have a stereotyped sequence. First come the tables of measurement; then the soups, salads, etc. To my mind, no cookbook can start without flavor as a basis—and particularly no Health Food Cook Book. In cooking for Health, the pleasure of well-savored flavor is every bit as important as nutritional quality, as it makes mealtime more enjoyable and helps digestion.

Good cooking is the combination of two great fields of human experience - science and art. The science of food tells us what is good nutrition. The art of preparing food requires learning the art of flavor, using herbs, garlic and 100% whole, fresh, live foods.

Stock, the Foundation of Flavor

Flavor can only be as good as the stock on which it is based. Good stock, properly used, is the difference between excellent and mediocre cooking. When the stock (or consomme) is excellent, the creation of fine flavor is comparatively easy. When it is not, meals can taste flat and dull to the palate.

In foreign lands mention of stock in a Cook Book would be superfluous. But in our land it is a little-known and little-practiced principle of the basic art. There are several reasons for that: Unless a great deal can be prepared at a time, the cooking of stock is too time-consuming and expensive. If a great deal is prepared, it is difficult to keep for any length of time. You will find the simple procedure in the chapter on "Canning and Quick Freezing" (page 314). Although three quarts can be made at one time, some stock should be frozen in ice cube trays, when hardened transfer to freezer bags to use on an as-needed basis for small amounts. Place remaining stock in quart and pint jars.

A pressure cooker is a great time-saver in the preparation of

---

What sculpture is to a block of marble, education is to the soul.
—Addison, The Spectator

stocks. By using one, the cooking time can be divided by 10. This means that the recipe for "Meat Stock" below, which requires 16 cooking hours, can be reduced to about 1½ with a pressure cooker, and the "Chicken Stock" can be reduced from 8 hours to from ¾ to 1 hour cooking time.

There are many kinds of stock that the interested cook will learn to create with experience. Some of the variations are the "white consommés" for fowl, soups, and the base of white sauces; the "brown consommé or stock" (which in this book is called "meat stock"), the bases of brown sauces, gravies, and meat foundations; the "fish stocks"; and many others.

Here are the two most important stocks for the good Health food cook. Master these and then create your own repertoire.

Meat Stock

3 *lbs. beef (flesh and bone) Bones broken into small pieces. Any of the following may be used: shin of beef, shanks of beef, beef-marrow bones with meat attached, or any of beef meat-and-bone combination*

3 *lbs. veal (flesh and bone) Bones broken into small pieces. Use shin of veal or knuckle of veal.*

1 *lb. marrowbone Bones broken into small pieces*

⅓ *cup each diced celery, turnip, carrot, and minced onion*

3 *sprigs thyme or ½ teaspoon dried thyme*

3 *sprigs parsley*

½ *bay leaf*

4 *quarts water*

Remove meat from bones. Sprinkle bones with a little fat from the meat and brown thoroughly in the oven, turning repeatedly. Sauté celery, turnips, carrot, and minced onion in a little butter or vegetable oil. Put bones, vegetables, and herbs in a heavy soup pot with water and bring to a boil. As soon as it reaches a boil, remove scum and wipe the sides of the pot, removing any scum that may cling. Reduce to very low heat and allow to simmer gently with lid half on for about 12 hours. (At the 6-hour point add more water if necessary to keep the quantity to 4 quarts. Do this again at the 12-hour point.) Strain, cool, and remove fat, saving a little for browning meat. Set aside. Cut meat into large cubes. Brown in some of the fat left from bone stock. Drain off *all* fat. Add 2 cups of the prepared bone stock to the meat and allow to simmer very slowly in a covered pan for 1½ hours. Pour all remaining bone stock into the pan, bring to a boil. Reduce heat immediately and simmer with slowest possible fire until meat is well cooked. Strain again, cool, and remove fat.

Stock should never be salted, because it is never used in its original state. Either it is further reduced in combination with other ingredients or it is cooked with meat which may have been salted before combining with the stock. This recipe will make 3 quarts.

The Clarification of Stocks

A great point is made by master chefs in the clearing of the stock so that it will be transparent and the color of "fine burnt amber." This can easily be done by dropping a little egg white and eggshell into the stock, but I do not believe it is good Health food cookery. The egg white and shell draw to them some of the juices that have become coagulated by the heat. By removing these meat juices, you may make the stock more attractive to the eye, but you lose great nutritive value. I have never found that stock needed clarification in the finest of recipes. This is a case where eye-appeal is sacrificed for both flavor and nutrition

Chicken Stock

NOTE: Although this recipe may contain veal and turkey as well as chicken, the stock is referred to throughout the book as "Chicken Stock" for the sake of simplification.

6 *lbs. veal (flesh and bone) Bones broken into small pieces.*

1 *or 2 chicken or turkey skeletons (use all bony parts)*

6 *to 10 chicken feet (this is optional but adds very greatly to the richness of the stock)*

½ *cup diced carrots*
¼ *cup sliced onion*
¼ *cup leeks*
½ *cup diced celery*
2 *tablespoons minced parsley*
1 *bay leaf*
1 *sprig thyme*
1 *tablespoon Bragg Aminos*

Boil chicken feet very rapidly for five minutes. Remove. Hold in clean cloth in hand (to prevent burning hand) and slip off the horny scales. The nails can be easily removed by bending back. Remove meat from veal bones. Place veal bones, chicken bones, and chicken feet in heavy saucepan with 4¼ quarts of water (17 cups). Bring to boil rapidly, remove scum. Reduce to lowest possible heat and simmer gently for five hours. Add vegetables and herbs and more water if necessary to keep the quantity to 4 quarts. Cook very slowly and gently for another three hours. Strain, cool, and remove grease. This recipe will make 3 quarts.

Herbs and Spices

Among all of nature's great gifts to the human palate, none takes a more aristocratic place than the lowly herb. It is true the body can be nourished on good healthful food without flavoring of any kind. And yet good natural spices and piquant herb flavoring play a great role in stimulating digestion and contributing nutrition to the body.

For real adventure in food, one need not go to China, Borneo, Malaya, or Egypt. With a good stock of choice herbs on the pantry shelf, the wise cook can transform ordinary foods into exquisite delicacies. Dishes can be prepared that have come to us from far countries and far times and been translated into the true style of modern Health cookery. Herbs were the first medicine of man, and although they are a little-practiced art today, they still give hint of luscious feasts and dishes redolent of aromatic fragrances, and this is their real function. They are true vegetable substances with pungent quality, and belong very definitely in good nutritional cookery.

Few modern kitchens rely upon the old-fashioned herb garden, although fresh herbs are far more choice than dried. It is very seldom that the desired sprig of rosemary or sweet basil can be obtained from the vegetable market. I am going to tell you how to plant and grow a small kitchen herb garden; if you do not have the space nor the facilities for that, the only course left is to stock your pantry with a wide variety of dried herbs.

To be Used Sparingly

An abundance of herbs for your kitchen shelf does not mean that large quantities should be used in preparation of foods. Herbs should be used very cautiously. The hint of delicate flavor they impart is much better than a blatant combination of strong, predominant flavor. Don't overload your food with flavor. The finest herb cookery is that in which the herbs used remain a mystery. If the flavor is so strong and distinct that it can be detected instantly, the dish is not a success. Of course, there are several exceptions to this rule; special egg and chicken dishes require pronounced tarragon flavor, and where dill is used, it is not supposed to be subtle. But a good general rule for the experimenter is to use extreme caution to avoid over-flavoring.

The Use of Herbs and Spices

Nothing can be more unpleasant or confusing to the taste than the improper or unwise use of herbs and spices. Certain foods have marked affinities for particular herbs and spices that lift them out of the realm of amateur cookery. But use those same flavoring plants in other foods and there is a clash of temperament that screams with indignation.

On page 382 you will find a complete chart and guide for the proper combination of foods with "sweet" herbs, herb seeds and spices. This will be your most valuable guide in learning the magic touch that the finest gourmets cherish as their secret key to the art of delicious food. Consult this chart in the preparation of any food. You will find it conveniently arranged so that you may simply select the class of food desired, such as "Soups," and tell at a glance which herbs or combination of herbs will blend in harmony. Use this chart constantly until you become expert in the selection and tasteful blending of flavors.

To Remember in Using Herbs

Average Quantities. The warning to use herbs sparingly must again be emphasized. Always remember that herbs are an accent of refined charm. It is not always wise to follow exactly recipes calling for herbs. So much depends upon the strength of herbs. When you buy a new container of dried herbs, they are supposedly full strength. The longer you keep them on the shelf after you have broken the seal of the package, the weaker they become. Herbs of greater strength must obviously be used with more caution than the older, more exposed, weaker variety. A good guide, although one to be used with discretion, is to use about ½ teaspoon of dried herbs in a dish designed to serve 8 people, decreasing or increasing according to the number of desired servings. If you are fortunate enough to be able to use fresh herbs and your recipe is written in terms of the dried variety, substitute three or four times the amount. Fresh herbs may be reduced to terms of dried by taking approximately one fourth.

To Prevent Herb Specks in Food. Flecks of herbs can be very attractive in some dishes and undesirable in others. If you want to have the finished dish clear, use the herb packet; that is, tie the required herbs in a bit of cloth. The packet can be removed before serving.

To Use in Uncooked Food. Herbs should be placed in the liquid long in advance. It is sometimes best to let them stand overnight to obtain the full release of flavor. This is particularly true of fresh or canned vegetable juices.

To Use in Cooked Food. Herbs should be added only during the last hour of cooking unless the recipe calls for other treat‐ment.

Moistening Herbs. If herbs are to "kiss" the dish—that is, to be used for only a short time in preparation—they should be pre‐moistened. Do this by allowing them to stand for three fourths of an hour slightly moistened by water, a little oil, or a drop of milk. The herbs must not float in liquid, but simply be dampened. If time is short, the same effect of quicker flavor-releasing may be obtained by tying the herbs in a packet and dipping for a few seconds into boiling hot water and then into ice-cold water. Drain before using.

Herb Butter

Cooking with herb butter is an entire art in itself. It improves almost any vegetable, meat, fish, fowl, or egg dish. It should be used as a topping for vegetables, meats, fish, and game just shortly before serving. It is often used in the preparation of egg dishes or can be used simply as a topping. It is delightful for sandwiches, for toasted breads, or for addition to other sauces for unusual flavor-quality.

The basic proportions are ⅛ pound of butter to 1 tablespoon finely chopped fresh herbs or ½ teaspoon of dried herbs, and ¼ teaspoon lemon juice. Cream the butter, blend herb in well, and add lemon juice. Cream again thoroughly and let stand for several hours before using. If desired for topping for hot foods, melt before using. If to be used for sandwiches, toasts, or hot breads, use as a solid spread.

Almost any of the "sweet" herbs can be used, such as basil, thyme, chervil, rosemary, marjoram, chives, watercress, or any attractive combination. Dill and fennel are delicious with fish.

How to Keep Herbs

Although it is very desirable to have a large variety of herbs on your pantry shelf, do not buy them in large quantities. They don't improve with age. For the best effect they should be at their peak of flavor and aroma. And that means they should be as fresh as possible. They should be kept in small, air-tight containers. If you can't buy them that way, transfer them to small, tight jars or cans before you place them upon your condiment shelf. Do not expose them to air any longer than necessary. They should be opened only at the moment of using, and then immediately closed tightly. If when you open them they do not send out a fresh, strong aroma, they should be discarded and replaced with fresh herbs.

How to Grow a Savory Herb Garden

A kitchen herb garden with a full, fresh variety of growing flavor can be yours if you have a small plot of ground or space for a window box. You'll find full directions on page 394.

The Herb Packet

Certain herbs blend more desirably than others, and there are many combinations for different purposes. These combinations can be placed in little packets so that they are easily available to the busy housewife. These little packets are simply small cheese-cloth bags about the size of a nutmeg, tied with a string. One end of the string should be left about 3 or 4 inches long, and looped to make it easy to remove with a fork or cooking utensil at the precise moment the desired flavor of the dish is achieved. They can be tossed into the stew or other dish while it is cooking, and removed before serving. Here are several excellent combinations to prepare:

FOR MEAT
1. *A bay leaf. A few chives, chopped. Parsley.*
2. *Tender leaves of sweet basil, marjoram, and rosemary.*
3. *Thyme, summer savory, sweet basil, a few coriander seeds.*
4. *Chervil, rosemary, sage, savory.*
5. *Tarragon and basil.*

FOR FISH

1. Dill, fennel, tarragon
2. Sweet basil, bay leaf, chervil
3. Mint, chervil, fennel
4. Cilantro, basil, tarragon

FOR POULTRY

1. Basil, tarragon, thyme
2. Rosemary, tarragon, sage
3. Marjoram, chervil
4. Poultry seasoning (herbs)

FOR EGGS

1. Basil, chervil, rosemary
2. Marjoram, chervil, savory
3. Thyme, chervil, basil
4. Salad herbs

FOR SOUPS

1. Chervil, thyme, savory, bay leaf
2. Rosemary, bay leaf, marjoram
3. Basil, rosemary, savory
4. Italian herbs

Herbs combine nicely with any of the onion family: onions, garlic, chives and shallots. Very often a little lemon juice brings out the flavor of the herbs in blending.

WANTED - For Robbing Health & Life

KILLER Saturated Fats
CLOGGER Salt
DOPEY Caffeine
PLUGGER Frying Pan
DEATH-DEALER Drugs
JERKEY Turbulent Emotions
GREASY Overweight

CHOKER Hydrogenated Fats
DEADEYED Devitalized Foods
HARD (Inorganic Minerals)Water
CRAZY Alcohol
SMOKEY Tobacco
LOAFER Laziness
HOGGY Over-Eating

What Wise Men Say

Wisdom does not show itself so much in precept as in life -- a firmness of mind and mastery of appetite.   - Seneca

Govern well thy appetite, lest Sin surprise thee, & her black attendant Death.- Milton

Our prayers should be for a sound mind in a healthy body.   - Juvenal

Health is a blessing that money cannot buy.
                              - Izaak Walton

Health consists of temperance alone. - Pope

I saw few die of hunger... of eating, a hundred thousand.   - Ben Franklin

Let nature be your teacher.   - Wordsworth

The natural healing force within us is the greatest force in getting well.
          — Hippocrates, Father of Medicine

Of all the knowledge, that most worth having is knowledge about health. The first requisite of a good life is to be a healthy person.   —Herbert Spencer

Section Two: Recipes

PATRICIA BRAGG, Life Extension Nutritionist, enjoys her home in Santa Barbara, California, where she has organic gardens . . . including even delicious fruit-bearing banana trees.

Take time
for **12** things

1 **Take time to Work—**
   it is the price of success.

2 **Take time to Think—**
   it is the source of power.

3 **Take time to Play—**
   it is the secret of youth.

4 **Take time to Read—**
   it is the foundation of knowledge.

5 **Take time to Worship—**
   *it is the highway of reverance and washes the
   dust of earth from our eyes.*

6 **Take time to Help and Enjoy Friends—**
   it is the source of happiness.

7 **Take time to Love—**
   it is the one sacrament of life.

8 **Take time to Dream—**
   it hitches the soul to the stars.

9 **Take time to Laugh—**
   it is the singing that helps with life's loads.

10 **Take time for Beauty—**
   it is everywhere in nature.

11 **Take time for Health—**
   it is the true wealth and treasure of life.

12 **Take time to Plan—**
   *it is the secret of being able to have time to
   take time for the first eleven things.*

*From the Bragg home to your home we share our years of health
knowledge—years of living close to God and Nature and what joys of
fruitful, radiant living this produces—this my Father and I share
with you and your loved ones.*

With blessings for Health and Happiness,

Patricia Bragg

Chapter 2

Salads

Even in the early days of the cave man, some instinct led him to the search for vitamins in salad greens. But today we make the horrible mistake of concluding that only lettuce is salad. Oh, some more adventuresome cooks will go as far as romaine, and perhaps cabbage once in a while; but after that they have exhausted their full repertoire of salad-making.

Nature has almost as many variations of the salad leaf as she has variety in plant life. We as a nation have educated our grocers and vegetable stores into carrying only the more commonly accepted types of salad leaves, but it is possible in some markets to purchase the more delicious leaves, and perhaps also to grow a small garden of the delightful herb and salad leaves for your own kitchen.

Take the unique sorrel, fennel, and cresses. They are delectable salads in themselves. Then the escarole, dandelion greens, nasturtium leaves, the tender young leaves of the buckwheat, purslane, chicory, and the many, many varieties of lettuces and romaine, aside from the ordinary accepted ones.

We have many fascinating salads in our Health-food repertoire: the vegetable salad, fish salad, meat salad, and fruit salad; but the king of all salads is the green leaf salad and its blood brother, the wild, and cultivated, seasoning herb.

Do not cut your vegetables too fine, as the cut portions, when exposed to air, lose vitamin content. Serve as fresh and crisp as possible, not only from the standpoint of taste and appearance, but from the nutritional standpoint as well.

It is impossible to name the countless variations and combinations of greens and herbs in this book. But there are some very delicious recipes given here, and the good cook is always interested in experimenting and creating true adventures in delightful eating.

THE GREEN LEAF SALAD

Spring Salad Bowl

1 *large head lettuce*	1 *sliced cucumber*
½ *cup sliced radishes*	1 *clove garlic*
½ *cup sliced carrots*	3 *green onions, cut fine*
2 *large, ripe tomatoes*	

Rub salad bowl with garlic clove cut in half, until all the clove is rubbed into the bowl. Wash and dry thoroughly the head of lettuce, separating and tearing into pieces in the bowl. Add the radishes, carrots, and green onions. Peel tomatoes and add. Slice cucumbers, retaining the skins. The skins are not only nutritious, but colorful in the serving. Use any lemon mayonnaise. Serves 4.

Romaine with Garlic Bread

2 *heads romaine*	2 *tablespoons salad oil*
4 *slices whole-wheat bread,*	1 *tablespoon lemon juice*
sliced thick	2 *ripe tomatoes*
3 *cloves garlic*	

Break romaine into salad bowl. Peel tomatoes, section, and place in salad bowl. Then prepare garlic bread as follows: Crush garlic cloves into oil and lemon mixture; allow to stand for some time to get a thoroughly saturated ingredient. Meanwhile, toast the whole-wheat bread hard and dry. Pour garlic oil and lemon juice over the bread when toasted, cut into cubes, and toss with the salad with French dressing. (For those who do not like too strong a flavor of garlic, the garlic bread can be removed before eating, as it will leave a delicate flavor in the salad itself. However, most people like to eat the garlic bread right along with the salad.) Serves 4.

NOTE: If a strong French dressing is used, a very good thing is to break a slightly soft-boiled egg over the mixture before serving. This tones down the sharp flavors of lemon and garlic and makes a delightful blend.

Summer Herb Salad

Combine mustard greens, watercress, spinach, and lettuce leaves with summer savory, tarragon, marjoram, and rosemary. Add some celery seed to the French dressing.

Tarragon Salad

¼ *cup spinach leaves*
½ *cup consisting of very tender*
tips of beet tops, tips of broc-
coli, tips of radishes, young
onions, or baby carrots
¼ *cup minced parsley*

12 *tarragon leaves, chopped fine*
¼ *cup chopped chives*
1 *pimiento, chopped*
1 *green pepper, chopped fine*

Toss all ingredients with French dressing. Serves 4.

Romaine → ## Escarole Salad Escarole →

½ *cup escarole*
½ *cup endive*
½ *head romaine*
½ *head lettuce*
½ *cup celery*   Endive →

¼ *cup tarragon, minced if fresh*
or ½ teaspoon powdered tar-
ragon
¼ *cup chervil, minced if fresh,*
or ¼ teaspoon powdered
chervil

Mix all ingredients together. Add French dressing and toss. Serves 4.

Buckwheat Salad

Use only the tender young leaves by themselves. Add French dressing and toss. The young, tender buckwheat leaf has a delightfully
distinctive flavor that should not be blended with any other flavor.

Purslane Salad

Use the purslane leaves alone; do not combine with other salad
leaves for best flavor. If desired, however, it can be combined best
with romaine. Top with salad dressing and serve.

Lamb's Lettuce Salad

2 *cups lamb's lettuce*
1 *cup celery*
¼ *cup grated cheese*   *French dressing*

Toss all ingredients together and serve. Serves 4.

Dandelion Salad

½ *head lettuce*
½ *head romaine*
½ *cup dandelion leaves*   *a few fresh mint leaves*
¼ *cup chopped dandelion stems*

Toss torn leaves together,
add French dressing, and toss again. Serves 4.

Nasturtium Salad

½ *head lettuce*   4 *or* 5 *nasturtium flowers*
½ *head romaine*   1 *teaspoon nasturtium seed*
1 *cup fresh nasturtium leaves*

Tear, do not cut, the lettuce and the nasturtium leaves into small
pieces. Cutting with a knife or kitchen shears often gives a bitter
flavor to the salad leaf. Toss salad with nasturtium flowers. Chop
the nasturtium seed; add to the French dressing and toss together.
Save several nasturtium flowers for decorations. Serves 3.

Gourmet Mixed Green Salad

The mixed green salads we get in the restaurant today are often a
joke. It is true they do include, besides the usual lettuce, cabbage,
or romaine, a little watercress and perhaps a little chicory. But here
is a *real* mixed green salad that will delight the real salad gourmet.

All these leaves should be thoroughly washed, dried, crisped in a
cool place, and torn into small pieces—never cut with a knife or
kitchen shears.

½ *cup buckwheat leaves*   ½ *cup escarole*
¼ *cup dandelion greens*   1 *cup purslane*
¼ *cup watercress*   1 *cup romaine*
½ *cup young, tender spinach*   ½ *cup lettuce*
  leaves   *a few dock leaves*
¼ *cup fresh mint leaves*   ¼ *cup chopped chives*
  a few wood-sorrel leaves

Toss all these greens with French dressing or add a bit of grated
cheese, if desired, before tossing with the French dressing. Ob-

viously it is difficult to assemble all these greens at one time, but the trick of this salad is to use as many as you can possibly obtain. Serves 6.

Spring Herb Salad

Use any combination of tender young salad leaves, such as tips or tops of the various vegetables just coming into the market or peeking up through the ground in the garden. Sprinkle these leaves with a little mint, or any of the greens from the whole spring landscape of wildflowers. Don't be afraid to use wildflower leaves if you know what the flowers are. There are shepherd's purse, wild rocket, sour dock, even the fresh young sprouts of the spring milkweed, the dandelion, the oxalis, the wood sorrel, and, of course, all the fresh new things from the vegetable garden: turnips, radishes, and mustard greens. Use as many combinations as you can find, and toss with a French dressing.

THE VEGETABLE SALAD

Famous Vegetable Salad

2 *stalks celery*
¼ *green pepper*
¼ *cucumber*
3 *medium-sized tomatoes*

6 *green onions*
1 *large avocado*
a few sprigs mint
1 *pint cottage cheese*

Dice avocado and tomatoes. Chop all vegetables fine. Mix thoroughly and add cottage cheese. Mix thoroughly through vegetables and serve. Serves 4.

Avocado Tomato Salad Bowl

4 *tablespoons olive or salad oil*
4 *tablespoons lemon juice*
3 *tomatoes, cut into eighths*
1 *avocado*
½ *bunch watercress*

1 *clove garlic, cut into halves*
½ *head lettuce*
½ *head chicory*

Pour olive oil and 2 tablespoons lemon juice over tomatoes; chill. Cut avocado lengthwise into halves, remove stone, pare, and cut

into crescents. Sprinkle with remaining lemon juice.   Rub salad
bowl with garlic . . . toss shredded salad greens together in
bowl with tomatoes and avocado. Serves 6.

Mint and Carrot Salad

9½ *cups grated carrot*
¼ *cup lemon juice*
1¼ *teaspoons orange-blossom*
honey

1¼ *tablespoons   mint   leaves*
(minced)
12 *ripe olives*
⅔ *cup almonds, ground*
⅔ *cup coconut, grated*

Mix carrots with lemon juice and honey. Add coconut, almonds,
and mint and mix thoroughly. Add ripe olives for effective
garnish. Serves 6.

Skin Beautiful Salad

4 *firm lettuce leaves*
1 *tablespoon shelled green*
peas
2 *young spinach leaves*

1 *carrot*
½ *small leek*
3 *radishes*
1 *small tomato*

Wash vegetables carefully. Shred carrot and leek. Slice the radishes
thin. Chop the spinach leaves and green peas separately. Cut unpeeled tomato into small pieces. Arrange four lettuce cups on
platter. In center cup place tomatoes—in others the prepared vegetables. Sprinkle a little lemon juice and a few drops of olive oil
over the vegetables. Serves 1.

Stuffed Artichoke Salad

4 *globe artichokes*
1½ *cups dry whole-wheat bread*
crumbs
3 *tablespoons grated Parmesan*
cheese

¾ *clove garlic, minced*
¾ *tablespoon minced parsley*
¼ *cup olive oil*
lettuce or chicory
½ *teaspoon Bragg Aminos*

Boil artichokes 15 minutes. Combine next 5 ingredients and fill
the petals with the paste. Place in uncovered baking pan, add
water and Aminos to depth of 1 inch, bake in a hot oven (425°F.)
for ½ hour. Serve hot on shredded lettuce or chicory. Serves 4.

Cabbage Salad Bowl

*1/2 head cabbage, either red
  or green, mixed makes a
  colorful salad
2 small onions
1/2 teaspoon honey (opt.)*

*1/2 cup minced onion tops
pinch salad herbs
2 tbs lemon or orange juice
1/3 tsp Bragg Aminos
parsley or watercress garnish*

Shred cabbage, add thinly sliced onions, herbs and seasoning.
Combine all ingredients and toss well before serving. Serves 2-4.

Fresh Mushroom Salad

*1 small head romaine
1/2 bunch chicory
1/2 bunch watercress
1/4 tsp Bragg Aminos*

*fresh mushrooms, about 8-10
2 tomatoes
pinch salad herbs*

Saute sliced mushrooms lightly in butter with herbs. Then
combine all ingredients in salad bowl, add salad dressing of choice
and toss. Serves 2-4.

Sprouted Soybean Salad

*1/2 head lettuce
1/4 head cabbage
1 cup soybean sprouts*

*1/4 cup green or red bellpepper
2 tomatoes
1/4 cup minced onion*

Shred or slice lettuce and cabbage; add chopped bellpepper and
other ingredients. Add sprouts, raw or lightly sauteed. Toss with
a dash of Bragg Aminos and salad dressing of choice. Serves 2-4.

Mexican Guacamole Salad

*3 avocados, mashed
2 garlic cloves, mashed
6 green onions, chopped
6 tomatoes, quartered
1/2 lemon, juiced*

*lettuce or cabbage, sliced
1 tsp health mayonnaise
dash of Bragg Aminos
pinch of salad herbs*

Mash avocados and garlic, mix in chopped green onions, lemon
juice and seasonings. Place mixture on a bed of sliced lettuce or
cabbage and garnish with tomatoes and any available fresh sliced
vegetables desired. Serves 4-6.

Grand Slam Salad

The purpose of this salad is to see how many varieties of vegetables you can put into one salad. Not only do almost all vegetables combine to give a delightful flavor, but, more important, it will serve your family a variety of vegetables which they badly need. Each vegetable in nature's galaxy has its own purpose. Some are rich in vitamin A; some in iron content. Some pique the appetite. Others add light, porous bulk to the diet. Each one has its specialty in the nutritional field, and a rich, well-rounded combination of vegetables in a salad can make any meal a real Health meal. If it is impossible to include all the vegetables named below, do not worry, but the more varieties you can work in, the better the salad will be nutritionally.

3 *cups salad greens (make this as wide a variety of salad greens as you can find, including many of the following: lettuce, romaine, chicory, watercress, escarole, endive, chives, leek, spinach, nasturtiums, purslane, lamb's lettuce, corn salad, buckwheat, dandelion greens, wood-sorrel leaves or any vegetable tops or wild salad leaves you can gather)*

½ *cup chopped carrots, or cubed carrots if preferred*

½ *cup cubed raw eggplant*

¼ *cup chopped edible pea pods*

½ *cup of any or all of the following: broccoli, chopped string beans, asparagus tips (either raw or cooked), chopped or cubed turnips, parsnips, lima beans*

1 *peeled ripe tomato*

1 *cucumber, cubed or sliced, but with the peel retained*

sliced radishes

1 *tablespoon chives*

1 *cup thinly sliced Chinese cabbage*

3 *stalks chopped celery*

artichoke hearts

½ *cup grated young tender beets*

½ *cup chopped celery root*

a few flowerets of cauliflower

½ *cup raw, tender new peas*

½ *green pepper, chopped*

½ *pimiento, chopped*

½ *avocado*

6 *pods chopped okra*

This salad can be varied by using raw vegetables one time and cooked vegetables the next. Do not hesitate to use all of the above list of vegetables raw. You will find a little adventuring along this line an interesting experience. Serves 8-12.

THE FRUIT SALAD

All of the following fresh fruits can be combined into delicious all fruit salads: apples, bananas, cherries, figs, currants, grapes, grapefruit, oranges, mangoes, papayas, mulberries, peaches, pears, apricots, tangerines, mandarins, plums, nectarines, pineapple, prunes, strawberries, boysenberries, blackberries. Cantaloupe, watermelon and melons of all kinds may be used alone or mixed within the melon family independent of other fruits. Almost any fruit can be used in a fruit salad, and combined either with lowfat cottage cheese, lemon mayonnaise, shredded coconut, honey or yogurt. A good health food cook will do their own experimenting.

Cherry & Berry Salad

1 pint blackberries
1 pint raspberries
3/8 lb black cherries, pitted
1 pint boysenberries

1-1/2 cups cottage cheese
2 tablespoons nuts of choice
1 head lettuce
yogurt, lowfat or non-fat

Wash berries and cherries. Pit and slice cherries and mix all ingredients in bowl. Serve on lettuce leaf and garnish with yogurt. Serves 6.

Tropical Hawaiian Delight

1 large pineapple, fresh
4 kiwis, or 1 papaya, or 2
  mangoes, or 4 guava or
  mix any tropical fruit

1 pint strawberries
1 tablespoon pistachio nuts,
  chopped
yogurt, lowfat

Quarter pineapple lengthwise. Do not peel. Cut away hard core. Scoop out inside. Chop fine. Add sliced kiwi fruit, guava, mango or any tropical fruit in season and refill shells. Hull strawberries and slice. Lay on top of pineapple to cover top. Garnish with raw chopped nuts. Serves 4.

Papaya Hawaiian Salad

2 cups papaya, diced   3/4 cup celery, sliced
1-1/2 cups fresh pineapple, diced   2 tbs yogurt
1-1/2 tablespoons finely chopped mixed raw nuts or seeds
  (almonds, sunflower, peanuts, pistachio, sesame, etc.)

Prepare fruit, combine diced celery and yogurt and add your favorite raw nuts and seeds, chopped. Serve on crisp lettuce leaves. Serves 4-6.

Cranberry Mold Delight

1/3 cup almonds, sliced   1/4 cup lemon juice, fresh
1/2 cup soy or goat cheese   1/4 cup apple juice
  diced   1/4 teaspoon cinnamon
1/3 cup honey   1 teaspoon gelatin or
3 cups cranberries, cooked   arrowroot dissolved in
                                   1/4 cup hot distilled water

Cook cranberries, then blend smooth. Add lemon juice, dissolved gelatin or arrowroot, honey and almonds. Allow to semi-cool, then add cheese. Pour into wet molds and put into refrigerator to harden. When hardened and ready to serve, cut in squares and place on a bed of shredded lettuce or cabbage and top with non-fat yogurt. Serves 4-6.

Pear and Grape Salad

6 lettuce leaves   6 pear halves, fresh or canned
3 tablespoons soy cream   1-1/2 lbs white seedless grapes
2 oz soy cheese or soft tofu   2 oz yogurt, non-fat

Cover salad plates with lettuce leaves. Place a pear half on each leaf, flat side up. Blend soy cheese or tofu (soft) and yogurt and soy cream and spread pears generously. Cut grapes into halves and arrange flat-side down on the covered pear, close together to resemble a bunch of grapes. Place a piece of grape stem in large end of pear. Serves 6.

Ambrosia

7 bananas, sliced
3 oranges, sliced
1 cup pecans, chopped

1 pineapple, sliced or 1 can
   unsweetened pineapple
1 cup coconut, grated
   orange-blossom honey

Mix fruits, pecans, coconut and add orange-blossom honey to taste. Serve in chilled bowl and top with non-fat yogurt or nut or rice cream if desired. Serves 4 to 6.

Fruit Bouquet

1 medium pineapple
2 grapefruit
1 cup grapes

2 fresh pears
3 oranges

Chill all fruits. Dice pineapple. Remove sections from oranges. Remove grapes from stems. Cut unpeeled fresh pears into cubes. Combine all fruits and serve in chilled sherbet dishes. Garnish with non-fat yogurt if desired. Serves 4.

Rhythm Salad

1 cup apple, cubed
1/2 cup raw carrots, shredded
3/4 cup prunes, stewed
3/4 cup apricots, stewed

1/4 cup raisins
1/4 cup peanuts, chopped
1 cup cabbage, shredded

Cook prunes and apricots, remove pits, slice; mix with apples, carrots, raisins and cabbage. Toss with lemon mayonnaise, sprinkle chopped peanuts over the top. Serves 6.

The Fish Salad

Fish and its flavors do not appeal to everyone. Some of these people can be tempted with fish added to a delicious salad — this is one way to introduce this important food into their diet.

◇◇

Tuna-Fish Salad

1 (7 oz.) *can tuna fish*	*lettuce*
¾ *cup celery, chopped*	2 *tomatoes*
½ *cup green pepper, chopped*	*juice of one lemon*
½ *cup onions, chopped*	*mayonnaise*
2 *hard-cooked eggs*	*ripe olives*

Mash tuna fish; add lemon juice and mayonnaise. Mix in chopped vegetables. Place on beds of lettuce. Garnish with quartered tomatoes and ripe olives and sliced hard-cooked eggs. Serves 4.

Crab Salad

1 *cup flaked crab meat*	½ *teaspoon chervil*
½ *cup chopped celery*	½ *teaspoon tarragon*
3 *large peeled tomatoes*	*lemon mayonnaise*

Mix all ingredients together and serve quickly after mixing. Serves 3.

Lobster Salad

1 *cup flaked lobster meat, or,*	*French dressing*
if desired, 1 *whole lobster*	¼ *cup sweet basil leaf or*
cubed	½ *teaspoon powdered basil*
½ *teaspoon marjoram*	

Mix all ingredients and serve. Serves 2.

Salmon Salad

2 *cups flaked salmon*	1 *cup lettuce*
1 *fresh pimiento, chopped or*	1 *cup romaine*
1 *canned pimiento, chopped*	¼ *cup watercress*
2 *teaspoons capers*	

Mix all ingredients; serve with desired dressing. Serves 4.

Avocado Filled with Salmon

2 *avocados*	1 *cup diced celery*
2 *tablespoons lemon juice*	1 *cup flaked salmon*
⅛ *teaspoon Bragg Aminos*	½ *cup mayonnaise*

Cut avocados lengthwise into halves, remove seeds, and sprinkle cut portion with lemon juice. . .Combine Bragg Liquid Aminos celery and salmon with mayonnaise to moisten. Other suggestions for this salad are as follows: 1 cup crab meat, lobster, shrimp, or oysters instead of salmon. Serves 4.

Shrimp Salad

1 *cup fresh or canned shrimp*	½ *teaspoon celery powder*
1 *teaspoon capers*	2 *cups romaine*
1 *teaspoon sweet basil*	¼ *teaspoon Bragg Aminos*

Strain and dry shrimp; remove intestinal veins; add to salad ingredients and toss with French dressing, adding celery-seed powder to the dressing before tossing. Serves 2.

SALAD WITH FOWL

Pineapple-Chicken Salad

¾ *cup shredded or diced pine-*	¾ *cup chopped celery*
apple	*romaine*
1¼ *cups cooked chicken*	*pimiento*

Mix pineapple, chicken, and celery. Add lemon mayonnaise to moisten. Arrange on romaine leaf; top with mayonnaise and decorate with strips of pimiento. Serves 2.

Chicken Salad in Aspic

5 *slices tomato* (½ *inch thick*)	2½ *tablespoons mayonnaise*
	1¾ *tablespoons chopped green*
1 *tablespoon unflavored gela-*	*pepper*
tin	⅓ *cup slivered blanched*
¼ *cup cold water*	*almonds*
1½ *cups seasoned chicken stock*	1¾ *tablespoons diced celery*
lemon juice	1¼ *cups chopped cooked*
	chicken

Marinate tomatoes in seasoned lemon juice. Chill. Soften gelatin in cold water for 5 minutes. Heat chicken stock to boiling. Add gelatin and stir until dissolved. Cool. When syrupy in consistency, add remaining ingredients and place in individual molds. Chill until firm. Unmold each portion on a slice of tomato and serve with lettuce hearts and mayonnaise. Serves 5.

Artichoke Chicken Salad

2 *cups diced chicken*   1 *cucumber, diced*
4 *artichoke hearts*   *lemon mayonnaise*
8 *small sprigs of rosemary,*
  about 1 inch long (if dried,
  use about ½ teaspoon)

Mix all ingredients and moisten with mayonnaise. Place on salad leaves and top with a dab of mayonnaise and a pinch of minced parsley. Serves 4.

Almond Chicken Salad

1 *cup chicken, cooked*   1 *chopped red pepper or pi-*
½ *cup quartered almonds*   *miento*
1 *cup cut celery*

Moisten all ingredients and mix with lemon mayonnaise. Serve on salad leaves. Serves 3.

Duck and Orange Salad

2 *cups cooked duck*   2 *tablespoons truffles or mush-*
2 *cups sliced oranges*   *rooms cut in small pieces*
                                 1 *cup diced cucumbers*

Mix all ingredients with lemon mayonnaise and serve on salad leaves. Serves 4.

Apple-Turkey Salad

2 *cups cooked turkey*   1 *dozen pecan halves*
1 *cup diced apple*   1 *ripe tomato*

Peel tomato and cut into small pieces. Mix all ingredients with lemon mayonnaise and serve on salad leaves. Serves 3.

CHEESE SALADS

Cottage Cheese and Onion Salad

1 cup cottage cheese , low fat
1/2 cup chopped young green
  onions, including tops

1/2 cup chopped celery
dash of Bragg Aminos
chives, minced

Mix all ingredients except chives, arrange on lettuce, cabbage, parsley or watercress leaves and add salad dressing of choice, or juice of orange or lemon. Top with a small amount of minced chives. Serves 2.

Cottage Cheese and Green Pepper Salad

1 cup cottage cheese, low fat
1/4 cup watercress, chopped

1 green bellpepper & seeds,
  chopped

Mix all ingredients; arrange on salad leaves and top with any preferred salad dressing. Serves 2.

Cottage Cheese and Endive Salad

Arrange cottage cheese on a bed of crisp endive; top with French dressing to which 1/2 teaspoon marjoram has been added.

Cottage Cheese with Pimiento

1 cup cottage cheese, low fat
1/2 cup pimiento, chopped

1/4 cup parsley, chopped
1/4 cup onion, chopped

Mix all ingredients; add salad dressing of choice; arrange on salad leaves. Serves 2.

Cottage Cheese and Beet Salad

1 cup cottage cheese, low fat
1 cup beets, cooked & diced

1/2 teaspoon thyme
1/4 cup chives

Mix all ingredients with mayonnaise dressing, yogurt or sour-cream dressing; arrange on sliced lettuce or cabbage leaves. Serves 2-4.

◇◇◇

Cottage Cheese Salad

Cottage cheese is delicious to top apricots, peaches, pears, nectarines, pineapples, or any citrus fruit salad. Arrange fruit attractively on salad leaves, top with cottage cheese and add lemon mayonnaise or a lemon and honey dressing.

Gourmet Mixed Green Salad de Luxe

To recipe for *Gourmet Mixed Green Salad,* add 1½ cups crumbled Roquefort cheese.

Pear and Camembert Salad

¼ cup Camembert cheese   2 *pears*
¼ cup cream   4 *pecans*

Mash Camembert with cream until smooth. Cut pears in half and core, hollowing out centers. Stuff with Camembert cheese; top with lemon mayonnaise and garnish with pecans. Serves 4.

Gorgonzola-Pineapple Salad

½ *fresh pineapple*   *preserved kumquats*
½ *cup crumbled Gorgonzola*   *French dressing*
   (*Italian cheese*)

Slice pineapple in spears, sprinkle over with crumbled Gorgonzola; add French dressing and garnish with several preserved kumquats. Serves 2.

Peach Brie Salad

¼ *cup Brie cheese*   1 *whole sprig sweet basil, or*
½ *cup cream*   ½ *teaspoon dried basil*
    2 *large, fresh peaches*

Mix Brie cheese with cream and basil until smooth. Halve and pit peaches; stuff with cheese mixture. Serve on salad leaves with French dressing. Serves 4.

◇◇

Chapter 3

Salad Dressings

Honey French Dressing

⅔ cup olive oil   6 tablespoons lemon juice
⅔ cup honey

Mix all ingredients except honey. Add honey slowly and beat
vigorously. Will make 1½ cups.

French Dressing with Tomato Juice

⅓ cup lemon juice   1 cup tomato juice
⅓ cup olive oil   1 clove garlic
1½ tablespoons honey   ½ teaspoon sweet basil
 1 tablespoon Bragg Aminos   ½ teaspoon rosemary

Blend well; allow to stand. Remove garlic before serving. Will
make 1⅔ cups.

Grapefruit French Dressing

4 tablespoons olive oil   ¼ teaspoon paprika
1 tablespoon grapefruit juice 1 tablespoon finely crumbled
½ tablespoon lemon juice   Roquefort cheese

Blend ingredients, beat vigorously. Allow to stand one hour before
serving. Will make ¼ cup.

Honey Soy-Oil Dressing

¼ *medium onion, grated*
5½ *tablespoons lemon juice*
 1 *cup soybean oil*
 3 *teaspoons celery seed*
 1 *teaspoon dry mustard*

½ *teaspoon paprika*
½ *cup orange-blossom honey*
 1 *teaspoon dry mustard*

Measure dry ingredients into small mixing bowl. Add honey and blend thoroughly. Add grated onion and small amount of lemon juice. Beat mixture; add oil and remaining lemon juice alternately and then celery seed. Store in a covered jar in a cool place. Will make 1½ cups.

Tomato-Juice Dressing

 1 *cup tomato juice*
½ *cup vegetable oil*
 3 *tablespoons lemon juice*
 1 *teaspoon Bragg Aminos*

¾ *teaspoon dry mustard*
 1 *teaspoon minced onion*
 1 *teaspoon chives*
 1 *clove garlic*

Mix all ingredients until well blended, with the exception of the clove of garlic. Beat thoroughly. Run a string through the clove of garlic, leaving one long end. Place in jar with garlic clove in dressing, string extended over the rim of the jar. Let stand overnight. Remove the garlic clove before using. Will make 1½ cups.

French Dressing with Onion Sauce

½ *cup olive oil*
¼ *cup lemon juice*

½ *teaspoon Bragg Aminos*
½ *teaspoon onion juice*
½ *teaspoon thyme*

Blend ingredients; beat vigorously in oil and let stand one hour before serving. Will make ¾ cup.

Dill-Seed Dressing

½ *teaspoon dry mustard*
¼ *teaspoon honey*
¼ *cup whipped cream*
½ *teaspoon Bragg Aminos*

 1 *hard-boiled egg yolk*
 1 *uncooked egg yolk*
¾ *tablespoon lemon juice*
½ *cup olive, soy, or peanut oil*
½ *teaspoon dill seed*

Rub cooked egg yolk through a sieve, add uncooked egg yolk. Beat in oil gradually, add lemon juice and seasonings. Just before serving fold in whipped cream and dill seed. Makes 1 cup.

Roquefort Dressing

½ *lb. Roquefort cheese*
lemon juice
olive, soy, or peanut oil

Mash Roquefort cheese with fork adding lemon juice to give the cheese a thick yet smooth consistency; add enough oil so that it is smooth. Will make 1 cup.

Lemon Mayonnaise

2 *cups soy, peanut, or olive oil*　　1 *teaspoon dry mustard*
½ *cup lemon juice*
2 *egg yolks*
¼ *teaspoon thyme*

Combine dry ingredients with unbeaten yolks in a mixing bowl and beat together until stiff. Add part of the oil, beating it into the mixture drop by drop at first, then proceeding more rapidly, keeping the mixture firm. When it begins to thicken, add a little lemon juice alternately with the oil. Makes 2½ cups.

Russian Dressing

½ *cup lemon mayonnaise*　　1 *tablespoon chopped pi-*
¼ *cup chili sauce*　　　　　　　*miento*
1 *tablespoon celery seed*　　½ *teaspoon anise seed*
1 *tablespoon chopped green*
　pepper

Blend ingredients; beat vigorously and allow to stand for one hour before serving. Will make ¾ cup.

Sour-Cream Dressing

1 *cup sour cream*　　　　　　½ *teaspoon orange-blossom*
2 *hard-boiled egg yolks*　　　　*honey*
1 *teaspoon lemon juice*

Press yolks through a sieve and blend into sour cream or you can substitute yogurt. Blend in lemon juice, honey. You can vary seasonings as desired. Makes 1-1/4 cups.

Quick Tofu or Yogurt Dressing
For Raw Vegetable Salads and Cooked Vegetables
To one cup soft tofu or yogurt, add the juice of one fresh lemon or lime, 1 tsp raw honey and any salad herbs desired. Blend well and serve with salad. Also excellent garnish for salads and sandwiches.

Quick Yogurt or Sour Cream Dressing
For Fruit Salads or Compotes
To above recipe, substitute fresh orange or unsweetened pineapple or fruit juice in place of lemon. Add small amount of honey and finely grated unsweetened coconut if desired.

French Tofu or Yogurt Dressing
For salads, sandwiches and dressings. Blend 1 cup soft tofu, lowfat yogurt or sour cream with small amount of French tomato dressing. For variation, add minced chives, ripe olives, watercress or fresh blended cucumber.

Tofu Delight Dressing or Spread
For salads, vegetables and sandwiches. Blend or mash 1/2 lb well drained soft tofu, 2 tbs canola oil, 2 tbs apple cider vinegar, 1 tbs honey, 1/2 tsp Bragg Aminos and pinch of salad herbs. Mix all ingredients until smooth and creamy. For variety, add 1 tbs unsweetened pineapple or fruit juice and flaked coconut.

◇◇◇

Mustard Dressing

1/3 cup lemon juice, fresh *1 teaspoon mustard powder*
2/3 cup olive oil *1 tablespoon raw honey*

Blend all ingredients and allow to stand one hour before serving.
Makes 1 cup. Opt: Substitute apple cider vinegar for lemon juice.

Avocado and Cottage Cheese Dressing

2 mashed avocados *juice of 1 lemon*
1 cup lowfat cottage cheese *dash of Bragg Aminos*

Mix mashed avocados and lowfat cottage cheese thoroughly, add
lemon juice and Bragg Aminos. Beat to a creamy consistency.
Makes 2 cups. A delicious garnish for vegetable and rice dishes.

Lime Dressing

4 tablespoons olive oil *pinch celery seed*
2 tablespoons fresh lime juice *1 teaspoon raw honey*
pinch salad herbs

Blend ingredients. Allow to stand for one hour before serving.
Makes 1/4 cup. Opt: Substitute apple cider vinegar for lime juice.

Pineapple Delight Dressing

yogurt, non-fat *pineapple juice, unsweetened*
honey of choice

Add enough pineapple juice to yogurt to give the consistency of
whipped cream. Add enough honey to sweeten to your taste. This
is a delicious fruit salad dressing. Makes 1 cup.

Orange Tofu Dressing

1 lemon (juice only) *1 orange (juice only)*
3 ounces tofu (well-drained) *1 teaspoon honey (optional)*

Blend tofu, lemon and orange juice. Makes 1 cup.

Delicious Tofu Nut-Butter Dressing or Spread

1/8 cup lemon juice, fresh *1 tablespoon raw honey*
1 tablespoon pure maple syrup *1/4 cup nut butter of choice*
  or mix with seed butters

Mix the above ingredients thoroughly. Makes 1/2 cup.

PERCENTAGE OF CALORIES FROM PROTEIN

LEGUMES

Soybean sprouts	54%
Mungbean sprouts	43%
Soybean curd (tofu)	43%
Soy flour	35%
Soybeans	35%
Soy sauce	33%
Broad beans	32%
Lentils	29%
Split peas	28%
Kidney beans	26%
Navy beans	26%
Lima beans	26%
Garbanzo beans	23%

VEGETABLES

Spinach	49%
New Zealand spinach	47%
Watercress	46%
Kale	45%
Broccoli	45%
Brussels sprouts	44%
Turnip greens	43%
Collards	43%
Cauliflower	40%
Mustard greens	39%
Mushrooms	38%
Chinese cabbage	34%
Parsley	34%
Lettuce	34%
Green peas	30%
Zucchini	28%
Green beans	26%
Cucumbers	24%
Dandelion greens	24%
Green pepper	22%
Artichokes	22%
Cabbage	22%
Celery	21%
Eggplant	21%
Tomatoes	18%
Onions	16%
Beets	15%
Pumpkin	12%
Potatoes	11%
Yams	8%
Sweet potatoes	6%

GRAINS

Wheat germ	31%
Rye	20%
Wheat hard red	17%
Wild rice	16%
Buckwheat	15%
Oatmeal	15%
Millet	12%
Barley	11%
Brown Rice	8%

FRUITS

Lemons	16%
Honeydew melon	10%
Cantaloupe	9%
Strawberry	8%
Orange	8%
Blackberry	8%
Cherry	8%
Apricot	8%
Grape	8%
Watermelon	8%
Tangerine	7%
Papaya	6%
Peach	6%
Pear	5%
Banana	5%
Grapefruit	5%
Pineapple	3%
Apple	1%

NUTS AND SEEDS

Pumpkin seeds	21%
Peanuts	18%
Sunflower seeds	17%
Walnuts, black	13%
Sesame seeds	13%
Almonds	12%
Cashews	12%
Filberts	8%

Data obtained from Nutritive Value of American Foods in Common Units, U.S.D.A. Agriculture Handbook No. 456. Reprinted from John Robbins, Diet for a New America (Walpole, N.H.: Stillpoint Publishing 1990) (by permission of the author.)

Chapter 4

Soups

"Vitamin" and Pot Liquors

THE MODERN nutritionist is beginning to look with respect on the tales of the magic potions of the Dark Ages: soups brewed of herbs of the forest and animal organs. Where he was wont to scoff, he now agrees that very probably the witches' broth had practical curative remedies rather than the supposed supernatural charms.

Through long periods of history, Europe and the Orient suffered from a shortage of food supply. Rather than roam the forest hunting for game and eating wild berries and herbs, the European crowded into small communities and concentrated his efforts on wars and munitions rather than on food. Death rather than life was paramount. Is it any wonder that the magician with his vitamin-rich herb pot and the old crone with her love potions brewed from forest remedies could work miracles? Of course today we know they were not miracles—in a sense. And yet, in another sense, all the richness of nature's gift to man, the living, growing things to nurture his body, was a miracle in itself.

The foreign custom of having the soup pot on the back of the stove (into which all water left from cooking meat and vegetables, as well as the odds and ends of the meat and vegetables themselves were tossed) is one of the most healthful practices in nutritional cookery. Far too many people "murder" their food. First they take the poor carrot, scrape all the vitamin-rich skin off it, toss it in large quantities of boiling water, boil the life out of it, and then throw all the water into which the vitamins and minerals have escaped down the drain pipe. Yes, we feed the American sink on nature's richest gifts and keep the dead, lifeless remainder for our own fare. Isn't that ridiculous?

Save all those celery tops, the few extra spinach leaves, the green lettuce leaves that are perhaps a little too dark to serve on the table, the tomato skins, the skin from any vegetable you feel you absolutely must peel—all the little odds and ends and leftovers that you would normally throw away—toss them into the soup pot. I always call it my "vitamin pot." And, above all, save those precious liquors that remain in the pot after cooking. You will find no more delicious soup in the world than the rich soup made of pot liquors and mixtures of vegetables that you would ordinarily discard. That, above all, is your basic soup recipe. But here are some others you will enjoy.

CONSOMMÉ

To the modern cook, almost any clear broth is a consommé, but actually a good rich consommé is the most difficult of all soups to prepare. It is also the most delicious, and can be made to take on endless variations by the addition of rice, marrow balls, and other choice ingredients. Here is a basic recipe for consommé. It is not, as is so often supposed, an inexpensive dish. As a matter of fact, it is one of the most expensive to prepare, and is considered a real delicacy both by those who know good food and by the nutritionist.

2½ *lbs. lean beef*	2 *medium-sized carrots*
2 *lbs. beef knuckles*	1 *large turnip*
1 *lb. veal knuckles*	⅓ *cup diced celery*
1½ *lbs. marrowbone*	1 *large onion*
1½ *quarts chicken stock*	1 *tablespoon Bragg Aminos*
1 *chicken skeleton, bones left from a previously cooked chicken. The skeleton of any fowl may be used.*	4 *qts. cold water*

If fresh herbs are used, use the following: 1 sprig of basil, 1 bay leaf, 2 caraway leaves, 1 sprig of marjoram, 1 sprig of rosemary, 2 sprigs thyme. If dried herbs are used, use the following: 2 cloves, ⅛ teaspoon basil, ½ bay leaf, ⅓ teaspoon marjoram, ⅛ teaspoon rosemary, ¼ teaspoon thyme, ¼ cup chopped parsley.

Cut beef into small pieces and brown half of it. Place in soup kettle with the rest of the meat and bones and allow to stand for 15 minutes in the cold water. Heat quickly to the boiling point, remove scum, and simmer very slowly for 4½ hours. Prepare vegetables, and cook slightly in a little butter or vegetable oil. Add to other ingredients with herbs and spices, and allow to cook for another 2 hours. Cool to remove fat, and then strain.

To some people it is very important to have a clear consommé. Personally, I do not see that this makes any difference, but if you wish a clear consommé, use this procedure. For each quart of stock, prepare an egg white by beating it slightly with 1 tablespoon of cold water, add this slightly beaten egg white, with eggshell, to the stock. Bring to a boil, stir constantly, and boil for a few minutes. Let stand for half an hour to cool naturally, and strain through cheesecloth.

The cook must be sure that the consommé is strongly seasoned if it is going to be clarified and strained, as many consommés lose their best flavor in this process.

Consommé is the most basic of soups. It has endless variations. Here are some of the most popular, healthful, and delicious.

Consommé with Vegetables

To consommé, add cooked vegetables such as carrots, turnips, asparagus tips, string beans, celery, cut in fancy shapes. Tiny pieces of half-cooked vegetables often give a satisfying crunchiness to the consommé. Garnish with a sprinkling of parsley.

Consommé with Chicken

To consommé, add small particles of diced chicken, turkey, or other fowl and green peas. Garnish with ⅛ teaspoon per serving of grated lemon rind.

Consommé with Cheese Croutons

Cover whole-wheat, rye, or any whole-grain bread or wafer with a thick coating of cheese. Cut into small squares. Brown under broiler until golden and crisp. Float on consommé with sprinkling of finely chopped parsley.

Where there is no vision, the people perish. — Proverbs 29:18

Consommé Pimiento

3 *tablespoons pimiento, sieved*　¼ *teaspoon Bragg Aminos*
½ *cup egg whites*
½ *cup cream*

Drain canned pimiento. Rub through sieve. Beat cream and egg whites separately until both are stiff. Combine. Add pimiento and Bragg Liquid Aminos...Blend well. Add about ¼ cup pimiento mixture to about 3 cups of consommé. Simmer for 10 minutes. This can also be served chilled and cubed. Makes 3 cups.

Consommé with Dumplings

To consommé, add whole-wheat dumplings.

Iced Consommé

Add 2 tablespoons lemon juice to 4 cups of consommé. Chill. Cut in cubes and serve with slight sprinkling of chopped parsley and lemon slices.

Consommé with Marrow Balls

To consommé, add marrow balls, prepared as follows:

1 *or 2 oz. marrow from bones*　1 *teaspoon chives*
used in consommé　¼ *teaspoon chervil*
½ *teaspoon Bragg Aminos*　1 *cup toasted whole-wheat bread crumbs*

Remove marrow from bones, warm, and mash as smooth as possible. Beat egg, add bread crumbs, seasoning, and marrow. Roll lightly into ball, drop one at a time into boiling consommé. Reduce heat for cooking. Boil gently for 12 to 15 minutes.

Ox-Tail Soup

1 *ox tail*　2 *tablespoons soy oil*
whole-wheat flour　2 *tablespoons lemon juice*
5 *cups consommé stock*　1 *teaspoon Bragg Aminos*
1 *cup water*
⅓ *cup diced onions, celery, turnips, and carrots*

Clean and wash ox tail, cut into small pieces. Dry thoroughly with damp cloth. Dredge in whole-wheat flour that has been mixed with seasoning. Brown in soy oil in bottom of soup pan; add water and consommé stock and simmer slowly for 1 hour. Add vegetables and lemon juice and continue cooking until both meat and vegetables are tender. Serves 4 to 6.

Creole Consommé

1 *quart brown meat stock*	2 *tablespoons chopped onions*
2 *cups tomatoes*	1 *teaspoon Bragg Aminos*
3 *tablespoons chopped green peppers*	¼ *cup whole-wheat spaghetti*

Cook the peppers and onion in butter for five minutes. Add stock and tomatoes. Simmer fifteen minutes, strain and season. Add cooked whole-wheat spaghetti. Serves 4.

SOUPS

Chicken Gumbo

1 *medium stewing chicken*	5⅓ *cups okra, chopped or sliced*
3 *tablespoons whole-wheat flour*	2⅓ *cups tomato pulp*
1⅓ *onions, chopped*	*few sprigs parsley, chopped*
4 *tablespoons fat, melted*	6 *cups water*
	1 *teaspoon Bragg Aminos*

Clean chicken and cut into serving portions. Dredge lightly with whole-wheat flour and saute with onion fat. When chicken is browned, add okra, tomatoes, parsley, and water. Season to taste with Bragg Liquid Aminos. Simmer until chicken is tender and okra well cooked—about 2½ hours. Add water as needed during cooking. Serves 8.

Turkey Mushroom Soup

1⅓ *carrots*	2⅔ *onion slices*
1⅓ *celery stalks*	½ *cup brown rice*
roast turkey bones	2⅔ *cups cooked mushrooms*
8 *cups water*	*sliced Brazil-nut meats*

Scrub carrots; slice. Chop celery. Combine carrots, celery, turkey bones, water, and onion. Cover; simmer 2 hours. Strain. There should be 4 cups stock. Wash rice, add to stock; simmer until tender. Add mushrooms. Heat. Garnish with nut meats. Serves 6.

Hamburger Chowder

1 tablespoon fat or oil	1½ cups sliced potatoes
1 lb. ground beef	1 cup diced carrots
1 medium onion, chopped	3 cups water
1 cup canned or chopped fresh tomatoes	

Put fat or oil in saucepan; add beef and onion, and cook, stirring constantly until lightly browned. Add remaining ingredients; cover and cook about 20 minutes until vegetables are tender. Serves 6.

Royal Soup

3¾ cups potatoes, diced	1½ cups asparagus tips
1½ quarts boiling water	4½ tablespoons chopped chives
1½ cups peas	3 tablespoons butter
½ teaspoon Bragg Aminos	¼ teaspoon thyme

Cook potatoes in boiling water for 15 minutes or until tender. Drain, reserving liquid; press potatoes through a sieve and add to liquid. Add peas and well-washed asparagus tips; boil gently about 10 to 15 minutes or until tender. Add chopped chives, butter, Bragg Liquid Aminos and thyme. Add more seasoning if desired. Makes about 9 servings.

Spring Broth

1 cup finely chopped celery	1 cup chopped zucchini
1 cup chopped raw spinach	2 quarts water
1 cup chopped parsley	1 teaspoon Bragg Aminos
1 cup grated carrots	

Boil the celery and carrots for about 20 minutes, then add spinach, parsley, zucchini and boil 10 minutes longer. Drain, reserving liquid. Serves 8.

Meatless Vegetable Soup

1⅓ cups potatoes, diced
2 tablespoons butter
1 tablespoon Bragg Aminos
⅓ cup onion, sliced
⅓ cup leeks, sliced
⅔ cup celery, sliced
2 tablespoons whole-wheat flour
1⅓ quarts cold water

⅛ teaspoon thyme
⅔ cup carrots, diced
½ cup white turnips, diced
⅔ cup peas or string beans
⅔ cup outside lettuce leaves
¼ cup whole-wheat or soy macaroni, broken into small pieces (optional)
¼ cup condensed tomato soup

Boil potatoes in water to cover until tender; drain, reserving liquid; press potatoes through sieve and return to cooking liquid. Heat fat; add onion, leeks, and celery; simmer about 10 minutes or until soft and lightly browned. Add whole-wheat flour; stir until smooth; remove from heat and slowly add water, stirring until smooth. Return to flame; add seasonings, vegetables, and macaroni. Boil gently for 20 minutes or until vegetables are tender. Add tomato soup and potato stock and reheat. Makes about 6 servings.

Basic Creamed-Soup Recipe

2 to 2½ tablespoons minced onion
2 tablespoons butter
2 tablespoons whole-wheat flour
1½ cups milk (or ¾ cup water and ¾ cup half milk, half cream, or, for a very rich soup, ¾ cup milk and ¾ cup half and half)
⅔ cup vegetable juice or water in which vegetables have been cooked
1 tablespoon Bragg Aminos

grinding of pepper or ⅛ teaspoon powdered pepper
1 cup finely chopped or puréed vegetables
½ cup meat stock or chicken stock
paprika
desired herbs
1 tablespoon chopped watercress

Cook onion in the melted butter until tender. Place in double boiler, blend with flour until smooth, and add all liquid. Cook until slightly thickened and smooth. Add vegetables, herbs, and seasonings. Garnish with dash of paprika. Add a small lump of butter to each soup dish before serving. Serves 4.

Creamed Spinach Soup

To Basic Creamed-Soup Recipe, add 1 cup of puréed cooked spinach as the vegetable. Use ¼ teaspoon chervil as the herb flavoring.

Creamed Celery Soup

To Basic Creamed-Soup Recipe, add 1 cup cooked finely chopped celery as the vegetable. Use 1 teaspoon fresh chopped mint as the herb flavoring.

Creamed Carrot Soup

To Basic Creamed-Soup Recipe, add 1 cup cooked finely chopped or puréed carrots as the vegetable. Use 1 tablespoon fresh chopped parsley as the herb flavoring.

Creamed Broccoli Soup

To Basic Creamed-Soup Recipe, add 1⅓ cups cooked chopped or puréed broccoli. Sprinkle with Parmesan or dry grated American cheese before serving.

Creamed Corn Soup

Substitute milk for all liquid in Basic Creamed-Soup Recipe. Add 1¼ cups kernels of corn, either fresh or canned. Use 1 tablespoon fresh chopped parsley as the herb flavoring.

Creamed Pea Soup

To Basic Creamed-Soup Recipe, add 1 cup cooked puréed peas, fresh or canned. Use ¼ teaspoon dried sweet basil and 1 tablespoon finely chopped fresh mint as the herb flavoring.

Creamed Watercress Soup

To Basic Creamed-Soup Recipe, add 1 small bunch finely chopped watercress. Substitute chicken stock for vegetable juice. Cook watercress 10 minutes before adding as the vegetable in this basic recipe.

Creamed Asparagus Soup

To Basic Creamed-Soup Recipe, add 1 cup cooked asparagus. Flavor with 1 teaspoon finely chopped parsley.

Cream of Tomato Soup

2 cups milk
2 cups tomatoes, fresh or canned
5 tablespoons butter
2 tablespoons whole-wheat flour
2 teaspoons minced onion
1/8 teaspoon celery seed

1/8 teaspoon pepper
1 clove
1/4 bay leaf
1/8 teaspoon basil
1/8 teaspoon tarragon

Purée tomatoes or rub through sieve. Cook tomatoes with onion, and all herbs and seasonings. Thicken to a paste by adding blended flour and butter and recook. Heat milk to scalding. Be sure tomato mixture is the same temperature as milk before adding, and then add it to milk very slowly. Serve at once. If heated milk and heated tomato mixture are not the same temperature and are not combined slowly, they will curdle. Serves 4.

Cream of Mushroom Soup

1/2 pound fresh mushrooms
4 tablespoons butter
1 tablespoon minced onion
1 teaspoon lemon juice
2 tablespoons minced celery
3 cups chicken stock
2 tablespoons whole-wheat flour

1 cup milk (or half and half)

1/8 teaspoon powdered pepper or 2 grindings of pepper-corns

Wash mushrooms (do not peel) and chop. Simmer in 1 tablespoon butter with onion and celery until tender. Rub through sieve. Add chicken stock. Blend flour and remaining butter, and add milk and seasonings, stirring until smooth and thick. Add mushroom purée and chicken stock mixture. Simmer for a few minutes and serve. Serves 4 to 6.

Cream of Lettuce Soup

1 *head lettuce, shredded*
3 *cups mild meat stock, prefer-*
  ably veal
¾ *cup cream or rich milk*
1½ *tablespoons butter*
1 *egg yolk*

½ *tablespoon minced onion*
⅛ *teaspoon nutmeg*
⅛ *teaspoon freshly ground pep-*
  percorn
dash of paprika

Beat egg; add to meat stock and cream. Sauté onions in butter until golden brown. Add onions and lettuce to stock. Cook very slowly for 40 minutes; 15 minutes before finishing, add nutmeg and peppercorns. Serve in soup bowls and add dash of paprika over top for coloring just before serving. Serves 4.

Cream of Potato Soup

1 *tablespoon butter*
1 *medium-sized potato*
1 *carrot*
2 *cups milk*

3 *stalks celery*

paprika
1 *onion*

Dice vegetables and cook together. Add milk. Boil gently for 10 minutes, add butter and seasoning. Serve at once. Serves 2.

Corn Chowder

1 *small onion, sliced*
1 *tablespoon butter*
1 *tablespoon honey*
1½ *cups cooked fresh or canned*
  corn

3 *cups potatoes, diced*
1 *cup cream or milk*
1 *cup canned or fresh toma-*
  toes
1 *quart boiling water*

Add the onion to the butter and cook slowly for 5 minutes without browning. Add seasoning, water, and vegetables; cook until tender. Slowly add milk or cream, and honey, and serve hot. Serves 6.

Avocado Soups

Avocado soups are great favorites in the tropics. The avocado is used frequently and generously in all kinds of meat soups. It is generally diced into small cubes and added to the soup just before it is served.

Avocado Clam Soup

1 *can of minced clams*   ½ *cup diced avocado*
1 *can tomato juice*

Heat clams. Heat tomato juice. Dilute separately with two cans of water, letting the clams simmer until thoroughly heated. Mix the clams and tomato juice. Just before serving add the avocado. Serves 4.

Avocado Tomato Soup

Dilute tomato juice with a small amount of butter and desired amount of diced avocado added just before serving.

Chinese Cabbage Soup

¼ *to* ½ *lb. beef, sliced and cut*   2 *or* 3 *slices of fresh ginger*
  in strips   *root*
6 *cups thin meat broth*
2 *cups coarsely cut Chinese or*
  celery cabbage leaves

Boil meat in broth for a few minutes, then simmer 30 minutes longer. Add seasoning and cabbage. Cook only 4 to 5 minutes, and serve. Serves 6.

Turnip Soup

6 *white turnips*   4 *cups stock, consommé, or*
2 *tablespoons butter*   *chicken broth*
2 *cups water*   ½ *cup brown rice*
                       small amount of milk

Slice the turnips fine and put into a saucepan with the butter. Cover and simmer for fifteen minutes. Add brown rice, stock, and water. Cook for one hour over a low fire. Strain through a sieve and return to fire, adding desired seasoning and a little milk if necessary, until desired thickness is obtained. Serves 4.

Cincinnati's Famous Split-Pea Soup

2 cups dried peas
2 quarts water
2 cups celery and leaves
1 cup chopped parsley
3 tablespoons soy, peanut, or
    salad oil, or butter
1 cup chopped onions
1 leek (optional)
⅓ teaspoon thyme
1 teaspoon Bragg Aminos

Boil peas for one hour and keep skimming foam from top of pan. Add rest of ingredients and simmer for half an hour. Add seasonings and oil or butter, and cook for five more minutes. May be made with lentils. Serves 8.

Soybean Soup

1 cup soybeans
¼ cup diced celery
4 cups cold water
½ small onion
1 tablespoon butter
1 tablespoon whole-wheat
    flour
¼ teaspoon thyme
⅛ teaspoon dry mustard
1 hard-cooked egg, sliced
½ lemon cut into thin slices
1 teaspoon Bragg Aminos

Soak the beans overnight. Drain, add celery and cold water. Cook 4 hours or until tender and rub through a strainer. Cut onion into thin slices and brown sightly in the butter; add whole-wheat flour, Bragg Liquid Aminos and bean puree. Reheat, strain, and pour over egg and lemon slices. Serves 4 to 6.

Black Soybean Soup

1 pint black soybeans, soaked
    overnight
1 medium onion, minced
3 stalks celery, including ten-
    der parts of leaves
8 cups cold water
2 tablespoons potato flour
1 tablespoon Bragg Aminos
⅛ cup lemon juice
1 teaspoon finely chopped
    lemon rind
⅛ teaspoon peppercorn, freshly
    ground
¼ cup chopped parsley
¼ teaspoon mustard
2½ tablespoons butter

Sauté onion until golden brown; add water, beans, celery, and parsley, and cook until beans are tender, or about 4 hours. Add more water if necessary. Strain through sieve, add flour and seasonings. Mix well and simmer slowly for 15 minutes before serving. Serves 6.

Lentil Soup

4 *cups lentils*
9 *cups water*
3 *lbs. brisket of beef*
1 *large onion, chopped*
¼ *cup celery, chopped*
1 *lb. spinach, chopped*

⅓ *cup peanut oil*
1 *tablespoon lemon juice*
½ *teaspoon finely chopped lemon rind*
1 *teaspoon Bragg Aminos*

Soak lentils overnight. Drain. Combine with beef and boil slowly in water for 3 to 4 hours. Add celery and onions and simmer slowly for another hour. Add seasonings, oil, spinach, and lemon juice, and cook until meat and lentils are tender. Serves 10.

New England Clam Chowder

2 *cups shucked clams, with liquor*
3 *cups potatoes, pared and cubed*
2 *tablespoons vegetable oil*
2 *medium onions, sliced*

4 *tablespoons butter*
1 *quart scalded milk*
6–8 *whole-wheat or rye wafers*
1 *tablespoon whole-wheat flour*
1 *teaspoon Bragg Aminos*

Pour a small amount of water over clams, about ½ cupful. Pick clams over carefully, removing any shell particles. Drain liquor into saucepan. Bring to a boiling point and strain through a piece of cheesecloth or extra-fine sieve. Set liquor aside. Remove the hard portions of the clams and chop fine. Sauté onion in oil.. Add potatoes and seasonings. Sauté until golden brown, stirring frequently. Add the chopped portion of the clams. Sprinkle all with whole-wheat flour and dredge. Add 2 cups boiling water and cook until potatoes are tender. Add the milk, the soft portions of the clams, and butter. Soak whole-wheat or rye wafers or crackers in a little milk until soft. Add to chowder. Reheat and bring to boiling-point and, at the same time, bring the clam liquor to the boiling-point. Try to keep both mixtures the same temperature to prevent curdling. Combine and, if desired, thicken further with a little flour and butter precooked together. Serves 6.

Manhattan Clam Chowder

2 *cups shucked clams, with liquor*
2 *tablespoons oil*
1 *onion, minced*
2 *cups diced potatoes*
2 *diced carrots*
4 *cups boiling water*
2 *cups tomatoes, stewed or canned*

¼ *teaspoon thyme*
¼ *teaspoon marjoram*
1 *teaspoon parsley*
1 *teaspoon Bragg Aminos*

Pour a small amount of water over clams, about ½ cup. Pick clams over carefully, removing any shell particles. Drain liquor into saucepan. Bring to a boiling point and strain through a piece of cheesecloth or extra-fine sieve. Set liquor aside. Remove any hard portions of the clams and chop fine. Sauté onion in oil until tender. Add carrots and potatoes and sauté for 5 minutes. Strain excess oil from pan. Add water, herbs, and seasonings. Cook until potatoes are nearly tender. Add tomatoes. Simmer until potatoes are tender. Add soft portion of clams and heated clam juice. Reheat. Simmer for 3 minutes and serve at once. Serves 5.

LAW OF LIFE

Man's body was created according to the laws of physics and chemistry, which are the Creator's own laws. They never vary. His law is written upon every nerve, every muscle, every faculty, which has been entrusted to us. These laws govern the cells, tissues, and organs of the body as they carry on their various functions. They operate largely through the complex network of nerves that run throughout the body. They act through the central nervous system, from which nerve impulses originate, and through the autonomic nervous system, that part of the network not under the direct control of the will.   -Henry W. Vollmer, M.D.

Little things are like weeds—the longer we neglect them, the larger they grow.

California Clam Chowder

1 *quart veal stock, chicken broth, or other meat stock*
1 *cup clams cut in very small pieces*
½ *cup clams, left whole*
1 *large onion, chopped fine*
⅓ *cup celery, chopped fine*
1½ *cups stewed or canned tomatoes*

⅓ *cup olive oil*
1 *cup diced potatoes*
3 *peppercorns ground fine*
1 *cup boiling water*
¼ *teaspoon thyme*

Place oil and onions in bottom of soup pot and allow onions to brown lightly. Add the meat stock, celery, tomatoes, and clams, and simmer slowly for 10 minutes. Add the potatoes, water, and seasonings. Cook until potatoes are done. Serves 5.

Fish Purée

1½ *small onions minced*
1½ *quarts milk*
6 *tablespoons butter*
6 *tablespoons whole-wheat flour*

¼ *teaspoon thyme*
3 *cups cooked fish*
paprika
1 *teaspoon Bragg Aminos*

Scald minced onion in milk. Melt butter, blend in whole-wheat flour, Bragg Liquid Aminos and thyme, and add milk gradually, stirring constantly. Force fish through sieve and add to sauce. Serve hot, garnished with paprika. Serves 8.

Baked Oyster Soup

4½ *pints rich milk*
3 *tablespoons butter*
2 *stalks celery, diced*
½ *teaspoon Bragg Aminos*

18 *slices toasted whole-wheat bread, crushed*
4½ *dozen oysters*

Bring milk to boil. Add butter, celery, and toasted whole-wheat bread crumbs. Add Bragg Liquid Aminos . . . .Drop in the oysters, two or three at a time, and as soon as the milk is almost ready to boil again, pour into a large baking dish and put in the oven. Let brown. Stir under, and brown again until the dish has become golden brown three times. Serve immediately. Serves 8.

Oyster Stew

I call this "nature's mineral dish," because there are good quantities of calcium in the milk and iodine in the oysters. It is a splendid food to serve periodically, and is often enjoyed by those who usually do not care for shellfish.

> 1 *qt. oysters, with liquor*
> 5 *cups scalded milk*
> ⅓ *cup butter*　　　　　　　⅛ *teaspoon peppercorns,*
> 1 *tablespoon minced onion*　　*freshly ground*
> 1 *teaspoon chives*　　　　*dash of mace*

Sauté onions lightly in 1 teaspoon butter; add to scalded milk, with oysters and seasonings. Simmer slowly until oysters are plump. Place pieces of butter at bottom of plate before serving the stew. When the oyster soup is poured into the plate, the butter will melt and float to the top, making a golden heading for this delicious soup. Serves 6.

Lobster Chowder

> 1 *medium-sized lobster*　　　2 *tablespoons minced onion*
> 4 *tablespoons butter*
> 4 *cups liquid (consisting of all*
> 　*milk, all chicken stock, or*　　¼ *teaspoon thyme*
> 　*half and half)*　　　　　　1 *teaspoon parsley*
> 1 *cup water*　　　　　　　*paprika*
> 3 *tablespoons whole-wheat*
> 　*cracker crumbs*

Remove the lobster meat from the shell. Simmer all body bones with thyme and parsley in the water for 15 minutes. Strain and reserve liquor. Dice lobster meat, chopping claw and tail meat fine. Cream the liver of the lobster (the green part) in half the butter. Combine lobster meat, creamed liver-butter mixture, and cracker crumbs. Scald the milk with the onion. Remove the onion and add to lobster mixture. Add strained, lobster-bone liquor and reheat. Sprinkle with paprika. Serves 3.

Peanut-Butter Soup

1 *quart milk*
2 *tablespoons peanut butter*
1 *grated apple*

1 *lemon, juice only*
cinnamon, nutmeg, or a pinch
of ginger

Scald milk and add peanut butter softened with the lemon juice.
Let stand in a warm place for 15 minutes. Add grated apple. Beat
well, and add spices. Serve piping hot in heated bowls. Serves 4.

Sweet-Potato Soup

1 *pint cold mashed sweet pota-*
toes
1½ *pints stewed strained toma-*
toes

½ *cup cream*

Add cold mashed sweet potatoes to strained tomatoes. Rub through
a colander or sieve, add cream. Heat and serve. Serves 3.

Onion and Cheese Soup

¾ *lb. sharp aged cheese*
3 *onions*
2 *tablespoons butter*
2 *tablespoons peanut oil*
1½ *tablespoons potato flour*
4 *cups milk*

2 *tablespoons chopped chives*
⅛ *teaspoon fresh ground pep-*
percorns
3 *caraway seeds*
⅛ *teaspoon chervil*

Cook onions lightly in butter until golden brown, work in flour.
Scald milk and add finely chopped cheese. Blend in seasoning.
Cook until mixture is smooth and thoroughly blended. This can
best be done in a double boiler. It should be served immediately
before the cheese lumps or thickens the soup. Serves 4.

Tasty Cheese Soup

⅔ *cup finely chopped onions*
5 *tablespoons butter*
5 *tablespoons whole-wheat*
flour
5 *cups milk*
5 *cups chicken stock*

1¼ *cups cooked chopped car-*
rots
1¼ *cups cooked chopped celery*
chopped parsley
¼ *teaspoon paprika*
⅔ *lb. natural cheese, finely cut*

Sauté onions in butter until tender and glassy. Add whole-wheat flour, blending well. Add stock and milk gradually, stirring constantly. When boiling, add carrots, celery, paprika, and cheese. Cook over low heat until cheese is melted.
Serve hot with finely chopped parsley. Serves 6.

Banana Soup

3 *bananas*	½ *tablespoon brown sugar*
3 *cups milk*	½ *tablespoon butter*

Peel and slice bananas and boil with the milk, butter, and brown sugar in a double boiler for ten minutes. Mash through a coarse sieve. Serve at once. Serves 3.

Chestnut Soup

3 *cups blanched chestnuts*	⅓ *teaspoon sage*
4½ *cups water*	¼ *teaspoon (scant) celery seed*
3 *cups milk, scalded*	*dash nutmeg*
3 *tablespoons minced onion*	1½ *cups cream*
6 *tablespoons butter*	*chopped parsley*
3 *tablespoons whole-wheat flour*	

To shell and blanch chestnuts: wash and discard those that float. Dry and with a sharp knife make a cross on both sides of the shell. Place in a baking dish with 1 teaspoon shortening and bake in a very hot oven (450°F.) about 10 minutes. Cool, remove shell and brown skin with a knife. Cook chestnuts in water until tender. Press through a sieve and add milk. Cook onion in butter until tender but not brown. Blend in whole-wheat flour . . . . .sage, celery seed and nutmeg. Add milk and chestnut mixture gradually, stirring constantly. Cook 5 minutes, add cream. Heat to boiling, garnish with parsley, and serve. Serves 8.

Ripe-Olive Soup

4½ *cups milk*	⅓ *teaspoon paprika*
1½ *tablespoons grated onion*	½ *cup cooked diced celery*
2¼ *tablespoons butter*	1 *cup diced ripe olives*
2¼ *tablespoons whole-wheat flour*	2 *teaspoons Bragg Aminos*

Combine milk or substitute with onion and bring to boil, then strain. Melt butter, blend in whole-wheat flour, Bragg Liquid Aminos and paprika, add strained milk, celery and olives and continue to heat for 10 minutes on low. Serves 6.

Orange Bouillon- Chilled

1 tablespoon unflavored
 gelatin
1 tablespoon distilled water
3 cups orange juice
1/3 cup honey

1 tablespoon lime or lemon
 juice
3 oranges
1 tablespoon grape juice

Soak gelatin in warm distilled water for 5 minutes and stir until dissolved. Stir in honey, add orange juice (3 cups) and lime or lemon juice. Chill. When mixture begins to congeal, blend in blender. Cut oranges in halves, scoop out the pulp and chop it fine; combine with orange mixture and add grape juice. When ready to serve, blend thoroughly again. Serve in bouillon cups garnished with orange sections and sprigs of mint or parsley. Serves 6.

Chilled or Hot Red Currant Soup

1/2 cup natural barley
1-1/3 quarts red currants
1/2 cup honey

2/3 cup water, distilled
1-1/3 sticks cinnamon
1/4 teaspoon Bragg Aminos

Soak natural barley overnight in distilled water. Wash and stem the currants, add honey, water and sticks of cinnamon. Cook currants over low heat for 15 minutes. Drain and put through a coarse sieve. Add soaked barley with 2/3 cup water and Bragg Aminos, simmer until barley is soft and juice thickened. Blend currents and barley — serve soup warm or chilled. Serves 4-6.

Every man is the builder of a temple called his body . . . We are all sculptors and painters and our material is our own flesh and blood and bones. Any nobleness begines at once to refine a man's features, any meanness or sensuality to imbrute them. — Henry David Thoreau

◇◇

Jellied Tomato Soup

4 *cups canned or fresh*
  tomatoes
1 *cup water*
1 *teaspoon honey*
1 *small onion, sliced*
3 *cloves*
1 *tablespoon lemon juice*

1 *teaspoon Bragg Aminos*
1½ *tablespoons unflavored*
  gelatin
½ *cup cold water*
minced parsley
lemon slices or whipped cream

To water add tomatoes . . . . sweetening, onion, cloves, lemon juice and Bragg Liquid Aminos. Cook for 20 minutes. Strain through a fine sieve to get 3 cups of juice. Soak gelatin for 5 minutes in cold water. Dissolve in hot tomato juice. Chill in large bowl. Force through a ricer or break with fork. Garnish bouillon cups with finely minced parsley, a slice of lemon, or a teaspoon of whipped cream. Serves 6 to 8.

Ponce de Leon,

Searched for the "Fountain of Youth".

If he had only known —

— it's within us...

Created by the food we eat!

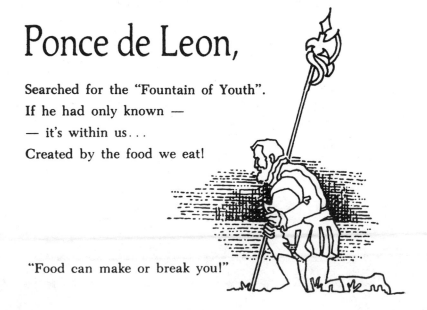

"Food can make or break you!"

Chapter 5

Vegetables

Vegetables Are a Menu "Must"

VEGETABLES as well as fruit, both raw in salads and properly cooked, are among the "protective" foods, and should represent at least three fifths of the diet. These foods not only contribute vitamins and minerals to the diet, but add the bulk required for proper body functioning, in addition to helping maintain the alkaline reserve of the body. They add variety, color, flavor, and texture to the diet.

To a long generation of Americans, vegetables have been a colorless, unappetizing, and uninteresting food, and no wonder. The accustomed method of boiling all the life out of the most succulent garden-picture vegetables and serving them straight from a swimming pool of surplus cooking water is certainly an unappetizing way to serve nature's delicacies. Any cook with ingenuity can prepare a vegetable to be the rarest of foods in delicacy. There is no better way to discover the unsurpassed quality of fine foods than by experimenting with herb cookery in vegetables, by preparing them properly to conserve all the vitamins, minerals, and food values and by bringing out their true qualities of flavor pointed up by harmoniously blended seasoning. It is not necessary to have them rich and heavily spiced. They can be standard items of fine food, delicately flavored and served in entirely new ways designed to excite the palate with a new adventure.

Cooking with herbs is a delightful and healthful experience. Of all foods, herbs are designed to point up the flavor of vegetables more intriguingly. For that reason, the chapter on cooking with herbs and this section devoted to vegetables should be used interchangeably. Then vegetables can become one of the real delicacies served at your table, rather than the humdrum, everyday foods to be regarded with distaste.

Buying Organic Vegetables for a Small Family

It is often very difficult to buy vegetables for a family of two or even of four people without running the risk of having leftovers. Of all foods, vegetables have least food value after they have been standing in cooked form. Vegetables are made to be eaten as soon as possible after cooking to obtain the utmost in their vitamin and mineral content. Avoid saving vegetables for a second meal or a second day. Try instead to buy wisely and cook carefully to avoid waste or leftovers.

The following chart indicates approximate servings:

Fresh Vegetables	For Two People	For Four People
Asparagus	1¼ lbs.	2½ lbs.
Beets (including beet tops)	1¼ lbs.	2½ lbs.
Broccoli	1¼ lbs.	2½ lbs.
Brussels sprouts	¾ lb.	1½ lbs.
Cabbage	¾ lb.	1½ lbs.
Carrots	½ lb.	1 lb.
Cauliflower	1 small head	1 large head
Corn on the cob	2 - 4 ears	8 ears
Greens (such as spinach, mustard, Swiss chard)	1¼ lbs.	2½ lbs.
Lima beans	1¼ lbs. unshelled	2½ lbs. unshelled
Onions	1 lb.	2 lbs.
Parsnips	1 lb.	2 lbs.
Peas	1¼ lbs. unshelled	2½ lbs. unshelled
Potatoes (white)	1 lb.	2 lbs.
Potatoes (sweet)	1 lb.	2 lbs.
Squash (almost any kind)	1 lb.	2 lbs.
String beans	¾ lb.	1½ lbs.
Turnips	1¼ lbs.	2½ lbs.
Zucchini	¾ lb.	1½ lbs.

How to Select Healthy, Fresh Vegetables

Although canning has become almost an exact science, fresh vegetables still outrank canned foods in all possible aspects in flavor and vitamin and mineral content. So buy all the fresh vegetables you can in season. You will find many in the market all the year round, as modern scientific agriculture has extended the season of many previously limited vegetables. Some of the vegetables, when out of season, may lack freshness and flavor. Today frozen foods have overcome this handicap. Learn to buy your vegetables when they are fresh, firm, and ripe. Avoid the moldy, withered, bruised, over-soft, over-hard, or colorless-looking vegetables. They not only lack flavor, but contain less of the vitamin and mineral content.

There are five classifications of vegetables, and each should be selected with attention to their characteristics of freshness and quality.

1. The root vegetables, such as carrots, potatoes, turnips, etc., should be firm, not withered. They should never have sprouts. And such root vegetables as potatoes and turnips, etc., should not be green.

2. Stem vegetables, such as asparagus, bean sprouts, celery, etc., should be true to their characteristic color, crisp, and fresh.

3. The leaf and flower vegetables represented by the green and salad vegetables, such as spinach, Swiss chard, lettuce, etc., should be deep green in color, crisp and fresh and, if in head form, solid.

4. Fruit vegetables are represented by the squash family: eggplant, okra, and tomato. They should be deep in their characteristic color, firm, and fresh.

5. The seed vegetables are corn, peas, beans and other legumes. These should be fresh and firm.

The stem, leaf, and fruit vegetables, which are easily distinguishable as those vegetables which are grown above the ground, are usually lower in starch content than the root vegetables, and the smaller the root vegetable, the less the starch content. If you are counting your calories or are on a low-starch or restricted-starch diet, select small carrots, beets and turnips as being more suitable. Not only do the smaller-sized root vegetables provide lower starch content for the diet, but they are more delectable in flavor. For general purposes, the medium-sized vegetables are usually preferred. These have not over-extended their growth, nor have they failed to achieve full maturity.

How to Keep Vegetables
before Preparation

The sooner vegetables are cooked after buying or picking, the better they are. If it is impossible to cook them at once, they should be put in the refrigerator immediately. Peas and corn, if at all possible, should be cooked very soon after they are gathered.

Greens and other crisp vegetables should be thoroughly washed, dried, placed in well-covered enamel or glass containers, and stored in the refrigerator.

If it is necessary to store your salad vegetables for any length of time, do not wash them until shortly before using.

Some vegetables, such as squash and sweet potatoes, require a little warmer place than the other vegetables.

How to Clean Vegetables
before Cooking

There is great danger in commercially purchased vegetables, unless they are properly cleaned. This is because many sprays are used in truck gardening, and it is also possible because of irrigation with unsanitary water in some areas, to obtain vegetables with infectious forms of bacteria. For these reasons it is absolutely essential to wash all vegetables thoroughly.

There are several good methods to remove spray. Use one to two tablespoons of hydrochloric acid to a gallon of water, and wash all your vegetables thoroughly in that. If that is not practical for you, simply get a dishpan full of mild soapsuds and give your vegetables a thorough scrubbing. Yes, even lettuce and leafy products. They can be rinsed thoroughly so that there is no trace of the soap remaining. Scrub them well and use a metal sponge to remove dark spots. In most cases they should not be scraped, nor their skins removed, as the richest portion of their food content often lies just beneath the skin covering. When you peel potatoes, carrots, turnips, and other vegetables, you are destroying a tremendous part of their food value. Boil, roast, or bake vegetables in their skins.

You will also find that many salad vegetables can be served with their skins intact. Cucumber salad, for example, when made of small slices of cucumber with the skin intact, is not only delicious but also attractive to the eye.

◇◇

Healthy Cooking of Vegetables

Vegetables should always be prepared with the least amount of water (distilled is purest and best to use) to retain the protective elements. In fact, steaming, baking and also woks are preferable because they conserve more vitamins and minerals. The new cookers and small convection ovens are ideal for health cooking and there are great ones available that enable you to cook by baking or steaming. (We do not endorse microwaves.)

Health Methods of Cooking

There are several excellent methods of cooking without water or using a very small amount.

1. Any good **heavy stainless steel, enamel, glass or iron pan** with a tight-fitting cover will do. You may or may not use a stainless steel steamer basket that fits in most pans; we prefer to use these but more water should be used and the remaining liquids should be served with the vegetables in shallow soup bowls and any excess saved, see pg. 29. For new taste delights try a dash or spray of Bragg Aminos over these steamed vegies. The pan used should be a size suited to the amount of vegetables you are preparing. If the vegetable is cut or sliced in small pieces and the utensil filled to the brim, it will require very little water. Carrots or beets prepared this way usually require only a few tablespoons of water. Always cover tightly and cook over medium heat.

2. **Casserole Cookery** may be applied to this health method by grating root vegetables and slicing, dicing or chopping the more succulent vegetables. This fast method uses a tablespoon or two of distilled water and a half to one teaspoon of olive oil or oriental sesame oil, fresh sliced garlic, Bragg Aminos and herbs. You can bake in a moderate oven.

3. **Steaming and Baking.** There are new hot air circulating convection oven-cookers that prepare fast healthy meals. They can steam, bake, wok and even saute ... from vegetables, potatoes, eggs, soups, breads, poultry, meats, fish and will even bake breads, cookies and pies.

4. **Wok and stir frying** are popular healthy methods for preparing vegies and main entrees. Woks originated in the Orient and have been used for centuries. We enjoy this fast, easy, almost waterless method of preparing our foods.

A Few Important Points
to Remember

1. While the vegetable is cooking, do not remove the lid. By removing the lid you allow the steam to escape, and often this contains the vitamins and minerals. Also, you are allowing the water in the vegetables, or the "self-cooking liquids," to escape.

2. Low heat should be used whenever possible and the vegetables should be cooked the shortest possible time to tenderize them.

3. Do not be afraid to eat vegetables slightly crisp. It is not necessary to cook vegetables to a pulpy mass to make them palatable.

4. Vegetables may be prepared in a variety of ways such as broiling, sautéing, baking, boiling, or steaming. Never fry vegetables.

5. Never use soda to preserve color, because it destroys some of the vitamins.

6. Do not allow vegetables to stand in water any length of time before cooking as the minerals dissolve and are lost in the water.

7. Cut vegetables shortly before cooking, as the cut vegetables when exposed to air lose vitamin C.

ASPARAGUS

Asparagus, with its delicate flavor, is one of our early spring vegetables. It is low in food value but high in minerals and vitamins.

Select medium or large, crisp stalks. Snap off stalks as far down as they will snap easily. Wash thoroughly, removing all excess scale. Steam or cook with as little water as possible. One excellent way is to tie in bundles and cook upright in a narrow kettle. Add boiling water, making sure pan is filled about 1 to 1½ inches; cover and cook about 20 minutes or until tender. Cooking time depends upon the tenderness and freshness of the asparagus stalk. About 2½ pounds of asparagus will serve 4.

Life cannot be maintained unless life be taken in, and this is best done by making at least 60 percent of your diet raw and cooked vegetables, with a plentiful supply of fresh juicy fruits. — **Patricia Bragg**

Buttered Asparagus

Remove coarse ends from stalks of asparagus. Steam tips until tender and serve on toasted bread with melted butter.

Baked Asparagus

2 *lbs. asparagus*
¼ *cup butter*
1 *egg*

1 *cup dry whole-wheat bread crumbs*

Snap, wash, and tie asparagus into 4 bundles. Roll in bread crumbs, dip into egg
then roll again in the bread crumbs. Place butter in baking dish, arrange bundles of asparagus, and bake until tender. Serves 4.

Sour-Creamed Asparagus

2 *lbs. asparagus (fresh or canned)*
6 *slices toasted whole-wheat bread*

1 *cup sour cream*
grated carrots to garnish

Place cooked asparagus on whole-wheat toast. Add 3 tablespoons of sour cream over each serving. Garnish with grated raw carrots. Serves 4.

Asparagus Hollandaise

Cook as in recipe for Buttered Asparagus. Add hollandaise sauce before serving.

ARTICHOKES

Contrary to popular belief, the artichoke has important food value. The globe artichoke contains more protein than most vegetables and a form of starch that is not readily utilized by the body, which makes it excellent for the restricted or low-calorie diet.

Do not confuse the globe artichoke with the Jerusalem. The globe is the green clustered bud type and the Jerusalem is a root vegetable resembling a small potato or yam.

◇◇

Artichokes with Garlic & Herbs

4 artichokes
4 cloves garlic, sliced
3 tablespoons lemon juice

1 teaspoon Bragg Aminos
1/4 cup olive oil
1/3 teaspoon Italian herbs

Wash artichokes thoroughly. Cut 1 inch off the tops. Remove stems & slice in 1/2 inch sections. Place sliced stems and sliced garlic between the leaves of the artichokes. Mix herbs, oil, Aminos and lemon juice and sprinkle over artichokes. Stand artichokes on end in a saucepan using steamer basket. Steam for 30 minutes or until tender. Serve hot or cold, whole or halved, with health mayonnaise. Serves 4-8.

Scalloped Globe Artichokes

6 cooked artichokes
1-1/2 tablespoons lemon juice
1 cup dry whole-wheat
   bread crumbs

1/8 teaspoon Italian herbs
1 teaspoon Bragg Aminos
2 eggs, beaten
1 cup soy or evaporated milk

Scrape edible portion from cooked artichoke leaves, remove choke and dice heart. Mix artichoke scrapings, whole wheat bread crumbs, eggs, milk and seasoning. Place in greased baking dish. Bake in moderate oven (375°F) about 15 minutes or until browned. Serves 6.

Stuffed Artichokes

4 artichokes
1/3 cup melted butter or olive oil
1/4 cup bread crumbs

4 cloves garlic, sliced
pinch sweet basil
1 tsp Bragg Aminos

Wash artichokes, insert sliced garlic in between the leaves. Place upright in steamer basket and steam until thoroughly tender (30-40 mins). When done, remove all leaves, scrape the choke out of the heart leaving rounded hollow. Discard choke. Scrape all the leaves of the artichoke, then mash this portion of the leaves with the melted butter or olive oil, bread crumbs and seasoning. Stuff artichoke heart. Place under broiler to brown. Serves 4.

(Note: This recipe can be varied by using rosemary or chopped fresh sweet basil leaves.)

<><><><><><><><><><><><><><><><><><><><><><><><><><><><><><><><>

BEANS

Nearly all legumes belong to the family of "life-builders." They are very high in protein — blood, muscle and tissue builders of the body. For that reason they can be used not only as a vegetable but as a protein dish in place of meat, eggs and other proteins.

Baked Lima Beans

3 cups lima beans, cooked
3 tablespoons butter or olive oil
2 tablespoons arrowroot flour
1 cup milk or soy milk

1 teaspoon Bragg Aminos
2 beaten eggs
1/2 cup whole-wheat bread
  crumbs

Add arrowroot flour to melted butter. Add milk gradually and stir until thick. Puree beans and add to sauce. Add seasoning and beaten eggs. Place in buttered casserole, cover with bread crumbs and butter. Bake 15 minutes in moderate oven. Serves 4.

Lima Beans with Cheese

2 cups dried beans, cooked
  (lima or other beans
  may be used)
2 tablespoons olive oil
2 tablespoons onion, chopped

1 cup milk or soy milk
2 tablespoons chopped
  green bellpepper
grated parmesan cheese
1 teaspoon Bragg Aminos

Place olive oil in wok or pan, add beans, milk, onions, bellpeppers and seasonings. When thoroughly heated, sprinkle grated parmesan cheese over top and stir. Allow to stand for a few moments before serving. Serves 4-6.

Baby Limas Marjoram

3 cups baby limas, cooked
1/3 teaspoon marjoram
2 tablespoons parsley
1 small onion, chopped
3 garlic cloves, chopped

2 tablespoons olive oil
2 large tomato, diced
pinch Italian herbs
1/2 teaspoon Bragg Aminos

Combine garlic and onion with olive or oriental sesame oil and saute in wok or pan for 2 to 3 minutes. Add diced tomato and remaining ingredients, cook 5 to 10 minutes until done, stirring frequently. Serves 3-6.

Baked Beans Basic Recipe

(This can be used for kidney beans, pink beans, navy beans, etc. all garden peas or any variety of similar legumes.)

1 qt. beans
1/2 cup olive oil
2 tablespoons brown rice syrup
1/2 teaspoon dry mustard
pinch Italian herbs

1/4 to 1 cup unsulphured
molasses (vary amount
to taste)
1 teaspoon Bragg Aminos

Cover beans with cold water and soak overnight. (This reduces cooking time.) Drain, cover with water again, place in bean pot, crock pot or iron kettle and heat slowly. Add other ingredients, keeping below boiling and always keeping enough water to cover the beans. When skin begins to burst, cover the bean pot and bake 1 to 2 hours in a medium oven until done. You can also prepare beans in a crock pot overnight on low. Serves 6 to 8.

Green Beans

1 lb of green beans serves 4.

Select tender beans. This can be tested by gently pulling off the ends. If they snap easily, they are young, fresh beans. Wash thoroughly, remove the ends and string; cut lengthwise or cross-wise into thin pieces, or leave whole if desired. Cook or steam in a small amount of water until tender. The cooked beans can be used in the following recipes:

Green Beans with Cheese

3 cups green beans, cooked
2 tablespoons cheese, grated
(parmesan is best)

2 tablespoons melted butter or
olive oil
1 teaspoon Bragg Aminos

Place all the above ingredients with the exception of half the cheese in a greased baking dish. Stir well; top the dish with the remaining cheese and a little butter. Bake in a hot oven for about 5 minutes. Serves 4-6.

Green Beans with Herbs

2 lbs string beans
3 tablespoons olive oil
1 teaspoon Bragg Aminos

2 cloves garlic
pinch Italian herbs
pinch parmesan cheese

String and cut beans. Steam or cook with a minimum of water over a slow fire. Saute in wok or pan whole garlic and herbs lightly in the olive or oriental sesame oil, add cooked beans and Bragg Aminos. Saute 2 minutes & sprinkle with parmesan. Serves 6-8.

Green Beans with Mint

3 cups cooked green beans
1/4 cup chopped mint
3 tablespoons olive oil

1/2 teaspoon Bragg Aminos
pinch salad herbs
sweet basil, fresh

Combine ingredients and seasoning and heat in wok. Serves 4-6.

Green Beans with Mushrooms

3 cups green beans, cooked
1 cup mushrooms, sliced
1-1/2 tablespoons melted
butter or olive oil

1/2 teaspoon Bragg Aminos
3 garlic cloves, minced
3 tablespoons yogurt as garnish

Saute the garlic & mushrooms in wok or pan with olive or sesame oil, then add beans & garnish with yogurt and serve. Serves 4-6.

Green Beans with Yogurt

3 cups cooked green beans
1 cup yogurt
3 tablespoons chopped onion
3 tablespoons melted butter
3 tablespoons potato flour

2 tablespoons lemon juice
2 tablespoons honey
3 tablespoons chopped parsley
1/2 teaspoon Bragg Aminos

Saute onions in butter, blend in the potato flour. Add bean-pot liquor and stir until it thickens. Add seasoning, honey, yogurt and lemon juice. Add the beans and heat thoroughly. Garnish with chopped parsley. Serves 4-6.

Spanish Snap Beans

2 *medium sliced onions*
2 *cups fresh or canned*
   tomatoes
1 *green bellpepper,*
   diced with seeds
1 *pinch, Italian herbs*
2 *garlic cloves, sliced*

2 *teaspoons olive oil*
2 *tablespoons whole-wheat*
   flour
2 *lbs. cooked snap beans, cut in*
   1-inch pieces
1 *cup water, distilled*
1 *teaspoon Bragg Aminos*

Combine the tomatoes, onions, bellpepper, herbs & garlic. Simmer for 10 minutes. Blend olive oil with a dash of oriental sesame oil for flavor with the whole-wheat flour & stir into tomato mixture. Cook until smooth & thick, stirring frequently. Add cooked beans and heat well for 5 minutes. Serves 4 to 6.

§ § §

SOYBEANS

The soybean is one of the richest foods in protein and in nutrients. It also makes a very delightful addition to health meals. It has an ancient heritage, having been used for thousands of years by the people of the Orient. Only in recent years have Americans and Europeans become awakened to the soybean's possibilities as a meat substitute, a milk substitute, and sprouted, and also to its great value as a healthy main food staple.

How to Make Sprouts
Soybeans, Sunflower, Alfalfa, Lentil, Mung Beans, etc.

The sprouts of these beans and seeds are used as a salad vegetable, to replace salad greens and in sandwiches to replace lettuce. Soybean sprouts are a wonderful addition to omelets and meat dishes of all kinds and are, of course, popular in Oriental cookery such as chow mein, chop suey, and the like.

◇◇◇

These sprouts can be obtained either from soybeans, mung beans, or other seeds and are delicious and nutritious. These sprouting seeds and beans can easily be made at home and their preparation is not difficult.

It is very important to have the finest-quality beans and seeds for sprouting. These can usually be found at your Health Food Store. They should not be over one year old.

With the proper beans and seeds obtained for sprouting, you can create a vegetable in any climate, winter or summer, that is fresh, matures quickly (within a few days), does not require extensive soil cultivation or variations of sunshine and has tremendously healthy high food value.

The U.S. Department of Agriculture gives a very excellent method for sprouting beans and seeds:

"Soybeans, mung beans and other seeds can be sprouted in a glass jar, flower pot, a sink strainer or any container which you can drain from the top or bottom and can be covered with cheese cloth or mesh. Be sure the container is large enough, because the beans or seeds may swell from 6 to 10 times their original bulk as they sprout. Soak overnight and next morning put them in the container, cover and leave them in a warm place. Flood with lukewarm water at least three or four times each day during the sprouting period. In four to six days, the sprouts will be two to three inches long. Then they should be kept in a cool place or the refrigerator, just like any fresh vegetable until served."

"The sprouts are very tender. To hold their crispness, it's best not to add to hot mixtures until a few minutes before serving."

Note: See Salad Section for recipe for Soybean Sprout Salad.

Soybean Sprouts en Casserole

3 cups sprouted soybeans
3 sliced onions
3 / 4 cup celery, diced
1 / 2 cup whole-wheat bread
  crumbs
3 tablespoons butter or
  olive oil

1 cup milk or soy milk
2 tablespoons soybean flour
1 / 2 cup grated parmesan cheese
2 egg yolks
1 teaspoon Bragg Aminos

Lightly saute onions and celery first, then last minute add sprouts. Add this to beaten egg yolk, milk, flour, bread crumbs & seasoning. Put mixture in buttered casserole & top with grated parmesan cheese. Bake in moderate oven 5 to 8 minutes, or until delicately brown. Serves 4-6.

Sprouted Soybean Omelet

4 *eggs*	2 *tablespoons butter*
4 *tablespoons milk*	2 *cups sprouted soybeans*
½ *teaspoon Bragg Aminos*	½ *cup onion tops*

Beat whole eggs lightly, adding milk and seasoning. Melt the butter in the omelet pan. Pour in mixture, bean sprouts and chopped onion tops. Lift cooked part slightly from time to time, to allow the uncooked part to run under it and brown. Allow pan to heat quickly so that it will brown quickly. Serves 6.

Soybean Sprouts with Onions
and Mushrooms

3 *cups sprouted soybeans*	3 *tablespoons butter*
½ *cup onion tops, chopped fine*	1 *tablespoon Bragg Aminos*
1 *cup mushrooms*	

Saute onion tops, bean sprouts, and mushrooms lightly in butter. Pour Bragg Liquid Aminos over the mixture and allow to simmer for a few moments before serving. Serves 5.

Soybean Recipes

There are so many variations of preparing the magic soybean that we can only give a basic preparation for each type.

Green Soybeans

Allow soybean pods to stand 10 minutes in boiling water. Drain and shell the beans. For each cup of the shelled beans, add ½ cup of boiling water. Bring to a boil and cook until beans are tender (10 to 15 minutes). Drain and season in any manner desired.

Dried Soybeans

Soak the beans overnight. In the morning pick them over and wash again. Drain and put in 3 times the original amount of boiling water;

in other words, if you have one cup of beans to start with, add 3 cups boiling water. Cook slowly at a simmer for about 2 hours or overnight in crock pot. Soybeans will not cook into a soft, mushy mass. They will remain firmer and hold their shape better than the ordinary dry beans.

Canning and Quick-Freezing Soybeans
(See Chapter 24 Canning and Quick Freezing)

Soybeans Are Used In A Variety of Products that are Delicious, Nutritious and Ideal Meat Substitutes
(See Chapter 9 Vegetarian Entrees, and see the Bragg Vegetarian Gourmet Cookbook. See back pages to order.)

Soy Milk
(There are many varieties available in Health Stores)

Soy milk resembles cow's milk but is made from soybeans. It's healthier, contains no cholesterol, nor its problems. It can be used in any recipe calling for cow's milk in the same proportions as cow's milk.

There are many ways of making soy milk. This is one of the simplest and most practical and workable recipes: Soak beans overnight. Measure three times the amount of liquid in proportions to the soaked beans. Grind the beans in a food processor or blender while adding some of the liquid, proportioning the liquid so all of it is used up by the time you have ground all the beans.

Take this pulpy mass and boil it slowly for 1 hour. Strain.

Add pure vanilla, honey or other sweetening, as desired.

Soy Cheese
(There are many delicious varieties available in Health Stores)

To prepare soy cheese, allow soy milk to curdle just as you would ordinary milk. Set the soy milk in a warm place. When it is soured and thickened, cut it into sections and bring to a boil in a saucepan. Then strain.

The remaining cheese can be seasoned with Bragg Liquid Aminos, onions, chopped chives or other forms of seasoning.

BEETS

One of the most economical vegetables nutritionally is the beet. Both the root and the leaves can be used and are an excellent source of nutrients and iron. It is old-fashioned nutritional waste to simmer whole beets for hours, then skin and pickle them with vinegar. We prefer to steam them in their skins, served buttered or sliced. We also love beets raw, grated in our salads.

Baked Beets — Whole, Sliced or Grated

Select medium-sized tender beets. Remove tops. Wash and do not peel. Bake whole, sliced or grated. If grated, fill casserole very full, sprinkle with a small amount of water. Cover tightly and bake in a moderate oven. The grated beets will bake in 10 minutes after they are thoroughly heated, whole and sliced beets 20-40 minutes in a casserole dish. Remove cover, season and serve with butter.

Julienne Beets, Baked

Remove 6 beet tops and save them to cook as greens. Then take washed medium-sized beets (do not peel) and cut into julienne strips. Put in baking dish or casserole. Add 1/2 cup boiling water. Bake at a temperature of about 350°F. for about 30-45 minutes with a tight-fitting cover. After removing from the oven, add 1 teaspoon fresh lemon or lime juice, 1 tablespoon butter and a dash of Bragg Aminos. This will serve 4 people. (Carrots can also be cooked in the same manner.)

Lemon Beets, Pickled

small beets	*1 tablespoon pickling spices*
1 cup lemon juice	*2 tablespoons honey*
1/2 cup water	*1 tablespoon Apple Cider Vinegar*

Mix lemon juice and Apple Cider Vinegar with water, bring to a boil and cook for 10 minutes with 1 tablespoon of regular pickling spices tied in a little bag. Cool, sweeten with about 2 tablespoons of honey or to taste. Cook small beets with skins until tender; plunge into cold water and slice. Cover with seasoning mixture in a bottle and allow to stand for 12 hours or longer. Store in refrigerator.

Orange Beets

3-1/4 cups cooked beets,
  sliced
3/4 cup orange juice, fresh
1-1/4 teaspoons grated
  orange rind

3/4 cup distilled water
2 tablespoons potato flour
  or arrowroot flour
2 tablespoons butter
2 teaspoons honey

Stir the potato or arrowroot flour into the butter; add the water slowly. To this add orange rind, orange juice and honey. Cook together until smooth and thick, then add beets the last 3-5 minutes, stirring constantly. Serves 4-6.

Beet Greens

Nothing is more delicious than the tender young greens of beets. If you have a vegetable garden, you can eat beet greens as you thin your beets, and this can be very soon after they pop out of the ground. For those not fortunate enough to have a garden, select beets with care when you buy them so that they have tender green tops. Wash thoroughly and steam or cook covered, in their own juices for a few minutes or until tender. Season with a dash or spray of Bragg Liquid Aminos, butter or olive oil and a dash of apple cider vinegar is delicious and your favorite seasonings. Serve with sour cream or yogurt topping.

Sour Cream or Yogurt Beets

Cook as for Baked Grated Beets (see recipe on page 96). Serve topped with thick yogurt or sour cream. These are a natural accompaniment for hot or cold beets (also Russian Beet Soup) and may be used in any way desired.

§ § §

BROCCOLI

The rich green broccoli florets, leaves and stem have a delicate flavor that is delicious and also helps keep you healthy with its rich source of vitamins, minerals and nutrients.

Broccoli with Cheese

1 *lb. broccoli*
½ *cup grated cheese*
2 *tablespoons olive oil*
2 *cloves garlic*

½ *teaspoon Bragg Aminos*
⅓ *cup dried whole-wheat bread crumbs*

Wash broccoli thoroughly, removing tough end parts of the stem. Place in saucepan or casserole, with small amount of boiling water. Cook slowly until tender. Sprinkle grated cheese, seasoning, and bread crumbs over the top. Brown garlic slowly in oil, remove garlic, pour oil over the top, and bake in oven for 20 minutes. Serves 4.

CABBAGE

Cabbage is one of our richest vegetable sources of vitamin C. The deeper green the color, the better quality nutritionally.

Seven-Minute Cabbage

1 *large head green cabbage*

¼ *teaspoon Bragg Aminos*
3 *tablespoons butter*

Wash cabbage thoroughly. Quarter or cut in large pieces.   Cook with cover 7 to 12 minutes, add butter and Aminos .   Serves 4.

Green Buttered Cabbage

In cooking cabbage, remove only the toughest of the outside leaves. The outside leaves contain most of the vitamins and food values. Remove the tough stalk. Slice finely, put in buttered baking dish, cover with whole-wheat bread crumbs, ¼ cup butter. Add a few tablespoons liquid, either milk or water, and bake until tender. Brown for a few moments under broiler before serving.

Red Cabbage

2 *lbs. red cabbage*	2 *tablespoons honey*
2 *tablespoons peanut oil*	2 *large apples, peeled and*
½ *teaspoon nutmeg*	*quartered*
⅛ *teaspoon Bragg Aminos*	½ *cup lemon juice*
½ *cup water*	

Slice cabbage; add apples, lemon juice, spices, honey and water. Cook until just tender . . . . . (If desired, ½ teaspoon powdered clove and a small amount of sliced onion may be added during cooking.)

ℰ❧

CARROTS

Every time you serve carrots you are enriching the family table. They are a valuable source of vitamin A.

In cooking carrots, as with all vegetables, use the smallest possible amount of water. Then, if you are serving carrots in a sauce, be sure to include the cooking water in that sauce, making it part of the liquid content. It gives a real "lift" to the flavor.

Carrots and Celery

3 *cups thin-cut strips carrots*	2 *tablespoons melted butter*
3 *cups (small pieces) celery*	2½ *tablespoons finely chopped*
¼ *teaspoon thyme*	*parsley*
⅛ *teaspoon Bragg Aminos*	

Add the smallest amount of boiling water possible to the combined carrots and celery in a saucepan. Add herbs and seasoning. Cover tightly and simmer until tender . . . . toss with parsley and butter. Serves 8.

VARIATIONS: ¼ teaspoon celery seed or marjoram can be used to vary the flavor, instead of the thyme. Or a small amount of chopped chives or tender young onions can be used to point it up.

Spiced Carrots en Casserole

15 *small carrots*
¼ *cup butter*
2 *tablespoons honey*
¼ *teaspoon cinnamon*
¼ *cup boiling water*

Wash carrots thoroughly (do not scrape or pare) and place in casserole. Blend butter, honey, and cinnamon together, adding water and mixing thoroughly. Pour this mixture over the carrots, cover tightly, and bake in a moderate oven for about 1½ hours or until tender. After 1 hour add a small amount of boiling water, if necessary. Serves 5.

Caramelized Carrots

2½ *lbs. carrots cut into sticks*
or slices
1½ *tablespoons honey*
2½ *tablespoons butter*

Put the cut carrots into a buttered casserole; add seasoning and honey. Top with melted butter. Cover tightly and bake in a hot oven for about 50 minutes. Serves 8.

Glazed Carrots with Honey

6 *carrots, halved*
2 *tablespoons butter*
2 *tablespoons honey*
¼ *tablespoon grated orange rind*

Wash carrots thoroughly; cut in half. Cook until tender in the smallest possible amount of water. Allow to drain. Blend the honey, butter, orange rind and seasoning in a saucepan. Bring to a boil, then add the carrots and continue to simmer for a few minutes. Serves 3.

Carrots with Turnips

4 *carrots*
2 *turnips*
2 *cloves garlic*
3 *tablespoons vegetable oil or butter*
2 *small onions*
1 *teaspoon marjoram*
⅓ *teaspoon Bragg Aminos*
2 *tablespoons parsley*
3 *tablespoons grated cheese*
¼ *cup water*

Wash carrots and turnips thoroughly, cut into small pieces. Place olive oil or butter in a wok or pan with chopped onions and minced garlic. Cook slowly for 3 minutes. Add the carrots and turnips, then the seasonings and water. Cook very slowly. When carrots and turnips are almost tender, add the rest of ingredients and allow to stand for a few minutes before serving to blend in the cheese and the parsley. Serves 4.

Carrots Parsleyed

1 bunch new carrots   *1 tablespoon parsley, chopped*
2 tablespoons butter   *1 teaspoon honey*

Wash the carrots and slice in rounds. Add small amount of distilled water and cook in a covered pan until tender. Allow the cooking water to evaporate rather than draining it from the carrots by covering the pan and increasing the heat. Watch carefully to see that the carrots don't burn. When practically dry, add the butter, honey and parsley. Serves 3-5.

Baked Carrots

16 small carrots   *2 tablespoons olive oil*
1/4 cup honey or brown   *or butter*
* rice syrup*   *1/3 teaspoon cinnamon*
1/3 cup boiling water   *1/4 teaspoon Bragg Aminos*

Scrub carrots well and place in oiled casserole dish. Blend olive oil or butter with honey or brown rice syrup, cinnamon and Bragg Aminos. Add water and blend well. Pour over carrots, cover and bake in moderate oven (350°F) until tender. Serves 4-6.

§ § §

CAULIFLOWER

Remove florets from cauliflower head, and slice leaves and stems, it's all delicious. Wash thoroughly. Prepare as follows:

3 *cups cauliflower flowerets*   ½ *cup buttered whole-wheat*
1 *clove garlic*   *bread crumbs*
                                                      2 *tablespoons vegetable oil*

Brown garlic in oil, add seasoning. Remove clove of garlic; place
cauliflower flowerets in a baking dish, cover with garlic-seasoned
oil and buttered bread crumbs. Pour in one cup liquid, either milk
or water, bake in a moderate oven till tender. If desired, cauliflower can be browned under the broiler before serving. Also,
½ cup grated cheese can be added as a topping, just before putting
under the broiler. Serves 5.

CELERY

Green celery is higher in vitamin A than white or bleached celery,
although all types of celery are excellent nutritionally.

Braised Celery

2 *large onions, sliced*   ¼ *cup water*
4 *cups celery, cut fine*
4 *tablespoons melted butter*

Place onions in baking dish. Brown celery in melted butter. Combine with onions, ¼ cup water, and seasoning and cook for 5
minutes. Then bake in slow oven (325°F.) about 1 hour. Serves
6 to 8.

Celeriac and Wild Rice

⅓ *cup wild rice*   1⅓ *cups water*

Boil briskly for 20 to 30 minutes. Do not stir. Drain off water and
steam until fluffy.

½ *cup meat stock*   1 *celery root (celeriac)*
3 *tablespoons chopped onion*   ⅓ *cup peanut oil*
                                                      1 *beaten egg*

Mix and pour in buttered casserole and bake in 350°F. oven for
½ hour, or until celeriac is tender. Serves 4.

CORN

Corn should be cooked as soon as possible after being picked, as that is when the flavor is best. Steaming is best and usually takes 6-10 minutes.

Serve with a dash or spray of Bragg Liquid Aminos, olive oil and then sprinkle Brewer's yeast flakes over each corn or serve with fresh butter or onion butter. (See recipe for onion butter under "Sauces and Gravies.")

§ § §

EGGPLANT

Eggplant, perhaps more than any other vegetable, lends itself to a variety of preparations. Almost any seasoning and herb within the boundary of the imagination can be put to use by the inventive cook with this delightful vegetable.

Eggplant, skin and all, can be prepared as an entree, as a meat substitute and as an accompanying vegetable. It can be boiled, baked, broiled and prepared in so many delicious ways that it can be the "luxury" dish of the meal.

Only a few of the hundreds of recipes for eggplant can be included here, but the good cook should experiment with this delightful food above all others.

Eggplant with Herbs and Cheese

1 eggplant	*1/2 cup chopped chives or*
1/2 teaspoon marjoram	*tender green onion tops*
1/2 teaspoon rosemary	*2 garlic cloves*
1/4 teaspoon oregano	*1 tablespoon chopped parsley*
2 tablespoons olive oil	*1 cup tomato juice*
2 teaspoons lemon juice	*1/4 cup grated cheese*

Bake sliced eggplant in oiled casserole. Pour about 1/3 cup

of boiling water over it. Allow to cook slowly while mixing sauce of all other ingredients. Pour the sauce over eggplant, cover, and allow to cook about 30 minutes in all. When done, sprinkle with grated cheese and allow to brown under the broiler. Serves 4.

Eggplant and Okra

1 eggplant, unpeeled	1 tbs chopped bellpepper
2 large tomatoes	1/4 cup chives or
2 cups sliced okra	tender green onion tops
1/2 teaspoon Bragg Aminos	2 cloves garlic, sliced
1 teaspoon olive or sesame oil	1 tomato, diced

Saute in wok or pan all ingredients together until tender. Takes about 10-12 minutes, then sprinkle with parmesan cheese before serving. Serves 4-6.

Scalloped Eggplant

1 large eggplant	1 quart chopped tomatoes
4 tablespoons olive oil	pinch Italian herbs
1/2 teaspoon Bragg Aminos	1 cup grated unprocessed
2 medium onions, chopped	cheese
1 clove garlic, minced	1/4 teaspoon sweet basil

Slice eggplant in 6 slices without peeling, brush with oil. Broil until partly tender, turning once. Saute onion and garlic in remaining oil; add tomatoes and seasonings. Simmer until thickened, stirring often. Arrange eggplant slices, cheese and sauce in layers in greased casserole and bake in a slow oven about 30 minutes. Serves 6.

Stuffed Baked Eggplant

1 large firm eggplant	1 cup dry whole wheat
2 tomatoes	bread crumbs
2 teaspoons grated cheese	1 cup celery, finely cut
1 green pepper, minced	2 tablespoons onion, minced
1/2 teaspoon Bragg Aminos	1 tablespoon olive oil

Cut eggplant in half, remove pulp, leaving thick layer in hulls. Cut pulp into bits, mix well with other ingredients.

◇◇◇

Fill eggplant hulls, place in baking dish with one cup hot water and bake ½ hour. Serves 6.

GREEN LEAVES
Nature's Choicest Vegetables

All green leafy vegetables: spinach, Swiss chard, mustard greens, beet tops, turnip tops, etc., an infinite variety, can be prepared delightfully to the king's taste. These are all rich in nature's coloring element, chlorophyll, as well as the vitamins and minerals.

They are excellent foods to add light, porous bulk to the diet, and variety, color, and eye-appeal to the table.

All greens adapt themselves to the same basic recipes. For that reason, recipes below can be used interchangeably with any of the green, leafy vegetables.

The cooking time of these vegetables will vary. Mustard greens must be cooked longer than spinach leaves, for instance. But all can be cooked by following a basic pattern recipe, and cooked until tender.

Preparation of Green Leafy Vegetables

All green leafy vegetables, particularly spinach and Swiss chard, contain a lot of sand and dirt. They must be washed very thoroughly. They should be rinsed in 8 to 10 waters or until all sand and dirt are removed. They should then be placed in a saucepan, filling pan, without any water, using the water left on the leaves from the washing to act as a steam agent. Cover well, steam thoroughly, and cook until tender. All green leafy vegetables should be cooked slowly in a heavy pan.

Basic Greens Recipe No. 1

2 *lbs. greens*	¼ *teaspoon Bragg Aminos*
2 *tablespoons butter*	1 *small onion*
dash of mace	*dash of nutmeg*

Cook leaves. Drain, chop if desired. Add butter, minced onion, dash of mace and nutmeg before serving. Serves 4.

Basic Greens Recipe No. 2

2 cups cooked greens
2 tablespoons chopped green
pepper
1 tablespoon chopped pimiento
2 tablespoons finely chopped
onion

5 tablespoons vegetable oil
½ teaspoon Bragg Aminos
2 tablespoons lemon juice

Sauté green pepper, pimiento, and onion in vegetable oil. Add cooked greens. When thoroughly heated, add lemon juice before serving. Serves 3.

Basic Greens Recipe No. 3

2 lbs. greens
2 cloves garlic
4 tablespoons vegetable oil or
butter

1 tablespoon chervil
1 tablespoon chives
¼ teaspoon nutmeg
¼ teaspoon Bragg Aminos

Cook and drain greens. Prepare garlic in vegetable oil, browning it slightly. Put greens in saucepan. Add chervil and chives. Pour garlic and oil over the greens; stir in nutmeg. Serves 4.

Basic Greens Recipe No. 4

2 lbs. greens
2 cloves garlic
¼ teaspoon Bragg Aminos

4 tablespoons vegetable oil or
butter
2 tablespoons lemon juice

Brown the garlic in oil or butter, then add lemon juice. Remove garlic and pour over cooked greens before serving. Serves 4.

Basic Greens Recipe No. 5

2 lbs. greens
½ cup chopped parsley
¼ cup chopped green onions
¼ teaspoon Bragg Aminos

1 tablespoon butter or
vegetable oil
1 teaspoon rosemary

Cook greens with parsley, onions. Drain. Place in buttered . . . casserole, add rosemary, and bake in oven until tender. Serves 4.

Basic Greens Recipe No. 6

2 *lbs. greens*
2 *cloves garlic*
½ *cup thick consommé*

4 *tablespoons butter sauce*
4 *tablespoons peanut oil*
⅓ *teaspoon Bragg Aminos*

Cook greens. Prepare sauce by crushing garlic thoroughly and adding to consommé butter sauce and peanut oil. Heat sauce thoroughly; pour over greens before serving. Serves 4.

KALE

Kale and Sour Cream

4 *cups cooked kale*
1 *tablespoon butter*
1 *teaspoon honey*

1 *teaspoon lemon juice*
1 *cup sour cream*
¼ *teaspoon sweet anise*

Place kale in saucepan, add butter, honey, and lemon juice. Heat thoroughly. Reduce heat and gradually stir in sour cream . . . Serves 6 to 8.

LEEKS

Leeks au Gratin

1 *bunch leeks*
boiling water
½ *teaspoon Bragg Aminos*

½ *cup grated unprocessed cheese*

Wash and trim leeks. Cook until tender, about 25 minutes, in boiling water to cover. Drain. Arrange in oiled baking dish, sprinkle with a dash of Bragg Aminos and grated Parmesan cheese. Heat under broiler until cheese is melted. Serves 4.

MUSHROOMS

The popular button mushroom is the most widely used and is readily available fresh or canned. Oriental mushrooms are also high in protein and have greater health benefits. Shiitake, Reishi, Oyster, etc., are available dried and fresh in many whole-food supermarkets, health stores and supermarkets. Oriental markets have more fresh and dried varieties. Mushrooms are a delicious accompaniment to pastas, vegetables, soups, casseroles, etc. They can also be used as an entree as well as a vegetable.

Mushroomed Oysters

Thoroughly wash mushrooms, place cap side up on a large oyster and dot with butter. Cook in a hot oven until oysters are plump.

Broiled Button Mushrooms

8 large mushrooms, fresh   *1 tablespoon butter or*
dash Bragg Aminos   *olive oil*

Wash mushrooms and remove stem (save stems for soups). Place caps in oiled pan, cap side down, about 3 inches below source of heat. Broil 3 minutes, then turn over and broil 3 minutes longer. Put butter or oil and dash of Bragg Aminos in each cap, broil until butter melts. Serve on whole-grain toast or bed of shredded lettuce. Serves 2-4.

Avocado and Mushrooms

1 ripe avocado, diced   *desired amount of sliced*
10 mushrooms, sliced   *pimiento, fresh or canned*
2 tablespoons butter   *1 teaspoon Bragg Aminos*

Wash mushrooms, slice and saute with butter in wok or pan 7 to 8 minutes until tender, then add diced avocado and pimiento and serve on warmed corn tortilla or pita bread or whole-grain toast. Garnish with Parmesan cheese and Brewers yeast flakes. Serves 4.

OKRA

Okra has a peculiar property of being a gentle, slippery bulk, which makes it excellent for those whose diets cannot include roughage. Because of its blandness, it should be combined with vegetables of decided flavor or a pungent vegetable seasoning.

Tomato Okra

1 lb. okra, sliced
1/2 teaspoon Bragg Aminos
pinch Italian herbs

1 tablespoon olive oil
1 cup tomatoes, chopped

Cook okra until tender; add tomatoes, seasonings and simmer until done. This recipe is also delicious with 1/2 teaspoon sweet basil added during cooking. Serve in small bowls. Serves 2-4.

Okra Specialty

2 cups okra, sliced
1 large onion, sliced
2 large tomatoes, diced

1 teaspoon Bragg Aminos
2 cloves garlic, sliced
pinch Italian herbs

Cut and mix ingredients. Add enough distilled water to steam until tender. Serve in shallow bowls. Serves 4.

§ § §

ONIONS

Onions and Tofu

2 cups onions, sliced
1 package firm tofu, sliced
pinch salad herbs

1 tablespoon olive oil
1 teaspoon Bragg Aminos

Lightly saute in wok onions, tofu and seasoning in olive oil 4 to 6 minutes. Cover and let steam for 10 minutes, or until onions are slightly browned. Serves 4-6.

Onions with Cheese

6 *medium-sized onions*
¾ *cup grated, aged cheese*
¼ *teaspoon Bragg Aminos*

Boil onions until tender. Place in greased casserole dish. . .Sprinkle with pepper, and Bragg Liquid Aminos . . . and cover with grated cheese. Bake in moderately hot oven for a few minutes, or until the cheese is golden brown. Serves 6.

PARSNIPS

It has been customary to prepare parsnips with sweeteners, but the sugar content of parsnips is higher than that of most root vegetables and for that reason does not require inordinate amounts of added sweetening. Doubtless the parsnip is unpopular today because it has been improperly cooked. Either method of preparation given here is to be chosen as preferred.

Baked Parsnips (sweet style)

3 *cups cooked parsnips*   ⅓ *cup honey*
¼ *cup minced parsley*
¼ *cup melted butter*

Mix and place in a buttered casserole. Bake in 400°F. oven for 20 minutes. Serves 6.

Parsnip Patties

6 *to 8 parsnips*   3 *or 4 tablespoons minced*
2 *tablespoons butter*   *onion*
                          whole-wheat Melba toast
                          crumbs

Wash and cut young parsnips into pieces. Cook in small amount of water until tender. Mash and add seasoning, butter and a small amount of very finely minced onion. Mix well; shape into small patties. Dip and roll in whole-wheat Melba toast crumbs; place in oven until thoroughly heated. Serves 6.

PEAS

Peas, like beans, are the muscle-builders of the vegetable kingdom because they are high in protein.

Peas Basque

2 *lbs. very tender young peas*   3 *leaves lettuce*
1 *tablespoon butter*

Place butter in saucepan; add peas and cover with lettuce leaves that have been rinsed in cold water. Cook very slowly until tender.

Peas en Casserole

6 *small onions*   4 *cups fresh or canned peas*
½ *teaspoon chopped mint*
1 *cup hot water*
2 *tablespoons butter*   ½ *teaspoon thyme*

Put the onions and mint in a casserole. Add hot water, cover, and cook in a slow oven for 40 minutes. Add the peas, seasonings, and butter. Cover and bake 20 minutes in moderate oven. Serve from the casserole. Serves 5 or 6.

Peas in Onion-Butter Sauce

2 *lbs. shelled peas*
1 *finely chopped onion*
6 *tablespoons butter*   ½ *teaspoon cumin seed*

Cook peas until tender in a small amount of water. Sauté chopped onions in butter. Add seasoning, cooked peas, and cumin seed. Heat in a covered pan slowly. Serves 6.

Peas with Thyme

2 cups peas
½ cup finely chopped celery

½ teaspoon thyme

Cook all ingredients together in a minimum of water until tender. Add butter and serve. Serves 2.

POTATOES

Potatoes are a vegetable low in roughage, which makes them practical for people on soft diets. They are easily digested and assimilated. Many of the minerals are just beneath the skin, and for that reason the skin should be used. One of the best ways of preparing the potato is the simple baking process.

Potatoes au Gratin

Pare potatoes and cut into cubes. Slice thin about 2 small onions. Arrange in layers in a greased baking dish, a layer of potatoes, a layer of onions, and a layer of grated unprocessed cheese. Make the last layer cheese. Bake in a moderate oven until done.

Cheese-Stuffed Potatoes

3 potatoes

¼ lb. unprocessed cheese, grated

Scrub and dry potatoes. With an apple-corer remove a cylinder from the center of each potato. Fill each cavity with cheese. Seal ends with tiny pieces of cylinders which have been removed. Bake in a moderate oven (350°F.) until tender, about 45 to 50 minutes. Serves 3.

Zesty Potato Casserole

2 cups diced raw potatoes
¾ cup canned or fresh tomatoes
2 tablespoons butter or soy butter
¼ cup water

½ teaspoon paprika
½ clove garlic, sliced
¼ cup chopped parsley

Alternate layers of potatoes and tomatoes in a casserole. Combine butter or soy butter, water, seasonings, garlic, and parsley. Pour over potatoes and tomatoes. Cover and bake in moderately hot oven (375°F.) 40 minutes or until potatoes are tender. Serves 3.

Health Baked French Fries

5 *large white potatoes* ¼ *teaspoon Bragg Aminos*
5 *tablespoons melted butter*

Cut each potato into eight or ten lengthwise strips, ½ inch wide and ⅜ inch thick. Arrange in baking pan so they don't overlap. Pour melted butter over them. Bake in hot oven at 450°F for 30 minutes, or until tender, turning them occasionally. Serves 4.

ၗ∾

SWEET POTATOES

Maple Candied Sweet Potatoes

3 *medium sweet potatoes*   ½ *cup unsweetened apple juice*
¼ *cup maple syrup*   ¼ *cup water*
½ *tablespoon butter*

Steam potatoes in jackets until nearly tender. Peel and slice into baking dish. Heat remaining ingredients to boiling, pour over potatoes, and bake in slow oven (300°F.) 1 hour. Serves 3.

Sweets in Apples

2 *tablespoons butter*   2 *medium yams or sweet pota-*
3 *large apples*   *toes cooked, mashed*
2 *tablespoons honey or raw* 2 *tablespoons raisins*
  sugar

Remove slice from top of each apple, and core. Scoop out apples, leaving a substantial shell. (Scallop edge with a sharp knife, as desired.) Chop pulp. Add butter, mashed sweet potatoes, honey or raw sugar, and raisins. Mix well. Fill apple shells. Place in baking dish with a small amount of water. Bake in moderately hot oven (375°F.) 45 minutes. Serves 3.

★Sauerkraut Stuffed Pepper

3 *medium green peppers*	½ *cup sauerkraut*
½ *cup dry whole-wheat crumbs*	1 *thin slice onion*
½ *teaspoon Bragg Aminos*	¼ *teaspoon paprika*

Cut a piece off the stem end of each pepper and remove the seeds and partitions; then parboil in boiling water for 5 minutes. Mix the remaining ingredients and fill the peppers. Place in a buttered dish, top with whole-wheat bread crumbs, and pour ½ inch of water or stock into the pan. Bake in a moderate oven for 30 minutes. Serve hot. Serves 3.

★ Read the Bragg Book "Salt-Free Sauerkraut Recipes," & learn how to make your own raw sauerkraut. It's so delicious, easy-to-make & nutritous for your health. See back pages for ordering.

Of all the knowledge, that most worth having is knowledge about health. The first requisite of a good life is to be a healthy person.
— Herbert Spencer

The human body has one ability not possessed by any machine — the ability to repair itself.   — George E. Crile, Jr. M.D.

I'm on the Army Diet. Everything I eat goes to the front.

A reminder: What's on the table soon becomes what's on the chair.

PEPPERS

Spinach with Peppers

1½ tablespoons minced green pepper
½ tablespoon minced pimiento
1½ tablespoons minced onion
3 tablespoons butter or oil

1½ cups cooked spinach
1 teaspoon Bragg Aminos
1 tablespoon lemon juice

Cook green pepper, pimiento, and the onion in butter or oil. Add spinach, heat thoroughly, add lemon juice and Bragg Liquid Aminos. Serves 3 or 4.

SQUASH

Baked Acorn Squash

3 acorn squashes
½ cup honey

½ cup melted butter
olive, soy, or peanut oil

Cut three washed acorn squashes in halves lengthwise. Remove seeds. Brush with olive, soy, or peanut oil. Lay cut side down in a baking pan. Bake 30 minutes in moderately hot oven (400°F). Turn face up; brush with ¼ cup honey mixed with ¼ cup melted butter. Bake until tender and golden, about 30 minutes longer, brushing frequently with honey and butter mixture. Serves 6.

Squash and Limas

3 cups fresh or frozen lima beans
2 cups boiling water
6 cups sliced zucchini
¾ teaspoon paprika
1 teaspoon Bragg Aminos

3 tablespoons butter, or soy or peanut oil
¾ cup minced onion
3 tablespoons whole-wheat flour
½ teaspoon thyme

Combine the lima beans, Bragg Liquid Aminos and boiling water in a saucepan. Cover, bring to a boil. Cook 5 minutes. Add the squash, sliced thin, and continue cooking, covered, 10 minutes longer or until tender, stirring occasionally. Drain, reserving liquid. Meanwhile heat butter in skillet; add onion and sauté until tender. Blend in remaining ingredients. Measure 1 cup of the reserved liquid; add to the onion mixture and cook until thickened, stirring constantly. Pour over the squash and beans. Heat and serve. Serves 6 to 8.

Squash Surprise

1½ lbs. summer or zucchini
   squash
2 large tomatoes, chopped
½ teaspoon dill seed
1 large onion, chopped
1 teaspoon Bragg Aminos

Cut and mix ingredients. Steam until tender in a little water. Serves 6.

Zucchini with Herbs

1 lb. zucchini
¼ cup butter
2 tablespoons vegetable oil
1 clove garlic
1 small onion, chopped
2 tablespoons chopped parsley
1 teaspoon sweet basil
½ bay leaf
5 tomatoes, peeled and cut up
1 tablespoon Bragg Aminos

Wash and cut zucchini into thin rounds. Do not peel. Sauté onion and garlic in the melted butter and oil until slightly brown. Add zucchini and all seasonings and herbs, together with ½ cup boiling water. Cook a few minutes. Add tomatoes. Cook a few minutes more. Add chopped parsley and serve. Serves 8.

Zucchini and Chard

This delightful combination can be made exactly as in the recipe above, using chard instead of the fresh tomatoes and substituting ½ teaspoon of chives for a bay leaf.

When you realize that each body cell is a small factory, needing constant recharging through the food you eat, you'll begin to really think about diet.
—Dr. J.D. Nolan

TOMATOES

Tomatoes are rich in Vitamin C and nutrients. They are a sturdy vegetable, in spite of their delicate flavor and perishability. They are one of our most adaptable vegetables and can be used either as a dish in themselves, properly flavored or combined with small amounts of other vegetables or dishes to act as the flavoring quality itself.

Baked Tomatoes

Pick firm, medium-sized tomatoes and cut out a little of the hard part of the stem end. Lay close together in a baking pan. Put a small piece of butter or olive oil and a dash of Bragg Aminos in each cavity. You may also stuff the tomatoes by scooping out half of the insides and filling with whole-wheat bread crumbs or soft tofu or soy cheese or tuna. Bake in hot oven until done.

Broiled Tomatoes

1 tomato for each serving *whole wheat bread crumbs*
melted butter *1 egg*

Wash ripe tomatoes and halve crosswise. Seal top with melted butter and a dash of Bragg Aminos. Dip into beaten egg then in whole-wheat bread crumbs. Place face-up under broiler for 8 to 10 minutes, or until delicately browned.

Tomatoes Creole

3 green bellpeppers, chopped *5 tablespoons butter or olive oil*
6 large tomatoes *pinch Italian herbs*
1 large onion, minced *1 teaspoon Bragg Aminos*
1 garlic clove, minced

Cut green bellpeppers into medium-sized pieces; quarter the tomatoes. Add minced onion and garlic to the oil or butter and saute in wok or pan for 3 to 5 minutes. To this add tomatoes, green bellpeppers, seasoning and herbs. Mix well and cook slowly until the bellpeppers are tender. Serves 4-6.

Onion-Tomato Bake

15 green onions and tops	1 tablespoon raw honey
6 ripe tomatoes	1/3 cup whole-grain bread
1 teaspoon Bragg Aminos	crumbs
1 tbs grated Parmesan cheese	2 tablespoons butter or oil

Cut the green onions and tops into small circlets. Cut tomatoes into small sections; combine onions, tomatoes, Bragg Aminos and honey in buttered casserole. Sprinkle with whole-grain bread crumbs and top with butter or oil. Bake about 20 minutes in a slow oven. Garnish with grated Parmesan cheese and Brewers yeast flakes. Serves 4-6.

Spinach Tomato Parmesan

6 large ripe tomatoes, halved	1/2 onion, finely chopped
2 cups cooked spinach	1 teaspoon Bragg Aminos
2 tablespoons butter or oil	pinch salad herbs

Prepare tomatoes for stuffing—scoop out half of insides. Carefully wash spinach, stems and drain. Lightly steam without added water. The small amount of water left on the leaves from washing is enough to cook spinach in its own juice. Cook very quickly a few minutes to bring the leaves just to tenderness. Combine cooked spinach with butter or oil, finely chopped onion and seasonings. Stuff tomato shells, place in buttered casserole, bake 10 to 15 minutes in moderate oven. Garnish with grated Parmesan or Romano cheese and lowfat yogurt before serving. Serves 6.

Sprout Seeds & Beans for Super Nutrition & Added Protein

Sprouts are delicious, nutritious and can be easily grown at home. Mix equal amounts of items (dry) from the list below in a jar and then when you want to sprout some they are ready - soak 1 tablespoon of mix in water in glass jar, no lid. Drain excess water and allow sprouts to grow. It takes 2-3 days, rinse twice daily, when sweet, tender, 1/2 sprouted, refrigerate and enjoy as needed! You can expose the sprouts to filtered sun on your windowsill a day to green them up.

Alfalfa Seeds	Garbanzo Beans
Sunflower Seeds	Mung Beans
Navy Beans	Pinto Beans
Soy Beans	Brown Lentils

Wheat, Buckwheat & other Grains

◇◇

Sweetbread Tomatoes

4 *tomatoes*	¼ *cup whole-wheat bread*
2 *green peppers*	*crumbs or whole-wheat*
sweetbreads	*cracker crumbs*
1 *tablespoon Bragg Aminos*	½ *onion*
	4 *slices whole-wheat bread*

Wash ripe tomatoes and remove small portion from the stem end. Remove the seeds, liquids and part of the pulp. Allow to drain upside down for about half an hour. Prepare onions by mincing finely and sauteing in butter for a few minutes. Prepare peppers by removing and chopping into small pieces. Add a brown sauce (see section on "Sauces and Gravies"). Blend the brown sauce, onions, and chopped peppers. Line the hollowed-out portion of the tomato with this mixture, allowing it to extend over the edges. Prepare sweetbreads by allowing them first to stand 1 hour in cold water, then drain and parboil in boiling water to which Bragg Amino seasoning has been added. Also, 3 tablespoons of lemon juice should be added to each quart of water used. The sweetbreads should cook for only 20 to 25 minutes, then be drained and cubed. Place cubes in hollowed-out tomatoes over the lining mixture. Top with cracker crumbs and bake 12 to 15 minutes in hot oven. These can be served on toasted, buttered whole-wheat bread and covered with a small amount of butter, if desired, for extra topping. (NOTE: Although primarily a vegetable dish, this may be a delightful maincourse dish also.) Serves 4.

🌱🌱🌱🌱🌱
In the Beginning . . .

To find out what really happened when the earth was created, engineers spent weeks gathering information, checking and rechecking it, and feeding it into the computer. The great moment came: all was complete, everybody gathered around, a button was pressed, the great computer spun into action, relays opened and closed, lights flashed and bells rang, and finally a typed message emerged: "See Genesis 1:1." — The Anglican Digest

Having heard the word, keep it, and bring forth fruit with patience. —*Luke 8:15*

Chapter 6

Meats

Organically Fed
hormone and
chemical free
meats are best!

Proteins, the Backbone of Body Chemistry

MEATS are protein foods. Our muscles, heart, blood, liver, tissue and other parts of the body are made of protein. It is important that we have protein foods (animal or vegetarian) to keep the body growing and in repair. The proteins are the tissue-builders, the makers of rich, red blood cells, organs and muscles.

We hear a great deal today about amino acids and my father Paul C. Bragg pioneered the use of amino acids over 75 years ago. The link between protein and body tissue is amino acids. When the aminos enter the bloodstream, they are carried to every part of the body, where they set to work repairing, rebuilding and maintaining body tissue, building up rich, red blood and conditioning the various body organs. This is why my father created Bragg Liquid Aminos. Amino acids are found in both animal proteins and vegetable proteins. Bragg Liquid Aminos are made from soybeans that are rich in amino acids. .. see page 28 for details.

Animal or vegetable protein is life itself. You cannot live a healthy life without proteins in your diet. There are several ways of obtaining proteins. They can be obtained from vegetable sources such as soybeans, tofu, tempeh, beans, lentils, nuts, seeds, sprouts, etc... and the animal protein from meats.

In this chapter we have shown you how to prepare meats properly to make them as digestible, appetizing and nutritious as possible.

FOR VEGETARIANS: We have the Vegetarian Gourmet Recipes book, see back pages for ordering. The Bragg main diet is vegetarian.

— Patricia Bragg

How to Buy Organically Fed Meat for a Small Family

Since protein is one of the most expensive items, care must be given for proper buying. Many Health Food Stores and Wholefood Supermarkets can supply you with healthy, "hormone and chemical free" beef. We suggest having red lean meat not more than 1-2 times a week, as beef does contain more cholesterol (fat). The following hints will be of assistance in buying for the small family.

Amounts given in chart are for three to four people.

Beef

CHUCK		
ground	1 lb.	
pot roast	3 lbs. boned	
Swiss steak	1 lb.	PORTERHOUSE
stew	1 lb.	
CLUB STEAK	2 steaks, 1½ in. thick	
CUBE STEAK	2 steaks, ¾ to 1 in. thick	
FILET MIGNON	2 steaks, 1½ in. thick	
FLANK		
ground	1 lb.	
stew	1 lb. boned	
steak	1½ lbs.	
MINUTE STEAK	1 lb. sirloin	T-BONE
NECK, STEW MEAT	1 lb. boned	
OX TAIL	2 lbs.	
RIB STEAK	2 steaks, 1½ in. thick	
ROUND STEAK		
ground	1 lb.	
pot roast	3 lbs. boned	
stew	1 lb. boned	
Swiss steak	1 lb. boned	
RUMP		ROUND
ground	1 lb.	
pot roast	3 lbs. boned	
Swiss steak	1 lb.	
stew meat	1 lb. boned	
SHANK		
stew	1 lb.	
SHORT RIBS	1 lb.	
SIRLOIN STEAK	1½ lbs.	SIRLOIN

How to Buy Meat for a Small Family (continued)

Lamb

BREAST			RIB	
ground	1 lb.		chops	4 chops
stew	1 lb. boned		SHANK	
FLANK			leg	2½ lbs.
ground	1 lb.		boiled	2 lbs.
stew	1 lb. boned		SHOULDER	
KIDNEYS	6		chops	2 chops
LOIN			ground	1 lb.
chops	4 chops		pot roast	3 lbs. boned
NECK			stew	1 lb. boned
ground	1 lb.		SIRLOIN	
stew	1 lb. boned		leg	2½ lbs.
			steak (leg cut)	1-in. slice

Veal

ARM			NECK	
pot roast	3 lbs. boned		ground	1 lb.
BREAST			RIB	
ground	1 lb.		chops	2 chops
stew	1 lb. boned		ROUND STEAK	
CALVES' LIVER	1 lb.		cutlet	1 lb.
FLANK			pot roast	3 lbs. boned
ground	1 lb.		roast	3 lbs. boned
stew	1 lb. boned		RUMP	
KIDNEYS	3		pot roast	3 lbs. boned
LOIN			roast	3 lbs. boned
chops	2		SHANK	
roast	3 lbs.		stew	1 lb. boned
			SIRLOIN STEAK	1 lb.
			SWEETBREADS	1 pair

Types of Organic (Chemical & Hormone-free) Meat

In Health Food Cookery we don't use smoked, pickled or preserved meat as it contains harmful preservatives. In buying meats you do not have to buy expensive cuts, there are many less expensive cuts of lean meat that provide nutritional value and taste appeal, if properly prepared. Use small amounts as they do in the orient and you'll be amazed at how you reduce your food bill and cholesterol.

Meat should never be fried, under any conditions. The best methods of meat preparation are broiling, roasting, and stewing.

Timetable for Cooking Meats

BROILED MEATS—CHOPS

Minutes per lb.				*Minutes per lb.*
LAMB, *Rib*			LAMB, *Shoulder*	
¾ inch	10		½ inch	16
1 inch	12			
1½ inch	20		PORK	
			¾ inch	50

STEAKS

BEEF, *Porterhouse*			*Club*	
(rare)			(rare)	
1 inch	7		¾ inch	15
1½ inches	10		1 inch	17
2 inches	20		(medium)	
(medium)			¾ inch	17
1 inch	9		1 inch	19
1½ inches	12		(well)	
2 inches	22		¾ inch	22
(well)			1 inch	25
1 inch	12			
1½ inches	15		*Round steak*	
2 inches	30		½ inch	12

ROASTS

BEEF (All beef roasts figured at 300°F.)

Standing rib roast			*Chuck*	27
(rare)	17			
(medium)	23		*Rump*	32
(well)	29			
			Tenderloin	
Rolled rib roast			(rare)	27
(rare)	30		(medium)	34
(medium)	36		(well)	42
(well)	47			

◇◇

Timetable for Cooking Meats (continued)   *Minutes per lb.*

LAMB (All temperatures figured at 300°F.)

Crown	34
Cushion	32
Leg	32
Rack	15
Flank shoulder	32
Rolled shoulder	43

PORK (Pork must always be cooked until thoroughly done. All temperatures are figured at 350°F.)

Butt	55
Cushion	38
End of cut	16
Loin—center cut	40
Shoulder—whole	32
Rolled, boned shoulder	45
Spare ribs	40
Whole loin	18

VEAL (All temperatures figured at 300°F.)

Leg	23
Loin	35
Rack	35
Shoulder	28
Rolled shoulder	43

HOW TO PREPARE MEAT

Broiling

Almost every modern home is equipped with a broiler. It is a very simple method of cooking and one of the best for retaining the juices, tenderizing the meat and making the protein available to the body in an easily digested form. Broiled meats lend themselves to a very fine collection of herbs that can be cooked as the meat cooks or spread fresh on the meat after preparation.

Pan Broiling

If you do not have a broiler, pan broiling is next best, and it may be done on any heavy pan or on a very heavy griddle. Heat dry pan very hot. Place prepared steak or chop in pan. Lower heat slightly and pan broil until brown on one side, then turn and brown other side. Cook steak to degree desired. Ground round or Salisbury steak can be prepared in this way. Marinate or mix into meat before broiling - minced onion, garlic, Bragg Liquid Aminos and any herbs desired for a delicious taste.

Roasting

Roasting is not as easy as broiling, but basic rules will produce good roasts from quality meats every time. Here are some of them:

- The meat should be thoroughly wiped with a clean, damp cloth.
- The bone side should be placed to the bottom of the roasting pan.
- Roasting time should be watched and good judgment exercised because of variability in meat, some being more tender than others and needing less cooking time.
- Stuff into slits in lamb or beef, slices of garlic and herbs.
- Cooking at low temperatures cuts down shrinkage and retains more juice and flavor.

Stewing

The best flavor comes from blending herbs, garlic, onions and Bragg Liquid Aminos in the cooking of stews. Use potato flour to thicken stews and pot pies.

BEEF

Steak with Herbs

There are delicious flavors with herbs that combine perfectly with steak. Any of the following methods of preparation may be used. Use 1 tablespoon lemon juice, pinch of meat herbs and 1/2 teaspoon Bragg Liquid Aminos to each steak and marinate with one bay leaf. Allow to marinate 2 hours or longer. Be sure each side is moistened with this herb liquid; broil.

Another Delicious Way to Cook Steak with Herbs

Crush 3 cloves of garlic in 1-1/2 tablespoons of olive oil for each steak, adding your favorite herbs. After the garlic has permeated the oil, brush the sides of the steak with this mixture and broil.

Also a delightful addition to this method is to sprinkle a small pinch of marjoram and tarragon over the oil just before broiling.

This method tenderizes steak and makes it delicious:

To 1/2 cup lemon juice and 2 tablespoons olive oil, add two crushed garlic cloves, 1/2 tsp rosemary, 1/2 tsp tarragon, 1/2 tsp thyme, and 1 tsp Bragg Aminos. Allow mixture to stand for 1 hour then pour into a shallow, flat pan; place steak in mixture, allow to remain for 1 hour or longer if possible, turning from time to time so that both sides are evenly permeated. Remove steak from liquid and place immediately into broiler.

Steak Rolls and Whole-Grain Pasta

1 lb chuck or rump steak,	*2 cups distilled water*
cut 1/2-inch thick	*1 cup onion, minced*
1-1/2 tablespoons oil	*1 teaspoon Bragg Aminos*
1/4 teaspoon thyme	*1/3 teaspoon paprika*
1/4 teaspoon leaf sage	*2 cloves garlic, sliced*
1/3 teaspoon basil	*12 oz. whole-wheat, soy or*
1/3 cup olive oil	*spinach noodles or*
4-1/3 cups fresh or canned	*whole-grain pasta*
tomatoes, chopped	*3/4 cups parsley, minced*
1/3 cup tomato paste	*pinch Italian herbs*

Blend seasonings and sprinkle over meat. Roll from short side, like a jelly roll; tie securely with string. Brown in heated oil in large saucepan. Add all remaining ingredients except pasta and parsley. Simmer uncovered 1 to 2 hours, until sauce is thick, add 1 tablespoon potato flour to thicken if needed. Meanwhile, separately cook and drain noodles. Toss in parsley. Remove steak roll from sauce, cut string and slice in 1/4-inch thick slices. Arrange pasta in center of plate and top with this sauce. Place steak rolls on top of pasta and garnish with grated Parmesan cheese, Brewers yeast flakes and a dash of Bragg Liquid Aminos. Serves 6-8.

Proper food molds one's personality and that of one's offspring.

Savory Swiss Steak

1½ lbs. lean beef
¼ cup whole-wheat flour
1 teaspoon marjoram
1 teaspoon Bragg Aminos

1 onion
1 clove garlic
¼ cup lemon juice
1½ tablespoons peanut oil
½ teaspoon summer savory

Mix flour and Bragg Liquid Aminos and pound into steak, getting as much flour into meat as it will stand. Set aside and repeat in about an hour until all the flour is absorbed. Heat peanut oil in a skillet. Into this place the crushed garlic and minced onion. In same pan quickly brown floured steak on both sides. Strew herbs over meat, pour over it the lemon juice and 2 cups water; heat to boiling-point. Place in Dutch oven, cover, and bake in oven for 2 hours, basting frequently. Add a little more liquid from time to time, if necessary. Serves 4 to 6.

Sour-Creamed Swiss Steak

2 lbs. round steak (2 inches thick)
whole-wheat flour
soy or peanut oil
½ teaspoon paprika

1⅓ sliced onions
⅓ cup water
⅓ cup sour cream
1⅓ tablespoons grated cheese
1 teaspoon Bragg Aminos

Dredge steak with whole-wheat flour and Bragg Liquid Aminos . . . . . Brown both sides in oil. Add remaining ingredients. Cover pan closely and simmer until meat is tender, about 2½ hours. Serves 4 to 6.

Beef Pot Roast

2 teaspoons whole-wheat flour
2 lbs. beef (chuck or rump)
⅔ chopped onion

1 teaspoon butter or oil
1⅓ cloves
1⅓ cups boiling water
1 teaspoon Bragg Aminos

Mix whole-wheat flour, Bragg Liquid Aminos . . . and dredge meat with this mixture. Brown meat and onion in butter or oil, add cloves and a small amount of boiling water. Cover and simmer

3 hours, or until tender, adding more water as needed . . . One hour before serving, potatoes and carrots may be added and browned right with meat. Serves 4.

Roast Beef

Rolled rib roast of beef

Wipe meat with damp cloth.

Place on rack in roasting pan and roast uncovered in slow oven (300°F.), allowing 35 to 40 minutes per pound. A 5- or 6-pound roast serves about 8.

Savory Beef Roast

Prepare a basting liquor as follows:

1 *cup chicken or beef consommé*
¼ *cup lemon juice*
½ *teaspoon thyme*
1 *teaspoon savory*
1 *tablespoon finely chopped onion*
½ *teaspoon Bragg Aminos*

Prepare the roast in the desired way. One very good way in this case is to rub the roast with butter.

Cover with whole-wheat flour and allow to brown in a hot oven; reduce the heat and bake until thoroughly done. Be sure to serve all the basting liquor left in the bottom of the pan over the roast, as this liquor is delicious.

Hungarian Goulash

⅔ *lb. lean beef*
⅔ *lb. lean veal*
⅔ *lb. beef kidney*
⅓ *cup soy or peanut oil*
⅓ *cup chopped onion*
2 *tablespoons diced green pepper*
1 *tablespoon Bragg Aminos*
⅔ *teaspoon paprika*
¼ *teaspoon thyme*
¼ *teaspoon marjoram*
⅔ *teaspoon caraway seeds*
⅔ *cup canned or fresh tomatoes*
2 *cups diced potatoes*
1 *cup diced carrots*

Cut meat in 1-inch cubes. Heat the fat in a heavy skillet; add meat and brown evenly on all sides. Add onion and green pepper; sauté until lightly browned. Add seasonings and tomatoes. Cover and simmer gently 40 to 45 minutes or until meat is tender. Add potatoes and carrots; cook 20 minutes longer or until tender. Add a little water, if necessary. Serves 6.

Hamburger on Toast

1 *lb. ground round steak*	6 *slices whole-wheat toast*
butter	1 *teaspoon Bragg Aminos*
2 *onions in thin slices*	

Toast whole-wheat bread on one side, butter on other side. Place thin slices of onion on toast. Divide ground round steak into patties and place on top of onion, pressing it so as to cover the whole surface of the toast . . . . Place under the broiler until done. Serves 6.

Kidney-Bean Surprise

1 *can kidney beans*	1 *teaspoon Bragg Aminos*
1½ *lbs. ground beef*	1 *green pepper, diced*
3 *potatoes, diced*	
2 *onions, diced*	

Sauté onions and green pepper in butter or oil. When slightly browned, add ground beef and seasonings. Add diced potatoes, cover pan, and cook until almost tender. Add can of kidney beans and simmer for 15 minutes. Serves 6.

Vitamin Meat Loaf

3 *lbs. ground beef*	⅓ *teaspoon dry mustard*
1⅓ *cups wheat germ*	⅔ *teaspoon poultry seasoning*
½ *cup minced onion*	3 *cloves garlic, crushed*
1 *egg*	¼ *teaspoon thyme*
1⅓ *teaspoons lemon juice*	⅔ *cup tomato sauce*
1 *teaspoon Bragg Aminos*	⅓ *cup milk*

Mix ground beef and wheat germ. Add onion, beaten egg, and lemon juice. Add seasonings to sauce. Add with milk to meat and mix well. Pack into a small loaf pan and bake at 325°F. about 1½ hours. Serves 9.

Sweet-Potato Meat Loaf

1 *lb. ground chuck beef*	⅔ *teaspoon celery seed*
⅓ *lb. ground lamb*	1⅓ *tablespoons lemon juice*
⅓ *cup whole-wheat cracker or*	¼ *teaspoon thyme*
wafer crumbs	1⅓ *lbs. sweet potatoes*
⅓ *cup milk*	*hot top milk*
¼ *seeded, minced green*	*paprika*
pepper	1⅓ *tablespoons minced onion*
1 *egg*	2 *tablespoons butter, or*
1 *teaspoon Bragg Aminos*	*peanut oil*

Combine beef, lamb, crumbs, milk, Bragg Liquid Aminos, green pepper, eggs, celery seed, lemon juice, and thyme and mix well. Turn into greased or oiled loaf pan. Bake in moderate oven of 350°F for 1 hour. Drain off liquid, and place loaf on ovenware platter. Meanwhile, cook potatoes until tender; peel and put through ricer, or mash well. Add enough top milk to fluff. Add vegetable seasoning to taste, paprika, and minced onion that has been sauteed in butter until tender. Spread over top and sides of loaf. Brown in broiler oven or in a very hot oven of 500°F. Serves 6.

STEWS

Savory stews are one of the oldest forms of cooking, and although they have been given a humble name on our menu, they actually represent one of the greatest arts in preparing foods. Stews must not be mixed helter-skelter, with anything "thrown in"; they must be blended with imagination, with knowledge of the herbs and vegetables with which they combine, and with an eye to retaining all the juices of preparation so that they can be served with the meat.

Beef Stew with Herbs

2½ lbs. stew meat
½ cup lemon juice
3 tablespoons chopped parsley
¼ teaspoon marjoram
½ teaspoon thyme
1 large onion, minced
1 clove garlic, crushed

2 potatoes
2 carrots
3 celery stalks
1 teaspoon Bragg Aminos
whole-wheat flour
¼ cup peanut oil
¼ teaspoon summer savory

Brown meat in peanut oil and Bragg Liquid Aminos with onion and garlic. Remove meat and roll in whole-wheat flour. Return to the oil, onion, and garlic mixture and brown slowly for 10 minutes. Add the herbs, lemon juice, and 1 cup of water. Cover and place in oven at about 350°F. temperature. Cook 2 to 3 hours, adding a little liquid from time to time. Add the vegetables one hour before serving. Serves 5.

Beef Stew

2 lbs. chuck beef
⅓ cup whole-wheat flour
2 tablespoons beef drippings
2 sliced onions
1 teaspoon Bragg Aminos

4 ripe tomatoes, quartered
2 cups boiling water
½ teaspoon thyme
1 cup green beans, cut in ½-inch lengths

Cut meat in 1-inch cubes; add seasonings to whole-wheat flour. Dredge meat in flour. Heat the drippings in a heavy skillet or Dutch oven; add the meat and brown on all sides in the fat; add the tomatoes and boiling water. Cover and simmer gently over low heat about 1½ hours. Add beans and continue cooking until meat and beans are tender. Serves 6.

Italian Spaghetti

¾ cup sliced onions
2½ tablespoons oil
1¼ lbs. ground chuck or ground beef
1¼ peeled clove garlic, minced
1¼ seeded green peppers, minced
4⅓ cups tomatoes
2 (8 oz.) cans tomato sauce
1 bay leaf

1 (8 oz.) can mushrooms, with liquid
1¼ cups water
1 tablespoon Bragg Aminos
¼ teaspoon paprika
1¼ teaspoons powdered sage
⅓ teaspoon powdered thyme
1¼ teaspoons rosemary

Sauté onions in oil until tender. Add meat, stirring frequently, until it loses red color. Add all remaining ingredients; simmer uncovered for 1½ hours or until sauce is desired thickness, stirring occasionally. Meanwhile, prepare the following:

1 lb. ground chuck or ground beef
¾ cup crushed whole-wheat cracker or wafer crumbs
1 egg, slightly beaten

1 teaspoon Bragg Aminos
¾ cup top milk
2½ tablespoons oil
1¼ lbs. whole-wheat or soy spaghetti

Combine first 5 ingredients and roll into small balls. Heat oil in skillet; then brown the balls. About 20 minutes before the sauce is finished, cook spaghetti in boiling water . . . . Add meat balls to sauce. Pour sauce over drained, hot spaghetti on a platter. Serves 8.

Stuffed Peppers

6 pepper cases
2½ tablespoons oil
6 tablespoons minced onion
¾ lb. ground beef
1 (8 oz.) can tomato sauce

1¼ cups cooked brown or wild rice
⅓ teaspoon curry powder
¼ teaspoon paprika
1 teaspoon Bragg Aminos

Combine above ingredients and stuff peppers. Set in greased casserole and pour tomato sauce over peppers; bake in a 350°F. oven for about 45 minutes. Serves 6.

LAMB

Roast Leg of Lamb

Mint is the proverbial herb to use with roast lamb, but rosemary (either fresh or dried) is a delightful variation. Also try sliced garlic and raisins stuffed into slits in lamb.

Prepare the following basting sauce:

*1 cup beef broth or
   distilled water
1/2 onion, minced
1/4 cup lemon juice
2 garlic cloves, minced fine
3 tablespoons fresh minced
   mint or rosemary*

*1 tsp apple cider vinegar
1 tsp Bragg Liquid Aminos*

*(Use one herb or the other, not
both. If you must use dried mint
or dried rosemary, use 1/2
teaspoon)*

Rub lamb with olive oil. Dredge in whole-wheat or potato flour; place in hot oven to brown, using small roasting or turkey pan or rotisserie, then reduce heat to 300°F. Cooking time of approx. 30 minutes per pound. (See page 124.) During last hour of roasting, if desired, add potatoes, carrots and onions around the base of lamb. Baste frequently with prepared basting sauce.

Ways to Prepare Lamb Chops

Some people prefer lamb chops hot from the broiler with no seasoning. This is good but some of these herb seasonings are a treat.

Prepare the following sauce:

*1/4 teaspoon rosemary
1/4 teaspoon savory
1/2 onion, minced*

*2 tablespoons olive oil
2 garlic cloves, minced
1/2 tsp Bragg Liquid Aminos*

Crush onion and garlic, mix all ingredients and allow to stand for a half hour. Spread over chops before broiling or use as marinade. This recipe will make a sauce-marinade for 4 chops.

Here is a Variation

*3 tbs safflower, canola,
   olive oil or mix
2 tbs lemon juice*

*1/4 tsp powdered marjoram
1/4 tsp tarragon
1/4 cup chives or mint, minced*

Mix all ingredients; allow to stand ½ to 1 hour. Spread over chops before serving.

Stuffed Breast of Lamb

3¾ *lbs. boned breast of lamb*
⅓ *teaspoon thyme*
1¼ *tablespoons minced onion*
¾ *cup diced celery*
¾ *cup butter*
8 *cups whole-wheat bread crumbs*
2½ *cups cold water*
¼ *teaspoon nutmeg*
½ *teaspoon Bragg Aminos*

2½ *cups whole-wheat cracker or wafer crumbs*
⅓ *teaspoon poultry seasoning*
1 *slightly beaten egg*
¾ *cup boiling water*
¾ *cup honey*
mint jelly
⅓ *cup lemon juice*
6 *tablespoons whole-wheat flour*

Sprinkle the lamb with 1 teaspoon of vegetable seasoning and half of the thyme. Saute the onion and celery in the butter. Add whole-wheat wafer or cracker crumbs, and cook about 1 minute, mixing gently. Remove from the heat and add the remaining ingredients ... thyme, sage, nutmeg, poultry seasoning, and egg, until well mixed. Place stuffing on one side of each piece of the lamb and fold the other side over the stuffing, making 4 rolls. Tie each roll and place in a covered baking dish. Bake uncovered in a hot oven (450°F) for 15 minutes. Add boiling water, cover, and bake in a moderate oven of 350°F for one and three quarters hours, basting frequently. Spread with mixed jelly and lemon juice. Bake uncovered for 30 minutes longer or until tender, basting frequently. Remove string and place the lamb on a hot plate. Skim off excess fat, leaving 6 tablespoons in the pan with the drippings. Blend in whole-wheat flour and add cold water. Cook until smooth. Season to taste and serve with the lamb.
Serves 8

Lamb Stew

2 *lbs. boneless neck or shoulder lamb cut in pieces*
1 *green pepper, seeded and diced*
3 *small peeled potatoes*
2 *diced carrots*

3 *stalks cut celery*
4 *tablespoons peanut oil*
¼ *cup chopped parsley*
½ *teaspoon thyme*
½ *teaspoon marjoram*
½ **teaspoon Bragg Aminos**

Brown meat in peanut oil to which minced onion has been added; cover with boiling water; let simmer 2 hours or until tender. Add vegetables and herbs one hour before meat is done. Serves 6.

Spicy Lamb Shanks

4 *lamb shanks*
potato flour
½ *cup cooked prunes*
½ *cup cooked dried peaches*
¼ *cup honey*
½ *teaspoon ginger*

½ *teaspoon cinnamon*
½ *teaspoon allspice*
3 *cloves*
3 *tablespoons lemon juice*
½ *teaspoon Bragg Aminos*

Dredge meat in potato flour and Bragg Liquid Aminos. Place in greased casserole in moderate oven (about 350°F) for about 2 hours or until meat is tender. Mix all other ingredients and heat to boiling-point. Do not boil. Simmer slowly for 10 minutes. Drain all the fat from the cooked meat; add the spicy mixture of fruit and spices, cover again, and bake in a hot oven (about 420°F) for 1/2 hour. Serves 4.

Lamb Casserole with Eggplant

2 *lbs. cubed breast of lamb*
4 *tablespoons potato flour*
¼ *cup peanut oil*
1 *small onion, minced*
¼ *cup minced parsley*
1 *teaspoon Bragg Aminos*

½ *cup chopped celery*
¼ *teaspoon cloves*
1 *small eggplant or* ½ *large eggplant*
1 *green pepper, seeded and minced*

Dredge lamb in potato flour and Bragg Aminos and brown quickly in peanut oil. Peel and cube eggplant. Place lamb, seasonings, and vegetables in deep casserole. Thoroughly cover with water. Bake in a moderate oven until tender. Serves 6.

Lamb Oregano in Cabbage Leaves

1 *head cabbage*
1½ *lbs. ground lamb*
½ *teaspoon oregano*   2 *ripe tomatoes*
1 *large onion, minced*   1 *cup meat broth*
1 *cup brown rice, cooked*

After cooking cabbage, separate leaves carefully; combine all other ingredients and roll into cabbage leaves. Secure ends firmly by turning under. Place in greased pan; cover with meat broth and bake in a moderate oven until tender. Serves 6.

VEAL

Veal Chops with Vegetables

4 *loin chops*   4 *cloves*
3 *medium-sized carrots*   1 *sprig rosemary or* 1 *dash of*
4 *celery stalks*   *dried rosemary*
½ *onion, chopped*   2 *tablespoons olive oil*

Place all ingredients in saucepan in boiling water; cook slowly until tender. Remove meat. Sauté meat slowly in olive oil until slightly brown. Remove; place in casserole with liquid saved from original cooking, and heat for 15 minutes. Serves 4.

Veal Stew with Brown Rice

1½ *lbs. boned breast of veal*   ½ *cup brown rice*
1 *clove garlic*   1 *cup chopped celery*
2 *tablespoons peanut oil*   4¼ *cups water*
2 *tablespoons soy sauce*
4 *onions*

Cut veal into cubes, or small pieces; season, dredge in potato flour, brown with minced garlic in peanut oil. Place in Dutch oven. Add water and brown rice. Cover and simmer for ¾ of an hour. Add the onions and celery. Re-cover and simmer again for 35 minutes. Add 3 tablespoons flour (potato flour, rolled oats, or whole-wheat flour) and ¼ cup warm water. Simmer slowly for 15 minutes. Serves 6.

Veal Garden Stew

¾ *lb. veal neck*
¾ *cup dried kidney beans*
1½ *cups cold water*
4 *cups boiling water*
1 *garlic clove, minced*
¼ *cup chopped chives*
¼ *teaspoon chervil*
1 *tablespoon olive oil*

¾ *cup finely chopped green cabbage*
¼ *cup chopped chicory*
2 *medium-sized tomatoes*
¼ *teaspoon powdered rosemary*
¼ *teaspoon sweet basil*
1 *teaspoon Bragg Aminos*

Soak beans overnight in cold water; drain. In the morning add veal, beans and Bragg Liquid Aminos to boiling water. Simmer for about 2-1/2 hours or until beans are tender. Remove meat and cut into small pieces. Saute slowly all seasonings and herbs in oil until blended, or about 10 minutes. Add vegetables; allow to cook very slowly for an additional 15 minutes. Serves 8.

Veal Paprika

3 *lbs. veal shoulder, boned*
⅓ *cup fat or oil*
¾ *cup onion, minced*
1 *large garlic clove, minced*
⅓ *teaspoon pepper*
1 *teaspoon Bragg Aminos*

1½ *teaspoons paprika*
1¼ *cups sour cream*
2½ *tablespoons whole-wheat flour*
⅜ *cup cold water*
2¼ *cups boiling water*

Cut veal in 1-inch cubes. Place fat or oil in heavy skillet. Add onion, garlic, and veal. Add Bragg Liquid Aminos, pepper, paprika, and 2-1/4 cups boiling water. Cover and cook at low heat until meat is tender, or about 1 hour. Remove meat to a hot platter and keep hot in oven. Add sour cream to the drippings in the heavy skillet. Blend the flour with the 3/8 cup cold water until smooth and add, stirring constantly until blended to the sour cream. Cook at a slow heat until smooth and thickened. Pour over meat as sauce. Serves 6.

Veal Scallopine

1 *lb. veal (use steak cut from the leg)*	¼ *cup lemon juice*
1 *cup meat broth*	½ *teaspoon rosemary*
4 *tablespoons butter or olive oil*	2 *tablespoons chopped parsley*
	1 *tablespoon chopped chives*
½ *cup tomato juice*	¼ *lb. sliced mushrooms*
1 *ripe tomato, peeled*	2 *tablespoons dry, grated cheese*
1 *clove garlic*	
¼ *cup scallions, chopped, including tops*	1 *teaspoon Bragg Aminos*

Cut slices of veal 1/2 inch thick; pound with wooden mallet, dredge lightly in whole-wheat flour. Brown meat slowly in skillet with oil. Remove the meat, mash garlic and onions, and mix with lemon juice, tomato juice, herbs, and meat broth. Simmer slowly 15 minutes. Put meat back in skillet, baste thoroughly, cover, and bake in slow oven (about 300°F) for about 35 minutes. Just before serving, sprinkle lightly with cheese. Serves 3.

Breaded Veal Cutlets

(Allow 1 medium-sized veal steak for 3 servings)

1 *medium-sized veal steak*	½ *teaspoon chervil*
1 *egg*	4 *tablespoons butter or olive oil*
1½ *cups whole-wheat flour or whole-wheat cracker crumbs*	½ *cup sour cream*

Cut veal steak into desired servings. Dry thoroughly. Add 1 tablespoon water to egg and beat. Dip veal in whole-wheat flour or bread crumbs that have been seasoned slightly with vegetable salt seasoning. Dip in egg; dip in flour again. Sauté very slowly in butter or oil. Add ½ cup water and ½ cup sour cream. Sprinkle with chervil. Place in oven and cook slowly, covered, until meat is tender. If necessary, add a little liquid during cooking.

Who is strong? He that can conquer his bad habits. —Ben Franklin

◇◇

Veal Birds

2½ lbs. veal steak (¼ inch thick)
1¼ cups sage or mushroom stuffing

whole-wheat flour
soy oil or peanut oil
1¼ cups milk

Cut veal into 2 x 4 inch pieces. Place a mound of stuffing on each piece, fold veal over stuffing, and fasten with skewers. Season, roll in flour, brown in fat, and add milk. Cover and simmer or bake in moderate oven (350°F.) 1 hour. Serves 8.

PORK

Good fresh pork, properly prepared, is very high in vitamin content and nutritional value; however, all the smoked pork meats, such as bacon and ham, are not considered good Health foods.

Spanish Roast Loin of Pork

3¾ lbs. loin of pork
1 cup minced green pepper
1 cup minced onion
1¼ peeled cloves garlic, minced
⅓ cup butter or oil
2 (8 oz.) cans or 2 cups tomato sauce
2½ cups cooked wild or brown rice (about 1 cup raw rice)

2 cups hot water
1¼ tablespoons chili powder
⅓ cup brown sugar, firmly packed
1 tablespoon Bragg Aminos
¾ cup sliced ripe olives
1 cup seedless raisins (optional)

Loosen port from rib bone, entire length of the loin, enough to form a pocket for stuffing or ask butcher to prepare. Saute pepper, onion, and garlic until tender. Add tomato sauce and 3/4 cup hot water. Bring to boil. Add chili powder, sugar, Bragg Liquid Aminos, olives and raisins. Boil 4 minutes. Add 1/3 cup of this sauce to rice. Stuff pork with mixture. Arrange pork in Dutch oven; bake covered in moderate oven (350°F) for 2 hours. Pour rest of sauce over roast, and continue baking, uncovered, for 1/2 hour. Baste roast; add rest of water, and bake 1/2 hour longer. Serves 6 or 7.

Scalloped Pork Chops
(with Cumin Seed)

4 *pork chops*	¼ *teaspoon cumin seed*
4 *medium-sized potatoes*	1 *tablespoon minced parsley*
2 *tablespoons olive oil*	1 *cup milk*
½ *teaspoon Bragg Aminos*	3 *tablespoons whole-wheat flour*

Roll chops in whole-wheat flour and brown in oil. Place in casserole with potatoes thinly sliced, seasoning, and flour. If desired, dot chops with a little butter. Pour in milk. Bake in a moderate oven for 45 minutes, covered. Uncover and bake another 45 minutes longer, or until tender. Serves 4.

Braised Pork Chops

Pork chops, no matter whether rib, loin, or shoulder, should be cut about ¾ to 1 inch thick. Sprinkle them with . . . Bragg Liquid Aminos a little whole-wheat flour, and brown well on both sides in a heavy hot skillet. Add 2 cups of boiling liquid (water or canned tomato juice) and a little minced onion if desired, and simmer slowly, covered, for about 1 hour or until chops are very tender. They may also be finished off by removing from skillet about 15 minutes before they are tender and placed in a casserole with pared apples or pineapple slices and some of the sauce from the pan. The cooking should be continued until both chops and apples are tender.

Spare Ribs and Sweet Potatoes

4 *lbs. spare ribs*	1 *cup minced celery*
2 *cups mashed sweet potatoes*	1 *cup finely chopped green cabbage*
½ *cup apple sauce*	
1 *tablespoon minced onion*	2 *tablespoons peanut oil*
½ *cup brown rice, cooked*	¼ *teaspoon Bragg Aminos*
1 *bay leaf*	

Mix sweet potatoes, onions, rice, celery, apple sauce. . .Add Bragg Liquid Aminos. . .Dredge ribs in whole-wheat flour. Spread mixture on the bony part of the ribs. Place in baking dish; cover the bottom of the pan with boiling water, put the bay leaf in the water. Cook in a moderate oven about 2 hours or until tender. This recipe serves 4.

Pork Tenderloin

1 *lb. pork tenderloin*   1 *tablespoon Bragg Aminos*
1 *tablespoon melted butter* ¼ *teaspoon rosemary*
1 *clove garlic*

Sauté garlic, seasonings, and Bragg Liquid Aminos for 10 minutes in butter. Cut pork tenderloin into slices about ½ inch thick. Pound with a wooden mallet till flat. Brush with the butter sauce, and broil until well done. Serves 3.

MEAT ORGANS

The organs of animals are not popular in the average home, but the brains, heart, kidney, liver, and sweetbreads are very high in nutritional value. There are hundreds of ways of preparing them. Here are some favorite recipes for these types of animal organs.

Scrambled Brains on Toast

1 *calf's brain*   ½ *tomato*
4 *tablespoons butter* 1 *teaspoon Bragg Aminos*
½ *cup white button mush-*
 rooms
2 *beaten eggs*

Wash brain; remove arteries and membranes and soak in cold water for 1 hour. Cover with water; bring to boiling-point, and simmer very slowly for about 30 minutes. Slice. Melt butter in saucepan, add cooked brains and all other ingredients. Cook very slowly, stirring frequently. This can be served on buttered, whole-wheat toast. Serves 3.

Broiled Liver

1 *lb. calves' liver*   1 *large onion sliced in rings*
¼ *teaspoon Bragg Aminos* 3 *tablespoons butter*

Wipe liver with damp cloth and remove all the outside skin and veins. Cut into slices 1/2 inch thick, place onion rings over top, brush with butter. Broil 5 minutes; remove onion rings, turn, and place onion rings on other side. Broil for few minutes more or until done. Serves 3.

Favorite Liver Dumplings

1⅓ cups whole-wheat cracker or wafer crumbs
1⅓ cups whole-wheat bread crumbs
⅔ lb. ground liver
4 eggs
⅔ teaspoon nutmeg
2⅔ medium-sized onions, chopped fine
5 or 6 pieces garlic, chopped fine
⅓ cup butter, or oil
whole-wheat flour
1 teaspoon Bragg Aminos

Mix the above ingredients and add enough whole-wheat flour to make mixture a little stiff. Make in balls; drop into a vegetable soup and cook about 10 to 15 minutes. Cut dumpling in half to see if cooked through, and serve with soup. These will be very light if correctly cooked. Serves 4.

Liver Ragout

1 large shredded carrot
1 large minced onion
1 large diced turnip
1 bay leaf
2½ tablespoons soy or peanut oil
1¼ tablespoons whole-wheat flour
3 lbs. liver (1 piece)
2½ cups water or stock
1 teaspoon Bragg Aminos

Brown carrot, onion, turnip, and bay leaf in oil. Add whole-wheat flour and blend, then add liver and water. Season and simmer for 1¼ to 1½ hours. Serves 8.

Stuffed Calves' Hearts

2 calves' hearts
½ cup dried prunes
½ cup dried apricots
3 tablespoons peanut oil
whole-wheat flour for dredging

Wash hearts; remove veins and blood clots. Cut out any hard parts. Dredge in whole-wheat flour; brown in peanut oil. Remove. Add chopped fruit mixture. Add 1-1/2 cups meat stock or water. (The meat stock will give and additional flavor.) Cover and cook slowly in baking dish in oven for 2 hours or until tender. Serves 4.

Lamb Heart Braised

Clean heart in fresh water, split, remove veins, arteries, and clotted blood. Roll in whole-wheat flour, and brown in hot fat. Place in small deep pan, half cover with boiling vegetable stock or water, cover closely, and bake about 2 hours at 300°F. Turn when half done. Remove heart when tender. Measure stock. For 1 cup stock, add 2 tablespoons whole-wheat flour blended with 3 tablespoons cold water. Stir and boil 5 minutes, season to taste with vegetable seasoning, and use as sauce for heart.

Kidney Stew

4 *veal kidneys*	1½ *cups meat stock*
4 *tablespoons butter*	2 *tablespoons lemon juice*
1 *tablespoon chopped onion*	½ *cup finely diced carrots*
3 *tablespoons whole-wheat flour*	¼ *cup finely diced celery*
1 *teaspoon Bragg Aminos*	½ *cup fresh mushrooms, quartered*

Plunge kidneys into boiling water, remove skin, then soak in cold salt water for 30 minutes. Slice, removing tubes and tissues; saute in half the butter for 7 minutes. Remove from butter. Place onions and mushrooms in butter and brown. Add flour and meat stock; boil for several minutes. Strain this mixture, add to kidneys, and let cook in oven for 5 to 10 minutes or until tender. Serves 4.

Lamb Kidneys

Basic Recipe for Grilling: Remove the fine skin. Cut in half without completely separating. Pierce with skewer to keep open during grilling. If desired, dip in melted butter and roll in whole-wheat

◇◇

bread crumbs. Broil, very quickly. Serve with any of the following sauces: Onion butter; Maître d'hôtel butter; Bordelaise sauce; Bercy sauce. Also can be served topped with broiled mushrooms. *Basic Recipe for Sautéeing:* Remove the fine skin. Cut in half. Cut into slices ¼ in. thick. Sauté in butter very quickly to avoid hardening. This should be done by tossing in hot butter over hot fire. Drain. Let stand for a few minutes to give off any blood they may contain. Reheat quickly with sauce, but do not boil in sauce to which they are added. They will harden. Sautéed lamb kidneys combine nicely with any of the following sauces: Bercy sauce; Herb sauce, cream style; Curry gravy; Bordelaise sauce; Basil sauce; Maître d'hôtel butter.

Veal Kidneys

Basic Recipe for Grilling: trim the kidney, leaving a small layer of fat around it. Cut in half without completely separating. Pierce with skewer to keep open during grilling. Broil under low heat, basting often with melted butter. Serve with any of the following sauces: Onion butter; Bordelaise sauce; Maitre de'hotel butter.

Basic Recipe for Casserole: Trim the kidney, leaving a small layer of fat around it. Cut in five or six slices. Toss lightly in butter over a hot fire. Place in a liberally buttered heavy skillet and cook gently over slow fire for 30 minutes, turning frequently. Place in a liberally buttered casserole and add any of the following sauces: Bercy sauce; Basic sauce; Herb sauce, cream style. Bake in meduim oven for 10 minutes.

Broiled Sweetbreads

1 pair of sweetbreads will serve 2 persons generously. When buying sweetbreads, always try to buy a pair connected. A pair consists of a heart sweetbread and a throat sweetbread. The heart sweetbread is more choice; therefore, try to avoid buying two throat sweetbreads.

1 *pair sweetbreads*	¼ *cup butter*
1 *tablespoon lemon juice*	½ *teaspoon Bragg Aminos*

Plunge sweetbreads into cold water and allow to stand for 1 hour. Drain. Boil.

Add lemon juice to boiling water. Cook slowly for 20 to 25 minutes. Drain and place in cold water again. Drain again. Slit crosswise, brush with melted butter, and broil for about five minutes until very delicately brown. The sweetbreads should be turned about 3 times during the broiling.

Fresh Mushrooms and Sweetbreads

1¼ lbs. sweetbreads
6 tablespoons butter
1¼ tablespoons whole-wheat flour
6 green onions, minced

2 sprigs parsley, minced
¾ lb. fresh or canned mushrooms, sliced
2 egg yolks, well beaten
¾ cup heavy cream

Precook sweetbreads. Melt 3 tablespoons butter, add whole-wheat flour, and brown. Add sweetbreads, onions, parsley, and 1 cup of stock from cooking sweetbreads. Simmer until sauce is quite thick. Meanwhile cook cleaned mushrooms about 5 minutes in top of double boiler with remaining 2 tablespoons of butter, then add sweetbread mixture. About 3 minutes before serving, add egg yolk mixed with cream. Stir continually until heated through and serve at once. Makes 6 servings.

UNCOMPLICATE YOUR LIVING

Living is a continual lesson in problem solving, but the trick is to know where to start. No excuses — start your Health Program Today.

"Living under conditions of modern life, it is important to bear in mind that the preparation and refinement of food products either entirely eliminates or in part destroys the vital elements in the original materials." — U.S. Dept. of Agriculture

"Now learn what and how great benefits a temperate diet will bring with it. In the first place, you enjoy good health.
— Horace, 65-8 B.C.

In health there is liberty. Health is the first of all liberties, happiness gives us the energy which is the basis of health. —Miel

"Your eyes shall be opened, and ye shall be as gods, knowing good and evil."
—Genesis 3:5

 # Fish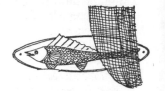

Chapter 7

FISH has been man's food since the dawn of time. It has all the excellent properties of a good protein food, and because it is usually very high in natural iodine, it has been handed down by tradition as "brain food." Whether or not the succulent lobster, the flaky crab, the delicious sea bass will make a mental wizard of you remains in the realms of debate. But the precious minerals it contains doubtless contribute to the proper maintenance of the nerve system, the brain tissue, and general well-being. It is also an excellent source of vitamins A, B, and D and contains iron, calcium, and phosphorus. Salt-water fish contain more iodine than any known common food.

Whether fresh, quick-frozen, or canned, fish should have a firm, elastic flesh and a fresh odor. Discard immediately any fish that has an offensive, heavy "fishy" odor. A fresh fish will sink rapidly in water.

Fish should be used as soon as possible, but if it is necessary to keep it a short time, it should be tightly covered in the refrigerator to avoid contaminating other stored foods with the fish odors.

Because of its delicate flavor, fish lends itself to the delicate seasoning of herbs and spices. It should never be fried. But baked, broiled, or boiled, it is one of nature's real delicacies.

Basic Recipe for Broiled Fish

The fish that lend themselves best to broiling are:

Bass	Halibut	Pompano	Sole
Bluefish	Mackerel	Salmon	Swordfish
Cod	Perch	Sand dab	Tuna
Flounder	Pike	Smelt	Whitefish
Haddock			

FOR VEGETARIANS: We have the Vegetarian Gourmet Recipes book, see back pages for ordering. The Bragg main diet is vegetarian. — Patricia Bragg

Clean and dry fish. Brush with butter. Arrange on greased broiler or shallow cooking sheet or pan.

Sprinkle pepper, and paprika if desired. Place under broiler about 2 in. below broiling unit. Broil on one side. Turn. Brush again with butter. Broil until flaky when tested with fork. Serve with chopped parsley and lemon wedges or with sauce.

Whether broiling fillets, fish steaks, small or medium-sized whole fish, the general basic recipe remains the same. The broiling time must be adjusted to suit thickness of size of fish. Broiling time ranges from 5 to 12 minutes on each side.

Suitable Sauces for Broiled Fish

Marguery sauce—page 259
Hollandaise sauce—page 257
Maître d' hôtel butter—page 258
Egg butter sauce—page 260
Onion butter—page 260
Cheese sauce—page 261
Basil sauce—page 263

Herb sauce for fish—page 264
Béarnaise sauce—page 257
Caper sauce, hollandaise—page 257
Caper sauce, maître d' hôtel—page 258

Steamed Fish

The fish that lend themselves best to steaming are:

Carp	*Haddock*	*Red snapper*	*Sole*
Cod	*Halibut*	*Salmon*	*Trout*
Flounder	*Perch*		

Use steamer or colander over a kettle of boiling water. Season fish with Bragg Liquid Aminos and garlic and herbs. Place in steamer. Cover tightly. Steam until fish is tender and flakes easily when tested with a fork. Allow approximately 15 minutes to the pound depending on the thickness of the fish. Do not overcook. Serve with chopped parsely and lemon wedges or with sauce.

Suitable Sauces for Steamed Fish

Hollandaise sauce—page 257
Egg butter sauce—page 260
Onion butter—page 260
Newburg sauce—page 260
Tomato sauce—page 261
Mexican sauce—page 261

Cheese sauce—page 261
Curry gravy—page 262
Basil sauce—page 263
Caper sauce, hollandaise—page 257

Basic Recipe for Baked Split Fish

The whole, split fish that lend themselves best to baking are:

Bluefish	*Halibut*	*Pompano*	*Shad*
Carp	*Mackerel*	*Red snapper*	*Sole*
Cod	*Perch*	*Salmon*	*Swordfish*
Flounder	*Pickerel*	*Sand dab*	*Trout*
Haddock			*Whitefish*

Clean and split. Place skin-side down in a shallow, buttered casserole. Brush with melted butter (about 1 tablespoon to each pound of fish) and season with herbs, garlic and Bragg Aminos, or paprika. Bake in a hot oven (about 425°F) for 25 minutes or until tender and flaky when tried. Place under the broiler for a few moments to brown. Garnish, stuff, or serve with sauce.

Suitable Sauces for Baked Split Fish

Marguery sauce—page 259
Mexican sauce—page 261
Curry gravy—page 262
Basil sauce—page 263
Herb sauce for fish—page 264

Caper sauce, hollandaise—page 257
Caper sauce, maître d'hôtel—page 258

Stuffing for Fish

3 *cups dry whole-wheat bread cubes*
1 *cup celery, cut fine*
2 *tablespoons minced onion*
2 *teaspoons poultry seasoning*

1 *teaspoon Bragg Aminos*
¼ *teaspoon pepper*
⅓ *cup melted butter*
2 *teaspoons chopped parsley*

Cook celery until tender in 1 cup boiling water (about 15 minutes). Drain thoroughly and reserve celery liquor. Sauté onion very lightly until transparent in color. Mix all ingredients together, using about 3 tablespoons of the celery liquor. Let stand for 15 minutes before stuffing fish. Will stuff about 3 to 4 pounds of fish.

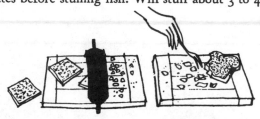

◇◇◇

Sole or Flounder Marguery

6 *fillets of sole (or flounder* ¼ *cup water*
 cut in fillets) 6 *clams (optional)*
¼ *cup lemon juice* 1 *small boiled lobster*
¼ *teaspoon paprika* *(optional)*
½ *teaspoon Bragg Aminos* ¼ *cup grated unprocessed*
  cheese

Place sole in buttered deep casserole. Sprinkle with paprika. Pour lemon juice and water over it, cover with buttered paper, and bake 15 minutes in a moderate oven (350°F). Arrange cooked fillets on ovenproof platter. Pour Marguery sauce (see page 259) over fish. Arrange slices of lobster and 6 clams for garnishing (optional). Sprinkle with cheese. Place in a slow oven (about 300°F) and bake until thoroughly heated. Serves 6.

Steamed Finnan Haddie

1½ *lbs. finnan-haddie fillets* 3 *tablespoons butter*

Steam fish over boiling water until tender, about 12 minutes. Serve with melted butter. Serves 4.

Baked Halibut with Herb Sauce

1½ *sliced small onions* ½ *teaspoon Bragg Aminos*
1½ *bay leaves* ¾ *cup whole-wheat cracker or*
 3 *lbs. halibut steak* *wafer crumbs*
4½ *tablespoons butter* 1½ *tablespoons melted butter*
7½ *tablespoons whole-wheat* ¼ *teaspoon paprika*
 flour
2¼ *cups milk*

Place sliced onion, bay leaves, broken into small pieces, and halibut in greased casserole. With a spoon, work together the butter, half of the whole-wheat flour, Bragg Liquid Aminos and herbs, and half the paprika; spread on top of fish. Bake in moderately hot oven (375°F) for 50 minutes, or until done. Drain off fat from baking dish into saucepan; stir in remaining whole-wheat flour. If there is not enough fat, add 1 tablespoon melted butter. Stir in milk and remaing paprika. Cook, stirring until thickened. Pour around the fish. Serves 6.

Savory Baked Abalone

3 *lbs. abalone, sliced*
3 *eggs, beaten*
whole-wheat cracker crumbs
olive oil
1½ *cups hot water*
1 *large onion, minced*

1½ *teaspoons dry mustard*
¾ *cup tomato juice*
1½ *lemons, juice only*
1½ *tablespoons minced parsley*
1 *teaspoon Bragg Aminos*
1½ *cloves garlic, crushed*

Trim off any dark parts of fish and cut into slices. Place on a board and with a wooden mallet pound the fish lightly until it becomes soft but not mushy. Dip into the beaten eggs, then crumbs, and sauté quickly in olive oil. When browned, place fish in a baking dish. Place remaining ingredients into the pan in which fish slices were sautéed and cook for 5 minutes, stirring constantly. Pour over fish and bake in a slow oven (300°F.) for 1 hour. Serves 8.

Fish with Herbs
(Baked in Paper)

Use several small, sweet fish per person. Trout is excellent for this recipe. The recipe is for 3 small fish. Multiply ingredients by number of servings desired.

3 *small sweet fish*
¼ *teaspoon fresh ground*
  peppercorn
¼ *teaspoon Bragg Aminos*

½ *teaspoon chervil*
½ *teaspoon sweet basil*
1 *teaspoon chopped chives*
olive oil

Clean, wash, and dry each fish thoroughly. Place fish on a large circle of heavy brown paper that has been oiled thoroughly with olive oil until saturated. Place fish in semi-circle—that is, on half the circle. Add the seasonings and herbs. Fold the other half of the circle down. Roll up edges and secure firmly. Bake in a moderate oven (350°F.) for about half an hour, brushing the paper with oil from time to time to keep it from scorching. The paper packages should be turned three times during the baking. Serves 1.

◇◇◇

Tomato-Stuffed Fish

¾ tablespoon chopped onion
2¼ tablespoons butter or oil
¾ cup whole-wheat cracker
  crumbs
1½ cups whole-wheat bread
  crumbs

¾ cup fresh or canned
  tomatoes
1 teaspoon Bragg Aminos
1½ lbs. fish steaks or about 2
  or 3 fillets (bass, flounder,
  or halibut may be used)

Simmer onion until soft in half of butter or oil. Add crumbs and brown slightly, stirring constantly. Remove from heat, add tomatoes. Mix well. Spread stuffing between the 2 slices of fish steak. Place on well greased plank that has been preheated 5 minutes in hot oven (400°F). Brush top of fish with remaining butter or oil. Bake in hot oven (400°F) 40 minutes. Serves 4.

Fluffy Salmon Loaf

⅔ lb. canned salmon
⅔ lemon (juice only)
¼ cup minced green pepper
⅛ teaspoon paprika
½ cup whole-wheat cracker
  crumbs

½ cup chopped celery
½ teaspoon Bragg Aminos
½ cup wheat germ
⅔ cup milk, or soy milk
¼ cup liquid from fish
2 eggs

Drain, bone, and flake fish. Sprinkle with lemon juice and seasonings. Combine with wheat germ, whole-wheat cracker crumbs, celery, and green pepper. Add milk and liquid drained from fish. Add well-beaten eggs, mixing well. Pack into greased loaf pan. Bake at 325°F. for 1¼ to 1½ hours or until loaf is firm and appetizingly browned. Slice and serve with tomato sauce. Serves 3.

Cuban-Style Fish

1¾ lbs. white fish or trout
½ teaspoon Bragg Aminos
2 tablespoons lemon juice
⅛ cup peanut, soy, or olive oil
¼ cup chopped toasted
   almonds
¼ cup finely chopped onion

1⅓ tablespoons hot water
⅔ medium-sized onion, sliced
⅔ tablespoon finely chopped
   parsley
⅛ teaspoon paprika
⅛ teaspoon thyme
⅔ bay leaf

Clean fish, sprinkle with Bragg Liquid Aminos and 1 tablespoon of lemon juice. In frying pan add 1-1/2 tablespoons of oil, almonds, chopped onion, hot water, and parsley. Simmer all together for 5 minutes. In a roasting pan put the remaining oil, the sliced onion, paprika, thyme, and bay leaf; place fish on top of this, cover with cooked mixture, sprinkle with remaining lemon juice. Bake in a moderate oven (350°F), cooking fish about 35 to 45 minutes. Keep basting to avoid dryness. Serves 6.

Fish Pudding

1 lb. fish fillets
¼ cup butter
1 tablespoon whole-wheat
   flour
⅔ cup milk
1 egg, slightly beaten

⅓ cup cream
½ teaspoon Bragg Aminos
¼ teaspoon paprika
⅛ teaspoon nutmeg

Wipe fillets with a clean wet cloth; put 2 or 3 times through finest knife of food-grinder. Heat butter; mix in whole-wheat flour. Add milk slowly and cook, stirring constantly, over low heat until thickened. Add cream, seasonings, and fish. Add a little of the hot sauce to slightly beaten egg; stir into remaining sauce. Pour into a greased casserole. Place in a pan of water. Bake in a moderate oven (350°F.) 30 to 35 minutes. Serves 4.

Tuna Fish à la Rice
and Cheese

1 (13 oz.) *can tuna fish*
1½ *cups cooked wild or brown rice*
2 *tablespoons parsley, chopped fine*
2 *tablespoons onion, chopped*

1 *cup grated unprocessed cheese*
½ *cup buttered whole-wheat crackers or wafers, rolled fine*
1 *teaspoon Bragg Aminos*

Drain and flake fish. Arrange fish and rice in layers in a greased casserole, sprinkling each layer with parsley and onion. Add grated cheese. Top with buttered whole-wheat cracker or wafer crumbs and a dash of paprika. Bake in a moderate oven (375°F.) about 25 minutes or until browned. Makes about 6 servings.

Baked Shad Roe

Parboil the shad roe, then press into a buttered pan with ¾ cup of tomato juice. Season with 1 teaspoon lemon juice, ¼ teaspoon Bragg Liquid Aminos and ¼ teaspoon freshly ground black peppercorns. Tarragon, chervil, or basil may be added if desired. Bake 20 minutes in a hot oven, basting every 5 minutes.

SHELLFISH

Broiled Oysters

2 *dozen raw oysters on half shell*
½ *cup whole-wheat toast crumbs*
¼ *cup melted butter*
2 *tablespoons chopped parsley*

¼ *teaspoon Bragg Aminos*
¼ *teaspoon pepper*
¼ *teaspoon thyme*
1 *teaspoon lemon juice*

Season toast crumbs with Bragg Liquid Aminos, garlic, pepper, and thyme; add chopped parsley. Mix thoroughly. Combine lemon juice and melted butter. Lift oysters from shell with silver fork. Dip in lemon juice and butter mixture and then in toast-crumb mixture. Replace gently in shell. Place on buttered broiler rack and broil until juices flow. Turn oysters in shell while broiling. If desired, sprinkle with a little grated cheese or serve with maitre de'hotel butter. Serves 8.

Roasted Oysters

Buy oysters in the shell. Scrub thoroughly. Arrange in dripping pan and cook in hot oven until shells open up. Season with any desired seasoning or sauce and serve in half shell.

Panned Oysters

⅜ *cup butter*	3 *tablespoons lemon juice*
1½ *pints oysters*	¼ *teaspoon Bragg Aminos*

Heat butter in a heavy skillet; add drained oysters and cook over low heat until the edges curl. Add lemon juice, Bragg Aminos and garlic to taste. Serve on hot buttered toast. Garnish with lemons quartered and parsley. Serves 6.

Poached Oysters

Clean oysters. Drain. Place in saucepan with liquor drained from them. Heat until oysters are plump and edges begin to curl. Drain and reserve liquor to be used if needed in any recipe you are using. Clean shells well and serve oysters on shells.

Oysters Mornay

Cover bottoms of shells with Mornay sauce. Place two poached oysters on each shell. Cover tops with Mornay sauce. Bake for a few moments either on bed of rock salt or on wire rack.

Oysters Florentine

Cover bottoms of oyster shells with shredded, cooked, buttered spinach. Place two poached oysters in each shell. Cover with Mornay sauce. Heat in oven.

Steamed Clams

Wash clams thoroughly, scrubbing with brush, changing water several times. Put into large kettle, allowing ½ cup hot water to 4 quarts clams. Cover closely and steam until shells partially open, but do not overcook. Serve with individual dishes of melted butter.

Roasted Clams

Clam bakes are very popular. The clams should first be washed in water and then placed on hot stones. To prepare the hot stones, burn wood over the stones, remove the ashes and sprinkle the stones with a thin layer of seaweed. After placing the clams on the stones, cover with seaweed and a piece of canvas to retain the steam.

Clams Nantaise

2 *dozen clams in the shell*
½ *teaspoon minced shallot*
5 *tablespoons butter*
2 *tablespoons whole-wheat flour*

½ *cup lemon juice*
¼ *cup finely chopped parsley*
3 *tablespoons Parmesan cheese*
¼ *cup cream*

Steam clams until shells open. Remove tough portions of clams. Reserve shells. Mince and add tender portions to minced shallot and sauté both in 2 tablespoons butter. Add lemon juice. Mix whole-wheat flour with remaining butter and add cream gradually. Sauté until flour is cooked. Add to minced clams and shallot with parsley and cheese. Stuff cleaned shells and bake in oven on bed of rock salt or oven rack. Serves 8.

Boiled Crab or Lobster

Lobster or crab should be tossed into a large kettle containing vigorously boiling water. ⅓ cup of rock salt should be added to each quart of water. The lobster and crab should be dropped in alive, with the tail end down, one at a time, and the water should come back to the boiling-point after adding each one. They should be entirely covered by water and boiled about 20 minutes. They can be seasoned with a butter sauce or Bordelaise sauce.

Lobster Newburg

2 lbs. lobster, boiled
¼ cup butter
dash of nutmeg
dash of cayenne pepper

⅓ cup cream
1 teaspoon Bragg Aminos
2 beaten egg yolks

Slice lobster meat and sauté slowly in butter for about 3 minutes. Add seasoning and Aminos and cook another minute. Stir in cream with beaten egg yolks. Cook until thickened. Serve on buttered whole-wheat toast. Serves 8.

Crabs with Rice

10 small crabs or ⅓ lb. crab meat
1⅓ cups boiling water
⅔ cup uncooked brown or wild rice
1 tablespoon Bragg Aminos

1 large onion, chopped
1 large carrot, chopped
⅔ tablespoon butter or oil
1⅓ bay leaves
1 whole clove
5 drops lemon juice
paprika

Wash crabs. Drop in boiling salted water, cover, and boil for 20 minutes. Remove crabs, cut off and crush the legs and cook in crab liquor for about 1 hour. Strain, and pour over brown or wild rice. Let stand for ½ hour and then cook until rice is tender. Remove meat from bony tissue. Cook chopped onion and carrot and spices in fat until slightly browned, then add flaked crab meat. Season with lemon juice, Bragg Liquid Aminos and paprika; add rice and cook together for 3 minutes. Serve hot. Makes 4 portions.

Crab Cakes New Orleans

1½ cups fresh-cooked crab meat or 10 oz. canned crab meat
3 eggs, separated
1½ tablespoons butter
¼ cup chopped onion

1⅛ tablespoons lemon juice
⅓ teaspoon dry mustard
½ teaspoon Bragg Aminos
⅛ teaspoon paprika

Pick over crab meat to remove any bony tissue. Beat egg yolks until thick. Fold in crab meat. Heat butter; add onion and cook over low

◆◇

heat about 10 minutes, or until soft and lightly browned. Mix with crab meat. Add lemon juice, mustard, Bragg Liquid Aminos and paprika. Beat egg whites until stiff but not dry. Fold into crab-meat mixture. Drop by spoonfuls into hot butter in skillet and brown lightly on both sides. Serve with favorite sauce. Serves 4-6.

Cioppino or Bouillabaisse

This famous dish loved by Italian fishermen is a whole meal. Boil a large crab until done. Clean, remove, shred body meat and crack legs. Cook two dozen unshelled prawns in salted water 15 minutes. Drain. Cook two dozen clams or cockles in their shells. Place clams in their shells, prawns in their shells and cracked crab legs in a tall pot. Over this spread shredded crab-meat. Then make this sauce:

1 large onion, minced	*1/2 cup water, distilled*
3 cloves garlic, minced	*1/2 bay leaf*
1/3 cup olive oil	*1/2 teaspoon thyme*
1 large can tomatoes	*1/2 teaspoon marjoram*
or 5-6 fresh large tomatoes	*pinch Italian herbs*
2 cans (8-oz) tomato sauce	*1 teaspoon Bragg Aminos*

Lightly saute onion and garlic in olive oil, add tomatoes, tomato sauce and seasonings. Simmer for about 1 hour. Pour over fish mixture, set for 5 minutes and serve in bowls. With a health salad this is a complete meal.

The Value of Vitamin C

The World Famous Vitamin C Scientist, Dr. Linus Pauling, in some of his important Vitamin C studies, found that study subjects who took 1,000 mgs of Vitamin C first thing in the morning helped reduce cholesterol levels and triglycerides. These amazing studies showed a great improvement in two to three weeks, where often some of the study members had difficulty lowering their cholesterol levels and triglycerides. It also helped them become more regular in their elimination.

Your body has 5 superpumps. Your heart is the masterpump (pumps 2,000 gallons daily), and the other four are your arms and legs that add to its strength. Example - Maestro's with their music & swinging arms...have stronger hearts & healthier longer lives.

Chapter 8

Poultry and Game

Organically-fed
hormone and
chemical-free
poultry is best!

Chicken Timetable

SCHEDULE (if chicken is taken directly from refrigerator before cooking, add 5 minutes more per pound):

3 to 4 lbs:	350°F. 40-45 minutes per pound, or 2 to 2-3/4 hours
4 to 5 lbs:	325°F. 35-40 minutes per pound, or 2-1/2 to 3 hours
5 to 6 lbs:	325°F. 30-35 minutes per pound, or 3 to 3-1/2 hours

To determine if done, hold end bone of drumstick. Move gently. If drumstick thigh joint breaks or moves easily, it is done. Do not let juices escape by piercing with a fork.

Roast Chicken

4 to 5 lbs tender chicken   *3 tablespoons whole-wheat or*
6 tbsp butter or canola oil   *potato flour*

Stuff chicken with whole-grain stuffing or pecan delight stuffing. Melt the butter or oil in roasting pan. Add flour and mix until creamed. Rub chicken well with mixture, spreading on breast and legs. Place in a hot oven about 450°F. for 10 minutes or until well browned. Reduce heat to about 350°F. and bake until tender. For basting use 1/2 cup mixed butter and canola oil mixed into 1 cup boiling water. When this is gone, use pan drippings with a little additional boiling water, if needed. Chicken should be basted every 15 minutes. (Refer to "Chicken Timetable" for cooking time.)

FOR VEGETARIANS: We have the Vegetarian Gourmet Recipes book, see back pages for ordering. The Bragg main diet is vegetarian.

— Patricia Bragg

Chicken Casserole

1 (3 lb) frying chicken, cut in pieces	1 / 3 cup whole-grain or potato flour
1 medium onion, sliced	2 cups distilled water
2 tablespoons canola oil	1-1 / 2 cups potatoes, diced
6 small carrots	1 / 3 cup celery, diced
1 small can mushrooms	1 teaspoon lemon juice
	1 teaspoon Bragg Aminos

Roll chicken in flour and brown in oil. Put chicken and remaining ingredients, vegetables, etc., in casserole. Cover and bake in a moderate oven (350°F.) until chicken is tender, about 60 minutes. Uncover last 15 minutes to brown. Thicken gravy with 1 tablespoon potato flour mixed with distilled water. For Hawaiian variety use unsweetened pineapple juice instead of water and 1 tablespoon honey. Serves 4-6.

Sauteed Chicken

1 small chicken, cut in pieces	whole-grain crackers, roll fine
milk of choice	1 tsp Bragg Aminos
1 egg, fertile, beaten	pinch Italian herbs
3 tbs butter or olive oil	1 tbs cilantro, minced

Dip cleaned bird in milk and well-beaten egg, then roll in crushed crackers. Place in heavy frying pan with melted butter or oil. Keep heat low and brown chicken. When it is brown, add small amount of water, herbs and Bragg Aminos. Cover. Bake 45 minutes in a 350°F. oven. This makes a very juicy and tender chicken. Serves 4.

"Every healthy horse has some gas!" stated American farmers. When people eat natural plant fiber foods (fresh fruits, vegetables, and whole-grains), they are cleaning, purifying and recharging their body machinery. Occasionally some gentle cleansing combustion (gas) will occur. There is a new enzyme product that helps with this (especially with beans) called Beano.

Chicken Paprika

2 young chickens, cut
1/2 cup chopped onions
1-1/2 cups soft tofu or
   sour cream
1 tablespoon olive oil

1 tablespoon Bragg Aminos
1 tablespoon chives, chopped
1 tablespoon paprika
pinch Italian herbs
1 tsp cilantro, chopped (optional)

Saute or broil chickens until almost done. In deep pan, lightly saute onions and seasoning. Stir in soft tofu or sour cream and add cooked chicken. Heat thoroughly and serve. Serves 8.

Chicken Tomato Delight

1 broiler chicken (2-3 lbs)
2 large ripe tomatos, peeled
1 teaspoon Bragg Aminos
4 tablespoons butter or
   olive oil or mix

1/2 cup parsley, chopped
2 garlic cloves, minced
1/2 teaspoon sweet basil
pinch Italian herbs
1/4 cup boiling distilled water

Cut chicken into serving pieces. Saute in oil until lightly browned. Slice tomatoes, add all ingredients and 1/4 cup boiling distilled water and simmer until tender (about 1 hour). Garnish with Parmesan cheese and Brewers yeast flakes. Serves 2-4.

Broiled Chicken

2 small broilers
1/2 cup butter or oil or mix
1/4 cup parsley, chopped

1/2 teaspoon chervil
2 garlic cloves, minced
1 tablespoon Bragg Aminos

Mix herbs, garlic, Bragg Aminos and oil. Split chicken and soak in mixture for 3 hours. Drain, saving mixture for basting. Place chicken on hot broiler, basting frequently with marinade. Broil about 50 minutes. Serves 4-6.

"We've never had a heart attack among our Framingham group in 35 years in anyone who maintains a cholesterol under 150. Three-quarters of the people who live on the face of this earth never have a heart attack."
*See page 345
   —Dr. William Castelli, M.D., Director famous Framingham Heart Study

Chicken with Brown Rice

1 *medium-sized stewing hen*	3 *tablespoons butter*
1 *cup brown rice*	1 *pimiento, minced*
2 *small onions*	*giblets from chicken*
3 *cloves garlic*	1 *tablespoon minced parsley*
1 *bay leaf*	¼ *teaspoon sweet basil*
1 *large ripe tomato*	*chicken stock*

Boil giblets and bay leaf until tender in enough water to yield 2½ cups hot chicken stock. Cut chicken into serving portions. Combine 1 minced onion and 2 cloves minced garlic. Cover with water and cook until tender (about 1 hour). Brown uncooked rice in butter, place rice and all remaining ingredients with chicken mixture and continue cooking until rice is thoroughly tender. Serves 5.

Roast Duck

Stuff and truss. Use stuffing for game birds (see page 165). (This stuffing recipe will fill a 2-lb. bird. Multiply by number of pounds of duck you wish to cook.)

1 *roasting duck*	¼ *cup peanut or olive oil*
¼ *teaspoon Bragg Aminos*	¾ *cup orange juice*
¼ *teaspoon cinnamon*	1 *orange*

Mix cinnamon, orange juice and Bragg Aminos. Rub inside of cleaned duck with some of mixture. Fill with stuffing and truss. Brush duck lightly with balance of mixture. Peel orange and place 4 thin orange slices over the breast of the duck, fastening with skewers or tooth-picks. Place in uncovered pan in hot oven for 20 minutes. Reduce heat to moderate oven. Baste frequently with oil and orange-juice mixture and roast until tender. Serves 4.

Tropical Duck

1 *duck, 3 to 3½ lbs.*	1½ *cups crushed pineapple*
1 *teaspoon Bragg Aminos*	½ *cup shredded apple*

Cut duck into serving portions, simmer in boiling water until tender. Add all other ingredients and cook for 20 minutes longer. Serves about 4.

Roast Goose
(6 to 8 lb.)

Wash and clean the goose thoroughly. Do not stuff or add any seasoning. Prick through to fat layers, especially around leg and wing portion. If goose is very fat, it is necessary to preroast it before stuffing. Place on rack with dripping pan in moderate oven about 375°F. about 15 minutes. Remove from oven and allow to cool at room temperature. Drain off fat. Repeat this process once more, draining off fat again. Then when cooled a second time at room temperature, stuff with the following stuffing:

> 8 *cups dried whole-wheat*
> *bread crumbs*
> 2 *chopped onions*   5 *large tart apples, diced*
> ½ *cup chopped celery*   ½ *cup brown sugar*
> 2 *tablespoons butter*   1 *cup cooked, mashed sweet*
> 1 *teaspoon sage*   *potatoes*
> ¼ *cup chopped parsley*   *giblets from goose*

Cook giblets until tender. Mix lightly with all other ingredients. Stuff goose. Return stuffed goose to roaster again and roast, uncovered, in a slow oven until tender.

Turkey Timetable

SCHEDULE (if turkey has been in refrigerator directly before cooking, add 5 minutes more per pound longer than if standing at room temperature):
8–10 *pounds*: 325°F. 13 *to* 15 *minutes per pound or* 3 *to* 3½ *hours*
10–14 *pounds*: 325°F. 18 *to* 20 *minutes per pound or* 3½ *to* 4 *hours*
14–18 *pounds*: 300°F. 15 *to* 18 *minutes per pound or* 4 *to* 4½ *hours*
18 *pounds*: 300°F. 13 *to* 15 *minutes per pound or* 4½ *to* 5 *hours*
20 *pounds*: 300°F. 13 *to* 15 *minutes per pound or* 5 *to* 6 *hours*

Turkey
(12 to 14 lb.)

Wash and clean turkey thoroughly. Remove leg tendons, or cut through the skin in the area of the turkey leg about 2 inches above the foot with a sharp knife or instrument and loosen from bone and muscle. Stuff, shape, and tie turkey. Rub the breast, leg, and wings with ⅓ cup of butter rubbed until creamy and mixed with ¼ cup whole-wheat flour ground fine. Dredge the bottom of the pan with flour; place in a hot oven about 450°F. When flour on the turkey begins to brown, reduce the heat to about 350°F. and baste every 15 minutes until turkey is done. This will be about 3 hours, depending upon the size of the turkey. Consult the "Turkey Timetable."

For basting liquor, use ½ cup melted butter in ½ cup boiling water to which a bay leaf has been added. After this liquor is used up, use the liquor left in the pan. Pour water in the pan during cooking as needed to prevent the flour from burning. During the cooking, turn the turkey frequently so that it will brown evenly. If the turkey browns too fast, cover with buttered paper or cheesecloth to prevent burning.

How to Cook Turkey
in an Electric Roaster

Preheat roaster to 450°F. Place turkey, already prepared, breast down on rack. Roast at that temperature until it begins to brown. Reduce heat to 350°F. or lower and roast until tender.

How to Cook Half a Turkey

The average turkey is much too large for the small family. Many butchers will split a turkey and sell half, or will divide a turkey for two purchasers. The turkey should be split right through the top of the breast. The half turkey should be cleaned thoroughly, washed and dried,
The skin around the cut portion of the turkey should be skewered to the edge bones to keep it from shrinking back and leaving the exposed meat. The leg should be tied securely to the tail, and the wing pressed flat against the breast. Lay the turkey, cut-side down, on rack in roasting pan. Brush thoroughly with the following mixture: ¼ cup melted butter, 1 bay leaf, ¼ teaspoon sweet basil. Dip a clean piece of cheesecloth in the remaining butter mixture, cover top of turkey. Consult "Turkey Timetable" for cooking time, and when half done, remove bird. Prepare a half portion of desired stuffing from any

of the stuffing recipes you wish to use. Place a piece of wax paper on roasting rack. Place dressing over wax paper, shaping to contour of the turkey. Return turkey to the roaster, placing it over dressing so that the dressing is completely covered. Finish roasting time, until tender. Baste from time to time, using fat from the bottom of the roasting pan to pour over the cheesecloth, keeping it moist.

DRESSINGS
Whole-Wheat Stuffing

3 *cups whole-wheat dried or*
    toasted bread crumbs
¼ *cup butter or oil*
¾ *onion, minced*
¾ *teaspoon sage*
¾ *teaspoon thyme*

1 *teaspoon Bragg Aminos*
⅓ *teaspoon paprika*
few minced celery leaves
1⅛ *cups diced celery*

Heat the whole-wheat dried or toasted bread crumbs in a very slow oven until thoroughly dry. Cook the minced onion and seasonings in the fat two or three minutes. Add the celery, celery leaves, and crumbs. Mix thoroughly. Let cool, then stuff the bird. Makes stuffing for 3½- to 4-pound chicken or duckling; triple it for a 10- to 14-lb. turkey.

Pecan Delight Stuffing

¼ *cup butter or oil*
1 *small onion, minced*
⅓ *cup watercress, minced*
⅔ *teaspoon thyme*
⅔ *teaspoon marjoram*
¼ *teaspoon paprika*

1 *teaspoon Bragg Aminos*
⅓ *cup chopped pecans*
⅓ *teaspoon celery seeds*
⅛ *teaspoon ground nutmeg*
4 *cups whole-wheat bread*
    crumbs

Cook the minced onion and seasonings for 2 to 3 minutes in the fat. Add the crumbs, watercress, and chopped nuts. Mix thoroughly, let cool, and stuff bird.

Thanksgiving Turkey Dressing

3 cups whole-wheat bread
crumbs, dried or toasted
1 egg, beaten (fertile)
4 tbs butter (salt-free)
2 onions, chopped

3/4 cup mushrooms, chopped
3/4 cup celery, chopped
1 teaspoon Bragg Aminos
1/2 teaspoon poultry seasoning
3 garlic cloves, minced

Mix all ingredients together. If not moist enough, add a few tablespoons distilled water, skim or soy milk. Ready for stuffing or baking. Any excess bake separately or freeze with the date and ingredients marked on package.

Stuffing for Game Birds

1/2 cup wild or brown rice
1 quart boiling water
1/4 tsp poultry seasoning
1/2 teaspoon Bragg Aminos

2 tablespoon butter, salt-free
1/2 cup fresh mushrooms, sliced
1 egg, beaten (fertile)

Cook the rice in boiling water until it is thoroughly tender. Then rinse and add beaten egg, mushrooms and seasonings. Blend thoroughly. Stuff bird and roast. This is enough stuffing for about a 2-4 pound bird. Any excess bake separately or freeze and store.

Walnut Stuffing

1/2 lb whole-grain bread
1/3 cup chives, chopped
1 bay leaf
1 cup boiling distilled water
2 cups walnuts, chopped
1 teaspoon Bragg Aminos

1 teaspoon sage
1/2 teaspoon thyme
1/2 teaspoon marjoram
giblets from the fowl
4 tablespoons olive oil or
salt-free butter, or mix

Cook the giblets, thyme and bay leaf together in boiling water until tender. Discard the bay leaf and drain giblets, retaining liquid. Toast whole-grain bread in oven until dry. Break into fine crumbs, combine all ingredients and mix thoroughly. Do not mash or squeeze — toss together lightly. Moisten the mixture with the liquor remaining from the cooking of the giblets. This will be sufficient stuffing for a 8 to 12 lb. fowl.

Chestnut Herb Dressing

*3 cups thoroughly dried
　whole-wheat bread crumbs
8 cooked, peeled chestnuts
1/2 cup minced celery and
　leaves
3 tablespoons butter*

*1 teaspoon Bragg Aminos
1 teaspoon sweet basil
1 teaspoon poultry seasoning
1 large onion, minced
2 clove garlic, minced
1/2 cup hot water*

Saute for 3 minutes the onion, garlic and celery slowly in butter. Add herbs, seasonings, 1/2 cup of hot water, then pour this mixture over bread crumbs; add diced chestnuts. Mix lightly by tossing. Any excess bake in pie pan. This will stuff a 5-8 lb. bird.

Melba Toast Celery Dressing

*3 cups Melba toast crumbs
1 cup celery, chopped fine
1 to 2 tablespoons onion,
　minced fine
3 tablespoons water*

*1 teaspoon Bragg Aminos
2 cloves garlic, crushed
3 tablespoons butter or olive
　oil (or mix)
1 teaspoon poultry seasoning*

Mix ingredients and moisten slightly with water. Stuff bird. Water chestnuts, chopped almonds, minced ripe olives or raisins may be added for variety.

Bragg Healthy Lifestyle Promotes Super-Health

Bragg healthy lifestyle consists of eating 70-80% of your diet from fresh live foods, raw vegetables, salads, fresh fruits and juices, sprouts, raw seeds and nuts, the home-prepared all-natural 100% whole-grained breads, pastas & cereals and the nutritious beans and legumes — and these are the no-cholesterol, no-fat, no-salt, just "live foods" body fuel for more health that make live people. This is the reason people become revitalized and reborn into a fresh new life filled with Joy, Health, Vitality, Youthfulness, and Longevity! There are millions of healthy Bragg followers around the world proving this works!

Chapter 9

Vegetarian Entrees and Cheese Dishes

Bean Patties

1 *cup whole-wheat bread crumbs*	2 *cups cooked or canned beans*
1 *beaten egg*	1 *tablespoon chopped parsley*
	1 *teaspoon Bragg Aminos*

Mix the above ingredients and form into patties. Bake for about 10 minutes. Any legumes may be used in this recipe. Serves 4.

Lentil Loaf

1½ *cups whole-wheat bread crumbs*	1½ *tablespoons chopped parsley*
1½ *cups milk or soy milk*	¾ *teaspoon Bragg Aminos*
	1½ *cups cooked lentils*

Mix the above ingredients well, put into greased pan, and bake in a moderate oven until firm. Beans or peas may be substituted for lentils. Cooked whole-grain cereal may be used in place of lentils. Serves 5.

Lentils with Walnuts

2 *cups lentils*	¾ *cup ground walnuts*
2 *tablespoons butter*	½ *teaspoon Bragg Aminos*
¼ *teaspoon thyme*	

Cook lentils until tender and quite dry. Put through colander or mash. Add ground walnuts and herbs.
Put in greased casserole and bake 20 to 30 minutes. Serves 3.

Lentils with Wild Rice
or Whole-Grain Cereal

1¼ cups lentils, puréed
1½ cups cooked wild rice or
    whole-grain cereal
2 tablespoons butter
½ cup milk

2 eggs
1 teaspoon Bragg Aminos
¼ cup chives
½ teaspoon rosemary
1 small onion, minced

Combine lentils and wild rice (or whole-grain cereal); add butter, milk and Bragg Liquid Aminos. Separate yolks and whites of eggs. Beat whites until stiff. Stir yolks into mixture and fold in whites and herbs. Place in buttered casserole in moderate oven, watching carefully until mixture is well set and top delicately brown. Serves 4.

Lima-Bean Loaf

1 egg, slightly beaten
1 teaspoon Bragg Aminos
1 cup dried lima beans
1½ tablespoons butter or soy or
    olive oil

1½ cups whole-wheat cracker
    crumbs
1 tablespoon minced pimiento
1 cup milk or soy milk
1 lemon, juice only

Wash and soak the beans overnight. Cook until soft, drain, and rub through a coarse sieve. Mix the other ingredients, place in greased casserole, and bake in a moderate oven. Baste with lemon juice and butter. Serves 5. May be prepared also with cooked whole-grain cereals instead of lima beans.

Soybean Loaf

3 cups soybeans
¾ cup whole-wheat crackers
3 eggs
¾ cup milk or soy milk
3 tablespoons grated onion
6 tablespoons butter or oil

1 teaspoon Bragg Aminos
¾ cup water
1½ tablespoons grated orange or
    lemon peel

Cook and mash the beans. Brown the whole-wheat cracker crumbs and sift. Mix all ingredients together thoroughly. Place in a greased bread pan and bake 30 minutes in a moderate oven. Serve hot or cold. Serves 8.

Soybean Macaroni Loaf

2¼ cups cooked soybeans
¾ cup cooked whole-wheat
   macaroni
¾ tablespoon chopped onion
1 teaspoon Bragg Aminos

3 tablespoons butter or soy oil
3 tablespoons whole-wheat
   flour
1½ cups milk or soy milk
¾ cup grated unprocessed
   cheese

Combine butter or soy oil, flour, and milk into a white sauce. Add cheese and stir until melted. Combine other ingredients and place in a greased casserole. Cover with cheese sauce. Bake in a moderate oven (350°F.) for 40 minutes. Serves 4 to 6.

Vegetable and Soybean Stew

1 cup or 1 (8 oz.) can meat
   substitute
3 cups cooked soybeans
2 cups fresh or canned
   tomatoes

2 onions, chopped
1 green pepper, chopped
1 teaspoon Bragg Aminos
paprika
4 raw potatoes, chopped

Cut meat substitute into small pieces and cook in a heavy skillet until slightly browned; remove from pan. Chop potatoes, onions, and green pepper into fat in skillet. Season with Bragg Aminos, paprika. Add soybeans and tomatoes. Top with meat substitute; cover, and cook very slowly about 1½ hours, adding liquid from soybeans or water if needed. Serves 5.

Soy Vegetable Roast

½ cup tomato juice
1 chopped onion
2 eggs
sage
½ cup whole-grain cereal

1½ cups cooked soybeans
1½ cups cooked carrots
1½ cups cooked celery
1 teaspoon Bragg Aminos

Grind or mash soybeans, celery, and carrots. Add cooked cereal, tomato juice, chopped onion, and beaten eggs. Mix and season to taste. This loaf should be moist; if too dry, add more tomato juice. Place in a buttered pan and bake 45 minutes in a moderate oven. Serves 6.

Vegetable Hash

½ *cup chopped ripe olives*
2 *cups cooked soybeans*
½ *cup cooked celery*
½ *cup cooked carrots*

½ *cup cooked onions*
½ *cup cooked beets*
1 *teaspoon Bragg Aminos*

Mix all together. Pour in a shallow, greased pan, cover with sliced tomatoes, and bake in hot oven until brown. Serves 5.

Boston Baked Soybeans

2½ *cups canned soybeans*
¼ *minced onion*
½ *teaspoon mustard*
2 *tablespoons unsulphured molasses*

3 *tablespoons peanut oil*
¼ *teaspoon ground fresh peppercorns*
1 *teaspoon Bragg Aminos*

Mix all ingredients together. Bake in a buttered casserole in a moderate oven (about 350°F.) 20 to 30 minutes. Serves 5.

Stuffed Peppers with Soybeans

4 *green peppers*
¼ *cup diced cucumber*
1 *cup canned soybeans*
1 *teaspoon Bragg Aminos*

¼ *cup diced celery*
2 *ripe tomatoes*
1 *teaspoon minced chives*
¼ *teaspoon thyme*
¼ *minced onion*

Remove seeds from green pepper by cutting off top near the stem and hollowing out. Boil very slowly for 5 minutes, ... add Bragg Liquid Aminos . Mash soybeans. Cook celery and cucumber until almost tender. Peel and section tomatoes, cut into fine pieces. Make a mixture of the beans, vegetables, and seasoning. Stuff peppers; cover top with a few whole-wheat buttered bread crumbs. Bake in hot oven for about 20 to 25 minutes. Serves 4.

◇◇

Vegetarian Loaf

1½ *cups cooked peas*
1½ *cups cooked beans*
1½ *cups cooked brown rice or
whole-grain cereal*
3 *eggs, beaten*

3 *tablespoons melted butter*
2¼ *cups tomato sauce*
⅛ *teaspoon celery seed*
1 *teaspoon Bragg Aminos*

Use fresh or dry beans and peas. While hot put them through a food-chopper. Add all the other ingredients but the hot sauce and shape into a loaf, adding more cooked brown rice or cereal if necessary. Season to taste. Bake in a moderate oven for 45 minutes. Serve with hot tomato sauce. Serves 8.

Baked Vegetable Loaf

1 *egg*
1 *cup milk*
dash *of fresh ground pepper-
corn*
2 *cups diced carrots*
½ *green pepper*
½ *onion*
2 *tablespoons melted butter*

1 *cup chopped, stewed prunes*
1 *cup peas*
¼ *cup unsulphured molasses*
1 *teaspoon Bragg Aminos*
1 *cup diced potatoes*
1 *cup whole-wheat bread
crumbs*

Cook carrots and potatoes, chop coarse, and mix with chopped green pepper and chopped onion; add peas and prunes. Add all the seasonings, beaten egg, butter, and molasses. Mix thoroughly, place in buttered baking pan, and bake in a hot oven (about 400°F.) for 1 hour. Serves 6.

Vegetarian Sausages

2 *cups cooked soybeans*
1 *cup cooked lima beans*
1 *cup cooked navy beans*
⅛ *teaspoon paprika*
1 *teaspoon Bragg Aminos*

⅛ *teaspoon powdered sage*
1 *egg*
1 *cup cornmeal or whole-
wheat cracker crumbs*
⅔ *cup milk or soy milk*
1 *teaspoon poultry seasoning*
1 *tablespoon butter*

Press the beans through a colander and mix in all the seasonings. Beat the egg with milk. Shape seasoned beans into sausage shapes, dip in egg mixture, then in cornmeal, and repeat. Place in dripping pan with butter or soy oil, and brown on all sides in a hot oven (500°F.). Serves 8.

California Baked Polenta

⅓ cup chopped onion
¾ small clove garlic, minced
⅛ teaspoon thyme
¼ cup soy, peanut, or olive oil
¼ lb. fresh mushrooms or
  1 small can
1 cup yellow cornmeal

¾ cup cold water
3¾ cups hot water
¾ teaspoon Bragg Aminos
⅓ lb. sharp natural cheese, grated
¼ lb. grated Parmesan cheese
2¼ cups drained, cooked tomatoes

Wilt onion and garlic in hot oil; add seasonings, sauté mushrooms lightly and add tomatoes. Simmer gently 1½ hours, stirring occasionally and adding more tomato juice if necessary. Prepare mush by combining cornmeal and cold water. Gradually add to the boiling water and cook, stirring until thickened. Reduce heat and cook slowly for 10 minutes longer. Spread a ½-inch layer of cornmeal in shallow baking dish; cover with ½ cup of sauce and add layer of thinly sliced or grated cheese. Repeat layers. Save some sauce for serving. Sprinkle top with grated Parmesan cheese. Bake at 300°F. for 30 minutes. Serves 4 to 6.

Eggplant Roast

¾ lb. pecans or walnuts
3 tablespoons butter or oil
1 large eggplant, cooked and diced
1 teaspoon Bragg Aminos

¾ cup minced onion
3 tablespoons minced parsley
3 cups cooked brown rice or whole-grain cereal
1½ lemons, juice only
watercress

Saute the nuts in the butter for 5 minutes; then turn them into an oiled baking dish. Cover with eggplant. Sprinkle eggplant with Bragg Liquid Aminos, lemon juice, onion, and parsley. Add a thin layer of chopped nuts and then a layer of brown rice or cereal. Repeat the layers until all material is used. Sprinkle top with buttered whole-wheat bread crumbs. Add a small amount of water and bake in 400°F oven until top is browned, about 20 minutes. Serves 8.

Yellow Corn Croquettes

2 *cups canned or fresh corn*
1 *cup milk or soy milk*
1 *egg, beaten*
2 *tablespoons butter or oil*
1 *tablespoon grated onion*
1 *cup whole-wheat bread crumbs*

1 *cup whole-wheat cracker crumbs*
2 *tablespoons grated celery*
1 *teaspoon Bragg Aminos*

Mix ingredients and shape into balls. Roll in dry cracker crumbs, then egg, then crumbs. Sauté in butter until golden brown. Serves 8.

Mushroom Loaf

3 *tablespoons butter or oil*
4 *egg yolks*
3 *tablespoons whole-wheat flour*
¼ *cup diced celery*

4 *egg whites, beaten stiff*
2 *lbs. mushrooms, sliced thin*
½ *teaspoon dill seed*
1 *teaspoon Bragg Aminos*

Cream the butter, add yolks of eggs, beat in flour and egg whites beaten stiff. Add Bragg Aminos, dill seed, and mushrooms. Mix well, pour into a buttered pan. Steam 1 hour, turn out, and serve with parsley. Serves 6-8

Vegetarian Chop Suey

3 *cups water*
1 *teaspoon Bragg Aminos*
1 *cup chopped onions*
3 *cups diced celery*
½ *cup wild or brown rice*

1 *cup mushrooms*
2 *cups gluten steaks*
2 *tablespoons butter or oil*

Brown chopped gluten steaks, add onion, celery, mushrooms and uncooked wild or brown rice , add Bragg Aminos and water. Cook together in skillet for a few minutes. Then bake in oven until the rice is cooked. The flavor is improved with 1 teaspoon honey. (Gluten steaks can be purchased in your Health food store.) Serves 6.

To work the head, temperance must be carried into the diet. — Beecher

Chestnut Croquettes

2 cups ground chestnuts
1 egg
1 cup diced celery
2 tablespoons melted butter
3 slices broiled pineapple
1 tablespoon soy, peanut, or olive oil

½ lemon (juice only)
½ tablespoon butter
½ cup whole-wheat cracker crumbs
1 teaspoon Bragg Aminos

Shell the chestnuts, boil, and remove the brown skin. Cool and put through a food-grinder. Add the eggs, celery, cracker crumbs, 2 tablespoons melted butter and Bragg Aminos. Mix and shape as desired. Place them in a dripping pan with soy, peanut or olive oil and bake in a hot oven until brown. Baste occasionally with lemon juice and remaining butter. Garnish with broiled onion or pineapple slices. Serves 6.

Cincinnati Mock Turkey

1 cup whole-wheat cracker crumbs
1 cup whole-wheat bread crumbs
1 cup milk or soy milk
1 tablespoon peanut or soy oil
¼ cup pecans, chopped fine
¼ cup walnuts, chopped fine
1 egg

a few sprigs of parsley, chopped fine
1 cup mixed cooked soybeans and lentils
2 tablespoons chopped onion
1 teaspoon Bragg Aminos
2 to 3 tablespoons whole-wheat flour

Put the chopped onion and the oil into a small saucepan and heat for a few minutes, but do not brown or fry. Add the milk. Bring to a boil and pour over the whole-wheat cracker crumbs and whole-wheat bread crumbs. Sift the whole-wheat flour into a pan and stir constantly over the fire until its color is light brown. Add chopped nuts and continue stirring until they are warmed through but not browned. Beat the egg and add it to the mixture. Add the browned flour and nuts. Run the cooked beans and lentils through a food-chopper. Mix all ingredients thoroughly. Pour mixture in bread tin lined with heavy oiled paper and bake in an oven of about 325°F. After

◇◇◇

baking, set aside for 20 to 30 minutes to cool.   Then turn out into a baking dish and pour over it a gravy made as follows.

1½ *tablespoons butter or oil*　　2¼ *tablespoons whole-wheat*
　1 *tablespoon onion, chopped*　　　*flour*
　fine　　　　　　　　　　　1 *teaspoon Bragg Aminos*
1¼ *cups boiling water*

Mix this to a very smooth consistency and pour over the baked mock turkey and place in the oven for another half hour to bake. This makes a very delicious vegetarian roast. Serves 6.

Boston Mushroom and Onion Pilaff

1½ *cups brown or wild rice*　　2½ *large onions, sliced thin*
　6 *tablespoons butter or oil*　　1 *teaspoon Bragg Aminos*
⅜ *lb. fresh mushrooms or* 1
　(8 *oz.*) *can*

Wash rice well and drain. Melt butter or oil in heavy frying pan. Add rice and cook over low heat until well browned. Add mushrooms and brown lightly. Arrange onion rings over top. Pour 3 cups boiling water over rice. Cover frying pan tightly. Turn heat low and steam, covered, about one hour or until rice is cooked and liquid completely absorbed although rice is still moist. Serves 6.

Jambalaya

　3 *cups cooked brown or*　　　6 *ripe, peeled tomatoes or*
　　wild rice　　　　　　　　1½ *cups canned tomatoes*
　3 *tablespoons butter or oil*　　¾ *green pepper, sliced thin*
1½ *medium onions, chopped*　　1 *teaspoon minced parsley*
　fine　　　　　　　　　　　½ *teaspoon sweet marjoram*
1½ *tablespoons whole-wheat*　　½ *teaspoon garlic*
　flour　　　　　　　　　　1 *tablespoon Bragg Aminos*
1½ *lbs. shrimp, cooked*

Melt butter in heavy kettle. Add onion and brown. Blend in flour to make a smooth paste. Cook until slightly brown. Add shrimp, tomatoes — green pepper, parsley, marjoram, garlic powder and Bragg Aminos.   Cook slowly for ½ hour, stirring frequently.   Add cooked rice. Simmer for about 7 minutes and serve. Serves 8.

Mixed Nut Loaf

⅜ cup chopped walnuts
⅜ cup chopped pecans
⅜ cup chopped, blanched
    almonds
⅜ cup chopped cashews
1½ cups crushed whole-wheat
    crackers

1½ teaspoons mixed herbs
3 cups tomato sauce
2 eggs, beaten
1½ cups dry whole-wheat bread
    crumbs
1 teaspoon Bragg Aminos

Combine all the ingredients and mix well, using only enough (about ¾ cup) of the sauce to moisten. Place in a greased pan, bake in a moderate oven from 30 to 35 minutes. Serve hot or cold with the remaining tomato sauce. Serves 6.

Cheese and Nut Roast

1⅓ onions, chopped fine
1⅓ tablespoons butter or oil
⅓ cup water
1 cup whole-wheat cracker
    crumbs
1⅓ cups grated unprocessed
    cheese

1 cup chopped walnuts
⅔ lemon (juice only)
2 eggs, well beaten
⅔ tablespoon peanut butter
1 teaspoon Bragg Aminos

Brown the onions lightly in the butter, add the water, . . and mix with the cracker crumbs. Add the cheese, nut meats, peanut butter, lemon juice, Bragg Aminos and eggs and toss together, mixing well. Add more seasoning if necessary. Turn into a greased casserole, top with crumbs, and bake in an oven of 400°F until brown. Serves 4.

Celery and Pecan Loaf

1¼ cups chopped pecans
1¼ cups celery, chopped fine
¾ cup whole-wheat bread
    crumbs
¾ cup whole-wheat cracker
    crumbs

1 teaspoon Bragg Aminos
1 cup scalded milk
1 teaspoon onion juice
2 tablespoons melted butter
2 eggs

Mix the above ingredients thoroughly together and bake in a buttered baking dish for 40 minutes in a 375°F. oven. Serves 6.

Creole Casserole

2½ cups cooked whole-grain
   cereal
⅓ teaspoon chili powder
2 tablespoons soy oil
5 tablespoons onion

4 tablespoons chopped green
   pepper
2½ cups canned tomatoes
1 teaspoon Bragg Aminos
¾ cup cubed cheese

Combine the cereal, one teaspoon onion, and chili powder. Spread this thin on a heat-proof platter. Heat the oil. Add the rest of the onion and cook till golden brown. Add the tomatoes and simmer until thickened. Pour the tomato sauce and Bragg Liquid Aminos on the cereal; top with the cheese.   Bake in a hot oven   (400°F.) about 15 minutes. Serves 6 to 8.

Green Spinach and Nut Loaf

¾ cup chopped walnuts
1½ lbs. spinach
2 eggs
1 onion, chopped fine

1¼ cups whole-wheat cracker
   crumbs
2 tablespoons butter or soy oil
1 teaspoon Bragg Aminos

Wash and cook spinach for a few minutes, chop and add to chopped nuts. Mix in beaten eggs, onion, and whole-wheat cracker crumbs. Add Bragg Liquid Aminos , butter or oil, and turn into a greased pan. Bake for half an hour in a moderate oven (375°F.). Serves 4.

Vegetable Stew

1 cup diced eggplant
1 cup chopped string beans
1 cup canned soybeans
1 cup diced zucchini
½ cup chopped okra
2 large tomatoes, peeled and
   diced
2 small onions, sliced

1 green pepper,
   chopped
½ cup sliced celery
1 tablespoon Bragg Aminos
¼ teaspoon thyme
1 bay leaf

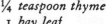

Cook all ingredients in heavy pan, add distilled water to barely cover. Add bay leaf but remove when mixture is half cooked. Simmer gently for 1/2 hour, remove from heat, cover with buttered whole-grain bread crumbs and bake covered in oven for 1/4 hour. Remove cover and allow to brown slowly for another 1/4 hour in a moderate oven. Garnish with Parmesan or Romano cheese and Brewer's yeast flakes. Serves 6.

Tomato Cheese-Tofu Sauce

1/2 lb grated cheese
1/2 cup whole-grain
    bread crumbs
1/2 cup tofu, diced
1/2 cup soy or dairy cream
2 tbs butter or olive oil

2 beaten eggs or egg replacer
3/4 cup tomato juice, warmed
1/2 teaspoon Bragg Aminos
1/4 teaspoon dry mustard
pinch Italian herbs

Melt soy or cheddar cheese in double boiler; add toasted bread crumbs, cream, and tomato juice, stirring constantly. Then add beaten eggs, tofu, seasonings and herbs. When mixture is thoroughly blended and melted, serve on whole-grain toast or pasta, with warmed corn tortillas or pita bread, or over fresh steamed vegetables. Garnish with Parmesan or Romano cheese and Brewer's yeast flakes. Serves 6.

Cheese Souffle

4 eggs, separated
1/2 teaspoon Bragg Aminos
1/8 teaspoon sweet basil
1/2 cup grated cheddar cheese
pinch salad herbs

2 tbs whole-grain
    or potato flour
4 tbs butter or oil
1 cup tomato juice, salt-free

Melt butter, add flour, stir and cook for a few moments. Add warm tomato juice and seasonings, herbs and cheese. Stir until smooth and melted. Remove from stove and cool. Beat egg yolks and add to mixture. Beat egg whites and fold in gently. Turn into oiled casserole, bake in moderate oven (325° F.) for 45 minutes. This will make the souffle very firm. If it is desired softer, cut down the time and increase oven temperature slightly. Serves 4.

Cottage Cheese

Use two quarts of whole milk. Pour milk into glass jar and lightly cover the top with waxed paper. Let stand for three days, or long enough to permit whey to appear. If milk has not clabbered sufficiently, let stand until of a light consistency, then place in a cloth bag to drip for 2 or 3 hours. Remove from bag into a mixing bowl, add the soured cream. Whip with a spoon until smooth.

Cup Cheese

4 *quarts sour milk*
3 *tablespoons butter*

Use very thick sour milk. Draw a knife through the milk 4 or 5 times, scoring separations. Then heat and scald until the curd becomes very dry. Place in a dampened cheesecloth bag, hang up to drip over sink or place under a heavy weight for about 24 hours until the cheese is dry. Put through a coarse sieve, store in a wooden bowl covered with a heavy cloth in a warm place. This should be kept about a week so that it will soften and ripen. It may be stirred several times during that period. After this ripening period, place in a heavy pan or skillet, cook very slowly stirring constantly until all lumps are blended. Add seasoning and butter.

Soybean Cheese

To prepare soybean cheese, allow soy milk to curdle, just as you would ordinary milk. Set the soy milk in a warm place, and when it is soured and thickened, cut into sections and bring to a boil in a saucepan. Then strain through cloth. The remaining cheese can be seasoned with Bragg Liquid Aminos, onions, chopped chives, or other desired seasoning.

Cheese Custard

1 *tablespoon melted butter*
½ *teaspoon mustard*
½ *teaspoon paprika*
1 *cup unprocessed grated cheese*

1 *cup soft whole-wheat bread crumbs*
½ *cup milk*
1 *well-beaten egg*

Melt butter, add seasonings, then add cheese and soft bread crumbs and milk. Cook 5 minutes, then add beaten egg and cook for a few minutes longer. Serve this on squares of toasted whole-wheat bread. Serves 6.

Chapter 10

Eggs and Egg Dishes

Fertile eggs are best from healthy free-range chickens fed on drug-free feed.

THERE IS NO one food so adaptable to the art of cookery as the fertile, healthy egg. It is complete in itself and yet can be blended with variety in innumerable dishes. It can be used as the base active ingredient or principal constituent and can be served as a main dish or an accompaniment or garnish to a meal.

Nutritionally, fertile eggs are high in protein, vitamins and minerals. The average adult can have 2 to 4 eggs weekly, more for the growing child and active person, less or none for the older, sedentary or egg allergic individual or anyone with high cholesterol levels. They can use egg-replacer products.

One egg contains about 250 mg of cholesterol. Preparing egg omelets and egg dishes use 1-2 tsp of lecithin granules as it acts like butter, but is a great fat (cholesterol) emulsifier. Also great over vegetables, casseroles, potatoes, etc.

Testing Eggs for Freshness

Fresh as possible eggs are desirable for flavor and food value. While shopping . . . it's difficult to determine the freshness of eggs. For that reason these simple tests are excellent:

1. Hold the egg in front of a candle flame in a dark room. The air space at the top determines the quality of the egg. The smaller the air space, the better quality the egg. The old superstition that a fresh egg will sink rapidly in a basin of cold water is not true. This has been disproved by authoritative government tests.

2. Another old-fashioned test that no-longer means anything is the texture test. A dull egg used to mean a fresh one; a shiny egg, the opposite. Now, however, most eggs are put through a sandblast to make them all appear dull, so do not be misled.

3. When broken, the egg should have no odor. The yolk should stand high in a semicircle and not flatten out.

4. Eggs obtained direct from the farmer may be accepted usually

as fresh if you know your farmer. Most farmers today candle their eggs for signs of spots, molds, and rots.

5. Although without a sign of staleness, eggs having heavy blood dots should not be used. They are often caused by a chicken being badly frightened. Small flecks are easily removed by touching them with a wet cloth or towel.

Soft-boiled Eggs

Place eggs in a pan with water to cover. Bring slowly to boiling-point. Reduce to simmering heat and allow to simmer for 3 minutes. Eggs at refrigerator temperature require longer cooking.

Hard-boiled Eggs

Cook as for soft-boiled eggs, allow to simmer for only 15 minutes.

Coddled Eggs

If eggs have been kept in refrigerator, allow them to warm to room temperature naturally. Slip gently into pan filled with boiling water. Cover tightly and remove from heat. Allow to stand from 4 to 8 minutes, depending upon consistency desired.

Poached Eggs

Use poacher or heavy shallow pan such as a heavy frying pan or buttered muffin tin. Fill pan or poacher ⅔ full of boiling water. Each egg should be broken individually into a saucer and gently slipped into the muffin pan or poacher. Water should cover the egg. Remove pan from heat and allow to stand for 5 minutes or more depending upon consistency desired. Remove carefully and serve on buttered toast.

Poached Eggs Vienna

Fill a small saucepan two-thirds full of milk. Bring milk to scalding point but do not boil. Milk should be maintained at this temperature throughout cooking. Break egg into sauce dish. Stir milk vigorously around the edge of the saucepan until a well is formed in the middle of the milk. Slip egg in gently. Coax egg into shape with a spoon until it is set. Only 1 egg can be prepared at a time. When done, lift egg out carefully and place on buttered whole-wheat or rye toast. Cover with a few tablespoons of the milk used for poaching. The milk imparts an unusual flavor to the egg, and the egg gives the milk an unusual character. Very little, if any, seasoning is needed.

Poached Eggs with Mushrooms

Arrange pieces of buttered toast to cover bottom and sides of buttered baking dish. Over this place a layer of fresh mushrooms slowly sautéed in butter. Top this with poached egg, 1 tablespoon of cream per egg, and grated cheese. Allow to brown in a moderately hot oven (375°F.), or brown slightly in broiler.

Poached Eggs with Chicken Livers

Use recipe as above, substituting chicken livers for the mushrooms and omitting the cream.

Eggs Benedict

Sauté a circular piece of vegetarian cutlet or meat substitute and place on a split, toasted, buttered whole-wheat muffin or buttered whole-wheat toast. Arrange a poached egg on top of this. Cover all with Hollandaise sauce. The meat substitute may be omitted if desired and a delicious variation is achieved with the use of caper sauce, Hollandaise.

Eggs Florentine

Season cooked spinach with butter
and lay in bottom of casserole. Sprinkle with grated Parmesan cheese. With a large spoon, make little nests in the spinach and into each one slip an egg. Cover the entire dish with Mornay sauce and bake in a moderate oven (325°F.) until the eggs are set.

Shirred Eggs

Butter an egg shirrer or small baking dish such as a custard cup. Mix 1 tablespoon heavy cream with 1½ tablespoons whole-wheat bread crumbs. Put half this mixture into baking dish, slip in egg, and top with remaining half of cream and bread crumbs. Bake in moderate oven (350°F.) until firm. This should be about 5 to 6 minutes.

◇◇

Eggs Robert

Slip eggs into heated, buttered omelet pan. Cook until whites are firm. Remove to hot platter. Pour Robert sauce over eggs and serve.

Eggs au Beurre Noir

Slip eggs into hot, buttered omelet pan. Sprinkle with pepper, and Bragg Liquid Aminos and cook until whites are firm. Remove carefully to hot platter. In the omelet pan brown 2 tablespoons butter, add 1 tablespoon vinegar, and pour over the eggs.

Scrambled Eggs with Avocado

Scramble eggs as usual and add diced avocado just before eggs are set. Serve immediately on toast

Scrambled Eggs with Mushrooms

6 *eggs*	¼ *cup mushroom liquid from*
6 *tablespoons cream*	*can*
½ *cup mushrooms (stems and*	1 *teaspoon minced onion*
pieces may be used)	2 *tablespoons butter or oil*
½ *teaspoon Bragg Aminos*	

Beat eggs and cream until frothy. Heat butter or oil in heavy pan. Add mushrooms, Bragg Liquid Aminos and onion . . . . . Simmer for a few minutes. Add mushroom liquid and simmer for another minute. Pour in egg and cream mixture, continue cooking at very low heat, scraping constantly from the bottom of the pan until desired texture is achieved. Serves 4 to 6.

Scrambled Eggs with Tomato

Peel and quarter tomatoes, remove seeds and excess juice, and cut into smaller pieces. Use in above recipe in place of the mushrooms or in addition to them, if desired.

Scrambled Eggs with Capers

To either of above recipes for scrambled eggs, add 1 tablespoon capers.

Scrambled Eggs with Cheese Bits

6 *eggs*
6 *tablespoons cream*
½ *cup crumbled cheese*

3 *tablespoons butter or oil*
1 *teaspoon Bragg Aminos*

Melt butter or oil and Bragg Liquid Aminos in heavy pan and allow to simmer a few moments. Beat eggs with cream; fold in cheese bits; pour mixture into pan and scramble to desired consistency . . . Serves 4 to 6.

Scrambled Olive Eggs

3 *eggs*
⅛ *cup cream or milk*
⅛ *teaspoon paprika*

¼ *cup minced ripe olives*
½ *teaspoon Bragg Aminos*

Beat eggs slightly with water. Add paprika. Pour this mixture into a slightly warmed frying pan, add olives, and cook slowly, stirring constantly until eggs are as firm as desired. Serves 2.

Chow Eggs

4 *eggs*
⅓ *cup cooked meat, chopped*
¼ *cup chopped mushrooms*
⅓ *cup chopped water chestnuts*

¾ *cup chopped bamboo shoots*
½ *teaspoon Bragg Aminos*

Beat eggs and add remaining ingredients. Cook as for scrambled eggs. Garnish with parsley. Serves 3.

Egg Delight

1 *small dry onion or*
    4 green onions, chopped
3 *eggs*

1 *teaspoon Bragg Aminos*

Saute onions and Bragg Liquid Aminos in a little butter or oil, until golden brown. Pour eggs over top of onions, and mix together with a fork. Serves 4.

Basic Omelet Recipe

6 *eggs*
6 *tablespoons rich milk or cream*

3 *tablespoons butter*
1 *teaspoon Bragg Aminos*

Use regular omelet pan or a large, heavy pan. Add Bragg Liquid Aminos and cream, beating lightly until blended. Melt butter in pan, pour in egg mixture. As the omelet cooks lift slightly with knife or spatula, allowing uncooked portion to run underneath. Cook until creamy in texture. Then increase heat to brown underneath. Crease center with knife and fold gently. Remove carefully from pan and serve. Serves 4.

Filled Omelet

Use above basic omelet recipe, but before folding spread the top with a mixture of 2 tablespoons cream blended with 1 tablespoon melted butter and any of the following fillings:

1. Cheese mashed with a small amount of thyme.
2. Sautéed chicken livers, cut in small pieces.
3. Pieces of cooked fish.
4. Diced, cooked chicken.
5. Chopped green peppers and chopped celery. This mixture should not be cooked, as crisp bits in the omelet will add to its character.
6. Peeled sections of tomatoes with most of the juice and seeds removed, and a small sprig of basil.
7. Mushrooms prepared in any manner without liquid.
8. Cooked kidneys cut into small pieces.
9. Cooked shellfish such as lobster, shrimp or crab.
10. Any vegetable mixture seasoned with herbs. Refer to Herb Chart on page 382 for proper herbs to use with egg mixture.
11. Fruit omelet can be made with desired bits of cooked or fresh fruit. It should be well drained.
12. Bits of cheese, with or without suitable herbs. See Herb Chart on page 382.

Variations for Basic Omelet Recipes

Instead of using any of the above mixtures as a filling, they can be added to the omelet itself by mixing with the egg before turning into omelet pan.

Herb Omelet

To basic omelet recipe, add ½ teaspoon minced parsley, chervil, chives, and basil, or alternate combination of herbs: watercress, parsley, sweet marjoram, and chives.

Spanish Omelet

1 lb. onions, chopped fine
2 cloves garlic
6 eggs
¼ cup parsley, chopped
1 green pepper, chopped fine
¼ lb. grated yellow unprocessed cheese
3 tomatoes, peeled and chopped
olive oil or butter

Cook the above ingredients in olive oil or butter, in a large iron frying pan. Add cheese last. Serves 4 to 6.

Eggs French Style

2⅔ tablespoons butter
5⅓ tablespoons whole-wheat flour
1⅓ cups milk or soy milk
½ teaspoon Bragg Aminos
⅛ teaspoon thyme
8 hard-cooked eggs
whole-wheat wafer crumbs
⅔ teaspoon paprika

Melt butter, blend in whole-wheat flour, and add milk or soy milk and seasonings. Cook until thickened, stirring constantly. Dip eggs into the sauce, cook and roll in wafer or whole-wheat cracker crumbs. Sauté in butter or oil until brown. Drain on absorbent paper. Serve with tomato sauce. Serves 4.

Baked Eggs on Spanish Rice

⅔ cup uncooked wild or brown rice
1¾ cups cooked tomatoes
⅓ small onion, sliced
⅓ cup buttered whole-wheat bread crumbs
½ bay leaf
1 teaspoon Bragg Aminos
1 clove
1⅓ tablespoons melted butter or oil
1⅓ tablespoons whole-wheat flour
4 eggs
1⅓ tablespoons grated unprocessed cheese

Cook wild or brown rice in boiling. . . .water until tender; drain and rinse with cold water. Simmer tomatoes, onion, bay leaf, Bragg Liquid Aminos and clove together for 10 minutes. Strain. Blend butter with whole-wheat flour in saucepan and add strained tomatoes, stirring constantly. Cook until thickened. Arrange layer of rice in greased casserole and make 4 depressions in the rice. Place an egg in each depression. Pour tomato sauce over all and sprinkle with cheese and whole-wheat bread crumbs. Bake in moderate oven (350°F) until eggs are firm, about 15 minutes. Serves 4.

Curried Eggs

4 *hard-boiled eggs*   ¼ *teaspoon curry powder*
1 *cup Mornay sauce*   ½ *teaspoon Bragg Aminos*

Cut eggs into quarters or eighths. Warm in Mornay sauce seasoned with curry powder. Serves 2.

Deviled Eggs

4 *hard-boiled eggs*   2 *tablespoons Parmesan or*
¼ *teaspoon mustard*   *grated cheese*
1 *teaspoon lemon juice*   ½ *teaspoon Bragg Aminos*
1 *teaspoon chopped pimiento*   3 *tablespoons melted butter*
¼ *teaspoon paprika*   1 *teaspoon minced onion or*
1 *tablespoon lemon mayon-*   *shallot*
  naise

Cut eggs in half. Remove yolks and mash. Add all ingredients, mix thoroughly. Add more lemon mayonnaise if necessary to shape. Fill whites and pile high in centers. Sprinkle with a little paprika. Serves 2 to 4.

Chapter 11

Cereals

NATURE'S greatest gift to mankind is the tiny, golden berry of grain. Whole wheat, rye, barley, oats—all the delicious nutlike grains impart much rich flavor to the menu and inestimable energy and food value to the diet.

In modern civilization our greatest crime against food has been committed against the whole grain. Since it contains elements that do not keep well in storage (for instance, the brans and the germs of the grains), we have established commercial practices of milling the bran and the germ right out of the grain and offering only the thin shell as an excuse for a rich, golden grain. We have robbed the grains of some of their life, their vitality, their vitamins, their minerals, by removing part of their most precious substances. The tiny golden flake, that is, the wheat germ, the rich, nutlike flavor of the bran, the full-bodied deliciousness of the completely blended grain flavor, are lost forever in the processing.

Although the whole grain has come more into prominence in recent years, we still do not take advantage of nature's rich variety of grain food. Wise farmers never plant the same grain year after year. If they do, it brings about soil starvation. And yet variety is more important to you than to the soil. If you habitually eat only one whole grain, such as whole wheat, you are not utilizing to the full the food essentials found in nature's variety of grains.

For that reason, I will give you a balanced blend of grains that is an excellent basic cereal mixture. You will note that most of the ingredients are thoroughly toasted.

My Favorite Blended Meal
or Cereal

NOTE: Health food stores carry cereals, already prepared, containing all the following ingredients:

◇◇

3/4 cup cracked whole wheat   *1/4 cup raw rice bran*
1/2 cup cracked whole rye   *1/4 cup raw oat bran*
1/4 cup cracked whole barley   *1/2 cup raw wheat germ*
1/2 cup cracked whole oats   *(vacuum-packed)*

Blend in food processor or blender the first four ingredients (whole grains) thoroughly in dry form. Place in shallow pan in very low oven (about 150°F) for 1 to 2 hours or until lightly done. Remove from oven and allow to cool to room temperature. Add last three ingredients (the brans and wheat germ) and blend thoroughly. This will yield about 3 cups of delicious toasted grains that can be used in many ways.

Methods of Breakfast Cereal Preparation

• No. 1: Stir 1 cup blended meal into 2 cups boiling water. Stir for 3 minutes. Remove from heat. Allow to stand 30 minutes.
• No. 2: Soak 1/2 cup blended meal overnight in 1 cup cold water. Cook in double boiler or heavy bottomed pan 20 to 30 minutes.
• No. 3: To 1 cup boiling water, add 1/3 cup blended meal. Cook in double boiler 20 minutes. Turn off heat and let stand for several hours — preferably overnight. Reheat for 15 minutes.
• No. 4: Soak 1/3 cup blended meal, raisins (optional) in 1 cup boiling hot water, sealed in large wide-mouth thermos overnight, so it's ready for morning. Allow 1-1/2 inches at top for expansion.

Toppings for Hot or Cold Breakfast Cereal

1. Honey and cream (lowfat yogurt, nut milk, soy or real cream)
2. Sliced bananas, honey and cream of choice
3. Berries, honey and cream of choice
4. Fresh, sliced figs, honey and cream of choice
5. Chopped dates, chopped pecans and cream of choice
6. Dried, cooked or soaked unsulfured apricots, pears, peach, prunes, figs with honey and cream of choice. Pecans, pine-nuts, walnuts go well with any of the unsulfured dried fruits
7. Butter (salt free) or lecithin granules for hot cereal
8. Any fresh fruit, natural sweetening and cream of choice
9. Any fresh fruit, sweetening and fruit juice in place of cream (try unsweetened apple, pineapple, grape or cranberry juice)
10. Honey, 100% maple syrup, low-fat yogurt, soy or nut milk

◇◇◇

CEREALS USED IN BAKING

New Orleans Bread

7 cups blended meal (7 grain)
$^1/_3$ cup soy oil
$^1/_2$ cup brown rice syrup or
  molasses

1 package quick-rise yeast
equals 1 cake fresh yeast or
Rumsford baking powder
$2^2/_3$ cups warm distilled water

Mix water & yeast. Add brown rice syrup or molasses and oil. Put into bowl, add the meal and remainder of water. Knead well on floured board for 10 minutes. Cover and keep in a warm place for several hours. Knead again. For variety in loaves, you may add 2 tbsps grated hard cheese in one, a pinch of French or Italian herbs, or raisins in others. Place dough in well-oiled bread pans. Let rise until dough doubles in size (30-60 mins). Bake 45 minutes or longer in moderate oven. Makes 3 medium-sized loaves.

Blended Meal Waffles or Pancakes

1 cup whole-wheat flour
1 cup blended meal (7-grain)
2 teaspoons baking powder
1 teaspoon brown rice syrup

2 eggs
$1^1/_4$ cups soy or skim milk
3 tablespoons butter or oil
1 ripe banana (optional)

Sift flour before measuring. Mix with blended meal, Rumsford baking powder, oil, and rice syrup. Beat egg yolks well. Add milk. Combine with flour mixture & beat smooth. Add melted butter or oil & fold in stiffly beaten egg whites. For variety you may add mashed ripe bananas, apricots, berries, minced nuts, etc. Bake in hot waffle iron or cook as pancakes. Makes about 6 portions.

California Muffins

2 cups blended meal
1 teaspoon brown rice syrup
2 teaspoons baking powder
1 ripe banana (optional)

$1^1/_2$ cups soy or skim milk
3 tablespoons butter or soy oil
1 egg
1 tablespoon oat bran

(Variations: $^1/_3$ teaspoon pure vanilla extract, $^1/_4$ cup raisins and currants or 1 tablespoon sunflower seeds)

Mix oil or butter and rice syrup. Add beaten egg, meal, Rumsford baking powder, mashed banana and milk. Mix well and bake in muffin tin. Bake in a moderate oven until light brown. Makes 10 to 12 muffins.

Cereal-Fruit Desserts

1 *cup cooked blended meal*
1 *cup stewed fresh or dried fruit*

2 *tablespoons honey or sweetening to taste*
1 *beaten egg*

Combine meal with stewed fruit. Stir in well-beaten egg and sweetening to taste. Bake in a greased baking dish in a moderate oven until set in the center as for custard. Serve hot or cold with cream. Serves 2.

RICE

One of our rich, nutritional cereals is whole brown rice—rice that has not been polished or processed to remove the golden bran. It is a food that is easily digested because the starch grains are very small, and the delicacy of their shell walls makes it easy for the body to assimilate the grain almost completely .

The delicious wild rice is so very expensive that it can be used only for festive occasions, as a rule, but it is one of our most palatable foods and one that was relished as a food by the Indians. Wild rice is not truly a rice, but the seed of a tall grass that grows along the streams of the Middle West, especially in the Mississippi Valley. Its expense is due to its very difficult harvesting. Harvesters must paddle slowly through the rice beds shaking the seeds into the bottoms of their boats or canoes. Another difficulty is that the "field" cannot be harvested all at one time, but must be gone over many times to catch the grains that ripen at different intervals.

Wild Rice Casserole

1½ cups wild rice (soaked 2 or 3 hours). Cook in boiling water 30 minutes. Drain. Beat 2 eggs with ¼ cup peanut, soy, or olive oil, adding oil slowly. Add 1 cup chopped parsley, 1 grated onion, 1 cup unprocessed American or Cheddar cheese. Add 1 teaspoon Bragg Liquid Aminos, 1 small can mushrooms and juice. Mix well and add some cheese for topping. Bake 30 to 40 minutes in a moderate oven. Serves 4 ro 6. This may also be prepared with brown rice.

Rice Burgers

*1 small onion
pinch poultry seasoning
1 cup whole-wheat cracker
   crumbs
2 cups cooked wild or brown
   rice (or mixed)*

*1 teaspoon Bragg Aminos
4 tablespoons whole-wheat
   flour
1/4 cup soy or skim milk*

Add 1/2 cup of the whole-wheat cracker crumbs, Bragg Aminos, soy milk, whole-wheat flour, onion and poultry seasoning (or Italian seasoning) to the cold rice. Mix lightly together. Shape into round balls and roll in remaining bread crumbs. Brush lightly with soy oil. Place in oiled baking pan and bake in moderate oven until golden brown. This may also be prepared with cooked whole-grain cereal, kasha, or bulgur in place of the rice. Serves 4-6.

Rice and Raisin Pudding

*1 cup brown rice
1/3 cup honey or
1/4 cup brown rice syrup*

*grated lemon rind
1/2 to 1 cup raisins
1 quart milk or soy milk or
   coconut milk*

Wash rice in hot water and place in baking dish. Add honey or rice syrup, sprinkle with grated lemon rind. Pour in milk, place in low oven and bake for several hours. Stir frequently to prevent the top surface from browning. If top should begin to brown, cover the baking dish. One hour before the pudding has finished baking, stir in washed raisins. When the rice is tender, remove from oven, cool and serve. (When the pudding is done, the grains of rice should be whole and the liquid should be of a creamy consistency.) If the pudding is too dry when cool, add a little more milk. When serving you may top with yogurt. Serves 4-6.

Chapter 12

Breads, Rolls, and Muffins

Health in the Whole-Grain Foods

THE whole grains, as said, are nature's richest gift to mankind, both in their delightful taste and in their high nutritional value. Locked within the cells of the golden grain is nature's vitamin and mineral capsule. They are rich in vitamin B₁, in iron, in phosphorus; above all things, they contain valuable oils and carbohydrates. At one time the home was the factory for food-production. Man grew his grain and, with his primitive gristmill, ground it into flour and cereals. There was no milling or refining of any kind. He got into his blood stream everything that nature had fused into the grain. But then man moved to the congested community, to the teeming city and the thriving village. He could no longer produce his own food, and this is where man ceased to eat Health foods, because large groups of people require food that will keep, food that has a shelf life. Those foods that are perishable, that are filled with vitamins and minerals and rich factors for Health-building, are more difficult to keep in storage. That is when the great crime was committed against food. The introduction of the rolling mill took from the grain a lot of the life-containing elements; the energy element, vitamin B, was partly taken out. The germ, which contains the moisture and lubrication, was removed. These factors were milled out of the grain because they were perishable. If man would make more intelligent use of the available modern nutritional knowledge, a new race of people would appear on the face of the earth. Our lives would be lengthened and our Health during the latter years of our lives would be materially bettered.

The difference between ordinary refined white flours defies comparison with the whole-grain foods. In the commercial

◇◇

variety 99% of the taste thrill has been lost. The nutty flavor is gone, and with it a lot of the nutrients and wheat germ, iron, phosphorus, which are so important to maintaining super health!

When you prepare rolls, breads, cakes, pastries and all baked dishes with the rich natural whole grains, you experience the discovery of an entirely different taste-appeal. Try it and prove to yourself how much more enjoyment you will receive from eating these natural whole-grains and products with the priceless germ (vitamin E) left in them. They are more nutritious and more satisfying. The reason for it is that you are getting what the Master Chemist put into the whole grain for your health!

When using any of the recipes in this cookbook, especially in this section on baking, be sure to use 100% natural whole-grain flours. Whole-wheat and whole-grain pastry flours are best used for cake, pie and cookie recipes. There are wonderful varieties of whole and multi-grain flours that are perfect for baked goods, pastries, pizzas, waffles, pancakes, etc. Here are some of our favorites; Whole-Wheat, Multi-Grain, Rye, Pumpernickel, Spelt, Quinoa, Millet, Triticale, Durham Wheat, Soy, Corn, Oat and Potato. Coarser whole-grain bread flours available in Health Food Stores may be used for bread, rolls, biscuits, muffins, etc..

How to Keep Whole-Grain Flours

Whole-grain flours should be stored in tight container and kept in refrigerator or freezer. They will also absorb odors from other foods and have a tendency to absorb moisture. Because they are "live" foods, they are perishable. They will not keep for long periods of time as will dead, refined, milled, lifeless flours. Grind your own or we suggest you buy only as needed from your Health Food Store.

 ## Measurements

It's important to measure accurately. Baking with whole-grain flours and natural sweeteners is an entirely different process from using ordinary commercial, highly processed, dead products. With natural sweeteners you can vary (adjust) up or down to your "sweet desires"!

MEASUREMENTS TO KNOW!

3 TSP = 1 TBS,   8 TBS = 1/2 CUP,   16 TBS = 1 CUP,   1 CUP = 8 FL OZ
2 CUPS = 1 PINT,   4 CUPS = 1 QT,   4 QTS = 1 GAL,   16 OZ = 1 POUND

For accurate measurements . . . all measurements are
level. Use a set of standard measuring spoons and cup.

YEAST BREADS AND ROLLS

For Yeast — Try Quick-Rise Dry Yeast instead of fresh compressed.
Baking Powders — Rumford, Featherlight, (aluminum free) are best.
Vegetable Shortening — Canola and Soy oils or salt-free butter.
Sweeteners — Raw honey, barley malt or brown rice syrups,
molasses and fruit juice concentrates are best.

100% Whole-Wheat or Multi-Grain Bread

*2 cups skim or soy milk,
or half distilled water
2 tablespoons soy oil
or salt-free butter
4 tbs. raw honey*

*1 package quick-rise yeast
2 tablespoons oat bran
7 cups whole-wheat, multi-
grain or pastry flour or
mix as desired*

Heat milk, add oil or butter, yeast & honey or sweetener of choice.
Cool. Beat in enough flour to make a stiff dough. Knead well.
Place in oiled mixing bowl, cover and set in warm place. Let rise
until double in size. Punch down and let rise again. Remove from
bowl, shape into loaves and for variety make 3 different loaves —
Try some grated cheese, zucchini, carrots, chopped nuts, seeds,
raisins, a variety of whole-grain flours, herbs & spices. Why? It's
fun to experiment with baking and cooking. Place in oiled bread
pans. Cover with towel and let rise until double in size. Bake in
pre-heated 375°F oven for 1 hour, cool on rack. Makes 3 loaves.

Whole-Wheat and Wheat-Germ Bread

*1 package quick-rise yeast
4 tablespoons honey
2 tablespoons melted butter
or soy oil
1 tablespoon oat bran*

*1 cup wheat germ, raw
(vacuum-packed)
6 cups 100% whole-wheat flour
2 cups lukewarm soy milk
or skim milk*

Sift and measure whole-wheat flour. Add yeast, milk, honey and
oil. Beat in whole-wheat flour, wheat germ and oat bran gradually. Knead thoroughly, keeping dough soft. Cover and set in a
warm place and let rise 1 to 2 hours. When double in bulk, form
into loaves, place in oiled pans. Cover and let rise again for 1 hour.
Bake in pre-heated 375°F oven for 1 hour. Makes 2 to 3 loaves.

Whole-Grain Bread Sticks

Using above batter make some 1/2" round ropes, cut into 6-9 inch lengths.
Place on oiled cookie sheet and brush with a beaten egg. For variety
sprinkle with sesame, poppy or chia seeds. Bake 12-15 minutes at 300°F.

Dutch Rye Bread

2 cakes fresh yeast
3 cups lukewarm milk
2 tablespoons melted butter
2 tablespoons honey

1½ cups whole-wheat bread or
   pastry flour
4 cups rye flour
1 cup wheat germ

Soften yeast in 1 cup lukewarm milk. Scald rest of milk and cool to lukewarm. Add shortening, honey, softened yeast, whole-wheat and rye flours, and wheat germ. Knead to a stiff dough. While kneading add, if desired, 2 or 3 tablespoons caraway seeds. Cover. Let dough rise in a warm place until double in bulk. Shape into loaves and place in greased bread pans. Let rise again and bake in a hot oven (375°-400°F.) for 20 minutes; reduce heat to moderate (350°F.) and continue baking 40 to 50 minutes longer. Makes 2 large loaves.

Barley Bread

2 cups whole barley flour
1 cup whole-wheat bread or
   pastry flour
2 tablespoons butter or oil

1 tablespoon honey
1 cake yeast
1 cup warm milk

Make a sponge by dissolving the yeast in the warm milk. Stir in wheat flour to make a soft dough. Set in a warm place to rise and add butter or oil, honey, and barley flour. Knead for 10 minutes and let rise again. Divide into two loaves and place in greased bread pans. Cover, and let rise until light, and bake 35 to 40 minutes in moderate oven. This bread bakes more quickly than other bread.

Brown Rice Bread

½ cup uncooked brown rice
1½ cups water
1 tablespoon honey
1 tablespoon oil
1 cake yeast

1 cup fresh lukewarm milk
6 cups whole-wheat bread or
   pastry flour
1 cup whole-wheat flour for
   kneading

Steam rice in a double boiler in 1½ cups water until soft and dry. Add the   honey, and oil and heat to lukewarm. Dissolve the yeast in lukewarm milk and add to the rice. Place all in a mixing bowl and stir in 2 cups of flour. Cover and let stand until light. Add the remainder of the flour and knead lightly. Let the dough rise until it doubles in bulk. Knead, shape into loaves. Place in oiled pans, cover, and when the loaves have risen sufficiently, bake for about 50 minutes in moderate oven. Makes 3 medium-sized loaves.

Oatmeal Bread

2 cups rolled oats
1½ cups boiling water
2 cakes fresh yeast
½ cup lukewarm water
½ cup molasses

1 tablespoon vegetable shortening
5 cups whole-wheat bread or pastry flour

Cover oats with boiling water, let stand 30 minutes. Soften yeast in lukewarm water. To oats add softened yeast, add molasses, shortening, and whole-wheat flour. Mix well, turn out on floured board, and knead until smooth. Place in greased bowl, grease surface of dough and allow to rise until double in bulk— about 1½ hours. Knead lightly, shape into 2 loaves, and place in greased pans. Grease surface of loaves and allow to double in bulk —about 1 hour. Bake in hot oven (400°F.) 15 minutes, then reduce heat to moderate (350°F.) and continue baking about 45 minutes, or until done. Makes 2 loaves.

Corn Bread
(with yeast)

1 cake fresh yeast
2 cups lukewarm milk

1 tablespoon honey
2 tablespoons oil

4½ cups whole-wheat bread or pastry flour
2 cups yellow cornmeal
1 cup whole-wheat flour for kneading

Soak yeast in ¼ cup of lukewarm water until dissolved. Heat the milk and cool it to lukewarm, then add   honey, dissolved yeast, and oil. Make a sponge using about 2 cups of the flour. Let rise until it doubles in bulk. Add cornmeal and the remaining flour to make a stiff dough. Knead, let rise again, and shape into loaves. Cover and let rise in the oiled pans until double in bulk. Bake about 45 minutes in moderate oven. Makes 2 loaves.

Whole-Wheat Rolls

2 *cakes fresh yeast*
2 *cups milk*
¼ *cup unsulphured molasses*
¼ *cup honey*
¼ *cup melted butter*

1 *egg*
1 *cup wheat germ*
1 *cup whole-wheat flour*
5½ *cups whole-wheat pastry flour*

Crumble yeast into mixing bowl. Add milk that has been scalded and cooled to lukewarm. Stir in molasses and honey, let stand until thoroughly dissolved and bubbly. Add egg, wheat germ, and bread flour. Beat until elastic. Add pastry flour and shortening to form soft dough. Turn out on floured board, let stand 10 minutes, then knead about 7 minutes. Place in greased bowl, grease surface of dough, cover, and let rise until double in bulk—about 1½ hours. Knead lightly and shape into clover-leaf or other rolls. Place in greased pans and brush with melted butter. Let rise again until double in bulk. Bake in hot oven (425°F.) about 15 minutes. Makes about 48 rolls.

Fluff Rolls

3 *cups coconut milk*
3 *tablespoons honey*
3 *cakes fresh yeast*
9 *tablespoons butter or oil*

⅜ *cup lukewarm water*
9 *cups whole-wheat flour*

Make a sponge of lukewarm milk, oil, honey, and 4 cups flour. When sponge is cool, add yeast dissolved in warm water, and add rest of flour. Make dough stiff enough to be stirred with a spoon. Cover, and set to rise in warm place. When light, stir down and let rise again. Put in greased muffin tins. Cover, and when double in size, bake in oven 375°-400°F. about 25 minutes. Makes about 60 rolls.

Three-in-One Bread Recipe
(basic dough)

6 *cakes fresh yeast*
3 *cups lukewarm milk*
1½ *cups lukewarm water*
⅜ *cup honey*

¾ *cup melted butter*
or oil
3 *eggs*
13½ *cups whole-wheat*
pastry flour

1

2

3

Soften yeast in lukewarm water and milk. Blend in honey, melted butter or shortening, and eggs. Gradually add sifted flour. Mix until dough is well blended and soft. Use one third of dough for *lemon tea drops* and chill remaining dough for *cinnamon loaf* and *dinner rolls*.

Lemon Tea Drops

Use ⅓ unchilled basic dough to make 36 small tea muffins. Fill greased 2-inch muffin pans ½ full. Mix ½ cup brown or raw sugar, 2 teaspoons lemon juice, and 2 tablespoons grated lemon rind. Sprinkle about 1 teaspoon over each muffin. Cover and let rise in warm place (80° to 85°F.) until light, or about 45 minutes. Bake at 375°F. for 20 to 25 minutes.

Cinnamon Loaf

Use ⅓ chilled basic dough. Roll dough in rectangle. Mix ¼ cup brown sugar and 1 teaspoon cinnamon. Sprinkle dough and roll as for jelly roll, starting with 8-inch edge. Seal edges and place in greased 9 x 4 x 3-inch pan. Cover and let rise in warm place (80° to 85°F.) until double in bulk, or about 2 hours. Bake at 375°F. for 1 hour.

Dinner Rolls

Use ⅓ chilled basic dough to make 27 dinner rolls. Mold into crescents or any desired shape. Cover and let rise in warm place (80° to 85°F.) until double in bulk, or about 2 hours. Bake at 425°F. for 20 minutes.

Date Fans

1 *cup chopped dates*
3 *tablespoons water*

¼ *cup honey*
¼ *cup chopped nut meats*

Simmer chopped dates, water, sweetening, and nut meats for 3 minutes. Roll chilled dough (basic dough) ¼ inch thick and cut with 3-inch floured cutter. Spread 1 heaping teaspoon of date mixture on half of each round, leaving edges free. Moisten edges, fold as for turnover, and press down edges. Cut three gashes ½ inch long in folded edge and place on greased baking sheet. Cover and let rise about 1 hour or until double in bulk. Bake in hot oven (425°F.) for 10 or more minutes. Makes two dozen rolls.

Speedy Pan Rolls

1 *cup lukewarm milk*
⅓ *cup melted vegetable short-*
   ening
1 *tablespoon honey*
2 *cakes fresh yeast*

1 *egg*
4 *cups whole-wheat pastry*
   flour

Mix milk, melted shortening, honey. Add yeast and mix well. Add beaten egg. Gradually add sifted whole-wheat flour and mix until dough is well blended and soft. Roll out on well-floured board and cut dough into 1 x 4-inch rectangles. Brush cut sides with melted butter. Cover, place in greased 12 x 8-inch pan, and let rise in warm place (80° to 85°F) until double in bulk, or about 30 minutes. Bake in hot oven (425°F) for 20 minutes. Makes 24 rolls.

Cheese Lemon Buns

¾ *cup milk, scalded*
¼ *cup melted vegetable short-*
   ening
6 *tablespoons honey or raw*
   sugar
1½ *teaspoons grated lemon rind*

½ *teaspoon mace*
1 *cake fresh yeast*
2 *eggs*
3¼ *cups whole-wheat pastry*
   flour
½ *lb. cottage cheese, sieved*
½ *cup seedless raisins*

Mix scalded milk, shortening, 4 tablespoons sweetening . . . lemon rind, and mace. Cool to lukewarm, add crumbled yeast. Stir until dissolved. Add 1 beaten egg and enough flour to make a soft dough. Turn onto floured board, knead until smooth—about 5 minutes. Place in a greased bowl; cover and let rise in a warm place (80° to 85°F) until light, or about 1 hour. Punch down; turn onto floured board and shape into balls 1½ to 2 inches in diameter. Place 2 inches apart in greased shallow pans. Cover; let rise until double in size – about 30 minutes. Meanwhile, combine cheese, raisins, and remaining 2 tablespoons honey or raw sugar, and 1 beaten egg. When balls are double in size, make a large indentation with back of teaspoon in center of each roll and fill with cheese. Bake in hot oven (425°F) 15 minutes or until brown. Makes 12 to 15 buns.

Hot-Cross Buns

1 *cup milk, scalded*	4 *cups whole-wheat pastry*
⅓ *cup vegetable shortening*	*flour*
½ *cup honey*	1 *cup wheat germ*
2 *cakes fresh yeast*	2 *eggs, beaten*
¼ *cup lukewarm water*	1 *teaspoon cinnamon*
	1 *cup raisins or currants*

Mix milk, shortening, honey or raw sugar and cool to lukewarm. Soften yeast in lukewarm water; stir and add to milk mixture. Add spice, eggs, and half of flour. Beat well. Work in enough of the remaining whole-wheat flour to make a soft dough. Turn out onto a lightly floured board and knead 10 minutes or until smooth and satiny. Place dough in a warm, greased bowl; brush surface with melted shortening; cover and let rise in a warm place (80° to 85°F) about 2 hours or until doubled in bulk. Turn out onto floured board. Knead in the fruit lightly. Shape into balls about 1½ inches in diameter. Place in a greased pan close together for soft buns and farther apart if individual round buns are desired. Gash the top in the form of a cross. Brush with diluted egg yolk; cover and let rise ¾ hour or until doubled in bulk. Bake in a moderately hot oven (375°F) about 30 minutes. Makes about 24 buns.

Date and Nut Bread

2 *cakes fresh yeast*	4 *cups whole-wheat pastry*
2¼ *cups lukewarm pineapple*	*flour*
or apple juice	1 *cup whole-wheat bread flour*
3 *tablespoons melted butter*	1 *cup wheat germ*
½ *cup unsulphured molasses*	2 *cups dates, chopped coarse*
	1 *cup nuts, chopped coarse*
	1 *cup currants or raisins*

Soften yeast in ½ cup lukewarm apple or pineapple juice. Add remaining pineapple or apple juice, shortening. . . . . and molasses. Beat in flours and wheat germ to make a stiff dough. Brush surface very lightly with melted shortening; cover and let rise in a warm place (80° to 85°F.) about 2 hours or until doubled in bulk. Turn out on lightly floured board. Dredge dates with flour, mix with nuts, and knead into dough. Knead for about 10 minutes or until smooth and satiny. Divide dough into two equal portions. Cover and let stand 10 minutes. Shape into loaves. Place in greased loaf pans (about 9½ x 5½ inches). Brush tops with melted shortening, cover, and let rise about 1 hour, or until double in bulk. Bake in a moderately hot oven (375°F.) for 45 to 55 minutes. Makes 2 loaves.

Jingle Bread

2 *cakes fresh yeast*
¼ *cup lukewarm milk*
⅓ *cup honey*
¼ *cup melted vegetable shortening*

1 *cup warm buttermilk or sour milk*
2 *eggs, well beaten*
4 *cups whole-wheat pastry flour*
1 *cup wheat germ*

To the yeast cakes softened in ¼ cup lukewarm milk, add sweetening. . . . . . . melted butter, and buttermilk. Mix; add eggs and yeast. Beat in wheat germ and whole-wheat flour for soft dough. Place dough in well-greased covered bowl. Let rise in warm place for 1½ to 2 hours or until double in bulk. Serves 8.

Jingle Filling

½ *cup honey*
½ *cup chopped dates*
½ *cup chopped nut meats*
½ *cup seedless raisins*

1 *teaspoon cinnamon*
¼ *cup grated orange or lemon rind, or half and half*
2 *tablespoons orange or lemon juice*

Mix all above ingredients well. Roll out Jingle Bread dough into about an 18-inch square, spread with fruit filling. Roll up as for a jelly roll. Cut into 1-inch slices and arrange disks in well-greased round pan. Cover and let rise in warm place about ½ hour. Bake in moderate oven (350°F.) for 1 hour. Remove from pan at once and cover top with any syrup in bottom of pan.

Pumpkin Brown Bread

1 *pint milk*
2¼ *cups cornmeal*
½ *pint water*
2 *cups cooked pumpkin*
¼ *cup maple syrup*

⅛ *cup melted butter*
3 *cups whole-wheat pastry*
flour
½ *cup honey*
1 *cake fresh yeast*

Mix milk, maple syrup, water, melted shortening, honey and pumpkin together. Dissolve the yeast in ¼ cup lukewarm water and add to mixture. Beat in ½ of the flour and cornmeal. Add rest of flour and beat again. Cover, set in warm place to rise until it has doubled in bulk. Stir down and put into oiled bread pans. Cover, let rise until light. Bake in a moderate oven (375° to 400°F.) for one hour. Put one quart of water in a pan and place in the oven with the bread. This gives the bread a glossy appearance. Dates, nuts, and raisins may be added if desired. Makes 2 loaves.

Favorite Fruit Breads
(basic refrigerator dough)

½ *cup scalded milk*
¼ *cup melted vegetable*
shortening
¼ *cup honey*

2 *eggs, well beaten*
2 *cakes fresh yeast*
¼ *cup lukewarm water*
3 *cups whole-wheat pastry*
flour

Mix milk, melted shortening, honey. Cool to lukewarm. Add eggs, yeast softened in lukewarm water, and gradually whole-wheat flour. Mix thoroughly. Place in greased bowl and cover. Let rise in a warm place (80° to 85°F) for about 1 hour or until dough doubles in bulk. Punch down and turn dough over in bowl, greasing top lightly. Cover with a slightly dampened towel and waxed paper. Chill in refrigerator or cold place until needed. Makes 2 small loaves.

Prune Ring

This is a variation that may be used with the basic refrigerator dough. Roll chilled dough to 12 x 16-inch rectangle. Spread with

1 cup cooked, chopped prunes sweetened with honey, and roll long way of dough as for jelly roll. Place in deep greased 9-inch ring mold, joining ends to form complete circle. Slash top of ring with deep crosswise gashes every 2 inches. Let rise about 1 hour or until double in bulk. Bake in hot oven (400°F.) for 25 minutes or until done.

Quick Breakfast Ring

1 *cup milk, scalded*
½ *cup honey*
1 *egg, well beaten*
¼ *cup vegetable shortening*
2 *cakes fresh yeast, crumbled*
¼ *cup lukewarm water*
3¾ *cups whole-wheat pastry flour*

Mix first four ingredients and cool to lukewarm. Stir in yeast, softened in water, egg, and 1 cup flour. Beat well with spoon. Add remaining flour and beat 3 minutes. Line bottom greased angel-cake pan with waxed paper. Fill with batter. Then make the topping by mixing ¼ cup honey . . . . ¼ teaspoon cinnamon, and ¼ cup chopped nuts. Sprinkle over batter. Cover; let rise in warm place (80° to 85°F.) until double in bulk, or about 1 hour. Bake in moderately hot oven (375°F.), about 40 minutes. Makes 1 ring.

Sour-Cream Coffee Cake

6 *cups whole-wheat pastry flour*
½ *cup honey*
½ *pint sour cream*
1 *cup warm milk*
½ *cup butter*
4 *eggs*
2 *cakes yeast*

Mix flour, honey and crumble yeast in flour. Beat eggs and cream well and add to flour; beat well. Melt butter in milk and when lukewarm, add to the rest and beat thoroughly, then put in refrigerator overnight. Roll dough out in sheet and spread with melted butter, cinnamon, and honey. Roll up and cut 1½ inches thick and put in buttered pans to rise until double in bulk and bake at 350°F for ½ hour. Makes about 24 cakes.

Behind the nutty loaf is the mill wheel; behind the mill is the wheat field; on the wheat field rests the sunlight; above the sun is God.
— James Russell Lowell

MUFFINS & QUICK BREADS

Delicious Whole-Grain Muffins

1-1/3 cups rolled oats
1/2 cup whole-wheat pastry
  flour
1/3 cup raw honey
2 tsp baking powder
1 beaten egg (fertile)

1/2 cup raisins
1/2 cup nuts, chopped
1/2 cup dates, chopped
1 cup buttermilk or sour milk
3 tablespoons melted butter

Sift flour, sweetening... and baking powder, add rolled oats, dried fruit and nut meats. Pour in buttermilk and beaten egg, stirring lightly. Fold in melted shortening. Fill greased muffin pans 2/3 full and bake in hot oven (425°F) 15 to 25 minutes, depending on the size of the muffins. Makes about 18 muffins.

Date Bran Muffins

1 cup 100% oat bran
1 cup soy or skim milk
1 egg (fertile)
1/4 cup molasses
6 dates, halved

2 teaspoons baking powder
1/4 cup butter or canola oil
1/2 cup dates, chopped
3/4 cup whole-grain pastry flour

Mix bran and milk; let stand 5 minutes. Beat egg; add with the molasses to bran mixture. Sift dry ingredients and add to mixture. Quickly stir in melted butter or oil. Add chopped dates. Fill oiled muffin pans 2/3 full. Place half date on top of each muffin. Bake in moderately hot oven (375°F) 30 minutes. Makes 12 muffins.

Pizza Whole-Grain Crust

Use any remaining bread doughs for future pizzas. Mold dough into sizes desired and freeze. When needed add mushrooms, tofu, sliced fresh vegetables, onions, olives, grated mozzarella cheese, dash of Bragg Aminos and Italian herbs. Bake in 400° oven until done. Garnish with Brewers yeast flakes.

Apple Corn Muffins

¾ cup whole-wheat pastry
flour
⅓ cup yellow cornmeal
3 teaspoons baking powder
3 tablespoons melted butter or
vegetable shortening

¼ cup finely sliced or grated
raw apple
1 egg, well beaten
⅓ cup milk
¼ cup honey

Sift whole-wheat flour, cornmeal, baking powder........together. Wash, pare, and cut apple. Mix egg, milk, and honey and add to dry ingredients, stirring only enough to dampen well. Stir in melted shortening. Fold in apple. Fill well-greased muffin tins ⅔ full and bake in moderately hot oven (375°F.) for 25 minutes. Makes 12 medium-sized muffins.

Corn Bread

1 cup whole-wheat pastry
flour
4 teaspoons baking powder
¼ tablespoon honey

1 cup yellow cornmeal
1 egg
1 cup milk
3 tablespoons melted butter

Sift whole-wheat flour, and baking powder, together. Add cornmeal. Beat egg well, add milk, honey......and melted shortening. Beat in whole-wheat flour mixture. Bake in a shallow greased pan in moderate oven 20 minutes or until golden brown. Serves 10 to 12.

Buttermilk Corn Bread

¾ cup whole-wheat pastry
flour
2 teaspoons baking powder
1½ cups buttermilk

1½ cups yellow cornmeal
¼ cup butter or vegetable
shortening
2 eggs

Sift the whole-wheat flour and measure; mix with the baking powder. Sift again and stir in the cornmeal. Cut in shortening and add beaten eggs and buttermilk. Mix slightly, just enough to moisten. Pour into a well-greased shallow pan, 8 inches square, and bake in a hot oven (425°F) about 30 minutes. Cut in squares while hot and serve. Makes twelve to sixteen servings.

Buttermilk Biscuits

2 *cups whole-wheat pastry flour*
2 *teaspoons baking powder*

4 *tablespoons vegetable shortening*
⅔ *cup buttermilk*

Sift whole-wheat flour and baking powder . . . . . together. Cut in shortening with two knives or pastry blender. Add milk gradually, to form soft dough. Turn out on floured cloth or board, and knead lightly 20 to 30 seconds. Roll or pat out to ¼-inch thickness and cut with small biscuit-cutter. Bake on ungreased baking sheet in very hot oven (450°F.) 10 to 12 minutes. Makes 12 biscuits.

Whole-Wheat Walnut Bread

2 *cups whole-wheat pastry flour*
1 *cup wheat germ*
1 *cup honey*

2 *teaspoons baking powder*
1 *egg, beaten*
1 *cup milk*
1 *cup walnuts, chopped coarse*

Sift whole-wheat flour, sweetening, and baking powder into mixing bowl. Add egg mixed with milk and beat well. Stir in walnuts. Pour into well-greased loaf pan and let stand 20 minutes. Bake in a moderate oven (350°F) about 65 to 70 minutes. Turn out on rack to cool. Makes 1 loaf.

Honey Nut Bread

2 *tablespoons butter or vegetable shortening*
1 *cup honey*
1 *egg, well beaten*
grated rind of 1 orange
2½ *cups whole-wheat pastry flour*

2 *teaspoons baking powder*
½ *teaspoon baking soda*
¾ *cup chopped walnuts*
¾ *cup orange juice*

Cream shortening; stir in honey and mix well. Add egg and orange rind; beat until creamy. Mix and sift whole-wheat flour, baking powder, baking soda, add walnuts. Add flour mixture and orange juice alternately to first mixture. Bake in a greased oven-proof glass loaf pan in moderate oven (350°F) about 1 hour. This is better the second day. Makes 1 loaf.

Rye Biscuits

2 *cups rye pastry flour*
3 *teaspoons baking powder*

6 *tablespoons vegetable*
  shortening
6 *to* 8 *tablespoons water*

Sift and blend dry ingredients. Cut in shortening and add water. Put on rye-floured board and roll to about ½-inch thickness. Cut with biscuit-cutter. Place on greased baking pan and bake in a hot oven (400°F.) for about 15 minutes. The biscuits should be watched during the last 3 minutes to see that they do not over-brown. Makes 12 biscuits.

Rye Muffins

2 *cups rye pastry flour*
4 *tablespoons honey*
4 *teaspoons baking powder*

1 *cup water*
2 *tablespoons vegetable*
  shortening

Sift dry ingredients together. Cut in shortening. Stir in water. Stir until all large lumps are blended, but do not beat. Place in greased muffin pans and bake about 35 minutes in a hot oven (400°F.). Makes 12 muffins.

Rye Fruit Muffins

Use the recipe for rye muffins, using only one half the honey. Stir in 4 tablespoons of fruit, such as berries or pineapple. If you have fruit juice, use that instead of water.

Graham Pineapple Loaf

1 *quart crushed canned or*
  fresh pineapple
1 *lb. graham crackers,*
  crumbled

lemon juice
2 *bananas*
¼ *lb. coconut or nuts, ground*

❖◇◇❖

Drain pineapple and mix with graham crackers. If more moisture is needed, use pineapple juice. Pour into a mold and let stand until it is set. Unmold. Mash the bananas, adding 1 tablespoon of pineapple or lemon juice to prevent discoloration. Cover loaf with mashed banana as you would frost a cake. Then sprinkle coconut or ground nuts over all. Cut in slices and serve. The same quantity of any desired fruit may be substituted for the pineapple . . . Serves 6 to 8.

Toasted Garlic Whole-Wheat Bread

½ cup butter
1 or 2 peeled cloves garlic
1 loaf whole-wheat bread

¼ teaspoon Bragg Aminos
¼ cup grated Parmesan cheese
paprika

Allow butter to stand at room temperature until soft. Add garlic and mash lightly with fork. Then let mixture stand for 30 minutes or until garlic flavor permeates butter as much as desired. Remove garlic. Slash bread diagonally into thick slices, being careful not to cut the bottom crust. Spread garlic butter generously between slices and on top of loaf. Sprinkle loaf with grated cheese and paprika. Bake in moderately hot oven (375°F.) for 15 minutes. Then snip slices apart with kitchen scissors. Serve immediately. Serves 6 to 8.

Gingerbread

¼ cup honey
½ cup butter
1 egg
1 cup unsulphured molasses
2½ cups sifted whole-wheat flour
1 cup raisins

1½ teaspoons soda
1 teaspoon cinnamon
1 teaspoon ginger
½ teaspoon cloves
1 cup buttermilk

Cream shortening and honey, add beaten egg, molasses, then dry ingredients, which have been sifted together. Add buttermilk last and beat until smooth. The batter is soft. Bake in greased shallow pan 35 minutes in moderate oven (325°–350°F.). Makes fifteen generous portions.

Chapter 13

Pancakes and Waffles

Baking Powders — Rumford, Featherlight, Cellu are best.
Vegetable Shortening — Soy or Canola oils or salt-free butter are best.
Sweeteners — 100% pure maple syrup, honey, molasses, barley malt
or brown rice syrups or fruit juice concentrates are best.

Blinchiki with Applesauce or Jam

2 eggs (fertile is best) *whole wheat flour*
1 cup milk or soy milk *2 tablespoons raw honey*
2 tablespoons melted butter

Beat all ingredients, adding just enough flour to make a thin
batter. Test batter by dropping a spoonful onto oiled frying pan
to be sure blinchiki will be very thin. Saute blinchiki, fill with
unsweetened applesauce or health jelly or jam and fold or roll and
put in buttered dish in oven until heated through. Serve with
lowfat yogurt or sour cream.

Cottage Cheese Blinchiki

Lowfat or dry cottage cheese blinchiki are delicious for dessert.
Saute blinchiki as above, then fill with the following:

1/2 lb dry cottage cheese *1 tablespoon raw honey*
1 egg (fertile is best) *sour cream or lowfat yogurt*

Beat egg, add cottage cheese, honey. Mix well, and fill sauteed
blinchiki. Fold or roll and saute lightly in butter to warm. Serve
with sour cream or lowfat yogurt and honey. Serves 2-4.

*__Shocking Facts:__ America's nationwide health care costs soared to
$700 billion in 1991 and this is expected to more than double by the
year 2000. This is all the more reason each American should lead a
healthy lifestyle to save our economy from this huge medical expense,
not to mention the premature death and suffering (physical, mental,
emotional and financial).*

Whole-Wheat or Multi-Grain Pancakes

3/4 cup soy/multi-grain flour *2 eggs (fertile are best)*
3/4 cup wheat germ, raw *3 tablespoons melted butter*
1-1/2 cups whole-wheat flour *3 tablespoons molasses*
1/2 teaspoon baking powder *3 cups low-fat buttermilk*

Sift and measure whole-wheat and soy flour. Resift with the other
dry ingredients. Beat eggs well and add the melted butter,
molasses and buttermilk. Stir into the dry ingredients. Beat until
smooth and bake on a hot oiled griddle. Serves 4-6.

Whole-Wheat Waffles

2 eggs (fertile are best)
1 cup milk or soy milk *1 cup whole-wheat pastry flour*
1/2 teaspoon baking powder *3 tablespoons butter or soy oil*

Beat eggs to a thick foam. Add milk and fold in sifted flour and
baking powder. Add melted butter or soy oil and beat well. Bake
in a hot waffle iron until golden brown. Makes 4 waffles.

Whole-Wheat Buttermilk or Yogurt Waffles

2 eggs (fertile are best) *1/2 cup whole-wheat*
1/2 cup buttermilk or yogurt *pastry flour*
1/2 teaspoon baking powder *2 tablespoons butter or soy oil*

Beat eggs to a thick foam. Add buttermilk or yogurt, sifted flour
and baking powder. Beat well, add oil and beat again. Bake in hot
waffle iron until golden brown. Makes 2 waffles.

Buckwheat Waffles

1-1/2 cups whole-wheat *1 teaspoon baking powder*
pastry flour *1/2 teaspoon brown rice syrup*
1/4 cup buckwheat flour *4 tablespoons melted butter*
1/4 cup wheat germ, raw *or cold-pressed soy oil*
1 cup milk or soy milk *2 eggs (fertile)*

Sift whole-wheat flour, buckwheat flour, wheat germ, baking powder and sweetening together in large mixing bowl. Beat egg whites and yolks separately and mix with sifted flour and other dry ingredients. Add milk (or you can substitute yogurt) gradually and beat vigorously until batter is thin. Lastly add the melted butter or oil. Bake on a hot waffle iron until golden brown about 3 to 5 minutes for crisp waffles. Serves 2-4.

Soy Flour Waffles

2 cups soy flour
1/4 cup wheat germ, raw
1 tablespoon honey
*   or 1 teaspoon fruit*
*   juice concentrate*

2 eggs (fertile)
2 tablespoons melted butter
*   or soy or canola oil*
1 teaspoon baking powder
1 cup milk or soy milk

Sift together flour and baking powder in a large mixing bowl. Beat egg whites and yolks separately and mix with sifted flour and other dry ingredients; then add milk and sweetener gradually and beat vigorously until the batter is thin. Add the melted butter or oil. Bake in a hot waffle iron for 3 to 5 minutes. Serves 2-4.

Fresh Fruit Waffles and Pancakes

Add mashed banana (our favorite), strawberries, blueberries or other fresh fruits alone or mixed to whole-grain batter. It's fun to experiment — then you can discover your favorite additions and toppings. 100% maple syrup is our favorite topping.

Nutty Waffles and Pancakes

Add nut or seed meats of your choice (pecans, walnuts, almonds, cashews or sunflower, sesame or pumpkin seeds) to the batter.

Sourdough Waffles and Pancakes

You can also add 1 package sourdough starter to your favorite batter for tangy, delicious sourdough waffles, pancakes & breads.

Enjoy the natural healthy taste of your food without added sweeteners. By slowly removing sugar from your diet you will find yourself enjoying the natural sweetness of foods such as fresh fruits, fruit pies, apple sauce and fresh fruit juices. Over a period of time by using natural sweeteners and fruit juice concentrates instead of refined sugar ... your taste buds will enjoy natural flavors more.

Chapter 14

Pies and Fillings

Baking Powders — Rumford, Featherlight, Cellu are best.
Vegetable Shortening — Soy, Canola oils or salt-free butter are best.
Sweeteners — Raw honey, barley malt or brown rice syrups,
raw brown sugar, date sugar or fruit juice concentrates are best.

Whole Wheat Pie Crust (1)

*2 cups whole wheat
   pastry flour
ice water*

*1/2 cup soy oil
1/2 teaspoon brown rice syrup,
   honey or barley malt sweetener*

Add soy oil to flour, add as much ice water as needed to form soft
dough. Wrap in wax paper and refrigerate for about two hours
before rolling out on floured board. Makes 2 crusts.

Whole Wheat Pie Crust (2)

*2-1/4 cups whole wheat
   pastry flour*

*1/2 cup soy oil
about 5 tablespoons ice water*

Mix oil into flour. Add water and mix to a soft dough. Roll on
floured board to desired shape and thickness. Makes 2 crusts.

Whole Wheat - Soy Pie Crust

*1-1/2 cups whole wheat flour
1/2 cup soy flour
1/2 cup soy oil*

*1/2 teaspoon honey, barley malt
   or brown rice syrup
ice water*

Mix oil into flour. Add water and sweetener and mix to a soft
dough. Wrap in wax paper and refrigerate for about 2 hours
before rolling out on floured board. Makes 2 crusts.

Graham-Cracker Pie Crust

18 *graham crackers, rolled fine*   ¼ *cup softened butter*

Mix graham-cracker crumbs and butter thoroughly. Press mixture firmly and evenly against sides and bottom of a greased pie tin. Bake in a hot oven (400°F.) 10 minutes. Cool and fill with desired filling.

Luscious Orange Pastry

1 *cup whole-wheat pastry flour*
½ *cup soybean flour*
½ *cup vegetable shortening*

1 *tablespoon grated orange rind*
3 to 4 *tablespoons orange juice*

Sift whole-wheat flour. Cut in shortening until very small pieces are obtained. Add orange rind, mix well; add juice and mix lightly Roll out ⅔ of the dough on lightly floured board. Place loosely in pan. Trim edges. Add desired filling. Top with ½-inch twisted criss-cross strips cut from remaining dough. Bake in hot oven (425°F) until crust is golden brown (20 minutes). Makes one 8-inch pie.

Pittsburgh Pumpkin-Pie Filling

2 *cups pumpkin* (*strained*)
½ *cups rich milk or cream*
1 *cup honey*
2 *eggs*

½ *teaspoon ginger*
2 *teaspoons cinnamon*
½ *teaspoon allspice*

Add milk, sweetening, beaten eggs, and spices to pumpkin. Stir for 2 minutes. Pour into pie tin lined with whole-wheat or whole-wheat soy pie crust. Place in hot oven at 425°F and bake about 45 minutes, or until filling is firm. Serves 6.

Pecan Pie

3 *eggs*
½ *cup honey*
1 *cup maple syrup*

1 *teaspoon pure vanilla*
¼ *cup butter, melted*
1 *whole-wheat pie shell*
1 *cup pecans*

Add honey, maple syrup, vanilla, and butter to beaten eggs. Put in pecans in a layer of pie pan lined with whole-wheat pastry. Add mixture. Bake in moderate oven (350°F) 50 to 60 minutes. The nuts will rise to form a topping. Serves 6.

Delicious Graham-Cracker Apple Pie

18 *graham crackers*
1 *well-beaten egg*
4 *tablespoons melted butter*
6 *tart apples*
½ *cup seedless raisins*

⅓ *cup honey or raw sugar*
½ *teaspoon grated nutmeg*
1 *teaspoon cinnamon*
½ *cup walnut meats*

Roll crackers fine. Add egg and butter and mix. Line a glass pie dish with the mixture, pressing it down tightly with the back of a spoon. Save ¼ cup of mixture for the top. If this is not left over from crust lining, roll more crumbs sufficient to make ¼ cup. Wash apples, peel and core, cut in half, and cook with raisins, honey or raw sugar, and spices in about 1 cup of hot water, till the apples are soft, but not mushy. The amount of water used in cooking the apples should be increased or decreased according to juiciness of fruit. If the apples are too juicy for the pie, press the juice out after cooking. Pour into the pastry-lined pan, sprinkle top with the nuts and remaining crumbs. Bake in a moderate oven (350°F.) 20 minutes. Serves 6.

Two-Crust Blueberry Pie

whole-wheat pastry
4 *cups fresh or quick-frozen*
   berries
⅔ *cup honey*
1½ *tablespoons cornstarch*

¼ *teaspoon nutmeg*

¼ *teaspoon cinnamon*
2 *tablespoons lemon juice*
½ *lemon, sliced paper-thin*

Line a 9-inch pie plate with whole-wheat pastry (see recipe). Trim edge even with plate. To make filling, mix honey and cornstarch, add berries, spices, lemon, and lemon juice. Pour in pie shell. Moisten edge of crust with water. Cover with crust of whole-wheat pastry leaving ½ inch overhanging edges. Fold edge of upper crust under lower crust all the way around. Press edges together with tines of fork dipped in flour. Bake in hot oven (425°F.) 50 to 60 minutes. Serves 6.

Lemon Chiffon Pie

1 package unflavored gelatin
¼ cup cold water
3 eggs
½ cup lemon juice

1 teaspoon grated lemon rind
⅔ cup honey

Soften gelatin in cold water .   Add ½ cup of honey or raw sugar, lemon juice, to beaten egg yolks. Cook in double boiler until custard-like. Stir constantly. Add softened gelatin and stir until dissolved. Add grated rind. Cool. Beat egg whites with remaining sugar until stiff and fold into mixture when it begins to thicken. Turn into baked 9-inch pie shell. Chill. Sprinkle with chopped nuts if desired . . . Serves 6.

Rum Chiffon Pie

1 tablespoon unflavored
  gelatin
4 tablespoons cold water
¼ teaspoon nutmeg
1 cup milk

1 teaspoon vanilla
3 egg yolks
½ cup honey
1 teaspoon rum flavoring
3 egg whites, beaten stiff

Beat egg yolks until light and add honey gradually. Soak gelatin in cold water. Scald milk in double boiler and pour over egg mixture. Add nutmeg and cook again in double boiler until the consistency of thick cream. Add soaked gelatin and vanilla. Cool until nearly set, then beat slightly. Add rum flavoring and fold in egg whites. Fill baked shell; top with whipped cream and sprinkle with grated, unsweetened carob .   Serves 6.

Carrot Chiffon Pie

1 tablespoon unflavored
  gelatin
¼ cup cold water
1¼ cups cooked carrots, puréed
¼ cup honey
½ cup milk
½ teaspoon ginger

½ teaspoon nutmeg
½ teaspoon cinnamon
2 eggs, separated
2 tablespoons honey or raw
  sugar
1 baked whole-wheat pie shell
  or 1 baked graham-cracker
  pie shell

Soften gelatin in cold water. Beat egg yolks and add pureed carrots, honey, milk, and spices. Cook in double boiler until thick. Add gelatin and stir until dissolved. When mixture begins to thicken, fold in egg whites beaten stiff with 2 tablespoons of honey.
Pour into baked pie shell. Chill. Serves 6.

Strawberry Chiffon Pie

4 *egg yolks*
1 *cup honey or raw sugar*
juice of 1 *lemon*
grated rind of ½ *lemon*
1 *tablespoon unflavored gelatin (softened in* ¼ *cup cold water)*

4 *egg whites*
1 *cup strawberries, cut in half*
1 *baked graham-cracker pie shell*

Blend well egg yolks, ½ cup honey, lemon juice and rind. Cook over boiling water, beating constantly until thick and foamy —about 3 minutes. Remove from heat, add gelatin. Cool. Beat egg whites until stiff, but not dry. Add remaining ½ cup honey or raw sugar gradually, beating after each addition until stiff. Fold into gelatin mixture. Fold in strawberries. Pile lightly into baked pie shell. Decorate with more berries. Chill several hours until well set. Serves 6.

Banana Cream Pie Supreme

1 *cooled baked 8-inch pastry shell*
1 *cup sliced bananas*
6 *tablespoons honey*

3 *tablespoons cornstarch or* 1½ *tablespoons arrowroot*
2 *egg yolks*
1½ *cups scalded milk*
½ *teaspoon vanilla*
½ *teaspoon lemon juice*

Mix honey or raw sugar, and cornstarch. Gradually stir into milk. Cook over hot water, stirring constantly until thick. Add vanilla and lemon juice; cool. Arrange sliced bananas in bottom of pastry shell. Cover with filling. Top with meringue. Bake in a moderate oven (325° to 350°F) for 15 to 20 minutes. Serves 6.

Meringue

2 egg whites (fertile)   *4 tablespoons raw sugar*

Have egg whites at room temperature. Beat until stiff but not dry. Beat in sugar, one tablespoon at a time, being sure that the sugar is dissolved during each beating. Spread meringue over filling, having edges touch the baked crust. Bake in a slow oven (300°F.) about 15 minutes.

Cream Pie

2/3 cup raw honey   *2-1/2 cups skim or soy milk*
1-3/4 tbs arrowroot powder   *3 egg yolks, slightly beaten*
or instant tapioca   *1 teaspoon pure vanilla*
graham-cracker pie shell,   *whole strawberries*
baked   *strawberry glaze*

Mix honey and thickener in top of a double boiler; stir in cold milk. Cook over boiling water until thickened, stirring constantly. Cover and cook 15 minutes longer. Stir a little of the hot mixture into slightly beaten egg yolks; add to remaining mixture in double boiler and cook for 2 minutes over hot (not boiling) water, stirring constantly. Cook and add vanilla. Pour into baked graham-cracker pie shell and cool. Place berries on top in a decorative manner. Cover with strawberry glaze (recipe below). Serves 6.

 # Strawberry Glaze for Toppings

2 cups crushed strawberries   *1-1/4 tbs arrowroot powder*
1/2 cup distilled water   *or instant tapioca*
1/2 cup raw honey   *1 tbs butter, salt-free*

Crush strawberries (fresh or frozen) and place in a saucepan. Add water, honey and thickener. Bring to a boil for 2 minutes or until clear. Add butter and strain. Pour glaze over the whole berries, making sure that all berries are covered. Chill before serving.

Desserts - Frozen Fruit Pops for Children of All Ages
You can freeze any fresh or unsweetened fruit juices in ice cube trays with a popsicle stick in each one. They are delicious and healthy for your children. For variety you may mix lowfat yogurt with fresh diced fruit and fruit juice concentrate — sugar-free apple, grape or tropical mix.

Glazed Apricot Pie

2 lbs very ripe apricots
1-1/2 tablespoons
  arrowroot or instant tapioca
1/2 cup raw honey

1 tablespoon lemon juice
whipped cream (optional) or
  non-dairy replacer
whole-wheat pie crust, baked

Bake a pastry whole-grain pie crust (There are so many varieties of flours available, try different ones.) and cool. Wash apricots, halve and remove pits (save pit kernals, rich in B-17). Place half of apricot halves, uncooked, in the pie crust cut side up and slightly overlapping so all can be used. Cook remaining apricots with 1/3 cup distilled water until soft. Mix thickener and sweetening, add to cooked apricots and cook until sauce is transparent. Remove from heat. Stir in lemon juice. While still hot, pour over apricot halves in pie shell. Cool then chill. Serve plain or topped with non-dairy cream or whipped cream or try lowfat yogurt. Serves 6-8.

Tasty Apricot Filling

1-1/2 cups dried apricots
1-1/2 tablespoons
  arrowroot or instant tapioca
1/2 cup raw honey
1 cup distilled water

1 cup raisins or currants
2 teaspoons lemon rind,
  grated
2 tablespoons butter, salt-free

Hot wash and scrub apricots to remove any mold. Cook in small amount of distilled water until tender. Mix in all other ingredients and cook until mixture thickens. Add drained apricots, cool mixture and place in baked whole-grain pastry shell. Chill. Serves 6-8.

Mock Mince Pie

2 apples, cored, unpeeled
1/2 lemon, unpeeled
1-1/2 cups raisins
  or currants
1/2 cup molasses,
  unsulphered
1 beef bouillon cube

1/2 teaspoon cinnamon
1/4 teaspoon allspice
1/4 teaspoon ground cloves
1/3 cup distilled water
1/4 cup raw honey
pastry for 9-inch, double
  crust pie

Chop apples. Put lemon and raisins (less 1/4 cup) through food grinder or processor. Combine all ingredients, including the 1/4 cup whole raisins. Bring to boil, simmer 30 minutes, stirring often. Cool slightly. Roll out bottom pie shell and fill with mincemeat. Cut ½-inch strips of dough and arrange in criss-cross pattern. Bake in hot oven (450°F.) 10 minutes, reduce heat to moderate (350°F.) for 30 to 40 minutes. Serves 6.

Prune Banana Roll Filling

1⅔ *cups cooked prunes*   1 *tablespoon honey*
1⅓ *cups sliced banana*

Mix and place in pastry shell.

PASTRY

4 *eggs*   6⅔ *tablespoons cold water*
¼ *cup honey*   2 *cups whole-wheat flour*
2 *teaspoons baking powder*   ⅔ *cup soy flour*
                                  1⅓ *teaspoons lemon extract*

Pit the prunes and cut into small pieces. Add the banana and honey or raw sugar and mix thoroughly. To make the pastry, beat the eggs until very light. Mix in the honey or raw sugar; add water alternately with the whole-wheat and soy flour sifted with the baking powder. Add the flavoring and mix thoroughly. Pour into greased shallow pan and bake 15 to 20 minutes in a hot oven (425°F). Turn out on damp cloth and roll, then unroll and spread with filling. Roll again and remove from the damp cloth. Spread top with sweetening or cream icing. Serves 8 to 10. Vary by mixing cooked apricots and walnuts with the prunes; or adding chopped dates or pecans.

Fig Tarts

⅔ *lb. dried figs*   1⅓ *tablespoons grated orange*
1⅓ *cups boiling water*   *rind*
⅔ *tablespoons honey*   ⅔ *teaspoon grated lemon rind*
                                 8 *unbaked tart shells*

Wash the figs and cut off any stems. Cover with boiling water and simmer for 30 minutes. Drain, saving the juice. Chop the figs. Boil the fig juice till it is cooked down to one half (about 5 minutes). Add orange and lemon rind, honey or raw sugar, and figs. Fill tart shells. Bake in a hot oven (400°F.) for 30 minutes. If meringue tarts are preferred, cover each baked tart with meringue and bake in moderate oven till the meringue is light brown. Serves 8.

Date Tarts

2⅔ cups chopped dates
2⅔ teaspoons grated lemon rind
4 tablespoons lemon juice
1⅓ tablespoons butter

1 tablespoon honey
2⅔ tablespoons milk
8 unbaked tart shells
whole-wheat flour

Mix chopped dates with rind, lemon juice, honey or raw sugar, and milk. Fill tart shells, sprinkle each with a little flour and dot generously with butter. Bake in a hot oven (400°F.) 25 minutes. Serve plain, or top with custard, cream, or meringue. Serves 8.

Whole-Wheat Cream Puffs

¾ cup boiling water
¾ cup whole-wheat pastry
flour

3 eggs, unbeaten
⅜ cup butter

Combine the butter and the water in a saucepan. Heat until butter melts. Then add whole-wheat pastry flour all at once, stirring vigorously. Cook, while stirring, until mixture leaves side of saucepan. Remove, and cool for 1 minute. Then add eggs, unbeaten, one at a time, beating with a spoon after each addition until smooth. Drop by rounding tablespoons, using a wet spoon, 2 inches apart, on a greased baking sheet, leaving shaped points in the centers. bake in hot oven (450°F) for 10 minutes, then at 400°F for 25 minutes. The cream puffs should be puffed high and golden brown. Makes 12 puffs. Cool. Slit and fill with cream filling or whipped cream.

Nutrition directly affects growth, development, reproduction, well-being and the physical and mental condition of the individual. Health depends upon nutrition more than on any other single factor. —Dr. Wm. H. Sebrell, Jr.

Cream Filling

7½ tablespoons whole-wheat   3 eggs
   flour or 3¾ tablespoons   1½ tablespoons butter
   arrowroot   1½ teaspoons vanilla
¾ cup honey   3 cups milk

Mix thoroughly in top of double boiler flour, half of sweetening, and gradually add scalded milk. Blend well and cook over boiling water, stirring constantly. Cook until smooth and thick—about 10 minutes. Pour slowly, beating constantly with a beater, over eggs which have been beaten with remaining honey. Return to double boiler; cook 1 minute over rapidly boiling water, stirring constantly. Remove, add butter, and cool. Add vanilla. For fluffy filling, fold in ⅔ cup whipped cream.

Peach Cream Filling

6 tablespoons honey   1 egg
3 tablespoons cornstarch or   1 cup milk, scalded
   1½ tablespoons arrowroot   ¾ cup sliced peaches, fresh or
½ teaspoon vanilla   canned
                                 2 tablespoons butter

Combine honey, dry ingredients and mix with beaten egg. Stir in enough hot milk to make a thin paste. Add paste to remaining hot milk and cook over boiling water five minutes, stirring constantly. Add butter. Cool and fold in fruit slices. Cook 10 minutes or until mixture is thickened, stirring occasionally. Add vanilla. Use as filling for cream puffs or cake filling.

Chapter 15

Cakes and Frostings

Vegetable Shortening: Cold pressed Soy and Canola oils or salt-free butter are best.
Baking Powders: Rumford, Featherlight, Cellu (aluminum free) are best.
Sweeteners: Honey, barley malt or brown rice syrups, molasses, raw brown or date sugars, concentrated fruit juices are best.

ALWAYS use 100% whole-wheat or other whole grain pastry flour for all cakes. Be sure to sift flour before measuring and several times before using, makes for a lighter cake.

Never-fail Spice Cake

1/2 cup raw honey
1 egg (fertile)
1 tablespoon butter or oil
1 cup skim or soy milk
1-1/2 cups whole-wheat
pastry flour

1 teaspoon cinnamon
1/2 teaspoon cloves
1/2 teaspoon nutmeg
1 cup raisins or currants
1/2 cup nut meats (optional)
1 teaspoon baking powder

Beat egg well. Add to creamed honey and shortening. Add milk. Sift flour, baking powder, cinnamon, cloves, nutmeg and add to the mixture. Stir in raisins or currants and nuts. Turn into a well-oiled pan and bake about 40 minutes in a 350°F oven. Use favorite icing. Suggestions: sunshine frosting or maple frosting. Serves about 8-10.

Fruited Spice Cake

1 cup dried figs, dates or
prunes - or mix
1 teaspoon cinnamon
1 teaspoon ginger
1 teaspoon cloves
3/4 cup water, distilled
1/2 cup vegetable shortening

3 eggs (fertile)
3 cups whole-wheat
pastry flour
2 teaspoons baking powder
1 cup milk or soy milk
1 teaspoon pure vanilla
1/2 cup honey or raw sugar

Wash dried fruit, dry and chop. Add cinnamon, ginger, cloves, and water and boil 3 minutes, stirring constantly. Cool. Cream shortening and sweetening until light and fluffy. Add one egg at a time, beating well after adding each egg. Sift remainder of dry ingredients together and add alternately with the milk to the creamed mixture. Do not overbeat—only until smooth. Fold in fruit mixture and vanilla. Turn into 3 greased 9-inch layer pans and bake in moderate oven (350°F.) 25 minutes, or if baked in a tube pan, 70 to 80 minutes. Serves about 8.

Toasted Spice Cake

1 *cup honey*
1 *cup butter or vegetable shortening*
3 *egg yolks*
1 *teaspoon cloves*
1 *teaspoon cinnamon*
1 *teaspoon nutmeg*
1 *teaspoon vanilla*

½ *teaspoon lemon extract*
1½ *cups sour milk or buttermilk*
2½ *cups whole-wheat flour*
1½ *teaspoons baking powder*

Cream butter and honey together. Add egg yolks, cloves, cinnamon, nutmeg, vanilla, and lemon extract. Then add buttermilk, or sour milk. Sift flour, baking powder, and combine. Pour batter into greased pan and top with the following:

Topping for Toasted Spice Cake

3 *egg whites*
½ *cup honey*

1 *cup nut meats*

Beat egg whites and blend in sweetening. Spread mixture over Toasted Spice Cake batter. Sprinkle nut meats over top. Bake for 40 to 50 minutes in 350°F. oven. Serves about 10 or 12.

Temptation Spice Cake

3½ *teaspoons baking powder*
1½ *cups whole-wheat pastry flour*
1 *teaspoon cinnamon*
½ *teaspoon nutmeg*
⅓ *cup honey*

¼ *teaspoon cloves*
½ *cup melted butter*
1 *cup milk*
1 *teaspoon vanilla*
½ *to* ⅔ *cup unbeaten eggs (2 large eggs)*

Sift all dry ingredients together. Add butter, milk, and vanilla. Using about 150 strokes per minute, beat mixture vigorously with a spoon for 2 minutes. Count only actual beating time, or strokes. If it is beaten by hand and it is necessary to rest a moment, the actual number of strokes will be assured. If an electric mixer is used, beat 2 minutes on medium speed. Scrape sides of bowl frequently to assure even mix. Add unbeaten eggs and beat for 2 more minutes, scraping sides of bowl for better blend. Turn into greased layer pans. Bake in a moderate oven (350°F.) for 35 to 40 minutes. Cover with desired frosting. Suggestion: sunshine frosting. Serves 8 to 10.

Upside-Down Cake

1 *cup honey*
3 *egg whites*
½ *cup melted butter*
pineapple rings, cherries or desired fruit

¾ *cup whole-wheat pastry flour*
1 *teaspoon baking powder*
3 *egg yolks*
5 *tablespoons juice from fruit used in cake*

Add ½ cup honey to butter melted in a large iron frying pan. Spread evenly over bottom of pan. Arrange fruit attractively on top of butter and honey and pour over this the dough mixed as follows:

Add ½ cup honey and fruit juice to beaten yolks of eggs. Mix and sift in flour and baking powder. Fold in egg whites beaten stiff.

Bake in a moderate oven 45 minutes to 1 hour. Turn out upside down on a large cake plate. Serves 6 to 8.

Topsy-turvy Pineapple Cake

4 *tablespoons butter*
1 *cup honey*
1 *small can sliced unsweetened pineapple*
3 *egg yolks*

1 *cup whole-wheat pastry flour*
1½ *teaspoons baking powder*
½ *teaspoon lemon extract*
⅓ *cup hot pineapple juice*

Add ¾ cup honey to butter melted in a 9-in. skillet. Stir until blended. Arrange pineapple pieces or slices attractively over butter and honey mixture. Beat egg yolks with ½ cup honey until very light. Slowly add hot pineapple juice and continue to beat. Fold in remaining dry, sifted ingredients. Stir in lemon extract. Pour batter over pineapple slices and bake in a moderate oven (350°F.) for 45 minutes. Turn out upside down. Serves 6 to 8.

Upside-Down Ginger Cake

Sift:

1 cup whole-wheat pastry flour	1 teaspoon cinnamon
1 teaspoon baking powder	1 teaspoon ginger
	¼ teaspoon cloves
	¼ teaspoon nutmeg

Add these dry ingredients to the following mixture:

¼ cup honey	1 beaten egg
⅓ cup unsulphured molasses	⅓ cup butter or vegetable
½ cup buttermilk	shortening

Mix all ingredients until blended.

Prepare topping by combining: 2 tablespoons butter and ¼ cup sweetening. . .in round 10-inch cake tin. Stir until melted and blended. Remove from fire and arrange the following attractively in bottom of pan:

1 orange, in sections	½ cup nut meats
2 teaspoons grated orange rind	¼ cup raisins

Turn gingerbread batter into pan on top of the fruit and nuts. Bake for 30 to 35 minutes in a moderately hot oven. Turn out upside down on a large cake plate. Serves 8 to 10.

Devil's Food Cake

1 cup honey	2 squares unsweetened, melted carob
½ cup butter or vegetable shortening	2 unbeaten eggs
1½ cups whole-wheat pastry flour	1 cup milk
1 teaspoon soda	1 teaspoon vanilla

◇◇◇

Measure flour after sifting and then sift together three times the flour, soda. Add sweetening gradually and cream thoroughly until light and fluffy in consistency. Beat in eggs one at a time . . . Melt carob and add. Mix well. Add a small amount of milk at a time alternately with the flour, beating after each addition until smooth. Add vanilla and bake in greased 9-inch-deep layer pans for 25 to 30 minutes in a moderate oven (350°F). Serves 10.

Milk Carob Cake

½ cup butter or vegetable
  shortening
½ cup honey
2 eggs
1 teaspoon vanilla
1 cup sour milk

2 squares carob
2 cups whole-wheat pastry
  flour
1 teaspoon soda
1 tablespoon lemon juice

Add sweetening gradually to butter, and cream thoroughly until light and fluffy in consistency. Beat in well one unbeaten egg and then another unbeaten egg, beating two minutes after each addition. Add vanilla, sour milk, melted carob . . . . and sifted, mixed dry ingredients. Add soda dissolved in lemon juice last and beat again. Bake in a greased tin for 30 to 35 minutes, at 375°F. Serves 10.

Angel Food Cake

1 cup honey
1 teaspoon baking powder
1 cup whole-wheat pastry
  flour

1 cup egg whites
1 teaspoon cream of tartar
1 teaspoon vanilla

Sift and measure whole-wheat flour and then sift together three times baking powder, and whole-wheat flour.

Add cream of tartar to egg whites beaten frothy and continue beating until stiff but not dry. Add a small amount of the honey over the egg whites and fold in. Continue this process until all the honey has been added. Fold in the whole-wheat flour mixture a little at a time until all has been added. Fold in vanilla. Turn into ungreased angel food cake pan and bake in slow oven (300°F) for 1¼ hours. Invert pan on wire cake rack to cool. Leave plain or use preferred frosting. Suggestion: sunshine frosting. Serves 8.

Orange Angel Food Cake

4 egg yolks
½ cup honey
½ cup orange juice

1 cup whole-wheat pastry
flour
1 teaspoon baking powder
4 egg whites, beaten stiff

Beat yolks of 4 eggs until creamy and lemon-colored. Add honey or raw sugar gradually, mix well, and add orange juice. Fold in sifted whole-wheat flour and baking powder. Beat egg whites until stiff but not dry, and fold into mixture. Pour into angel food cake pan and place in cold oven. Bring oven up to 350°F. and bake cake 45 to 50 minutes. Ice with boiled orange icing. Serves 8.

Tasty Sponge Cake

4 eggs
¾ cup honey
¼ cup cold water
¾ cup whole-wheat pastry
flour

2 teaspoons baking powder
1½ tablespoons cornstarch
¾ teaspoon lemon extract

Add honey gradually to egg yolks beaten until thick. Beat until smooth. Add water. Sift together dry ingredients and add gradually to the first mixture. Blend in lemon extract. Fold in egg whites which have been beaten until stiff but not dry. Pour mixture into 9-inch tube pan and bake in slow oven (325°F.) for 1 hour. Invert pan on wire cake rack until cool. Frost with favorite icing. Serves 8.

Honey Sponge Cake

6 egg whites
1 cup honey
2 teaspoons lemon juice
2 teaspoons grated lemon rind

6 egg yolks
1½ cups whole-wheat pastry
flour
1 teaspoon baking powder

Add egg whites and beat until stiff. Bring honey to boil and slowly pour into egg whites, beating constantly. Add lemon juice and rind to egg yolks and beat until very thick and lemon-colored. Fold egg yolks into egg-white mixture. Sift whole-wheat flour and baking powder together and fold into batter. Place in ungreased tube pan and bake in

◇◇◇

moderately slow oven (325°F) for one hour or until done. Invert cake to cool. May be served plain or frosted. Suggested icing: boiled orange icing. Serves 8.

Lemon Snow Cake

½ cup butter
½ cup honey
3 egg whites
1 teaspoon vanilla

1¾ cups sifted whole-wheat pastry flour
2 teaspoons baking powder
¾ cup milk

Blend butter, sweetening, and vanilla. Add sifted dry ingredients gradually alternately with milk. Beat egg whites until stiff but not dry. Fold in carefully. Turn batter into two greased 8-inch layer pans lined with waxed paper. Bake in moderate oven (360°F) 30 to 35 minutes. remove from pans; peel off paper and cool. Ice with sunshine frosting. Serves 8 to 10.

Pineapple Feather Cake

½ cup vegetable shortening
½ teaspoon grated lemon rind
1 egg yolk
2 cups whole-wheat pastry flour

1 cup unsweetened pineapple juice
4 egg whites
3 teaspoons baking powder
¼ cup honey

Combine shortening, lemon rind, and egg yolk and mix well. Add honey or raw sugar gradually, creaming until light and fluffy. Sift flour and baking powder together and add alternately with pineapple juice, blending well after each addition. Fold in egg whites beaten stiff. Bake in 2 greased 9-inch layer-cake pans in moderate oven (350°F.) 30 minutes. Frost with pineapple frosting. Serves 10 to 12.

Daffodil Cake

4 eggs, separated
½ cup honey
¼ cup cold water
1 teaspoon vanilla
¼ teaspoon almond extract

¾ cup whole-wheat pastry flour
¾ teaspoon baking powder

Beat yolks with beater until thick and lemon-colored. Add honey .....gradually while beating. Blend well. Combine water and extracts. Add alternately in thirds with whole-wheat flour, sifted three times. Beat whites until almost stiff. Add baking powder and continue beating until stiff. Fold in egg whites. Pour into an ungreased 9-inch tube pan and bake in a moderate oven (350°F) for 50 to 55 minutes, or until done. Invert on cake rack to cool. Serves 10. Remove from pan and fill with:

Almond Cream Filling

2 *eggs*	1 *tablespoon plain unflavored*
1½ *cups milk*	*gelatin*
½ *cup honey*	¼ *cup cold water*
½ *teaspoon almond extract*	1½ *teaspoons vanilla*
	1 *cup whipping cream*

Beat eggs, milk, honey or raw sugar, together in top of double boiler. Cook over hot (not boiling) water, stirring constantly until mixture coats a silver spoon. remove from heat and stir in gelatin that has been soaked for 5 minutes in cold water. Cool; add extracts. Chill until partially set. Fold in whipped cream. Cut daffodil cake crosswise in 3 layers. Place largest layer top down on cake plate. Pile a little more than half the mixutre on largest cake layer. Chill in refrigerator until quite firm. Then place the next largest cake layer on top. Pile remaining filling on this. Chill until nearly set. Then place third layer on top. Chill until firm and sprinkle top with grated chocolate.

Fruit Cake (No. 1)

1 *teaspoon nutmeg*	1 *lb. pineapple*
1 *lb. walnuts, chopped coarse*	(*cut in wedges*)
1 *lb. blanched almonds,*	6 *cups whole-wheat pastry*
chopped coarse	*flour*
1 *lb. pecans, chopped coarse*	1 *teaspoon cinnamon*
2 *lbs. raisins*	1 *teaspoon allspice*
½ *lb. citron, sliced thin*	1 *teaspoon cloves*
1 *lb. lemon and orange peel*	1 *lb. butter*
1 *cup grape juice, unsweet-*	½ *lb. honey*
ened	12 *eggs*
1 *cup unsulphured molasses*	2 *teaspoons baking powder*

Mix fruits and nuts. Pour unsweetened grape juice over mixture and let stand overnight. Sift whole-wheat flour before measuring. Sift again with spices. Cream butter and honey. . . . . .adding eggs one at a time. Beat well after each addition. Add fruit and nut mixture. Mix in flour a little at a time alternately with molasses. Grease pans and line with heavy waxed paper to ½ inch of rim. Bake at 275°F. about 2 to 2½ hours for one pound. 10- to 12-lb. cake takes about 4 to 4½ hours.

Fruit Cake (No. 2)

1 *lb. Brazil nuts*
1 *lb. pecans*
½ *lb. candied cherries*

½ *lb. candied pineapple*
2 *lbs. dates (pitted)*

Put whole in dish except for pineapple, which is cut in smaller pieces.

Beat:

1 *cup honey*
1½ *cups whole-wheat pastry flour*

1 *teaspoon baking powder*

Beat 4 large eggs and add to above. Pour batter over fruit and nuts and stir. Bake in loaf tins at 350°F. for one hour and fifteen minutes. Serves 12.

Fresh Fruit Cake

1¼ *cups whole-wheat flour*
¼ *teaspoon baking powder*

¼ *lb. butter*
1 *egg*

Cut shortening into dry ingredients and add egg last. Then pat crust into coffee-cake tin. You may use any fruit or berries desired. Pour 1 cup of sugar or equivalent of honey over fruit. If a juicy fruit is used, such as raspberries, strawberries, or blueberries, make a custard using 1 egg and ⅓ cup cream and add about ten minutes before removing from oven. Bake in moderate oven at 375°F. about an hour. Serves 6.

Behind the nutty loaf is the millwheel; behind the mill is the wheat field; on the wheat field rests the sunlight; above the sun is God. — James Russell Lowell

Banana Cake

½ cup butter
1½ cups honey
2 well-beaten eggs
1 teaspoon vanilla

½ teaspoon soda
¼ cup sour milk
1 banana, mashed
2 cups whole-wheat
pastry flour

Cream butter and honey, add eggs and vanilla, beat until fluffy. Add sifted dry ingredients alternately with sour milk and banana pulp, beating after each addition. Bake in loaf pan in moderate oven (350°F.) for 50 minutes. Cool. Cover with caramel frosting. Serves 8.

Raisin Nut Cake

⅓ cup butter
3 eggs
¼ lb. chopped nut meats
2½ cups whole-wheat pastry
    flour

1½ cups honey
½ cup milk
1 lb. raisins
3 teaspoons baking powder
1 teaspoon lemon extract
1 teaspoon almond extract

Mix butter and honey until creamy, then add eggs one at a time, beating thoroughly. Sift whole-wheat flour, then resift, adding all the dry ingredients. Add fruit and nuts which have been floured with ½ cup of the flour, alternately with milk and sifted ingredients. Pour into well-oiled loaf tin and bake in slow oven about 1 hour. This cake keeps well. Serves 8.

Honey Cakes

1 cup honey
1 cup butter
2 eggs

2 teaspoons soda
1 teaspoon vanilla
3½ cups whole-wheat pastry
    flour

Cream butter and eggs, add other ingredients, and mix well. Leave in refrigerator overnight. Roll one teaspoonful of dough into a ball and place 2 inches apart on oiled cookie sheet. Bake in 300°F. oven until brown. May be put together while warm with honey or raw sugar, jam, or jelly. Makes about 24 small cakes.

Prune Nut Bars

4 *eggs*	
1 *cup honey*	1⅓ *teaspoons baking powder*
1⅓ *teaspoons grated lemon rind*	2 *cups chopped prunes (un-*
1⅓ *cups whole-wheat pastry*	*cooked)*
flour	

Beat eggs until thick and lemon-colored; add honey and lemon rind. Beat well. Sift together whole-wheat flour, and baking powder and add to egg mixture. Fold in chopped prunes and nuts. Pour into pan 8 x 12 inches that has been greased, lined with waxed paper, and greased again. Bake in moderate oven (325°F.) 40 to 45 minutes. Turn out on cooling rack and remove paper. Cut in bars when cool. Frost with your favorite icing. Makes about 36 bars.

Blueberry Puffs

1 *tablespoon lemon juice*	2 *tablespoons vegetable short-*
2 *cups fresh or quick-frozen*	*ening*
blueberries	½ *cup honey*
1 *cup whole-wheat pastry*	1 *egg, unbeaten*
flour	½ *teaspoon lemon extract*
2 *teaspoons baking powder*	¼ *cup milk*

Sprinkle lemon juice over berries and fill 5 or 6 custard cups ⅔ full. Sift dry ingredients together. Cream shortening with spoon until fluffy. Add honey and beat until light. Add egg and lemon extract; beat well. Add milk and dry ingredients and stir until just mixed. Spread batter over berries. Bake in hot oven (400°F.) 30 minutes or until done. Turn out onto dessert plates and serve warm with cream. Serves 6.

Blueberry Squares

1½ *cups whole-wheat pastry*	4 *teaspoons whole-wheat*
flour	*pastry flour*
2 *teaspoons baking powder*	1 *egg, well beaten*
¼ *cup vegetable shortening*	½ *cup milk*
¾ *cup honey*	1 *teaspoon vanilla*
	1¼ *cups fresh or quick-frozen*
	blueberries

Sift whole-wheat flour, baking powder, three times. Cream shortening until fluffy, and gradually add honey or raw sugar and beat until light. Add egg and mix well. Add dry ingredients alternately with combined milk and vanilla, beating after each addition until smooth. Lightly toss blueberries with the four teaspoons of whole-wheat flour, and fold into batter. Bake in greased and floured 8 x 8 x 2-inch pan in moderate oven (350°F) for 60 minutes or until done. Cut in squares and serve warm. Makes about 36 squares.

Peanut-Butter Cupcakes

½ cup vegetable shortening
1½ cups honey
¾ cup butter
3 beaten eggs
¾ cup peanut butter

2¼ cups whole-wheat pastry
flour
3¾ teaspoons baking powder
1⅛ cups milk
1½ teaspoons vanilla

Cream shortening and 1 cup of honey or raw sugar. Add peanut butter and mix well. Add eggs beaten with ½ cup honey or raw sugar. Add sifted dry ingredients alternately with milk and vanilla. Fill greased cupcake pans half full. Bake in moderate oven (350°F.) for 25 minutes. Cover with maple frosting. Makes 12 to 14 cupcakes.

Banana Cupcakes

¾ cup butter or vegetable
shortening
½ cup honey
3 beaten eggs
2¼ cups whole-wheat pastry
flour

1½ teaspoons baking powder
⅜ cup sour milk
1½ cups mashed, sieved banana
1½ teaspoons vanilla

Cream butter or shortening and honey or raw sugar. Add eggs and beat well. Add sifted dry ingredients alternately with milk, banana, and vanilla. Fill greased cupcake pans half full. Bake in moderately hot oven (375°F.) for 20 minutes. Makes 45 cakes. Serve plain or with maple frosting.

Banana Gingerbread

¼ *cup butter*	½ *teaspoon soda*
¼ *cup honey*	½ *teaspoon ginger*
1 *egg, beaten*	½ *cup hot water*
½ *cup unsulphured molasses*	¾ *cup whipped cream*
1⅓ *cups whole-wheat pastry flour*	2 *sliced bananas*

Cream butter and honey, add beaten egg and molasses. Beat in mixed dry ingredients and hot water alternately in small amounts. Bake in two greased pans 25 minutes in moderate oven (350°F.). Cool. Slice one banana on bottom layer and cover with whipped cream. Top with other cake and cover with remaining sliced banana and cream. Serves 8.

Apple Sauce Cake

1 *cup apple sauce*	¾ *cup raisins*
2 *tablespoons butter*	2 *cups whole-wheat pastry flour*
½ *cup honey*	
¼ *teaspoon cinnamon*	2 *eggs*
¼ *teaspoon nutmeg*	½ *teaspoon soda*

Add well-beaten eggs to creamed butter and honey. Add apple sauce and spices. Sift the flour with the soda and mix with the other ingredients. Dust raisins with a little whole-wheat flour and add. Bake in a moderate oven (350°F.) for 40 minutes. Serve plain or with sunshine frosting. Serves 8.

Spice Crumb Breakfast Cake

⅓ *cup and 3 tablespoons butter*	1 *teaspoon nutmeg*
1 *cup honey*	1½ *teaspoons ginger*
2½ *cups whole-wheat pastry flour*	½ *teaspoon cloves*
	¾ *cup milk*
1 *egg unbeaten*	1 *teaspoon vanilla*
2½ *teaspoons baking powder*	1 *cup seedless raisins*

Blend 3 tablespoons butter, ¼ cup honey, and ½ cup flour to crumblike consistency. Sprinkle these crumbs in bottom of a greased and floured 8 x 8 x 2-inch cake pan. Cream ⅓ cup butter with a spoon until fluffy, add ¾ cup honey gradually, and mix until light. Add egg and beat thoroughly. Sift together remaining 2 cups of whole-wheat flour with. . .baking powder, nutmeg, ginger, and cloves. Add dry ingredients alternately in thirds with the milk, beating smooth after each addition. Stir in raisins and vanilla and pour into pan. Bake in moderate oven (350°F.) for 50 minutes. Serve warm or cold. Serves 6 to 8 persons.

Unusual Cake

12 *whole-wheat crackers*	2 *teaspoons baking powder*
½ *cup honey*	1 *cup chopped walnuts*
2 *cups chopped dates*	6 *egg whites*

Crush the crackers to make a fine meal. Mix with the honey, baking powder, nuts, and dates. Beat the egg whites to a stiff froth and add. Bake in a greased cake tin in a moderate oven (350°F.) for 45 minutes. Cool, slice, and serve with whipped cream. Serves 8.

California Cheesecake

2 *cups whole-wheat crackers, crushed fine*	1 *cup light cream*
1½ *cups honey*	3 *cups cottage cheese*
1½ *teaspoons cinnamon*	¼ *cup whole-wheat pastry flour*
½ *cup melted butter or vegetable shortening*	2 *teaspoons grated lemon rind*
4 *eggs*	¼ *cup chopped walnuts*
	1½ *tablespoons lemon juice*

Combine crumbs, ½ cup honey, cinnamon, and butter. Reserve ¾ cup of this crumb mixture. Press remainder to bottom and sides of a 9-inch spring-form pan. Beat eggs light, then beat in 1 cup honey gradually. Add lemon juice. . .cream, cheese, and whole-wheat flour. Beat until thoroughly blended. Strain through fine sieve. Add lemon rind and stir well. Pour into pan and sprinkle top with remainder of crumbs and nuts. Bake in moderate oven (350°F.) for 1 hour. Turn off heat, open oven door, and let cake cool in oven 1 hour. Chill and remove from pan. Serves 10 to 12 persons.

Strawberry Shortcake

2 *cups whole-wheat pastry flour*	2 *eggs*
1 *teaspoon baking powder*	⅔ *cup milk*
2 *tablespoons honey*	6 *tablespoons butter*
	1 *quart strawberries*
	1 *cup whipped cream*

Sift and measure flour. Add the baking powder, honey . . . . and sift twice. Cut shortening into flour. Beat the eggs and the milk and pour into the flour mixture. Mix well. It will be a soft dough. Place in greased cake tin and bake in a very hot oven (450°F.) until done. Remove from the pan, split, and butter the split sides. Cover the bottom half with strawberries. Put top half over it, cutside up, and cover with the rest of the berries. Top with whipped cream. Serves 8.

Date Shortcake

⅔ *cup butter or vegetable shortening*	2 *cups sifted whole-wheat pastry flour*
⅓ *cup honey*	2⅓ *cups rolled oats*

Work shortening, honey . . . . and flour into a crumbly mixture, add rolled oats, and mix well. Put half the pastry into a well-greased baking pan and pat into place. Spread pastry with date filling. Top with another layer of the remaining oatmeal mixture, again shaping gently. Bake in a moderate oven (350°F.) for about 35 minutes, or until done. Cool. Cut into bars 1 inch wide and 3 inches long. Yield: 43 bars.

Date Shortcake Filling

2⅔ *cups chopped dates*	2⅔ *tablespoons lemon juice*
⅔ *cup water*	½ *cup honey*

Mix ingredients and cook for about 5 minutes over low heat, stirring constantly until mixture is thick and smooth. Cool before spreading on pastry.

FROSTINGS

Sunshine Frosting

2 egg whites, unbeaten	1 teaspoon pure vanilla
1 cup raw honey	1/4 teaspoon lemon extract
5 tbs cold distilled water	1/8 teaspoon Arrowroot powder

Mix unbeaten egg whites, honey, cold water and Arrowroot powder in double boiler. Place over boiling water and beat with rotary beater until mixture will hold a peak (about 7 minutes). Remove from heat. Add vanilla and lemon extract and beat until thick enough to hold its shape when spread. Frosts one cake.

Pineapple Feather Frosting

2 egg whites (fertile)	5 tablespoons unsweetened
1/2 cup raw honey	pineapple juice
1 tsp pure maple syrup	1/3 teaspoon lemon rind, grated

Combine egg whites, honey, maple syrup and pineapple juice in double boiler. Mix thoroughly. Place over boiling water and beat 7 minutes or until frosting stands in peaks. Remove from heat, add lemon rind and beat until thick enough to spread. Frosts one cake.

Maple Frosting

3/4 cup raw honey	1 egg white (fertile)
2-1/2 tbs distilled water	1 teaspoon pure maple syrup

Cook egg white with sweetening and water in double boiler, beating constantly until frosting forms peaks (about 7 minutes). Remove from heat, add maple syrup and beat until thick enough to spread. Frosts one cake.

Fresh Orange Icing

1 cup raw honey	juice and grated rind of
1 egg white (fertile)	2 medium oranges

PREVENTION WORKS - IF EXERCISED!
Follow the Bragg Healthy Lifestyle
for achieving your health goals — start today!

Boil cup of honey or raw sugar with juice and grated orange rind until it spins a thread. Beat egg white until stiff. Gradually add syrup to egg white, beating constantly until the mixture is thick enough to spread on cake. Frosts one cake.

Carob Frosting

1/2 cup raw honey
2 egg whites, fertile
1 cup carob powder

2 tablespoons soy or cow's milk
1 teaspoon butter, salt-free
1/2 teaspoon pure vanilla

Combine egg whites, honey and mix well. Add powdered carob and cook in double boiler until mixture thickens (about 5 minutes). Add milk gradually and cook two minutes longer, stirring constantly. Remove from heat, add butter and vanilla. Blend well until it's of spreadable consistency. Frosts one cake.

Butterscotch Nut Frosting

1-1/3 cups raw honey
1/3 cup hot distilled water
1/8 tsp arrowroot powder

1/2 teaspoon pure vanilla
1/2 cup chopped nuts
1 egg white

Place honey and water in sauce pan and stir over low heat until honey is dissolved. Boil until syrup spins a thread (238°F.). Add arrowroot powder to egg white and beat. Pour syrup over egg white, beating constantly until icing stands in peaks. Add vanilla. Fold in chopped nuts or currants (pre-soak 1 hour) or mix. Frosts one cake.

Natural Fruit Filling

1 cup raisins, chopped
3/4 cup dried figs, apples
* or prunes, chopped*
1 cup hot distilled water

2 teaspoons orange peel, grated
2 teaspoons whole-wheat flour
* or arrowroot powder*
1/2 cup raw honey or
* juice concentrate*

Mix fruit, sweetener and thickener. Pour hot water over mixture. Add grated orange peel and cook until thick, stirring constantly. Chill before spreading. Enough filling for one cake. (Optional: Add mixed chopped nuts or seeds or mashed bananas before spreading.)

Chapter 16

Health Cookies

Vegetable Shortening — Soy and Canola oils or salt-free butter.
Baking Powders — Rumford, Featherlight *(aluminum free)* are best.
Sweeteners —Honey, barley malt or brown rice syrups, molasses,
date and raw brown sugars, concentrated fruit juices are best.

Golden Blossom Bars

1/2 cup butter or soy oil	*1 teaspoon baking powder*
1 cup honey	*1 cup nut or seed meats,*
2 egg yolks (fertile)	*chopped*
2-1/2 cups sifted	*1 teaspoon pure vanilla*
whole-grain pastry flour	*2 tablespoons lemon juice*

Cream butter or soy oil thoroughly. Add sweetening and egg yolks
gradually and beat until fluffy. Sift flour. Measure. Add baking
powder and sift again. Add gradually to the creamed mixture,
beating thoroughly. Add nut or seed meats (walnuts, almonds,
hazels or sunflower, sesame, pumpkin seeds, etc.), pure vanilla
and lemon juice. Spread batter in oiled 8 x 8-inch baking pan and
bake in hot oven (400° F) about 12 minutes or until golden brown.
Cool and cut in strips. Makes 30-36 bars.

Molasses Fruit Bars

1/2 cup butter or soy oil	*1/2 teaspoon soda*
1/2 cup honey or raw sugar	*1 teaspoon baking powder*
2 eggs, well beaten (fertile)	*1 cup soy or skim milk*
1 cup molasses or sorghum	*2 cups chopped nut meats*
3 cups sifted whole-wheat	*2 cups chopped raisins or*
pastry flour	*dates or mix*

**Prevent breads, pastries and cakes from sticking
to pans by using Liquid Lecithin or Pam
(corn oil & lecithin spray) instead of oil or butter.**

Cream shortening thoroughly, add sweetening gradually, and beat until light and fluffy. Add eggs and molasses and blend thoroughly. Sift whole-wheat flour once. Measure; add. . . .soda, and baking powder and sift again. Add to creamed mixture alternately with milk, a small amount at a time. Beat thoroughly after each addition. Add chopped nuts and fruit. Spread very thin in several large shallow greased pans. Bake in moderate oven (350°F.) 10 to 12 minutes. Cool and cut in two-inch squares. Makes about 8 dozen bars.

Butterscotch Bran Cookies

1 *cup butter or vegetable shortening*
2 *cups honey*
1 *egg*

3 *cups sifted whole-wheat pastry flour*
2 *teaspoons baking powder*
1 *cup bran*

Cream shortening and honey. Add egg and beat well. Sift whole-wheat flour, measure, and sift again with baking powder. Add with bran to creamed mixture, mixing well. Shape into long rolls 1½ inches in diameter. Wrap in wax paper and chill 5 hours. Slice ⅛ inch thick and bake on ungreased cookie sheets in a hot oven (400°F.) 10 minutes, or until brown. Makes about 7 dozen cookies.

Almond Sticks

⅓ *lb. butter or vegetable shortening*
⅔ *cup ground almonds*
1⅓ *teaspoons lemon juice*

1⅓ *cups whole-wheat pastry flour*
⅔ *cup honey*
4 *teaspoons orange juice*
1 *grated lemon rind*

Cut butter and almonds into whole-wheat flour and sweetening. Add remaining ingredients. Shape into crescents. Bake in slow oven (250°F.) for 30 minutes. Remove from pan and roll in powdered raw sugar or dextrose. Makes 3 doz. sticks.

Honey is Best

◇◇◇

Lemon Oatmeal Cookies

½ *cup butter or vegetable*
  shortening
1 *cup honey*
1 *egg, well beaten*
1 *teaspoon grated lemon rind*
2½ *cups steel-cut oats (un-*
  cooked)

2 *tablespoons lemon juice*
¾ *cup sifted whole-wheat*
  pastry flour

Cream shortening and honey thoroughly. Add egg and beat until
light and fluffy. Add lemon rind and juice. Sift whole-wheat
pastry flour . . . . add with oats to creamed
mixture. Drop with spoon on greased baking sheet and bake in a
moderately hot oven (375°F.) 12 to 15 minutes. Makes 36 cookies.

Bran Macaroons

6 *tablespoons butter or vege-*
  table shortening
1 *cup unsulphured molasses*
2 *eggs, well beaten*

3 *cups bran*
4 *tablespoons whole-wheat*
  pastry flour
¼ *teaspoon powdered allspice*
¼ *teaspoon powdered ginger*

Mix ingredients together. Drop with spoon on greased cookie sheet.
Bake in hot oven (400°F.) 8 to 12 minutes. Chopped nuts or raisins
may be added before baking if desired. Makes 3 dozen macaroons.

Gingerbread Boys

1½ *cups unsulphured molasses*
1⅛ *cups butter or vegetable*
  shortening
5¼ *cups whole-wheat pastry*
  flour

3 *teaspoons baking powder*
¾ *teaspoon soda*
¾ *teaspoon allspice*
2¼ *teaspoons ginger*

Heat molasses gently to bubbling and add butter. Cool and add
dry ingredients sifted together. Mix to smooth dough. Chill. Roll
out on floured board to ¼-inch thickness and cut with cookie-
cutter or make paper pattern of gingerbread man or Santa Claus
and cut out with sharp point of paring knife. Makes about 6 dozen
cookies.

Nut or Seed Butter Carob Brownie

1/2 cup soy or canola oil
1/2 cup peanut or nut butter
1-1/2 cups raw honey
3 eggs, beaten (fertile)

1-1/3 cups sifted whole-wheat
or whole-grain pastry flour
1/2 teaspoon baking powder
4 tablespoons carob powder
1 cup raw nuts and seeds

Mix oil with nut or seed butter (raw is best). Add honey gradually. Mix carob and eggs into nut butter mixture. Mix and sift dry ingredients, add to mixture. Add raw nuts and seeds, chopped, and mix well. Place in oiled, shallow pan. Bake 30 to 35 minutes at 350°F. Cut into squares while warm. Makes about 36 brownies.

Bragg Aminos-Nut and Seed Delights

Make a delicious topping for salads, fruits and vegetables, sandwiches casseroles, baked potatoes, omelets and other egg dishes from raw seed and nut meats. (Sunflower, sesame, pumpkin, almond, cashew, macadamia, etc.) In heavy warm skillet over medium heat, dry-cook mixture of raw nuts and seeds for 2-4 minutes; remove from heat and lightly spray with Bragg Liquid Aminos. Serve mix as a crunchy topping or as a delicious finger food.

Oatmeal Crisps

2-1/2 cups rolled oats
1 cup raw honey
1 cup canola or soy oil
2 eggs, beaten (fertile)
3 teaspoons pure vanilla

1-1/2 cups whole-wheat or
whole-grain pastry flour
2 teaspoons baking powder
1/4 cup soy or skim milk
1/2 cup oat bran

Mix oats, bran, honey, eggs and oil. Sift together whole-grain flour and baking powder. Add vanilla to milk and add dry ingredients and milk mixture alternately to first mixture. Drop level teaspoonsful of dough 2 inches apart on oiled cookie sheet. Flatten to 1/8 inch and

---

*Whole-grain bread strengthens man's heart and
promotes health . . . that is why it is called the staff of life*

decorate top with raisins or nuts. Bake in hot oven (400°F) for 10 minutes. Remove at once from pan. Makes 5 to 6 dozen cookies.

Coconut Macaroons

3/4 cup butter
3/4 cup honey
1-1/4 cups hot water

2-1/2 cups shredded coconut
2-1/2 cups whole-wheat
pastry flour
1/2 teaspoon baking powder

Mix thoroughly the butter, honey and hot water and stir in the dry ingredients. Shape or cut as desired. Place on a well-oiled pan and bake in a moderately hot oven for 1/2 hour. This should make about 3-3/4 dozen macaroons.

Orange-Blossom Honey Chips

7 tablespoons butter
or soy oil
1/2 cup orange-blossom honey
1 egg
1/2 teaspoon pure vanilla

1 cup whole wheat
pastry flour
1 teaspoon baking powder
1/2 cup grated carob
1/4 cup chopped nuts

Blend oil or butter and honey until fluffy. Add the egg and beat. Add vanilla. Sift dry ingredients and stir in. Mix in the nuts and carob. Cover bowl and chill for 40 minutes. Drop teaspoonfuls of dough on oiled cookie sheet. Bake in a moderate oven (350°F) for 10 to 12 minutes. Remove at once from pan and cool. Makes about 2 dozen honey chips.

Raisin-Filled Cookies

1/2 cup butter or soy oil
1/2 cup honey
1 egg
1 teaspoon baking powder

1 teaspoon pure vanilla
1/4 teaspoon nutmeg
2 cups whole wheat pastry flour
1/2 cup raisins

Cream butter or oil and honey, add egg and beat well. Add vanilla and flour. On dough board roll out mixture to about 1/4-inch thick and cut with cookie cutter. Cover with raisins and top with another cut-out cookie. Press edges together and bake in a moderate oven until brown. Makes 1 dozen cookies.

Raisin Cookies

1 cup butter or soy oil
1 / 2 cup honey or rice syrup
2 eggs
4 cups whole-wheat pastry
   flour

2 teaspoons baking powder
1 teaspoon cinnamon
2 / 3 cup soy milk or skim milk
2 teaspoons pure vanilla
2 cups raisins
1 cup chopped walnuts

Blend the butter or oil with the honey or rice syrup. Add the eggs and beat well. Sift flour before measuring and sift three times with the other dry ingredients. Add to the first mixture alternately with the milk. Add the vanilla, raisins and nuts. Mix and drop by spoonfuls on a greased cookie sheet or shallow pan. Bake in a moderately hot oven (375°F) about 15 minutes. Makes 5 to 6 dozen cookies.

Soft Molasses Hermits

3 cups sifted whole-wheat
   pastry flour
2 teaspoons baking powder
1 teaspoon cinnamon
1 / 2 teaspoon ground cloves
1 cup raisins

1 / 2 cup honey or rice syrup
2 eggs, well beaten
1 cup unsulphured molasses
1 / 2 cup sour milk or buttermilk
1 cup butter or soy oil

Mix and sift dry ingredients. Mix oil and sweetening. Add eggs and beat well. Add molasses. Add whole-wheat flour and milk alternately. Mix in raisins. Drop teaspoons of dough 2 inches apart on an oiled baking sheet. Bake in hot oven (400°F) about 10 minutes. Makes about 7 dozen cookies.

Carob-Bar Cookies

3 carob squares
1 / 2 cup butter or soy oil
3 cups rolled oats

1 / 2 cup honey or rice syrup
2 teaspoons pure vanilla
1 / 3 cup chopped nut meats

Melt carob and butter in top of double boiler. Add remaining ingredients and blend well. Pack firmly into greased square pan. Bake in hot oven (425°F) 12 minutes. Chill. Cut into bars. Makes 24-36 cookies, depending on bar sizes.

Icebox Cookies

1 cup butter or soy oil
1 cup honey
2 teaspoons baking powder
1 tablespoon pure vanilla
2 beaten eggs

1/2 teaspoon cinnamon
1/2 cup chopped nuts
3-1/2 cups whole-wheat
  pastry flour

Cream honey with the butter or oil. Add other ingredients in this sequence: vanilla, beaten eggs, sifted dry ingredients, nuts. Place on waxed paper and shape into roll. Wrap in waxed paper and place in refrigerator overnight or until ready for use. Slice thinly and bake on greased cookie sheet in hot oven (about 400°F) until delicately browned. Makes about 5 dozen cookies.

Molasses Strips

3 cups whole-wheat
  pastry flour
1/2 teaspoon baking powder
1 teaspoon cinnamon
dash of powdered cloves

1/2 cup unsulphured molasses
1/3 cup butter or soy oil
1/2 cup honey or rice syrup
1/4 cup boiling water
1/3 cup chopped pecans

Mix honey or rice syrup and butter or oil. Blend molasses with boiling water. Add to the mixture and fold in the sifted dry ingredients. Allow to cool. When at room temperature, place in refrigerator for half an hour. Turn out on whole-wheat-floured board and roll. Cut into desired shape, sprinkle with nuts and bake in a moderate oven. Makes 4 dozen cookies.

Many people go throughout life committing partial suicide — destroying their health, youth, beauty, talents, energies, creative qualities. Indeed, to learn how to be good to oneself is often more difficult than to learn how to be good to others.
— Paul C. Bragg

◇◇◇

Chapter 17

Health
Desserts

FRESH FRUITS FOR DESSERT

There is no finer dessert than organically grown fresh fruit. In Europe, fresh fruit is served with thin slices of natural cheeses or you may use the delicious non-dairy cheeses. The fruit bowl on the family table is graceful, beautiful, and nutritious. Luscious, pears, peaches, grapes, bananas, nectarines, plums, apricots, persimmons, pineapple, pomegranates, cherries and apples cannot be surpassed as a delicious, wise ending to a gracious healthy meal. Watermelons and melons are best served alone as a fruit snack or meal and not mixed with other fruits or food.

When your favorite fresh fruit is not in season, there are many other year around fruits available, bananas, apples, oranges, etc. and the wholesome, sun-dried fruit desserts may be substituted.

Sun-Dried Unsulphured Fruits

The natural unsulphured sun-dried fruits are rich in iron and other minerals and vitamins. Health Food Stores carry a wide selection of these popular health builders.

All sun-dried fruits before using should be scrub washed and soaked in hot water 3 minutes to remove any mold that might have developed during drying process. For preparing sun-dried fruit, just cook or soak overnight until tender in distilled water or unsweetened pineapple or fruit juice. Many dried fruits need no sweetening, cooking or soaking. If desired, add small amounts of honey or barley malt or brown rice syrup. If dried fruit is not to be cooked but eaten raw in time, store un-washed in covered jar in refrigerator, cellar or cold room.

Fresh Fruit Compote

You can vary or add to any of these combinations and serve as a fruit compote. If desired, sweeten with honey, natural sweeteners, unsweetened pineapple or fruit juices. Garnish with yogurt and / or grated coconut.

1. Apricots and red cherries
2. Black cherries and peaches
3. Berries and pineapple
4. Pears, plums and bananas
5. Dates, peaches and nectarines
6. Persimmons and pineapple
7. Berries, bananas and peaches
8. Melon balls—from your favorite melons
9. Peaches, nectarines, orange and grapefruit sections
10. Halves of seeded grapes, bananas, apples and plums

Pineapple Delight

1 cup crushed pineapple, fresh   *1 cup whipping cream*
or unsweetened if canned   *or non-dairy cream*

Beat cream until stiff. Fold in crushed pineapple. If more sweetening is desired, add 1 tbs honey or barley malt sweetener. Chill. Serves 2.

Fruit Whip

1 cup whipping cream   *1 cup mixed diced fresh fruit,*
or non-dairy cream   *such as bananas, strawberries,*
1 teaspoon pure vanilla   *apples, pears, peaches, apricots*
1 tablespoon honey   *pineapple and grapes*

Whip cream, add 1/2 tsp unflavored gelatin soaked in 1 tbs cold water to dissolve. Fold in vanilla, honey and fruit. Chill and serve. Serves 2-4.

Fresh Strawberry Sponge

1/2 cup strawberry juice   *1/2 tablespoon unflavored*
and pulp   *gelatin*
1/8 cup cold distilled water   *1/2 tbs fresh lemon juice*
1/4 cup hot distilled water   *1 egg white, beaten stiff*
1/2 cup raw honey   *1/4 cup cream, whipped*

Crush berries, add sweetening and allow to stand 1/2 hour. Soften gelatin in cold distilled water, add hot distilled water and stir until dissolved. Add berry mixture and lemon juice. Cool. When it begins to thicken, fold in whipped cream and egg white beaten stiff. Turn into sherbet glasses. Chill. Garnish with berries and whipped cream or delicious non-dairy cream (rice, soy or nut creams) if desired. Serves 3.

◇◇

Date and Nut Crumble

2 egg whites, beaten stiff	*1/4 teaspoon pure vanilla*
1/2 cup raw honey	*1 tablespoon soy or skim milk*
2 tbs whole-grain flour	*2 cups dates, chopped*
1/4 teaspoon baking powder	*1 cup nuts or seeds, chopped*

Add sweetening gradually to egg whites. Add sifted dry ingredients, dates and nuts or seeds, then milk and vanilla. Spread thin in oiled pan 9 x 9 inches. Bake in 250°F. oven for 35 minutes. Cool and break in small pieces. Pile pieces alternately with whipped cream, nut or rice creams in chilled sherbet glasses. Serves 4.

Grapefruit, Fresh or Broiled

Cut grapefruit in half. Remove fruit from skin, taking out in one whole section by cutting carefully around diameter and bottom. Carefully section fruit. Serve fresh or put under broiler for a few seconds until heated. Delicious as is or top with diced fresh fruit and lowfat yogurt.

Strawberry or Berry Custard

4 tablespoons raw honey	*2 eggs, fertile*
4 tbs whole-grain pastry flour	*2 cups soy or cows milk*
8 cups strawberries	*1 tsp almond or vanilla extract*

You can prepare the custard sauce the day before so it can be thoroughly chilled. Mix sweetening and whole-grain pastry flour in the top of a double boiler. Stir in unbeaten eggs until well blended. Gradually stir in milk. Cook over boiling water, stirring constantly, until smooth and thickened (about 5 minutes). Cool, add pure almond or vanilla extract, cover and chill. Pour chilled custard sauce over berries and serve. Serves 8. For variety try blueberries, blackberries, raspberries, etc. All berries are nutritious and delicious.

Raisin Pudding

1 cup whole-grain pastry flour	*1/2 cup soy or skim milk*
1 cup raw honey	*1 cup distilled water*
1 tsp baking powder	*4 teaspoons butter*
	1/2 cup raisins or currants

Sift whole-wheat flour, baking powder. . . . . . . and ⅔ cup honey into a mixing bowl . . . . Stir in raisins and milk. Spread batter in a greased baking dish or pan. Combine the remaining sweetening . . . . water, and butter in saucepan; heat until honey is dissolved, and pour syrup over batter. Bake in a moderate oven (350°F.) for about 45 minutes or until done. As pudding bakes, batter rises to top of syrup. Serve warm with syrup from pudding and plain or whipped cream. Serves 6 to 8.

Baked Bananas

4 *bananas*   ¼ *cup honey*
juice of 1 lemon   *nuts, chopped fine*

Peel bananas and place whole in baking dish. Mix honey and lemon juice and pour over bananas. Sprinkle with the nuts and bake until a delicate brown, 30 to 45 minutes. Serve hot. Serves 4.

Individual Plum Puddings

1½ *cups bran*   1½ *teaspoons baking powder*
¾ *cup whole-wheat bread*   1½ *teaspoons nutmeg*
   crumbs   ¾ *teaspoon cinnamon*
¾ *cup milk, scalded*   ⅜ *teaspoon cloves*
½ *cup honey*   ⅜ *teaspoon mace*
3 *eggs, separated*   1⅛ *cups chopped dates*
3 *oz. oil*   1½ *cups chopped seedless*
3 *tablespoons whole-wheat*   *raisins*
   pastry flour   4½ *tablespoons chopped citron*
                                    3 *tablespoons grape juice*

Soak bran and crumbs in milk 5 minutes.   Add sweetening, beaten egg yolks, and oil . . . . Mix dry ingredients; add to fruit and stir into first mixture. Add grape juice. Fold in egg whites beaten stiff. Fill 8 thin oven-proof glass custard cups ⅔ full. Decorate tops with almonds. Cover each cup with waxed paper, secured with an elastic band. Set on rack in a steamer or large kettle and fill kettle with boiling water to just above the top of the rack. Cover and steam 2 hours, replenishing water as needed. Cool puddings in cups, and decorate in holiday style. Serves 8.

Apple Sauce

4 cups apples, quartered   *3 tablespoons honey (optional)*

Cook apples until soft, adding a little distilled water to keep from sticking to the pan. When done, stir in honey if desired. Sweet apples usually need no sweetening. Serves 6.

> Try delicious fresh fruit frozen mock ice cream made with no sugar or cream. It's easy to prepare by freezing the fruit, then put through food processor, Champion juicer or blender. Serve immediately.

ICE CREAMS & SHERBETS

Honey Ice Cream

3 eggs, separated   *3 cups cream*
¾ cup orange-blossom honey   *1½ teaspoons vanilla*

Beat egg yolks until thick, adding honey gradually. Blend in cream and vanilla. Freeze until firm. Place in chilled bowl, add egg whites, beaten dry, and beat until smooth. Return to freezing tray and freeze until firm. Serves 9.

Banana Pecan Ice Cream

½ cup mashed ripe bananas   *⅛ cup honey*
1 teaspoon lemon juice   *½ cup heavy cream*
¼ cup milk   *½ teaspoon vanilla*
1 egg, separated   *¼ cup chopped pecans*

Mix bananas, lemon juice, ...and milk, stirring until well blended. Beat egg whites until stiff and fold in honey or raw sugar. Beat egg yolks until thick. Whip cream until thick enough to hold soft peak. Combine banana mixture, egg yolks, egg whites, cream, vanilla, and pecan meats. Pour into refrigerator tray and freeze until firm. Sprinkle additional nuts on top. Serves 4.

Prune-Delight Ice Cream

1½ teaspoons unflavored gelatin   6 eggs, beaten
1½ tablespoons cold water   1½ teaspoons vanilla
 3 cups prunes
1½ cups milk   1½ cups heavy cream
¾ cup honey

Soften gelatin in cold water 5 minutes. Wash prunes in hot water, cut from pits, and grind in food-chopper, using fine blade. Combine milk and honey or raw sugar and heat to boiling. Add gelatin and stir until dissolved. Pour hot mixture over eggs, stirring constantly; add vanilla, prunes . . . . . Chill. Beat thoroughly with rotary beater until fluffy. Whip cream until stiff enough to hold a soft peak and fold into whipped prune mixture. Pour into freezing tray and freeze until firm. Serves 9.

Angel Parfait

¾ tablespoon unflavored   3 egg whites, beaten dry
   gelatin   1½ cups cream
 3 tablespoons cold water   1½ teaspoons vanilla
¾ cup honey
¾ cup water

Boil the honey or raw sugar . . . and ½ cup water to a soft-ball stage. Pour slowly into egg whites, beating constantly. Soften gelatin in cold water. Add to the egg mixture and stir until dissolved. Stir over cold or ice water until mixture is cold and begins to set, then fold in cream and flavoring (lemon, orange, or almond may also be used). Turn into refrigerator trays and freeze without stirring. Serves 4 to 6.

Lemon Ice

1½ tablespoons unflavored   1 cup honey
   gelatin   1⅛ cups lemon juice
 6 cups boiling water
⅜ cup cold water

Make a syrup of boiling water and honey or raw sugar. Soften gelatin in cold water. Add to syrup and stir until dissolved. Add lemon juice . . . . . .cool and freeze. For fluffy ice, when mixture is partly frozen, add the whites of two eggs beaten stiff. Serves 8.

Grape-Juice Sherbets

1½ tablespoons unflavored gela-
    tin
¾ cup cold water
2¼ cups boiling water
1½ cups honey

6 tablespoons lemon juice
3 cups grape juice unsweet-
    ened
½ cup fresh orange juice

Make a syrup by boiling honey or raw sugar and hot water 10 minutes. Soften gelatin in cold water. Add to syrup and stir until dissolved. Cool slightly and add fruit juices . . . . . Pour into trays and freeze. Serve in sherbet glasses. Serves 4.

Lemon Milk Sherbet

3 eggs
⅜ cup honey
¾ cup lemon juice

3 cups milk
3 tablespoons grated lemon
    rind

Beat eggs and honey until thick and combine with remaining ingredients. Place in refrigerator tray and freeze at coldest. Stir or beat once during freezing. Serves 6.

Banana Sherbet

4 cups mashed bananas
½ cup honey
12 tablespoons lemon juice

2 egg whites
4 cups milk

Mix banana pulp with lemon juice. Add honey or raw sugar, and egg whites beaten stiff . . . . . Add mixture slowly to milk, stirring constantly. Place in freezing tray and freeze until firm. Stir once while freezing. Serves 4.

Fruit Sherbet

1½ quarts hot water
1¼ cups honey or thick maple
    syrup

4 bananas, mashed
juice of 4 oranges
juice of 3 lemons

Mix honey and water. Chill. When cold add fruit juices and mashed banana. Mix well. This may be served as a cold drink or frozen sherbet. Serves 6 to 8.

PUDDINGS & OTHER DESSERTS

Paskha

½ *pound very dry cottage*
  cheese
1 *hard-boiled egg*
⅛ *cup sweet butter*
¼ *cup honey*

¼ *cup seedless raisins*
½ *tablespoon grated orange*
  rind
⅛ *teaspoon vanilla*
1 *tablespoon sour cream*

Purée cottage cheese and hard-boiled egg, putting through sieve twice. Combine and mix thoroughly with the butter, honey, vanilla, raisins, orange rind and sour cream. Press firmly into mold, using plate with weight to hold in place. Chill in refrigerator for at least 12 hours before serving. Serve in small portions. Serves 6.

Baked Custards

6 *eggs*
6 *tablespoons honey*
3¾ *cups milk*
1½ *teaspoons vanilla*
grated nutmeg

Beat eggs until frothy. Add **sweetening** . . . . and beat until eggs are thick and lemon-colored. Blend in milk and vanilla. Turn into buttered custard cups; sprinkle top of each with nutmeg. Set in shallow pan of hot water and bake in slow oven (300°F.) about 1 hour, or until silver knife inserted in center comes out clean. Remove, cool, and chill. Serve as is, or unmold and top with berries. Makes about 8 custards.

For variation add 2 teaspoons maple syrup in bottom of each buttered custard cup. Carefully pour in custard mixture and bake as above.

Favorite Custard

2⅔ cups milk
4 eggs
⅔ scant cup honey

⅔ teaspoon vanilla
nutmeg

Scald milk but do not boil. Beat eggs slightly; add honey and vanilla. Stir milk into eggs. Pour into custard cups and sprinkle with nutmeg. Place in shallow pan with hot water. When water comes to boil, place lid on top of pan for about 3 minutes. Bake to soft custard or until a silver knife comes out clean when inserted in center.

Carob Custard

4 cups milk
6 eggs
2 tablespoons honey

1 teaspoon vanilla
1 cup carob powder

Scald milk. Add small amount of milk to carob . . . blend to smooth paste; add hot milk. Add honey and vanilla to slightly beaten eggs. Stir milk and carob mixture into eggs and bake as individual custards. Serves 10.

Yellow Corn Pudding

1 cup unsulphured molasses
½ cup yellow cornmeal
5 cups milk
½ teaspoon cinnamon

½ teaspoon nutmeg
½ cup butter
½ teaspoon vanilla

Scald 4 cups of the milk; mix with all other ingredients. Place in double boiler for 20 minutes, stirring frequently. Place in buttered baking dish, topping with 1 cup of milk. Bake in a very slow oven 2½ to 3 hours. This recipe serves about 8 to 10 people, and should be cut in half for a smaller family.

Sweet-Potato Pudding

1 cup grated sweet potatoes
½ cup honey
2 beaten eggs
4 tablespoons melted butter
2 cups milk
½ teaspoon nutmeg

¼ teaspoon ginger
½ teaspoon cinnamon
dash of aniseed
½ cup stewed dried apricots
½ cup chopped walnut meats

Mix all ingredients; turn into buttered baking dish and bake in a slow oven (about 300° F.) for about 1¼ hours. Stir occasionally. Serves 6.

God grant me
the serenity
to accept the things
I cannot change —
the courage
to change the things
I can —
And the wisdom to know
the difference —

Anonymous

"Why not look for the best — the best in others, the best in ourselves, the best in all life situations? He who looks for the best knows the worst is there but refuses to be discouraged by it. Though temporarily defeated, dismayed, he smiles and tries again. If you look for the best, life will become pleasant for you and everyone around you."

Chapter 18

Sauces and Gravies

Hollandaise Sauce

½ *lb. butter*	*few grains cayenne*
2 *tablespoons lemon juice*	4 *egg yolks*

Divide butter in thirds. Heat water in lower part of double boiler to boiling-point. Allow to cool slightly to steaming-point but not boiling, and adjust heat to keep at steaming-point. Place ⅓ of butter, egg yolks, and lemon juice in upper part of double boiler. Place over steaming water and stir constantly until mixture thickens. Add second piece of butter. As soon as it melts, add the third piece of butter, stirring constantly the entire time. When butter is all melted, remove from heat, add cayenne, and beat until glossy. Serve at once. Serves 6.

Béarnaise Sauce

To hollandaise sauce, add 1 tablespoon each finely chopped fresh parsley and fresh tarragon. If unable to obtain fresh tarragon, add ½ teaspoon dried tarragon.

Caper Sauce, Hollandaise

(for broiled, boiled, steamed, or baked fish or poached eggs)

To hollandaise sauce add 1 tablespoon capers.

Caper Sauce, Maître d'Hôtel
(for fish)

4 *tablespoons butter*
1½ *tablespoons lemon juice*
1 *tablespoon capers*

1 *teaspoon chopped parsley*
½ *teaspoon Bragg Aminos*

Melt butter. Add lemon juice, capers, parsley, and seasonings. Heat until sizzling. Pour over fish. Enough sauce for one medium-sized fish.

Maître d'Hôtel Butter

¼ *cup butter*
1 *tablespoon parsley, chopped fine*
4 *teaspoons lemon juice*

½ *teaspoon Bragg Aminos*
⅛ *teaspoon cayenne pepper*

Cream butter with wooden spoon until very soft in consistency. Add Bragg Liquid Aminos , parsley and lemon juice very slowly, stirring constantly. If desired, ¼ teaspoon sweet minced onion or shallot and/or 2 teaspoons minced pimiento or green pepper add greatly to the flavor. Serves 6.

Mornay Sauce

1 *cup meat stock*
1 *slice onion*
¼ *bay leaf*
1 *sprig parsley*
4 *peppercorns*
3 *tablespoons butter*
½ *teaspoon Bragg Aminos*

2 *tablespoons and* 1 *teaspoon whole-wheat pastry flour*
⅔ *cup scalded milk*
⅛ *teaspoon pepper*
1 *oz. Gruyère cheese, sliced thin*
1 *oz. grated Parmesan cheese*

Add onion, carrot, bay leaf, parsley, Bragg Liquid Aminos . . . and pepper to meat stock and cook slowly for 20 minutes or until stock is reduced to ⅔ cupful. Melt butter, add flour, and then blend in the milk and strained stock gradually. Return to fire in double boiler for 15 minutes to cook flour. Add Gruyère and Parmesan and whisk lightly through sauce. Put sauce on fire again for a few minutes to ensure melting of the cheese. Serves 6.

Bercy Sauce

1½ cups meat stock or chicken
  stock (or half and half)
4½ tablespoons garlic butter
1½ tablespoons minced shallot
  (small red onion can be substituted if necessary)

3 tablespoons whole-wheat
  pastry flour
1 tablespoon butter
¼ teaspoon Bragg Aminos
1 tablespoon lemon juice
¼ cup parsley

Sauté shallot in 1 tablespoon butter gently until thoroughly heated.
Blend in flour until smooth. Add stock gradually and then add remaining butter, lemon juice, seasonings, and parsley. Simmer over
a low flame for 5 minutes, stirring frequently. Serves 6 to 8.

Robert Sauce

½ cup chicken stock
2 teaspoons butter
3 shallots, minced
1 teaspoon whole-wheat flour
1 tablespoon lemon juice
1½ teaspoons capers, chopped

1½ teaspoons olives, chopped
½ teaspoon dry mustard
½ tablespoon Bragg Aminos
⅛ teaspoon cayenne

Add shallots and flour to melted butter and cook until flour is
done, about 5 minutes. Add all other ingredients and continue
cooking for about 12 minutes, stirring constantly. Keep warm in
double boiler until needed for service. Do not reheat. Serves 4 to 6.

Marguery Sauce
(for sole and other fish)

Bones and trimmings of any
  white fish
Bones of small lobster, 6 shrimp
  tails, and 6 clams (optional)
1 small cooked onion
¼ cup lemon juice
3 sprigs parsley
2 tablespoons butter
2 tablespoons whole-wheat
  pastry flour

1 teaspoon Bragg Aminos
1 teaspoon chives
¼ teaspoon dill
¼ teaspoon marjoram
¼ teaspoon powdered fennel or
  ¼ cup chopped cooked fresh
  fennel (sometimes known in
  the markets as "sweet
  anise")

At bottom of a thick, deep, buttered saucepan place cooked sliced onion and chopped parsley. Over this lay fish ingredients. Cover with lemon juice. Cover pan and cook on slow flame for 20 minutes to allow fish essence to exude. Shake pan frequently. Add two cups cold water, chives, dill, marjoram, and fennel and bring to boiling-point. Cook on a moderate flame until stock is reduced to 1 cup, or about 30 minutes. Blend melted butter and flour. Add stock to this mixture slowly, stirring until well blended. Bring to boiling-point and add ¼ cup of the liquid in which the fish has cooked. Strain. Serves 6.

Egg Butter Sauce

3 *hard-boiled egg yolks*　　　⅓ *cup butter, softened*
⅛ *teaspoon paprika*　　　1½ *tablespoons cream*
　　　　　　　　　　　　1½ *teaspoons lemon juice*

Force egg yolks through a sieve, add paprika and work in softened butter, cream, and lemon juice gradually. Makes ¾ cup sauce.

Onion Butter

¼ *lb. butter*　　　　　3 *tablespoons finely chopped onion*

Work onion into butter. (This recipe can be increased or decreased for desired quantity. Chives can replace the onion for more delicate flavor—or half and half can be used.) Makes ½ cup onion butter.

Newburg Sauce

1 *tablespoon butter*　　　½ *cup cream, milk, or soy milk*
1 *teaspoon whole-wheat flour*　　2 *egg yolks, beaten*
　　　　　　　　　　　　2 *tablespoons orange juice*

Melt butter, add whole-wheat flour, and cream, milk, or soy milk. Cook until thickened, stirring constantly. When ready to use, add to egg yolks and orange juice; blend. Makes ½ cup sauce.

Tomato Sauce

3 tablespoons oil
3 tablespoons whole-wheat
　flour
1½ cups cooked tomatoes
2 slices of onion

1½ bay leaves
4 cloves
⅛ teaspoon mace
½ teaspoon Bragg Aminos

Combine ingredients listed and simmer for 15 minutes. Strain. Serve hot. Makes 1½ cups sauce.

Mexican Sauce
(for fish)

2⅔ tablespoons chopped onion
⅔ clove garlic (optional)
⅓ lemon, sliced thin
⅔ tablespoon chopped celery
　leaves
⅔ tablespoon chopped parsley
⅔ tablespoon lemon juice
1⅓ teaspoons honey

⅔ tablespoon olive oil
1⅓ teaspoons whole-wheat
　flour
⅓ teaspoon chili powder
⅔ cup tomato purée
1 hard-boiled egg, chopped
1 teaspoon Bragg Aminos

Cook onion in oil until tender, add whole-wheat flour, and allow to brown. Add remaining ingredients except egg. Simmer about 10 minutes. Add egg and serve over fish. Makes 1 cup sauce.

Cheese Sauce

1½ tablespoons butter
1½ tablespoons whole-wheat
　flour
¾ cup grated unprocessed
　cheese

¾ cup milk or soy milk
⅓ teaspoon Bragg Aminos

Melt butter in double boiler. Stir in whole-wheat flour. Add milk while stirring. Cook until smooth and thickened. Stir in cheese. Makes 1½ cups sauce.

Herb Sauce
(cream style)

1 tablespoon butter or oil
1 tablespoon whole-wheat
flour
1 cup chicken broth
½ teaspoon Bragg Aminos

⅛ teaspoon paprika
⅛ cup minced green onions
1 tablespoon chopped parsley
1 tablespoon chopped fresh
tarragon

Melt butter in double boiler; stir in whole-wheat flour. Stir in chicken broth that has been made by simmering the neck, backbone and gizzard of a broiler chicken in 2 cups hot water for ½ hour and straining. Add all remaining ingredients and cook, stirring until thickened. Serve over broiled chicken. Enough for one broiled chicken.

Curry Gravy
(for leg of lamb, chicken, or fish)

1½ medium cooking apples
1½ medium onions, chopped
3 tablespoons butter
½ teaspoon Bragg Aminos

3 level teaspoons curry
powder
4 or 5 whole cloves
3 teaspoons lemon juice

Peel apple, add chopped onion, cook slowly to golden brown; then mash to paste. Add curry powder, cloves, and lemon juice. Cook until smooth. Makes 1 cup sauce.

Turkey Gravy

4½ tablespoons of drippings
4½ tablespoons whole-wheat
flour
1 teaspoon Bragg Aminos

3 cups liquid (approximately
1½ cups liquid from cook-
ing of giblets and 1½ cups
milk or water)

Pour the drippings from the roasting pan into a bowl. Skim off as much fat as possible; put three tablespoons of the drippings into a saucepan. Add flour and blend thoroughly. Add liquid and cook mixture over low heat, stirring constantly till thickened. Let it boil briskly about 5 minutes. Makes about 3 cups gravy.

Cranberry Mandarin Sauce

2 *cups honey*	8 *cups fresh cranberries*
4 *cups water*	4 *tangerines*

Boil honey. . . . . .and water together 5 minutes.
Add cranberries and boil, without stirring, until all the skins pop
open—about 5 minutes. Remove from heat. Peel, section, and seed
tangerines. Add to sauce and allow mixture to cool in saucepan.
Add a few slivers of tangerine skin to sauce. Makes about 10 cups.

Meat Sauce

1½ *lbs. ground beef*	1½ *cans tomato paste*
⅜ *cup chopped onion*	1 *teaspoon Bragg Aminos*
¾ *cup chopped celery*	⅜ *teaspoon thyme*
3 *cloves garlic (optional)*	1 *small bay leaf*
1½ *small cans mushroom stems*	¾ *teaspoon paprika*
and pieces	
6 *cups cooked tomatoes*	

Use oil or butter to brown ground beef, onion, celery, garlic and
mushrooms. Cook until lightly browned, stirring frequently. (Add
oil or butter if needed.) Add tomatoes, tomato paste, and seasonings; simmer over low heat about 1½ hours until thickened. Serve
with spaghetti. Serves 6 to 8.

Bordelaise Sauce

2 *tablespoons butter*	8 *peppercorns, freshly ground*
1 *shallot, chopped fine*	1 *clove*
1 *large slice onion, chopped*	1 *cup meat stock*
2 *teaspoons chopped parsley*	1 *teaspoon Bragg Aminos*
1 *bay leaf*	

Cook vegetables with seasoning in butter until well browned. Add
stock. Simmer for 8 minutes and strain. Serves 4.

Basil Sauce

1 *onion*	1 *teaspoon sweet basil*
1 *clove garlic, minced*	2 *tablespoons olive oil*
1 *can solid pack tomatoes*	1 *teaspoon Bragg Aminos*

Cut onion in half; cover with olive oil and broil under hot flame. Mince garlic clove, put over onion half, dress again with olive oil and continue to broil until golden brown. Add to tomatoes with sweet basil and let simmer until thick and creamy, then press through a strainer. This sauce is splendid for egg, meat or pasta dishes. Serves 6.

Herb Sauce for Fish

*1 cup butter or olive oil
  or blend*
*2 tablespoons lemon juice,
  fresh*
1/2 teaspoon chervil

*2 teaspoons parsley,
  minced*
*1 tablespoon chives,
  minced*
1 teaspoon Bragg Aminos

Cream or blend all ingredients and add a pinch of fish herbs. Allow to stand for 1 hour. Brush on fish just before serving. Makes 1-1/4 cups sauce. Delicious for fish chowders, pastas, etc. Any excess freeze in ice-cube trays for later use, marking with date and ingredients.

Barbecue Sauce

1/2 teaspoon paprika
1 tablespoon balsamic vinegar
1 teaspoon dry mustard
1/2 teaspoon thyme
3 cloves garlic, minced
1/2 cup tomato juice, salt-free

2 teaspoons minced onion
1 1/2 tablespoons honey
2 teaspoons Bragg Aminos
1/4 cup lemon juice, fresh
1/4 cup olive oil
pinch cayenne pepper

Blend all ingredients thoroughly and allow to stand several hours before using. Makes 1 cup sauce. Freeze excess in ice-cube trays for future use. After frozen, store in ziplock bag with the date and ingredients.

Basting Sauce for Meat or Poultry

2 tablespoons lemon juice
1/4 cup water, distilled
1 tablespoon melted butter
1 tablespoon olive oil
2 bay leaves

*1/2 teaspoon each of thyme,
  tarragon, and rosemary*
2 garlic cloves, crushed
1 teaspoon Bragg Aminos

Blend well. Let stand 1 hour and use for basting. Makes 1/3 cup sauce.

DESSERT SAUCES

Butterscotch Sauce

2¼ *cups honey*   6 *tablespoons butter*
⅜ *cup water*   ¾ *cup chopped nut meats*

Boil honey and water together to 234°F. or until a small amount of the mixture forms a soft ball when dropped in cold water. Add butter and nut meats. Makes about 3 cups sauce.

Choco-like Sauce

¾ *cup cold water*   1⅛ *cups honey*
3¾ *oz. carob*

Combine water and carob and cook over direct heat 4 minutes, stirring constantly. Add honey. Cook 4 minutes longer. Pour into an airtight jar and seal. Keep syrup and use as needed. Makes 1½ cups sauce.

Custard Sauce

3 *egg yolks*   2¼ *cups scalded milk*
⅜ *cup honey*   ¾ *teaspoon pure vanilla*

Beat eggs slightly; add sweetening . . . . Add milk gradually, beating constantly, and cook over hot water until mixture thickens. Chill and add flavoring. Makes 2¼ cups sauce.

Strawberry Sauce

¾ *cup honey*   1½ *cups crushed strawberries*
⅓ *cup water*

Boil sweetening . . . and water together about 12 minutes, add strawberries, cook 1 minute, and chill. Makes 1½ cups sauce.

Honey Peach Sauce

3 *cups sliced peaches*   ½ *cup honey (slightly over full*
¾ *cup water*   *measure)*

Cook the peaches until nearly done, then add the honey. Makes 4 cups sauce.

Orange Pudding Sauce

1 cup honey
4 tablespoons cornstarch
grated rinds of 2 oranges
1⅓ cups boiling water

2 eggs, *well beaten*
4 tablespoons butter
1⅓ cups orange juice
2 teaspoons lemon juice

Combine sweetening, . . . cornstarch, and grated orange rinds and mix well. Add boiling water and cook in double boiler for 10 minutes, stirring occasionally. Remove from heat and pour some of the hot mixture over beaten eggs; blend well. Return to double boiler, add butter, and cook for 2 minutes, stirring constantly. Add fruit juices and beat until well blended. Cool before serving. Makes 2⅔ cups sauce.

Pineapple Mint Sauce

½ cup drained, crushed un-
    sweetened pineapple
⅛ cup pineapple juice, un-
    sweetened

½ cup water
4 drops oil of peppermint
⅔ cup honey

Combine unsweetened pineapple, juice, **sweetening** . . . . and water and simmer about 10 minutes or until thickened. Cool. . . and add peppermint. Serve cold with roast lamb. Makes 1¼ cups sauce.

Quick Maple Syrup

Heat ½ cup of maple sugar. Add 1 generous teaspoon of butter. Serve hot in place of butterscotch or chocolate sauce. Very good on any apple dessert.

Maple Cream Sauce

½ cup maple syrup
1 egg yolk

½ cup heavy cream

Heat syrup in double boiler. Beat egg yolk well. Dilute with hot syrup while stirring and return to double boiler. Cook over boiling water, stirring constantly until mixture thickens (about 6 minutes). Cool . . . . Stir in cream whipped stiff. Delicious as sauce for hot brown rice. Add shredded rind of lemon to taste. Chill and mix with 1 cup diced fresh fruit or berries just before serving. Makes 2¼ cups sauce.

Chapter 19

One World Cookery

FROM the far corners of the world comes the heritage of good nutrition. Sometimes it is embodied in rare delicacies, but more often in the ordinary food of the common people. The peasants of many lands are often more expert in their methods of preparing and flavoring good food than are the famous chefs of the most exalted and fashionable restaurants. Wild animals are often more intelligent in their selection of foods than we are, and primitive man followed in their footsteps. That may be why we find the simple people, those closest to nature in natural living, more instinctively intelligent and intuitively adept with foods.

Foreign foods are not often, as is popularly imagined, heavy, rich, and over-spiced. They are usually standard interpretations of fine food, prepared delicately and compounded with intelligent nutritional logic. That they excite the palate is not the least of their appeal and, from the standpoint of Health, not their entire value. Nutritionally speaking, they stand firmly on their own good bodybuilding principles.

We should be much the loser if we ignored the marvelous combinations of vegetables of the Armenians, the ingenious uses of corn by the Mexicans, the full-bodied heartiness of the Russian interpretation, the symphonically blended French "marmites," and the subtle, slightly "undercooked" offerings of the Chinese. In the world of good nutrition we are not limited by differences of language, politics, or boundaries. Our only guide is the language of common sense.

Paul Bragg and daughter Patricia in their around the world health crusades always gather health recipes which they bring to you in this chapter.

OUR MEXICAN NEIGHBORS

Masa

Masa is the base of the tortilla, the tamale, and the enchilada. It is one of Mexico's greatest Health foods. This is the way to prepare it:

3 *lbs. shelled corn*	3 *teaspoons unslaked lime*
15 *cups boiling water*	(*this can be purchased in most grocery stores*)

Add the lime to one cup of water and allow it to dissolve and settle at the bottom. Add the corn to the rest of the boiling water. After the lime has settled in the cup of water, pour the top of this lime water into the container holding the corn. Cook the corn to boiling-point and then allow to cool.

Place the corn in a sieve or colander and keep washing it with running water. Wash it very thoroughly. You will find that some of the skin of the corn will come off. Get as much of the skin off as possible.

While the corn is still slightly moist, put it through a grinder. (Any kind of grinder will do; a meat-grinder may be used. However, the finer the masa is ground, the better it will be.) Sometimes it is advisable to put the masa through the grinder twice. You now have your basic material from which many Mexican dishes can be made.

How to Make Tortillas from Masa

Place a lump of masa between two pieces of cloth and pack into the shape of the tortilla. Many Mexican women are adept at patting the masa into shape with their bare hands, but this is rather difficult as it sticks to the hands. So for the amateur in the preparation of tortillas, I suggest the use of the two layers of cloth. When the masa is well shaped, place it on a heavy griddle without any grease. When it begins to show air bubbles on one side, turn and cook on the other side. It is not necessary for the tortilla to be brown—only to be well cooked.

Your tortilla is now ready to make tacos or to be used as we would use bread, toast, or wafers.

How to Make Tamales
from Masa

Mix masa with shortening and liquid. For liquid, either water or chicken or meat stock may be used. Proportions must be experimented with because of the various types of corn, but the "floating" test will determine when you have hit on the right consistency. If a small amount of the masa dropped in water will float, it is satisfactory. However, here is a suggestion to use as the starting-point of your experiment:

2 cups masa
½ to ¾ cup meat stock or water

1 cup shortening (peanut, corn, or soy oil)

The shortening and liquid must be beaten into the masa thoroughly and vigorously, but should be added only a little at a time until proper consistency is determined.

You will need cornhusks to make the real Mexican tamale. You will be able to buy them in the ordinary market, or in the Mexican market in your city. Wash them very thoroughly and use while they are still wet, so that they will be soft. Spread the cornhusks thick with masa, stuff with tamale stuffing (see recipe for *Gala Filling for Tamales*), and fold or roll. Tie ends of cornhusk firmly so that the masa and filling cannot escape in the cooking. Place in a pan suitable in size to the amount you are preparing and line the pan with cornhusks. Cook the tamales over steam for about one hour, or until tender. When the masa breaks away from the cornhusks easily, the tamale is done.

Gala Filling for Tamales

1 large onion, sliced
1 large tomato, peeled and sliced

½ cup lemon juice

Marinate onion and tomato in lemon juice for several hours. Soak ½ large green pepper in water for 1 hour.

Meanwhile, boil until tender:

1 lb. pork
¼ lb. veal

When tender, remove meat and mince finely. Save meat stock. Sauté the following:

2 *cloves garlic, minced fine*　　　½ *large green pepper (soaked*
1 *onion, minced fine*　　　　　　　　*as above mentioned) in*
　　　　　　　　　　　　　　　　　　　3 *tablespoons oil*

To sauté mixture add:

minced pork　　　　　　　　　½ *cup meat stock*
minced veal

Simmer for a few minutes. Then add:

1 *teaspoon chili sauce (see*　　　½ *teaspoon honey*
　recipes on page 271)　　　　⅛ *teaspoon rosemary*
1 *teaspoon lemon juice*　　　　⅛ *teaspoon cayenne*

Continue to simmer for a few minutes. Fill masa-lined husks with mixture, but before rolling and securing ends, add the following in the center of each tamale:

a few soaked raisins (these may　*a tablespoon of chopped tomato*
　be ground or whole and　　　　*and onion that have been*
　should have been soaked for　　*soaking in lemon juice*
　from 1 *to* 2 *hours)*　　　　*a piece of chicken if desired*
an olive

Roll as described in tamale recipe.

Using Masa for Sweet Tamales

Some of the most delicious Mexican tamales are the "sweet" or fruit-filled ones. The masa for these tamales is prepared exactly as in the recipe above, except that the masa base should be compounded as follows:

2 *cups masa*　　　　　　　　½ *to* ¾ *cup fruit juice or*
⅓ *cup honey*　　　　　　　　　*water*

For filling, see recipe Sweet Filling for Tamales.

Sweet Filling for Tamales

Almost any cooked, sweetened fruit makes a delicious filling for sweet tamales. Pitted cherries, apricots, peaches, apples, or pears (either dried or fresh), cooked and sweetened with raw sugar or honey, make an excellent filling.

Red Chili Sauce

6 *red peppers*
lemon juice for marinating
1 *onion, minced fine*
2 *teaspoons olive oil*

1 *teaspoon Bragg Aminos*
¼ *to* ½ *teaspoon oregano*
3 *cloves garlic, minced*

Marinate whole large red peppers in lemon and Bragg Liquid Aminos for two hours. Grind in food-chopper using fine knife. Add other ingredients when ready to serve.

Green Chili Sauce

2 *green peppers, small and hot*
6 *small green tomatoes*
¼ *green pepper, sweet*
½ *onion*
2 *tablespoons boiling water*
1 *teaspoon Bragg Aminos*

¼ *teaspoon oregano, finely powdered (also a few fresh leaves if possible, minced)*
¼ *teaspoon coriander, finely powdered (also a few fresh leaves if possible, minced)*

Grind all ingredients together. Add boiling water and mix.

Tacos

The tacos is the Mexican version of our sandwich, and to many is more delicious in every way. The tacos is prepared by using the tortilla already baked on the griddle and filling it with some of the following combinations:

1. Chopped cold chicken mixed with chopped olives, chopped celery, chopped green pepper, moistened with a little green chili sauce.

2. Cooked shredded tender pork mixed with a little fresh chopped onion, tomato, and green pepper, moistened with a little red chili sauce.

3. Chopped veal with chopped cucumbers, endive, and celery, moistened with a little chili sauce or mushroom sauce.

The fillings should be rolled in the tortilla and secured, if necessary, with two toothpicks. They should then be placed in the oven for a few minutes to brown. Or they can be covered with grated cheese and placed under the broiler for a few moments to brown.

It will be worth your while to prepare the true native Mexican dishes given above, but if you do not have the time or inclination for the various steps in these preparations, you may use the slightly Americanized version of the Mexican dishes and still have an excellent variety of enjoyable foods. Here are some of the more Americanized Mexican recipes:

Tamale Pie

1¼ *cups cornmeal*
6 *cups water*
1 *large onion*
1 *large green or chili pepper*
1 *teaspoon Bragg Aminos*

3¾ *tablespoons soy or peanut oil*
3 *cups cooked tomatoes*
2½ *cups ground cooked meat*
chili powder to season

Add cornmeal and Bragg Liquid Aminos to water in top of double boiler and cook for 45 minutes. Chop onion and pepper and sauté in hot oil. Add tomatoes, meat, and chili powder and cook until thickened. Line greased baking dish with half of the mush, pour in meat mixture, cover with remaining mush, and bake in 375°F. oven for 30 minutes, or until top is lightly browned. Serves 8.

Chili Con Carne

1¼ *cups dry kidney beans*
water
⅓ *minced onion*
1 *teaspoon Bragg Aminos*
3 *cloves garlic*

1¼ *tablespoons chopped green pepper*
2½ *tablespoons oil*
¾ *lb. ground beef*
3 *cups diced tomatoes*
¾ *tablespoon chili powder*

Wash and soak kidney beans several hours or overnight. Cook about 2½ hours in the same water. Add more water if necessary. Sauté onion and green pepper in oil until tender. Add beef and stir until beef is separated and browned. Add tomatoes, Bragg Aminos, chili powder and any other seasonings desired. Cook about 1 hour on low heat. Add precooked kidney beans and cook an additional 10-15 minutes. Add more chili powder if you like it hot. Serves 6-8.

Mexican Casserole

1/2 cup whole-grain cereal
2-1/4 cups boiling distilled
water
3/4 cup canned tomatoes

1-1/2 tbs olive, canola or soy oil
1 onion, minced
1/2 lb ground beef or tofu
1/3 teaspoon chili powder

Add whole-grain cereal to boiling water, stirring constantly for 3 minutes. Remove from heat, cover and let stand to cool. Mince onion and add beef or tofu (well drained) in oil and brown. Add tomatoes and chili powder, cook about 5 minutes. Spread half of cereal mixture in bottom of an oiled, shallow baking dish. Top with meat or tofu mixture and cover with remaining cereal mixture. Bake in moderate oven (375°F.) 45 minutes. Sprinkle with Bragg Aminos. Serves 6.

Avocado Mexican Soup

Soup Stock:
6 cups beef or chicken stock
or frozen stock cubes
1 onion, minced

Garnish:
1 tablespoon minced parsley
2 green mild chilis, diced
2 medium avocados
1/2 tsp Bragg Aminos

Cook onion in stock until tender, add parsley. Mash mild chili with avocados and top bowl of soup with one tablespoon just before serving. Delicious served with warm corn tortillas or pita bread. Serves 6.

CREOLE COOKERY

Despite the fact that New Orleans is the home of Creole cookery, it has a distinctive foreign characteristic due, perhaps, to its French and Spanish origins. It is a regional type of cookery that presents many foods at their finest in the light of good nutrition.

Gumbo Filé

1 medium boiling chicken, disjointed
2 dozen oysters and 6 cups oyster liquor (if not sufficient natural liquor, add water to make up this amount)
1 medium onion, chopped
½ teaspoon thyme
¼ cup chopped parsley
1 bay leaf
½ teaspoon chili powder
¼ cup peanut oil
3 cloves garlic
1 teaspoon Bragg Aminos
⅛ teaspoon pepper
⅛ teaspoon cayenne
2 tablespoons filé powder
1 cup brown rice
6 cups boiling water

Sauté chicken in peanut oil in large heavy soup skillet until golden brown. Add onion and sauté until brown. Add boiling water and hot oyster liquor (total liquid should equal 3 quarts). Add thyme, parsley, bay leaf, chili powder, Bragg Liquid Aminos, pepper, and cayenne. Boil briskly for 2 minutes. Reduce to low heat and simmer slowly for 2 hours. Remove chicken from stock, cut one cup of small cubes. Bring stock to a brisk boil again. Reduce to low heat and add chicken cubes and oysters. Simmer for just a few minutes or until oysters and chicken are heated through. Remove from fire. Add filé powder and mix thoroughly with stock. Place 1 tablespoon of cooked brown rice in center of soup plate. Ladle gumbo over rice and serve immediately. Serves 10.

Okra Gumbo

1 medium boiling chicken, disjointed
5 tomatoes, cut in half
1 medium onion, chopped
½ teaspoon chili powder
½ teaspoon thyme
¼ cup chopped parsley
2 cups okra pods, sliced
1 bay leaf
¼ cup peanut oil
1 teaspoon Bragg Aminos
⅛ teaspoon pepper
⅛ teaspoon cayenne
1 cup brown rice
3 quarts boiling water

Sauté chicken in peanut oil in large, heavy soup skillet until golden brown. Add onion and sauté until brown. Add boiling water, thyme, parsley, bay leaf, chili powder...Bragg Liquid Aminos, pepper, and cayenne. Boil briskly for 2 minutes. Reduce to low heat and simmer slowly for 1½ hours. Add okra pods and cook for another half hour. Remove chicken from stock, cut 1 cup of small cubes. Bring stock to a brisk boil again. Reduce to low heat and add chicken cubes. Simmer for a few minutes until chicken is heated through. Place 1 tablespoon of rice in center of soup plate. Ladle gumbo over rice and serve immediately. Serves 8.

Crab Jambalaya

1 *cup brown rice, cooked*
1 *cup shredded cooked crab meat (cooked, shelled shrimp may be substituted)*
1 *medium onion, chopped*
1½ *cloves garlic, minced*
3 *ripe tomatoes, peeled and quartered*
¼ *teaspoon chili powder*
⅛ *teaspoon pepper*
⅛ *teaspoon cayenne*
4 *tablespoons butter*
1 *teaspoon Bragg Aminos*

Sauté onion and garlic until light brown. Add tomatoes, crushing to a pulp while sautéing. Add crab, rice, and seasonings. Simmer in covered pan for 45 minutes, stirring occasionally. Serves 6.

Chicken Creole

1 *young fryer chicken*
3 *tomatoes, peeled and quartered*
1 *clove garlic, minced*
1 *large onion, sliced*
4 *green bell peppers, seeded and sliced*
1 *bay leaf*
¼ *teaspoon thyme*
4 *tablespoons butter*
1½ *cups chicken stock*
1½ *tablespoons whole-wheat pastry flour*
1 *teaspoon Bragg Aminos*

Sauté in butter in deep, heavy kettle, add onions and sauté until light brown. Add flour and blend with butter in bottom of pan. Add garlic, peppers, bay leaf, thyme, tomatoes. Cover and simmer for 15 to 20 minutes. Heat stock and add. Cover. Simmer for 50 minutes. Serve with rice. . .using remaining sauce to top both chicken and rice. Serves 6.

FROM FRANCE

It is often said that a Frenchman can take leftovers or poor cuts of meat and dress them up with superb sauces and flavoring until they are fit for a banquet. Whether that be true or not, the French do have a sense of appropriateness in seasoning that has been handed down from generation to generation until it is almost inbred. Their salads are famed world wide, and that is probably because they use variety. The endive, the escarole, the watercress, not just the plain lettuce or romaine, are all utilized in the French salad. They produce some of the most delicious cheese the world has known: Camembert, Roquefort, Brie, and many other varieties.

To top the list, they produce delicious soups without number, two of which are listed here because of their delicious flavor and high nutritional value.

Onion soup, as the French prepare it, is widely renowned, but their highest artistry in cooking culminates in that queen of all soups, Petite Marmite.

To the Frenchman, the art of eating, like love, is one of the higher intellectual pursuits, a great deal more far-reaching than the general American concept of physical pleasure in food. No small wonder that France has produced the finest in the art of flavor, cooking, serving, and food appreciation.

French Onion Soup

4 *cups consommé (see recipe*   2½ *tablespoons butter*
  in "Soups," page 62)   2½ *tablespoons dry, grated*
4 *medium onions (sliced very*   *cheese*
  thin)

Sauté onions in butter until golden brown and tender. Add to consommé stock. Simmer for a few minutes. Toast pieces (½ slice each) of whole-wheat bread until thoroughly dry, butter, and place at the bottom of a soup plate; pour onion soup over it and sprinkle with cheese just before serving. Serves 4.

Petite Marmite

This soup takes its name from the heavy earthenware pot in which it is prepared. *Petite marmite* means the "little soup pot." Marmites can be purchased and are the ideal utensil for this and other slow-cooking soups. The marmite also makes an attractive container from which to ladle the soup at the table. But lacking the marmite, any very heavy pot will do.

2 *lbs. broken veal bones*
2 *lbs. broken marrow bones*
marrow from bones
1 *medium-sized stewing chicken*
giblets from fowl
2 *lbs. lean brisket of beef*
⅓ *cup butter*
1 *tablespoon brown sugar*
4 *large leeks*
2 *bay leaves*
1 *clove*
1 *teaspoon Bragg Aminos*

¼ *teaspoon pepper*
3 *large onions*
3 *large carrots*
1 *large turnip*
1½ *cups chopped celery*
a few tender celery leaves
¼ *cup parsley, chopped*
1 *teaspoon fresh chervil or* ¼ *teaspoon dried, powdered chervil*
½ *teaspoon thyme*
grated cheese
parsley and chives for garnishing

Put chicken, beef, veal, bones, and giblets in a very heavy pot. Add pepper, clove, and bay leaves plus 3 to 4 quarts of water. Boil quickly; remove scum. Reduce heat and continue to simmer. Sauté onions gently, adding sugar to help them brown. Add to stock, then add all vegetables and seasonings and simmer for 4 hours. Sprinkle servings with grated cheese, parsley, and chives. Serve with small slices (halves or quarters) of thoroughly toasted whole-wheat bread. Serves 10.

Stuffed Scallop Shells

Ingredients for scallop stuffing:

1½ *lbs. fresh scallops*
6 *large scallop shells*
1¼ *cups fresh mushrooms, washed and sliced*

3 *tablespoons butter*
2 *tablespoons and* 1 *teaspoon minced shallots (small red onions may be substituted)*

Health is not quoted in the markets because it is without price.

Soup rejoices the stomach, and disposes it to receive and digest other food.
— Brillat Savarin

Ingredients for sauce:

3 *tablespoons whole-wheat flour*
3 *tablespoons butter*
1 *cup scalded milk*
1⅔ *cups juice of the scallops (if not sufficient, dilute with water to make up this quantity)*
1 *teaspoon Bragg Aminos*

¼ *teaspoon fresh ground pepper*
¼ *cup lemon juice*
¼ *teaspoon grated lemon rind*
4 *tablespoons grated cheese*
2 *tablespoons melted butter*
¼ *cup whole-wheat toast bread crumbs*
3 *cloves garlic minced*

Rinse scallops thoroughly. Dry on cloth. Cut into uniform pieces. Boil in water for 7 minutes and allow to stand in the water for 30 minutes. Sauté shallots and mushrooms in butter until shallots are golden brown.

To make sauce, blend flour with melted butter. Add scalded milk slowly, stirring constantly. Add pepper, lemon rind, and grated cheese. Simmer slowly, stirring constantly until flour is cooked. Add lemon juice, shallots, mushrooms, scallops . . . Stuff scallop shells, using extra sauce for topping . . . Brown whole-wheat toast bread crumbs in butter and sprinkle over top. Serves 6.

Peas with Lettuce and Thyme

4 *cups shelled tender green peas*
¼ *cup minced scallions (white portion only)*
1 *small head romaine*
3 *tablespoons melted butter*

¼ *cup chopped parsley*
1 *teaspoon honey*
3 *tablespoons butter*
¼ *teaspoon thyme*

Melt butter in heavy skillet. Lay romaine leaves on bottom of pan. Place peas, scallions, thyme, parsley, and sweetening over peas, well distributed . . . . Cover entire mixture with romaine leaves. Cover and simmer over very low fire, adding ¼ cup water from time to time if necessary to avoid dryness. Cook until peas are tender, Add butter just before serving. Serves 8.

FROM THE NEAR EAST

From Syria, Arabia, Armenia, Persia (Iran), Turkey, and all the Balkan countries come some of our greatest Health foods. The thin, hard black bread, the yogurts and honeys in generous abundance, were the heritage of these people long before Western civilization was dreamed of. Their specialties are the eggplant and lamb dishes, and delicious stuffings rolled in vine or grape leaves. Dates, figs, and fruits of all kinds are as much a part of the national diet as are our potatoes. They use nuts and seeds of melons or sunflowers as we would confections, and most of their conserves are prepared with the natural sugars and honeys.

All these things are common to most Near Eastern countries. The differences among them are primarily in manners, customs, and times of preparation and eating. They are past masters in the use of the whole grain, and the roasting of meats on the spit. Their desserts are usually simple: stewed fruits mixed with nuts, flavored with lemon juice and anise. But, above all, their foods rank with the world's great dishes in delicious flavor.

Armenian Stuffed Grape Leaves
(Dolma)

(If you are unable to obtain grape leaves, substitute cabbage.)

grape or cabbage leaves
½ lb. ground meat, preferably lamb
1 large onion, minced
2 level tablespoons brown rice, uncooked
⅛ teaspoon pepper, freshly ground

1 tablespoon minced parsley
½ teaspoon Bragg Aminos
1 tablespoon lemon juice
¼ cup meat stock
⅛ teaspoon oregano

Cook the leaves until tender. While cooking do not stir, as you need whole leaves and must avoid tearing them. Mix all other ingredients and put a small amount on a grape leaf or cabbage leaf, then roll the leaf, tucking end under to secure. Place in a casserole and barely cover with water. Cover the pan tightly and bake in the oven until meat is done. This should be about 1 to 1½ hours. Serves 4 to 6.

Armenian Wheat Pilaff

2 *cups Armenian processed wheat (This can be purchased at Greek or Armenian stores and is known as "bulgur." It is a precooked, sun-dried, whole-kernel grain.)*

4 *cups chicken, veal, or beef stock*
5½ *tablespoons oil or butter*
½ *large onion, minced*
⅛ *teaspoon Bragg Aminos*

Place oil or butter in very heavy skillet. Add the bulgur, or wheat. Add the onion. Cook until slightly browned. Add the seasoning and stock. Bake in a moderate oven for 35 minutes. At this point take out of oven and stir well. Then replace in oven and continue baking for 15 minutes. Serves 6.

Armenian Rice Pilaff

Use same recipe as for wheat pilaff, substituting rice for the bulgur.

Turkish Yogurt

Bring 1 quart of milk to a boil; pour milk into mixing bowl. Let stand until it cools to about 110°F. (just hot enough so it will not burn fingers). Put 2 tablespoons of ordinary commercial yogurt in center of milk. (This can be obtained at a Health food store.) Agitate slightly with spoon. Cover bowl with plate and wrap in heavy bath towel. After this stands for 5 hours, wrap towel around bowl, leaving only top open. Let stand for 12 hours. Do not disturb or move bowl. It is then ready to eat or place in refrigerator. (NOTE: If you save 2 tablespoons of this, you may use it in place of the commercial yogurt in making a new supply. Yogurt combines well with practically all foods.)

◇◇

Arabian Stuffed Eggplant

2 eggplants	1 cup whole-wheat bread
¾ lb. ground lamb	crumbs
1 clove garlic	2 tomatoes
1 small onion	½ teaspoon cinnamon
4 tablespoons minced parsley	¼ teaspoon pepper, freshly
1 egg	ground
½ cup peanut oil	½ teaspoon Bragg Aminos

Peel eggplants and cut into thick slices. Steam until almost tender.
Do not allow to become mushy. The eggplants must hold their
shape. Combine all other ingredients, mincing garlic, onion, and
parsley, and beating egg thoroughly before combining. Stuff layers
of eggplant with mixture. Pierce with skewers to hold in place.
Place in baking pan; pour oil over the eggplant and bake until the
stuffing is thoroughly cooked. This should be about 40 minutes in
a moderate oven. Serves 6.

Persian Kebab

2 lbs. meat from leg of lamb	¼ teaspoon pepper
or lean loin of lamb	⅓ cup lemon juice
2 large onions	2 tablespoons olive oil or vege-
2 tomatoes	table oil
½ teaspoon Bragg Aminos	¾ teaspoon oregano

Cut meat in inch cubes. Slice onion and place onion and lamb in a
mixture of lemon juice, oil, and seasoning. Marinate overnight.
Slice tomatoes. On long skewers place 1 piece meat, onion, tomato
and so on until the skewer is half filled. Then broil over a moderate flame or charcoal fire until all is well browned and done.
Serves 6.

Syrian Roast Stuffed Chicken

1 roasting chicken	½ teaspoon Bragg Aminos
2 cups rice pilaff	⅛ teaspoon pepper, freshly
¼ cup pine nuts	ground
1 carrot	1 tablespoon butter
1 branch celery	1 teaspoon cinnamon

Cut carrot and celery into small pieces. Mix with pilaff, pine nuts, seasoning, and melted butter. Moisten slightly with water. Clean chicken well. Stuff with mixture. Truss and roast in oven about 375°F. for 2 hours, or until tender and golden brown. Serves 4.

FOOD FROM THE FAR EAST

It is sometimes difficult to achieve the true Far Eastern flavoring because we do not always have the proper ingredients. It is very often difficult to secure fresh ginger root, for instance, or the very young garlic bulbs that do not have the strong pungency of the more matured garlic bulb, such as the Chinese use; or lotus leaves, small Chinese peas, or bamboo shoots, but many of these ingredients are becoming more available in the United States. Whenever you can find them, add them to your larder.

The Far East is the home of the soybean, the water chestnut, or the sesame seed and some of the world's finest Health foods. The people of the Orient, like their Western neighbors, have yielded too much to civilization. Too many of their foods are now prepared by deep-fat frying and other dietary practices in modern usage that are deleterious. But if we look for the best in Far Eastern cookery as we look for the best in our own, we will find a treasure house of delicious, wholesome food.

Chinese Omelet

  6 *eggs*
½ *cup shellfish, such as*
  shrimp, lobster, or crab,
  diced fine
½ *cup cooked chicken, diced*
  fine
¼ *cup sliced water chestnuts*
  1 *cup bean sprouts*

¼ *cup bamboo shoots, sliced*
½ *cup celery*
½ *cup minced onion*
¼ *cup sliced mushrooms,*
  canned (optional)
½ *teaspoon Bragg Aminos*

Mix well chicken, fish, onion, water chestnuts, bamboo shoots, bean sprouts, celery, mushrooms, and seasoning. Beat eggs; fold in vegetable and meat mixture and prepare as for regular omelet. Serves 6.

Korean Roast Duck

1 *roasting duck*
2 *cloves garlic*
2 *teaspoons chives*
1 *tablespoon honey*
1 *clove*

2 *tablespoons Bragg Aminos*
1 *teaspoon ginger*
3 *teaspoons lemon juice*
1 *cup water*

Wash duck thoroughly and dry. Mix all other ingredients with the exception of the honey and Bragg Aminos and boil for 5 minutes. Fill cavity of duck with this hot liquid, tying the duck at the neck and pouring the hot liquid inside. Secure opening so liquor will remain within the cavity. Blend honey with Bragg Aminos and rub over skin of duck to glaze. Roast in covered pan in hot oven until tender, basting frequently with liquor from bottom of pan. Serves 4.

Chinese Pork Shoulder

6 *lbs. pork shoulder, including skin and bone*
2 *tablespoons Bragg Aminos*
2 *cups cold water*

¼ *cup lemon juice*
1½ *tablespoons honey*
2 *slices fresh ginger*

Wash shoulder. Slash skinless portion with about 6 scorings of the knife. Place in heavy kettle with the water. Boil briskly and add all other ingredients. Boil for 5 minutes. Cover and simmer slowly for 3 hours or until tender, turning about 4 times during the cooking so that all sides cook immersed in the liquid from time to time. Serves 10.

Stuffed Mushrooms

1 *lb. large fresh mushroom caps*
½ *lb. ground pork*
2 *teaspoons minced onion*

2 *teaspoons cornstarch or arrowroot*
2 *teaspoons lemon juice butter*
½ *teaspoon Bragg Aminos*

Mince the stems of the mushrooms and mix with ground meat, and add all other ingredients . . . Wash mushroom caps thoroughly. Stuff caps with mounds of meat mixture. Place in steam over boiling water, in regular steamer or covered colander arranged over boiling saucepan. Steam for 10 minutes. Top each mound with a small piece of butter and place under broiler for a few moments. Serve immediately. Serves 4 to 6.

Chinese Spare Ribs

12 *spare ribs (get your butcher to cut them about 1 in. thick and as meaty a section as possible)*

2 *teaspoons Bragg Aminos*

2 *cups water*

1½ *teaspoons honey*

1½ *tablespoons lemon juice*

½ *cup crushed pineapple*

Boil ribs with Bragg Liquid Aminos . . . . . and water in a heavy kettle. Boil for 5 minutes. Simmer for ¾ hour or until tender. Add honey and boil briskly, stirring constantly until juice is reduced and meat saturated with sauce. Add pineapple. Place under broiler and brown. Serves 6.

Egg Fu-yung

8 *eggs*

1 *cup cooked lobster, crab, shrimp meat, pork, or chicken, shredded fine*

⅓ *cup chopped celery*

⅓ *cup sliced bamboo shoots (optional)*

⅓ *cup sliced water chestnuts (optional)*

2 *cups bean sprouts*

¼ *cup minced onion*

2 *teaspoon Bragg Aminos*

2 *teaspoons honey*

2 *tablespoons peanut oil*

3 *tablespoons canned, sliced mushrooms (optional)*

Sauté meat or fish shreds in peanut oil over hot fire, stirring constantly and quickly for about 3 minutes. Add celery, bamboo shoots, water chestnuts, stirring briskly for one more minute. Add the Bragg Liquid Aminos . . . . . honey and mushrooms. Stir briskly and cook for one more minute. Remove from fire. Remove to heated pan. Pour the eggs into the first pan. Then pour in vegetables previously sautéed and bean sprouts. Mix. Fold omelet in half. Cook each side about 1 to 2 minutes over a slow fire. Serves 8.

Japanese Salad

1 *cup shredded spinach leaves*	2 *tablespoons lemon juice*
1 *tomato*	1 *teaspoon Bragg Aminos*
⅛ *teaspoon fresh ginger root*	1 *tablespoon honey*
1 *teaspoon sesame seed*	

Cut up tomato and spinach leaves; prepare dressing of lemon juice, Bragg Liquid Aminos, honey, and ginger root and toss with salad. Serves 4.

Philippine Fruit Compote

1 *cup diced plums*	3 *tablespoons lime juice*
1 *cup diced pears*	3 *tablespoons pine nuts*
1 *cup diced apricots*	⅛ *teaspoon cinnamon*
3 *tablespoons honey*	⅛ *teaspoon ginger*

Mix honey, lime juice, spices, and nuts. Thin with a little water until of runny consistency. Use as a dressing for fruit, mixing thoroughly. Chill before serving. Serves 4.

RUSSIAN COOKERY

Russia affords more contrast in national foods than almost any other country. The borsch, or beet soup with sour cream, the kasha, a sort of mush made with buckwheat, and the wonderful fish and vegetable soups are exquisite nutritional delicacies. And yet these are the foods most often eaten by the peasants. Foods that are considered luxury foods in Russia, while good as a general rule, are often very rich and concentrated for the ordinary diet. But many of their national foods find their place in a real Health food cookbook.

Russian Borsch

1 *lb. soup meat*	5 *beets*
5 *cups boiling water*	2 *tablespoons lemon juice*
soup greens	2 *tablespoons butter or oil*
2 *onions, sliced*	½ *tablespoon whole-wheat*
¼ *head cabbage, shredded*	*flour*
1 *teaspoon Bragg Aminos*	1 *cup strained canned or*
	chopped fresh tomatoes

Wash meat and place in boiling water; add soup greens, onions, and Bragg Liquid Aminos. Simmer until meat is tender. Peel and cube beets. Put in separate pot with lemon juice and butter or oil. Cook until tender. Add whole-wheat flour to beets. Mix well, and add to strained meat broth. Add tomatoes and cabbage and boil for 10 to 15 minutes or until cabbage is tender. Serve 1 tablespoon sour cream with each portion. Serves 6.

Shashlik

2-3 *lbs. of young lamb rump or*   3 *tablespoons parsley*
    fat breast of lamb   1 *cup lemon juice*
½ *teaspoon pepper*   1 *cup water*
    2 *cloves garlic, quartered*   ¼ *cup oil*
    2 *onions*   ⅛ *teaspoon allspice*
½ *teaspoon Bragg Aminos*   *lemon wedges*

Cut lamb into squares about 2½ by 2½ inches and about 1 inch thick. Leave a small amount of fat on the lamb. Pack tightly into an earthenware crock or jar. Sprinkle with Bragg Liquid Aminos, onion slices, garlic, and parsley. Boil the lemon juice, water, and allspice. Cool and pour over meat. Let marinate overnight, or longer. When ready to prepare, remove the meat squares, dry on a towel, place on a skewer and broil in home broiler or over charcoal fire. Baste frequently with drippings. Serve with lemon wedges. Serves 6.

Beef Stroganoff

1½ *lbs. lean beef, preferably the*   4 *tablespoons butter*
    fillet   1 *teaspoon dry mustard*
    2 *cups meat stock*   5 *tablespoons sour cream*
¼ *teaspoon pepper*   1 *tablespoon tomato juice*
    1 *tablespoon whole-wheat*   1 *onion, minced*
    pastry flour   *mushrooms (optional)*
    1 *teaspoon Bragg Aminos*

Cut the meat into one-inch squares, about ¼ inch in thickness. Sprinkle with Bragg Liquid Aminos and pepper and let stand in a cold place for 2 hours. Melt 2 tablespoons butter in heavy

◇◇◇

skillet. Add flour, blend gradually, and brown. Bring stock to a boil. Add mustard. Stir in tomato juice and sour cream gradually. Sauté onion in remaining butter. Add meat squares and brown thoroughly on all sides. Add sautéed onion and meat squares to meat-stock mixture and simmer slowly for 15 minutes or until meat is tender. If mushrooms are used, brown mushrooms in pan in which you have sautéed onions and meat, and top dish with them before serving. Serves 4.

Cucumbers and Sour Cream

4 cucumbers
½ lb. ground meat
1½ cups cooked brown rice

½ teaspoon Bragg Aminos
½ cup sour cream

Scoop out seeds in center. Mix meat and rice and stuff cucumbers. Sauté in butter until brown on all sides. Add sour cream. Bake in oven until meat is done. Serves 4.

Russian Pirozhki

¼ lb. sweet butter
1 cup whole-wheat flour
sour cream
2 hard-boiled, chopped eggs
½ lb. ground beef

1 tablespoon oil or butter
1 small onion, chopped
½ tablespoon whole-wheat flour
¼ cup water
½ teaspoon Bragg Aminos

Make a simple puff paste of the sweet butter (reserving one table-spoon butter) . . . . 1 cup whole-wheat flour blended to a coarse consistency. Add sour cream to moisten. Roll dough on floured board. Cut reserved 1 tablespoon cold butter into bits and scatter on rolled-out dough. Fold in three thicknesses. Roll out. Fold again. Press down and wrap in waxed paper. Chill two hours or longer. Roll out again and cut in 2½-inch rounds.

Brown meat and sauté onion. Remove onion and add ½ table-spoon whole-wheat flour and ¼ cup water to meat pan. Cook to a thin, dark gravy. Combine all ingredients with eggs. Chill.

Place on pastry round, fold, and seal with milk. Bake at 450°F. until lightly browned. Serves 6.

Kulebiaka
(Pastry fish loaf)

Stuffing:

- 1 *lb. fresh salmon or other fish (boned and cut in ¾-in. squares)*
- ⅛ *teaspoon paprika*
- ¼ *teaspoon thyme*
- ¼ *cup onions, sliced fine*
- ½ *teaspoon Bragg Aminos*

- ¾ *cup fresh mushrooms, sliced thin*
- ⅛ *cup butter*
- ⅛ *cup minced parsley*
- ½ *teaspoon fennel seeds (pounded)*
- 1¼ *cups brown or wild rice, cooked dry*
- 2 *hard-boiled eggs, chopped*

Mix paprika, Bragg Liquid Aminos and thyme. Work into fish and let stand in refrigerator for one hour. Sauté onions and mushrooms in butter for 3 minutes. Add the fish and allow to brown, stirring frequently. Add parsley, fennel seeds, rice, and eggs. Allow to cool.

Pastry:

- 1⅜ *cups whole-wheat pastry flour*
- ⅛ *teaspoon paprika*

- 3 *tablespoons butter*
- 1 *egg, small*
- 2½ *tablespoons sour cream*

Sift flour, paprika . . . . Cut in 1½ tablespoons butter and egg, and mix to crumbly consistency. Add sour cream carefully; knead and roll out on floured cloth. Shape crust oblong to fit loaf pan. Place fish mixture still on cloth or napkin in center, fold edges of crust over it and close sides by moistening edges. Invert greased loaf pan over loaf on napkin so that closed edges touch bottom of pan. Prick tiny holes in top crust about 3½ inches from each end of pan. Insert small funnel in holes and drop 1½ tablespoons butter into filling. Brush top with cream. Bake until brown (about 40 minutes) at 375°F. Cut in small slices and serve hot. Serves 6.

FROM POLAND

One of the world's most delicious soups, and certainly one of the best on the list of Health food cookery, comes from Poland.

Polish Sour-Milk Soup

5 *cups sour milk*	4 *hard-cooked eggs*
2½ *cups sour cream*	2 *cups cooked veal, diced*
1¼ *cups beet juice*	*dash of poultry seasoning*
1¼ *cups cooked beet tops*	
few sprigs of dill, chopped	
2½ *cucumbers, sliced*	

Beat sour milk and cream separately until bubbles show on the surface, add juice, chopped beet tops, dill and cucumbers. Mix all together, adding the chopped hard-cooked eggs and veal. Season to taste, place on ice, and, when serving, place a piece of ice on each plate. Serves 6.

Mushrooms with Sour Cream

1 *lb. mushrooms, sliced*	¼ *cup minced onion*
1 *cup sour cream*	⅓ *teaspoon Bragg Aminos*
1½ *tablespoons milk*	*paprika*
4 *tablespoons butter*	

Sauté onion in butter. Add flour, blend, and sauté until golden brown. Add milk. Simmer briskly for 5 minutes. Add mushrooms and Bragg Liquid Aminos. Add ½ cup sour cream and continue to simmer until mushrooms are done. Add remaining sour cream and mix well. Serve immediately. Sprinkle with paprika. Serves 4.

FROM SWEDEN

The Swedish people use many dark whole-grain breads. Some of these are the crisp rye breads and thin, waferlike toast. Their practice of the smorgasbord, an assortment of tidbits of fancy fish, meat, cheese and vegetables before a dinner, is not for the average person. Here, however, is a recipe found on every smorgasbord that is ideal, nutritionally.

Swedish Meat balls

2 lbs ground beef or lamb
1/2 cup whole-grain
   crackers or bread crumbs

1 egg yolk (fertile)
1 carrot, finely grated
1 zucchini, finely grated
1/2 cup skim or soy milk
1 onion minced

Ingredients for Sauce

1-1/2 tablespoons potato flour
   tablespoon butter, salt-free
1-1/2 cups meat stock
1 tablespoon lemon juice
1 tbs cilantro, chopped

1-1/2 tablespoons fennel,
   chopped
1 tablespoon honey, raw
1 beaten egg yolk (fertile)
1 teaspoon Bragg Aminos

Combine ingredients for meatballs, mix well and knead with hands. Shape into small balls. To prepare sauce, add flour to melted butter in saucepan, stirring to blend thoroughly. Gradually add stock, seasonings, lemon juice and beaten egg. Cook slowly over low heat for 5 minutes. Arrange meat balls in casserole, cover with sauce, bake in oven until meat is done. Garnish with Parmesan cheese or Brewers yeast flakes. Serves 8.

Lamb Stew with Dill Casserole

2 lbs neck of lamb, cubed
4 tbs olive or canola oil
2 quarts distilled water
1 onion, sliced

1/2 teaspoon dill
1/2 teaspoon Bragg Aminos
2/3 cup celery, sliced
1 cup vegetable of choice

Brown cubed lamb on all sides in oil in heavy, deep skillet. Add water, seasonings and vegetables (onion, celery, potato, turnips, carrots, etc.). Simmer slowly for 2 hours or until tender. Serves 8.

Ten little two-letter words of action . . .

If it is to be, It is up to me!

FROM FINLAND

Finnish Fruit Soup

1 *cup prunes*
1 *cup apricots*
½ *cup raisins*
½ *cup currants*

1 *tablespoon unflavored gela-*
tin
¼ *cup honey*
2 *quarts water*

Wash fruits and cover with water. Soak overnight. Drain, saving water. Dice fruit and cook, using two parts retained water to one part fruit. Add honey and cook until fruit is very soft. Add gelatin that has been softened in a little cold water. Chill, beat, and serve. Serves 6 persons.

Fish and Turnips

2 *small white fish, boned*
2 *cups boiled yellow turnips*
3 *tablespoons chopped onion*
3 *tablespoons melted butter*
2 *cups milk*

3 *beaten eggs*
½ *teaspoon Bragg Aminos*
⅓ *cup whole-wheat toast*
crumbs

Place half of boned, skinned fish flat in buttered casserole. Sauté onion in 1 tablespoon butter until golden brown. Add turnips, eggs, Bragg Liquid Aminos . . . and mix thoroughly. Place a layer of this mixture on top of fish. Sprinkle with whole-wheat toast crumbs and 1 tablespoon melted butter. Put half of boned skinned fish on top as second layer. Again place a layer of turnip and egg mixture on top. Top again with remaining whole-wheat toast crumbs and melted butter. Pour milk around edges. Bake in a moderate oven (about 350°F.) for 40 minutes until browned on top. Serves 6.

FROM INDIA

A large portion of the people of India are vegetarians and are probably more adept at serving a wide variety of vegetarian foods than almost any other nation. They use coconut milk and ginger root abundantly, and prepare many curry dishes. One of their basic foods, the lentil, is one of our finest protein legumes.

Indian Eggplant

2 *cups diced eggplant*	1 *sprig lemon balm, minced*
4 *tablespoons lemon juice*	1 *teaspoon minced mint*
1½ *cups water*	¼ *teaspoon cayenne*
⅛ *teaspoon sage*	¼ *cup vegetable oil*
¼ *teaspoon thyme*	½ *teaspoon Bragg Aminos*
1 *teaspoon minced parsley*	

Place eggplant in water with herbs and 2 tablespoons of lemon juice. Cook until eggplant is tender; mix oil with two tablespoons lemon juice, cayenne pepper. Serve over eggplant after cooking. Serves 6.

Indian Curry Powder

1 *tablespoon turmeric*	¾ *teaspoon cardamom*
1 *tablespoon cumin*	¾ *teaspoon chili*
1 *tablespoon coriander*	¾ *teaspoon poppy seed*
½ *tablespoon pepper*	½ *tablespoon dry ginger*
¾ *teaspoon fennel*	

Try to buy all your ingredients ground to a fine powder. If you cannot, mix all ingredients thoroughly and grind to a fine powder in a mortar.

FROM HOLLAND

The Low Countries, the Netherlands and Belgium, have popularized the salad almost as much as has their neighbor France. Years of trade with their colonies in the Far East have accustomed them to the use of spices for flavoring, and as a rule their food has hidden delicate fragrances and nuances. Like their Scandinavian neighbors, they are a little too fond of pickling, smoking, and processing their meats, and perhaps overcooking a great many of their foods. Their best Health dishes are on the hearty side.

Dutch Vegetable Soup

1 *large soup bone*	½ *large turnip, diced*
cold water	½ *carrot, diced*
1 *cup tomatoes*	½ *onion, sliced*
1 *cup dried lima beans*	½ *teaspoon Bragg Aminos*
1 *cup grated corn*	½ *teaspoon whole-wheat flour*
1 *cup chopped cabbage*	¼ *cup milk*

Wash soup bone thoroughly, cover with cold water, and boil slowly for several hours. Skim off fat and add vegetables. Season to taste. Mix the flour with milk and stir into soup. Cook for one hour and serve hot. Serves 5.

Nutmeg Fish Cakes

1 *cup flaked and chopped cooked white fish of any kind*	6 *tablespoons butter*
	⅓ *teaspoon Bragg Aminos*
	½ *teaspoon nutmeg*
⅓ *cup soft whole-wheat bread crumbs*	¼ *cup scalded milk*
1 *beaten egg*	

Mix fish, bread crumbs, egg, Bragg Liquid Aminos and nutmeg. Shape into cakes. Sauté in 4 tablespoons melted butter until golden brown. Butter casserole generously with 2 tablespoons butter. Place fish cakes in casserole. Pour in milk and bake in moderate oven for 30 minutes. Serves 4.

THE SOUTH SEA ISLANDS

In the South Sea Islands, before the coming of the white man, Polynesians lived on an almost perfect Health food diet. To a certain extent that appetite has been depraved today, but the abundance of natural foods in the islands has made them almost an economic necessity in the diet. This is certainly fortunate for the Polynesian, who has but to draw on nature's generous supply to have his table loaded with luxury.

Tahitian Coconut Cream

Drain milk from coconut. Grind coconut meat. Combine milk and ground coconut. Allow to stand for 1 hour. Mix thoroughly and regrind or run through juice extractor. Coconut cream not only is a delicious beverage but can be used over fruit dessert. Coconut can be thoroughly broken up in a liquefier.

Malana Banana Poi

Mash banana; add grated coconut and honey to taste. Serve with cold coconut cream.

Rarotonga Coconut and Banana Whip

Whip coconut cream (or dairy cream as a substitute) with mashed banana and grated coconut to a stiff froth. Flavor with vanilla and season to taste with honey.

The longer you live the "Bragg Health Life"... the less prepared sweets will appeal to your taste buds! You will enjoy more fresh fruits and not the prepared pastries, desserts, jams, jellies, etc., even though they are prepared with natural ingredients, honey, etc., still it is best to keep your meals as simple, natural as possible!

— Patricia Bragg

Chapter 20

Candies

Peanut or Nut Honey Brittle

1 cup raw honey	*2 tbs salt-free butter*
1/2 cup raw brown sugar	*2 cups chopped raw peanuts*
1/2 cup molasses	*1/2 teaspoon soda*

Boil honey gently for 3 minutes, stirring constantly to prevent burning. Add raw sugar and molasses and continue to cook, stirring constantly until mixture is completely dissolved and syrup is thick, or when a few drops of syrup tested in cold water will form a hard ball. Remove from heat. Add soda and butter and stir until well blended. Add nuts and stir until well mixed. For variety add a few almonds, cashews and sunflower seeds to part of the mixture. Pour out in a thin sheet on a buttered slab or plate. Crack into sections when stiff.

Sugar Maple Creams

2/3 cup 100% maple syrup	*1 egg white (fertile)*
2 cups raw brown sugar	*1 teaspoon pure vanilla*
6 tablespoons hot water	*1 cup chopped nut meats*

Stir the maple syrup, raw sugar and water over slow heat until dissolved. Cook these ingredients quickly, without stirring, to the thread stage (238° F.). Beat egg white until stiff. Pour the syrup slowly on the egg white, beating constantly. Add the vanilla and nut meats. When candy is too stiff to stir, flatten it out on a greased tin. When cold, cut into squares.

California Carob Dates

¾ *lb. dates*
4 *squares carob*
⅓ *cup honey*

1½ *tablespoons boiling water*
½ *teaspoon vanilla extract*

Wipe the dates and extract the pits through a small lengthwise slit. . . . . Grate the carob into a small saucepan; add sweetening, boiling water, and vanilla. Heat without boiling until smooth, keeping mixture fluid by setting saucepan in a pan of boiling water. Fill dates with the carob mixture, gently pressing the edges together. Let stand to harden.

Carob Maple Fudge

¾ *cup maple sugar*
½ *cup honey*
4 *teaspoons butter*

5 *squares chipped carob*
½ *cup cream*
⅓ *cup shredded coconut*
⅓ *cup chopped nut meats*

Place the sweetening, butter, carob and cream. . . . . .in saucepan. Cook, stirring constantly, to 240°F., or to the soft-ball stage. Remove from heat, add the coconut, and beat until creamy. Pour into buttered pan, sprinkle nuts over the top, and mark into squares when cool.

Carob Molasses Caramels

2 *cups honey*
⅔ *cup butter*
⅔ *cup milk*

⅔ *cup unsulphured*
molasses
4 *squares chipped carob*
1 *teaspoon vanilla extract*

Place the sweetening, butter, milk, and carob. . . . .in a saucepan and cook, stirring constantly, to 252°F., or to the hard-ball stage. Add the extract and pour into buttered pans. When cool, cut into pieces with buttered scissors.

Nut Dreams

1⅞ *cups molasses*	1¼ *teaspoons almond extract*
1 *cup honey*	1 *cup pecan nut meats*
1 *cup butter*	1 *cup hickory nut meats*
2¼ *cups figs, chopped*	1 *cup walnut meats*
1¼ *teaspoons vanilla extract*	1 *cup Brazil nut meats*
1¼ *teaspoons lemon extract*	1 *cup cashew nuts*

Place the molasses and honey or raw sugar in a saucepan and cook, stirring constantly, to 260°F. or to the hard-ball stage. Add the butter and continue to cook, stirring constantly to 280°F., or to the soft-crack stage. Add the figs, extracts, and the nuts broken in small pieces. Pour into a well-buttered mold or pan. Allow to stand in a cool place for 12 hours or more. Turn out and cut slices. Wrap the slices in waxed paper.

Honey Nut Divinity

1½ *cups honey*	2 *egg whites*
1 *cup boiling water*	1 *teaspoon almond extract or*
4 *tablespoons butter*	*vanilla, as preferred*
	almonds or pecan nut meats

Place the sweetening, boiling water, and butter. . . . . .in a saucepan, stirring until dissolved. Cook slowly to 240°F., or to the soft-ball stage. Pour the syrup over the egg whites, beaten stiff, beating constantly. Add the extract and beat until creamy. Drop on waxed paper and decorate with nut meats.

California Sea Foam

1½ *cups brown or raw sugar*	1 *egg white*
⅜ *cup water*	½ *teaspoon vanilla extract*

Dissolve the brown or raw sugar in the water. . . . .Cook without stirring to 225°F., or to the hard-ball stage. Remove from heat and pour gradually over beaten egg whites, beating constantly. Add vanilla extract. Continue beating until candy cools and will hold its shape. Then drop by spoonfuls on waxed paper, or spread into buttered pan and mark in squares.

Persian Bonbons

1 *lb. dates*   1 *lb. nut meats*
1 *lb. raisins*   coconut

Use fresh, moist fruit. Run all ingredients through the meat-grinder and knead as for a dough. Pat out on a coconut-covered board, cut with small cookie-cutter, and roll in coconut. Wrap in waxed paper when dry.

Toasted Almonds

1½ *cups blanched almonds*
¾ *cup peanut or soy oil*

Cover the almonds with boiling water. Let them stand 2 minutes. Drain. Cover with cold water. Rub off skins and dry on a towel. Heat the oil in a small, heavy skillet and add enough nut meats at a time to cover the bottom of the pan. Stir until delicately browned. Remove from the oil, drain on absorbent paper. Repeat until all the nut meats are used.

Molasses Coconut Chews

½ *cup honey*   7 *teaspoons butter*
¾ *cup unsulphured molasses*   2½ *cups shredded coconut*
4 *teaspoons lemon juice*

Combine first 4 ingredients. Stir over low heat until mixture boils. Cook to 240°F. (soft-ball stage when tested in cold water). Add coconut. Drop from a teaspoon on waxed paper.

Raisin-Peanut Clusters

⅔ *cup unsulphured molasses*   4 *tablespoons butter*
½ *cup honey*   2⅔ *cups shelled peanuts*
1⅓ *teaspoons lemon juice*   1⅓ *cups seedless raisins*

Combine molasses, honey . . . . . . and lemon juice in a saucepan. Cook to 250°F. (hard-ball stage when tested in cold water). Remove from heat, add butter, stir until butter combines with syrup. Stir in peanuts and raisins. Drop by teaspoons on waxed paper. If candy hardens while working with it, set over very low heat and stir vigorously until soft.

Raisin and Nut Winks

¾ *cup maple sugar*   ¾ *cup raisins*
⅓ *cup water*   ⅓ *cup chopped nuts*

Boil sugar and water until they form a firm ball when tried in cold water. Chop the raisins and nuts and add them to the syrup. Cook until stiff enough not to run. Drop by teaspoon on oiled pan ½ inch apart to cool.

"Give us, Lord, a bit of sun,
A bit of work and a bit of fun.
Give us, in all struggle and sputter,
Our daily whole grain bread and a bit of nut butter.
Give us health, our keep to make
And a bit to spare for others' sake.
Give us, too, a bit of song
And a tale and a book, to help us along.
Give us, Lord, a chance to be
Our goodly best for ourselves and others
'Til all men learn to live as brothers."

— *An Old English Prayer*

"To preserve health is a moral and religious duty, for health is the basis for all social virtues. We can no longer be useful when not well."
— Dr. Samuel Johnson, Father of Dictionaries

God sends the food, man by refining and processing foods destroys its nutritional value. Eat only God's natural foods.—Patricia Bragg

Chapter 21

Drink Health the Juice Way
Live Raw Juices For Health Power

ALL OVER THE United States we hear about "cocktail hours" where beautifully colored alcoholic creations are used to produce new thrills, stimulate jaded appetites and bolster failing spirits.

We have a new kind of "cocktail," thanks to my dad Paul C. Bragg. It is not made of whisky, gin, rum or other alcoholic substance. There isn't a pickled cherry to be found in one of them. These live, recharging juices are made from fresh, organically grown vegetables and ripe fruits — the very life-blood of the plant – to boost your energy and immune levels. Dad imported the first hand juicers from Europe and with the Bragg Crusades introduced juice therapy across America. There is no liquor on the face of the earth so satisfying as the fresh live juice cocktail. Not only is it delicious but there is something more — the satisfaction and nourishment of the billions of cells that make up your body. When people take to the health cocktail habit, they are putting the plants' liquid life into their bodies to supercharge their health.

When we consider that fruits and vegetables have been grown naturally by solar energy (sunshine), they contain all of the elements that the sun and earth have buried deep into their fibrous cells, they are live cell foods. Juicing is a convenient and inexpensive method of obtaining the most concentrated form of nutrition available from the whole plant foods.

Select & Prepare Organic Foods for Juicing

Demand and buy organically grown fruits and vegetables whenever possible because commercial produce can contain deadly pesticides and petrochemical fertilizers. Yearly over 2.6 billion pounds of pesticides are dumped on American food crops. Choose deep-colored, ripe, firm fruits and fresh healthy vegetables. Use both the leaves and stems as well as the body of the vegetable. They yield an abundance of organic minerals. The tops of the carrots, for instance, contain phosphorus.

Because sprays of pesticides and herbicides are used on so many commercially grown fruits and vegetables, be sure to wash and scrub thoroughly with biodegradable soap as described on page 84.

Fruit and Vegetable Health Power Drinks

Raw, live fruit and vegetable juices can be purchased fresh from most Health Food Stores or prepared at home with one of the new wonderful juicers on the market. These health juices can be used full strength or diluted with distilled water individually or blended as below ... with vegetables and tomato combinations try adding a dash of Bragg Liquid Aminos or herbs — makes a delicious health drink.

In using herbs in these drinks, use 1 to 2 fresh leaves or pinch of dried herbs. A pinch of Dulse (seaweed), rich in protein and iron, is delicious with vegetable juice.

Here are some Powerful Juice Combinations:

1. *Beet, celery, alfalfa sprouts*
2. *Cabbage, celery and apple*
3. *Cabbage, cucumber, celery, tomato, spinach and basil*
4. *Tomato, carrot and mint*
5. *Carrot, celery, watercress, garlic and wheatgrass*
6. *Grapefruit, orange and lemon*
7. *Beet, parsley, celery, carrot, mustard green, cabbage, garlic*
8. *Beet, celery, dulse and carrot*
9. *Cucumber, carrot and parsley*
10. *Watercress, cucumber, garlic celery, carrot, kale or chard*
11. *Asparagus, carrot, and mint*
12. *Carrot, celery, parsley and cabbage, onion, sweet basil*
13. *Carrot and coconut milk*
14. *Carrot, broccoli, lemon, cayenne*
15. *Carrot, cauliflower, rosemary*
16. *Apple, carrot, radish, ginger*
17. *Apple, pineapple and mint*
18. *Apple, papaya and grapes*
19. *Papaya, cranberries and apple*
20. *Leafy greens, broccoli, apple*
21. *Grape, cherry and apple*
22. *Watermelon*
23. *Passionfruit and pineapple*

Healthy Herbal Teas

There is a wide variety of healthy, delicious herbal teas available in bulk and tea bags at Health Food Stores. Brew as you would regular teas in glass or stainless steel.

Carob Delight

1 cup milk or soy milk
1 teaspoon honey
1½ teaspoons powdered carob

1 mashed banana, or
   3 teaspoons coconut powder
½ teaspoon soybean milk
   powder
1 teaspoon honey

Put all in liquefier, or mix with hand beater. In a few minutes you will have a delicious drink. A meal in itself. Serves 1.

Grapefruit Foam

Beat an egg white until stiff. Add 2 teaspoons honey and beat thoroughly. Add 3 cups grapefruit juice and pour into glasses. Sprinkle with a dash of cinnamon or nutmeg. Makes 4 servings.

Mint Tinkle

¾ cup water
⅓ cup honey
18 sprigs mint, chopped
¾ cup fresh lime juice

3 cups unsweetened grape juice
¾ cup fresh lime juice

Combine water, honey; simmer 8 minutes. Pour over the chopped mint leaves. Cool; stir into combined fruit juices. Pour over ice in six glasses. Serve right away.

Apricot Ambrosia Punch

⅓ lb. dried unsulphured
   apricots
⅓ cup honey
3 cups fresh orange juice

⅔ cup fresh lemon juice
2 cups unsweetened apple juice

Cook apricots until tender; then press fruit and juice through sieve. Add honey and fruit juices and mix well. Chill. Just before serving, pour over ice in punch bowl. Garnish with orange and lemon slices. Makes 16 punch-cup servings.

Apple Lemonade

6 *cups unsweetened apple*   *fresh mint sprigs*
   juice   ⅜ *cup honey*
1⅛ *cups unstrained lemon juice*

Combine apple juice and lemon juice. Add honey and stir until the
sugar dissolves. Fill 5 or 6 glasses about ⅔ full with the apple lemon-
ade; then add enough ice to fill the glasses. Place a sprig of fresh
mint leaves in each glass. Serves 8.

Tomato Buttermilk

Mix ½ cup chilled tomato juice and ⅔ cup chilled buttermilk.

Grape Cooler

1 *cup honey*   2 *cups orange juice*
3 *cups water*   1 *cup lemon juice*
2 *cups grape juice*

Make a syrup of the honey and water; let cool. Add fruit juices. Pour
over ice in pitcher or tall glasses. Serves 12.

Pineapple Mint Julep

4 *sprigs fresh mint*   2¼ *cups unsweetened pineapple*
½ *cup honey*   *juice*
½ *cup fresh lemon juice*

Wash mint leaves, bruise with spoon; cover with honey. Add lemon
juice and let stand about 15 minutes. Add pineapple juice and mix.
Pour over ice in pitcher or tall glasses. Garnish with sprigs of mint.
Makes about 6 glasses.

Anise Milk

1 *quart milk*   1 *teaspoon aniseed, crushed*
1 *tablespoon honey*

Scald milk. Add honey and anise. Serve either hot or cold. Serves 4.

Honey Fruit Punch

2 cups distilled water
2 cups unsweetened grape juice
1/4 cup raw honey
1/2 cup fresh lemon juice
1/4 cup cherry juice
1/2 cup fresh orange juice
1 cup pineapple juice
1 ripe mashed banana

Blend thoroughly with an ice cube to chill. Serves 4-6.

Barley Water

Wash 1/4 cup natural barley and soak overnight. Drain. Add 1 quart distilled water and boil gently until the barley is thoroughly done and about 1-1/2 cups of liquid remain. Strain and serve plain or add soy milk and season to taste with honey, pure vanilla, etc.

Spiced Mint Tea

1 cinnamon stick
8 whole allspice
8 whole cloves
3 bags mint tea or
3 tbsp mint tea leaves
3-1/3 cups distilled water
1/4 cup raw honey
2/3 cup orange juice
1/3 cup lemon juice
1/3 cup grape juice

Combine water, spices and tea leaves or bags in saucepan, bring to bubbling boil. Remove from heat and steep for 10 minutes then strain. Add honey, stirring until well mixed. Cover and cool. Add fresh juices and serve in chilled glasses. Serves 4-6.

Bragg Health "Pep" Drink

Prepare in blender, add ice cube if desired chilled. Serves 2.

2 glasses fresh orange juice (fresh squeezed) or unsweetened pineapple, apple, cherry, cranberry, grape or tropical fruit juices (papaya, passionfruit, kiwi, etc.) or just pure distilled water is fine.

1-2 ripe bananas or papaya
1/3 tsp pectin powder
1/3 tsp vitamin C powder
1 tsp lecithin granules
1 tsp Brewers yeast flakes
1 tsp wheat germ vacuum-pack
1/2 tsp psyllium husk powder
1 tbsp raw oat or rice bran
1 tbsp soy protein powder
1/3 tsp chia or sesame seeds
1/3 tsp flax seeds, ground
1 tsp raw sunflower
   or pumpkin seeds
1/2 tsp honey (optional)
1/2 tsp vitamin powder (opt.)
1/2 tsp raisins (optional)

Note: In summer you can add fresh fruit in season - peaches, strawberries, berries, apricots or any other fresh fruit instead of bananas or papaya. In winter try (sugar-free) frozen fruits.

FOOD FOR THOUGHT

The Great Sin – Fear
The Best Day – Today
The Best Town – Where You Succeed
The Best Work – What You Like
The Best Play – Work
The Greatest Stumbling Block – Egotism
The Greatest Mistake – Giving Up
The Most Expensive Indulgence – Hate
The Greatest Trouble-maker – One Who Talks Too Much
The Most Ridiculous Trait – False Pride
The Most Dangerous Man – The Liar
The Greatest Need – Common Sense
The Greatest Thought – God and Mother Nature
The Greatest Wealth – Health
The Greatest Gift You Can Give or Receive – Love
The Greatest Race To Win – A Long Vigorous Life
Man's Greatest Companion and Friend – Good Books
Your Enemies – Envy, Greed, Self-Indulgence, Self-Pity
Life's Greatest Adventure – Growth on the Physical, Mental
  and Spiritual Plane
Most Disgusting – A Show Off
Most Repulsive – A Bully
Most Overbearing Manner – Arrogance
Man's Greatest Stumbling Block – Ignorance
The Greatest Sieve – Before You Say Anything, Say To Yourself,
  Is It Kind? Is It True? Is It Necessary?

THE WISEST PERSON

One Who Always Does What They Think And Feel Is Right.
Be A Wise Person!

Chapter 22

Canapes
Health Appetizers

"Appetizers" are a misnomer and, contrary to popular belief, do not point up the appetite but rather dull it. The very best health appetizer for a meal is a small glass of fresh fruit or vegetable juice or a delicious healthy salad. But for a gala occasion the so-called appetizers, or canapes, are nice to serve with fruit or vegetable juice cocktails, and they can be prepared the health way.

Canapes should never be substantial. They should be small, spicy tidbits and of distinctive flavor to pique the activity of the gastric juices. If they are to be served just prior to a meal, the soup course of the meal should be omitted. Ordinarily canapes contain some fatty substances—cheeses, spreads, and oils. To counteract, mix in some lecithin granules (a fat emulsifier). Soup, immediately following the canapes, adds additional fatty substances (cholesterol), causing a too rapid and false satisfaction which further dulls the appetite. Always start your dinner meal with a health salad, then have soup if desired.

Delicious health canapes can be made without the usual smoked, pickled or processed meats or fish. Most of the canape tidbits to follow may be served on small squares of dry, toasted whole-grain bread or crackers.

Knobby Cheese Balls

Blend or mix Tofu (well drained) or cream cheese, or dry cottage cheese with green and red bell pepper, watercress, chopped fine, cilantro or pinch of salad herbs. Form into small balls. Roll in poppy or sesame seeds, insert toothpick in each one and serve on bed of lettuce.

 ## Cheese Puffs

1 lb hard cheese, grated   *4 tbs butter, melted (salt-free)*
1/2 tsp powdered mustard   *4 egg whites, beaten stiff*
3 tbs Rumford baking powder

Grate cheese fine, add all other ingredients, and stir; add whites of eggs last. Place on whole-grain rounds of toast or wafers. Toast under broiler to puff up, serve while hot. Serves 8-10.

Snappy Cheese Balls

Use nippy cheese. Cut and form into balls or cubes. Roll in celery or mustard seed. Place one small leaf of watercress or mint on top of each ball or cube and stab into place with a toothpick. Serve on bed of lettuce or stick in large grapefruit.

Stuffed Celery

2 tbs Roquefort or soy cheese   *2 tbs tofu, well-drained*
1/4 tsp Bragg Aminos

Mash ingredients and blend thoroughly. Spread mixture on inside of celery stalk. Sprinkle top of cheese with celery, caraway, sesame, or anise seeds. (Do not combine seeds; use only one for your flavoring.)

Variations for Stuffed Celery

- Health unhydrogenated peanut or nut butter with minced apple.
- Mash avocado, add pinch minced chives and salad herbs.
- Any natural cheese blend with chives, parsley and salad herbs.
- Blend tofu or soy cheese with mustard and minced onion.

Avocado Paste

Blend avocado, minced chives and dash of Bragg Aminos. Sprinkle with lemon juice and mustard, sesame or caraway seeds.

Artichoke Hearts

Stuff artichoke hearts with mixture of soy or tofu cheese and whole-grain bread crumbs. Sprinkle with Bragg Aminos and celery, poppy or mustard seed. Place under broiler for few moments until brown. Cut in quarters, stab with toothpick, and serve on bed of lettuce or cabbage.

Grape Nippies

Select large, firm green grapes. Slit, remove seeds. Fill center with mixture of ¾ cream cheese to ¼ Roquefort cheese, with a few drops of lemon juice for blending. Remove excess paste around edges. Pierce through with long toothpick. Chill before serving.

Herb Toast

½ cup melted butter

¼ teaspoon of each of the following: chives, basil, marjoram, thyme

Allow herbs to stand in butter for 30 minutes. Reheat butter. Saturate several slices whole-wheat bread. Place in oven to brown, and toast slowly for about 20 to 25 minutes. Remove, cut in small pieces and serve.

Hot Clam or Oyster Canapés

2 dozen large clams or oysters in shell
1 full cup buttered whole-wheat bread crumbs
2 tablespoons grated nippy cheese

1 tablespoon lemon juice
3 tablespoons butter
¼ cup clam or oyster liquor
½ teaspoon chives
½ teaspoon parsley
⅛ teaspoon chervil
⅛ teaspoon thyme

Remove clams or oysters from shell. Set aside one dozen of the best-looking half shells. Remove neck and hard part from oysters or clams. Mash and blend with all other ingredients. Wash thoroughly the shells you have saved. Stuff with mixture; bake in oven until hot and brown. Serve in shells.

Cheese with Sardine Bits

Melt nippy cheese; cool. Blend in with the sardines and spread on toast squares.

Mushrooms

Broil mushrooms covered with butter and roll in chopped chives. Stab with toothpick.

Lobster, Crab or Shrimp Bits

Broil bits of lobster, crab, or shrimp dipped in butter until golden brown, turning frequently. Serve plain or sprinkled with very tiny bits of basil. Stab with toothpick and serve.

Asparagus Tips

Roll asparagus tips in grated nippy cheese and brown under broiler. Stab with toothpick and serve.

Camembert Capers

Spread small toasted squares with Camembert cheese, dot with 2 or 3 capers, place under broiler for a few moments.

Jack LaLanne and Patricia Bragg at Jack's new health retreat home at beautiful Morro Bay, California.

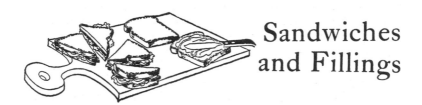

Chapter 23

Sandwiches and Fillings

Peanut Butter and Raisin Sandwich

Wash and chop or grind ½ cup raisins. Combine with ½ cup peanut butter, adding enough orange-blossom honey to moisten. Makes 6 sandwiches.

Celery and Peanut Butter Sandwich

Combine ⅓ cup chopped celery, ½ cup peanut butter, 2 tablespoons Health dressing. Makes 6 sandwiches.

Cottage Cheese and Vegetable Sandwich

Combine ½ cup cottage cheese, 3 tablespoons radishes, chopped fine, 3 tablespoons celery, chopped fine, 3 tablespoons cucumber, chopped fine, ⅛ teaspoon paprika, 1 tablespoon French tomato dressing. Mix until well blended. Makes 4 sandwiches.

Egg and Olive Sandwiches

Chop 3 hard-cooked eggs, and add ⅛ teaspoon paprika, and 12 sliced ripe olives. Mix 3 tablespoons of Health mayonnaise and 1 tablespoon of lemon juice, and add to egg and olive mixture. Toss together lightly. Makes 4 sandwiches.

Sliced Egg and Cucumber Sandwich

Slice 3 hard-cooked eggs. Combine ⅓ cup lemon juice, 2 tablespoons water, 1 teaspoon Bragg Liquid Aminos. . .and 16 to 20 thin slices of cucumber, half onion, minced, 1/4 cup parsley minced and pinch of salad herbs or fresh sweet basil. Mix well and marinate about 30 minutes. On whole-wheat, rye or multi-grain toast spread health mayonnaise, then arrange cucumber and egg mixture on top of toasted slices. Top with watercress, cabbage or lettuce. Makes delicious bread–lettuce sandwiches or topping for salads. Makes 4 sandwiches.

Tofu and Grated Vegetable Sandwich

Use 1 package soft tofu (well drained), add 1/4 cup grated carrot and / or mix zucchini, chopped cauliflower, broccoli, celery or any fresh vegetable of choice. Optional - add pinch of sunflower seeds. Mix with health mayonnaise and seasonings as desired. Makes 4 sandwiches.

Chopped Raw Carrot and Raisin Sandwich

Grate 2 raw carrots fine. Add 2 tablespoons chopped raisins and add enough health mayonnaise to moisten. Makes 2 sandwiches.

Tuna Fish, Almond and Celery Sandwich

Combine 1 can water-packed tuna fish and 1/2 cup celery, chopped fine, 1 teaspoon sliced almonds or sesame seeds and pinch of salad herbs. Add health mayonnaise to moisten. This also makes a great dressing-topping for salads. Makes 3 sandwiches.

Chicken and Vegetable Sandwich

Mix small amounts of chopped or grated celery, bell pepper, watercress, onions, cilantro, parsley, carrots, broccoli or any fresh vegetables desired. Add 3/4 cup chopped cooked chicken, combine with health mayonnaise or yogurt and seasonings as desired. Spread on sandwiches or fill pita pockets. Makes 4 sandwiches.

Tofu or Cream Cheese and Nut Sandwich

Use 1 cup soft tofu (well drained) or cream cheese or mix. Add 2 tablespoons minced raw nut or seed meats and some minced chives and onions. Spread on whole-grain toast, crackers, or fill pita pockets. Season as desired. Makes 4 sandwiches.

Banana Sandwich

Spread whole-grain toast with health mayonnaise or yogurt, then arrange sliced ripe bananas, top with raw nut or seed meats and honey if desired. Cover with lettuce or watercress, optional.

Peanut or Nut Butter and Banana Sandwich

Mash 1 ripe banana and work into 1/2 cup peanut or nut butter. If mixture is not thin enough add lowfat yogurt, mashed tofu (well drained), soy or nut milk. Makes 4 sandwiches.

Date Nut Seed Sandwich

Put 2 cups pitted dates and 1 cup raw nuts and seeds through grinder. Mix well with 1/4 cup pineapple juice. Makes 6 sandwiches.

Famous Roquefort Cheese Sandwich

Blend equal parts of Roquefort cheese and soft tofu (well-drained) or soy or cream cheese, moistened with a little health mayonnaise. Spread this on slices of whole-grain, lightly toasted bread. For variety top with sliced tomato, olives, red pepper, etc. Sprinkle with chopped parsley and watercress.

Sandwich Loaf

Take a loaf of unsliced whole-grain bread and cut horizontally into slices 1/2- to 3/4-inch thick. Olive oil or butter each slice lightly. Spread bottom slices with desired fillings (you may vary as desired with tofu or soy spread, tuna, date nut, etc.), cover with another slice and continue in the same fashion until loaf is complete. Spread top and sides of loaf lightly with soy or cream cheese softened with yogurt. One loaf usually requires three 3-ounce packages of soy or cream cheese and about 1/4 cup yogurt or soy cream. Chill loaf before serving. Garnish platter with lettuce, watercress, radish roses, tomato slices, etc. Decorate top with nuts, sliced olives, pimiento, etc. Cut loaf into thick slices just before serving. One sandwich loaf will yield 8 to 12 servings.

Sandwich and Pita Pocket Fillings

Egg filling: Combine 3 hard-boiled eggs (chopped fine), a little grated onion, minced parsley, cilantro and a dash of Bragg Liquid Aminos and health mayonnaise.

◇◇

Date filling: Grind 1 cup dates and 4 tablespoons nuts using sharp knife, coffee grinder or food processor. Add enough fresh orange juice to make the mixture of spreading consistency. A little fresh lemon or lime juice added will take away the too-sweet taste.

Nut butter and grated vegetables or fruits of choice: Combine nut butter and grated vegetables or fruit (raw carrots, celery, zucchini, etc. or apples, pears, bananas, etc.), season to taste.

Tuna: Drain excess water or oil from tuna fish. Flake fish and mix with 1/4 cup each of chopped celery and nuts, moisten with a dash of Bragg Aminos and lemon juice and mayonnaise if desired.

Raw vegetables: Mince 1/4 cup currants and 1/2 cup each shredded cabbage, carrots and apples. Add 1 tablespoon lemon juice and Bragg Aminos to taste. Moisten with dressing if desired.

Chicken: To 1 cup chopped chicken, add desired amount of celery, cucumber, olives, radishes and almonds chopped fine. Season with dash Bragg Aminos and moisten with health soy mayonnaise or low-fat yogurt if desired.

Toppings, Sauces and Dressings

Combine 1/2 pound soy cheese or soft tofu (well-drained) with 1 tablespoon chopped chives and 2 tablespoons low-fat yogurt. Mix well.

*****

Cream together 1/2 cup soft tofu (drain well) and 3 oz. of low-fat yogurt or tofu yogurt.

*****

Combine together ripe avocado with 2 tablespoons distilled water, season with minced green onions and tops, lemon or lime juice and salsa sauce or a seasoning to taste (salad herbs, kelp powder, fresh garlic or a dash of Bragg Liquid Aminos).

*****

Combine 1/3 cup raw cashews with 1 tablespoon brown rice syrup and 1 cup distilled water. Blend on high for 3 minutes.

*****

Blend together ripe avocado with 1 cup organic white grape juice for a sweet avocado sauce.

Statistics show that degenerative ills are increasing at alarming rates and attacking people at increasingly early ages. It is time the fact be recognized that diet is largely responsible for this increase, and that sugar, coffee, salt, refined and chemicalized foods — and the lack of exercise — are the major culprits.

Chapter 24
Canning and Quick Freezing
the Health Way

Although fresh foods cannot be equaled for flavor and nutritional value, canned and frozen foods have their purpose too. They provide a full larder of important food materials during the sparse winter season when fresh varieties are not so readily available.

Not all economy in food conservation is practical, but preserving the super-abundance of the summer organic vegetable garden, sun-ripened, fruit-laden trees and many other delicacies you cannot get during the winter is true economy, especially when it's from your own garden. It is true that canned or frozen fruits and vegetables can be purchased in the market inexpensively, but many times you will find these are not of prime health quality. Their greatest fault lies in the fact that they are often loaded with preservatives, chemicals or heavy, refined sugar syrup. Such foods are not Health Foods. There are excellent ways to do your canning and freezing at home the Health Way. Here are some of the more natural methods.

Nature's Delicious Sweeteners

Nature has provided us with many outstanding sweeteners that are entirely, nutritionally wholesome. Raw honey, barley malt and brown rice syrups, concentrated fruit juices, 100% maple syrup, molasses, raw brown sugars and date sugar. Paul C. Bragg pioneered the use of date sugar granules by using California sun-dried dates which are high in fiber and rich in vitamins and minerals. These sweeteners have not gone through the devitalizing process of heavy refinement. They have retained their natural minerals and vitamins. These sweeteners are not loaded with concentrated carbohydrates that burden the body as does entirely refined white sugar. Of course, discretion must always be used in arranging sweeteners in the diet. Even though healthful sugars are energy foods and vital to the body, if used to excess they can be harmful.

Honey, from all counts, nutritionally is nature's ideal sweetener. This sweet is predigested by the bees and is rich in one of our most valuable sugars, levulose (a fruit sugar). (A bee spends a lifetime to make one teaspoon of honey!) Honeys are best raw and uncooked. Select with care as some of them have been treated commercially, adulterated with syrup or overly cooked for clearness

For baking or for cereals, a wide variety of honeys can be used. But for canning or preserving fruits, many fruits needs no sweetening. For those that do, only the mildest sweetener should be used or the strength of the honey flavor will cover up the fruit flavors in the finished product.

Freezing

Freezing is an excellent way to store foods for later consumption — if it's done properly. Freezing foods must be done carefully to preserve the maximum amount of flavor and nutrition. Meat, fish, poultry, fruits and pre-cooked foods are quite easy to freeze. Vegetables mostly can be quick-frozen fresh without a quick dip in hot water (blanching) — most people blanch, but most often it's not necessary. Even taking the time to blanch, freezing takes a third to half the time and labor as canning.

The nutritional quality of foods that you freeze depends on the freshness of the foods, the temperature it is stored at in the freezer, and the manner in which frozen foods are thawed. Here are some tips for freezing and thawing foods.

First of all, make sure your freezer temperature is at 0°F. Use a freezer thermometer to check it. At warmer temperatures — even 10°F — the storage life of the food will be cut drastically.

Always let cooked food cool to room temperature before freezing. Chill soups rapidly over ice water. You can freeze stocks in ice cube trays for easy incremental addition to gravies and sauces. Main dishes are popular to freeze, but don't bother with starchy foods such as pastas — they cook quickly so prepare them as usual before eating. Don't freeze potatoes — add freshly cooked ones to soups before serving. Avoid freezing fried foods, as they tend to become rancid. Remember to slightly undercook foods that will be reheated later.

Excess air is the primary enemy of storage life and nutritional quality. Take great care in wrapping the items to be frozen. Foods wrapped poorly will suffer freezer burn (gray and white spots), which means the dry air of the freezer has drawn out some of the moisture. Use moisture-proof, airtight wrappings or use containers specifically designed for freezing. If there is ice inside the package, that means the item has been partially defrosted and then refrozen — something you want to avoid. Liquid foods must be stored in leakproof containers — be sure to leave enough room for expansion during freezing. It's a good idea to label each package and include the date frozen.

Quick freeze foods by placing them close to the outside freezer walls unstacked with air space all around them. You can stack items after they have been frozen 24 hours. Tray freeze cookies, pastries, crepes etc. by placing them unwrapped on a cookie sheet in the freezer until frozen. Then you can wrap them or put them in zip-lock freezer bags with date, etc., on label. They won't stick together so you can take as many as you want as you need them.

Always thaw foods in their original containers in the refrigerator to avoid spoilage. Foods thawed at room temperature have a higher risk of spoilage because micro-organisms, no longer inhibited by the cold, begin to grow again in the food. Use thawed food as soon as possible. Never refreeze food that has thawed completely. Defrosted food that has an off-odor should be thrown out.

Water-Pack Canning for Fruits

All fruit and fruit juices can be successfully canned without sugar. The sugar is used only to sweeten the food and does not keep it from spoiling. If you prefer to can by the water-pack method, your sweetening can be added at the time of serving, and any natural sweetening preferred can be used.

Precooking the fruit before packing will draw some of the juice out of the fruit and less sugar will be required to give the fruit the desired sweetness. All fruits may be canned without sugar simply by filling the jar to within 1/2 inch of the top with natural concentrated fruit juice or water; then process. There is no other change in the canning recipe. The sweeter fruits can be put up in their own juice and require little or no sweetening when served.

For All Methods of Canning

There are two principal methods of canning: the open kettle and the hot- or cold-pack method. (The latter method may include using a pressure cooker and steamer.) But there are some general steps to follow that apply regardless of method.

Two Hours from Garden to Can

All fresh fruits, vegetables, and meats contain substances called enzymes. They are valuable substances that bring about physiological changes in the food. They are the substances that bring about ripening and tenderizing of foods under nature's own influence. In other words, they are the developing factors in the foods. But valuable as they are, if they are allowed to go unchecked they cause decay and danger.

By storing foods in cold temperatures, the enzyme activity is somewhat checked, but it is not destroyed. The applied heat of canning destroys the enzyme activity entirely. For that reason food can be best preserved closest to its natural state if it is canned immediately after being picked or gathered.

The two-hour rule is an excellent one. If you can, can your foods within that period of time, you will be more assured of excellent quality. If that is impossible, your foods should be stored very carefully in a cool, well-ventilated location. Meats, if they are to be canned, should be kept in a refrigerator at 30° to 32°F. if they are to be held over for several days.

Dangerous Fermentation

Not all types of fermentation are dangerous, but they are all annoying because they cause spoilage. Food spoils when it comes into contact with unheated air. The bacteria yeasts and molds present in the food become extremely active under this exposure. Successful canning destroys them, but it must always be remembered that even after the canning process, food must be thoroughly protected from the air by a hermetic seal.

The most dangerous of the destructive bacteria is the *Bacillus botulinus*. These harmful elements are not destroyed in the canning process unless the processing is in every way adequate.

How to Avoid Dangerous Bacteria

A determination must first be made whether a food is acid or non-acid. These two classifications in terms of canning do not always carry the same meaning as they do in dietary terms. For canning purposes, the acid foods are considered the fruits, tomatoes, and rhubarb. The non-acid foods include practically all vegetables such as asparagus, peas, beans, and corn and also meat, fish, and poultry.

The acid foods may be canned by any of the three methods desired, but in order to prevent dangerous bacteria poisoning, the non-acid foods should be processed, preferably in a special cooker. The temperature applied should be from 240° to 250°F. at 10 to 15 pounds of steam pressure.

Safeguards in Using Home-Canned Foods

When opening jars of canned vegetables or meats, they should never be tasted before cooking.

If there is any doubt, never taste any canned food of any kind to see if it is spoiled. The small saving you will effect with the use of doubtful material is poor economy indeed.

Be certain the jars show no sign of leakage or fermentation.

If the liquid spurts when the jar is opened, do not use any of the contents of the jar.

The odor of canned food when opened should be fresh, pleasant, and characteristic of the product.

The food should be comparatively firm when opened and if the contents of the jar do not smell or look right, or the food is too soft or mushy, it should be discarded at once.

As an extra safeguard, be certain all the non-acid foods (this means all meats and all vegetables except tomatoes), are cooked to a boiling temperature at least 10 or 15 minutes in an open kettle before tasting or using in any way. This will avoid errors in judgment or detection when the jar is opened, as often the odors cannot be detected in the cold product but can be readily discovered when it is heated. If after you have boiled it, the food still does not smell or look right, do not taste it; discard it without tasting.

Open-Kettle Method

In the open-kettle method food is cooked until well done in an open kettle or pan as a means of killing the bacteria, and then packed, boiling hot, into a sterilized jar and sealed immediately. Only fruits, tomatoes, and some preserves can be cooked by this method. All other foods must be processed (or cooked) in the jar. I list this method here, although I do not feel it is as valuable as the hot- and cold-pack method because it sometimes causes loss of nutritional value before the jar is sealed, but it is the most practical method of canning for certain types of food.

1. Be certain you have first-class jars with no nicks, cracks, or

sharp edges. Wash them well in hot, soapy water and boil for at least 15 minutes in clear water. Scald them by pouring hot water over them and allow them to remain in the water until they are ready to use.

2. Carefully select fresh, firm products. Be sure they are at the proper state of ripeness, not overripe. Grade them according to size if uniformity is desired.

3. Prepare them according to recipe, and boil for the required length of time.

4. Fill one jar at a time to within ½ inch of the top with the boiling-hot product and liquid. Clean tops of jars and seal immediately, sealing each jar as filled and not waiting to seal a dozen jars at a time, or whatever number is being prepared. Place the rubber sealing band or sealing composition next to the glass and screw lid on over this tightly. Screw as tight as possible without using a mechanical aid.

5. Place jars on a cloth or towel and allow to cool in normal room temperature free from extreme heat, cold, or draft. It is not necessary to invert jars with sealing-compound lids. Jars with rubber rings may be set upside down to cool.

6. Test all jars thoroughly for seal when cool. For sealing-compound lids, take a spoon and tap the lids gently. If they are properly sealed, they will give a clear ringing note and there will be a slightly concave effect caused by the vacuum inside. If jars are not properly sealed, the sound will be dull and low in key. If the food touches the lid, the sound will be dull, but it will not be hollow or empty like that of the unsealed jar.

The Hot- and Cold-Pack Method

The cold-pack method is the process of placing the cold or raw product in the jar and then cooking it. The hot pack necessitates a short precooking time and then the boiling-hot product is placed in clean jars and cooked immediately. The hot pack is usually more successful for vegetables and meats.

1. Examine and wash jars as described in the steps for the open-kettle method.

2. Make proper selection of foods as described for the open-kettle method.

3. Prepare according to recipe.

4. Pack product into the clean jars not more than ½ inch from the top. An exception to this rule is corn, peas, lima beans, and

◇◇

meat. For these products fill the jars to within one inch of the top.

5. Add liquid.

For fruit: Syrup should be within 1½ inches of the top of the jar when fruit is packed cold; ½ inch of the top when the fruit is packed hot; for fruit juice or hot water to within ½ inch of the top.

For vegetables: Fill liquid to within ½ inch of the top of the jar. Seasoning may then be added.

For meat: For precooked meat, add 3 or 4 tablespoons of liquid. Meats packed raw do not require the addition of liquid.

6. Clean tops of jars and seal firmly as described for the open-kettle method.

7. Process the required length of time for the method of cooking used.

8. Remove the jars from the cooker or canner. Set the jars on cloth or towels and allow to cool at normal room temperature. Be sure the jars are not in a draft.

9. Test for correct seal.

How to Use the Pressure Cooker

The pressure cooker is an excellent utensil for canning, particularly for vegetables and meats and non-acid foods, as it gives a much greater margin of safety. However, if a pressure cooker is not available, other methods may be used, such as the hot-water bath and the steam cooker. These methods will be described later on.

Pressure cookers should be fitted with a rack in the bottom, a clean, tight cover, a petcock, and a pressure gauge.

1. Prepare and pack product according to directions for hot- and cold-pack canning.

2. Place rack in bottom of cooker and add boiling water to cover bottom of cooker to a depth of 1 to 2 inches.

3. Place the filled jars on the rack in the cooker. Prepare only enough jars at one time to fill the cooker. As soon as each jar is filled and cap adjusted, place it in the cooker. Do not allow jars to touch.

4. Adjust the cover of cooker and fasten securely by tightening opposite clamps or adjusting band.

5. Leave the petcock open until a jet of steam has been spurting from the petcock for 7 to 10 minutes. Then close petcock and start counting processing time from the minute the required amount

of pressure is reached on the pressure gauge. Keep pressure uniform throughout the processing period.

6. Process for required length of time (see timetables).

7. Remove cooker from the fire as soon as the processing time is up and allow the hand on the pressure gauge to return to zero. Then open petcock gradually.

8. Remove jars from cooker. Set jars on several thicknesses of cloth and allow to cool. Do not set hot jars in a draft.

9. Test for seal.

The U. S. Department of Agriculture recommends the use of a pressure cooker for canning non-acid vegetables and meats.

Hot-Water Bath

The hot-water bath is preferable for processing fruits and tomatoes. They are acid foods and can be canned safely at boiling temperatures and the texture and color of the finished product are better. A pressure cooker is recommended for processing vegetables, meats, and non-acid foods.

Equipment: A wash boiler or a large deep vessel that has a close-fitting cover may be used as a canner. The canner must be fitted with a rack made of laths, galvanized wire, or other perforated material. The rack must hold the jars at least ½ inch above the bottom of the canner. Have the water in the canner near the boiling-point when jars of food are placed in it.

Prepare and pack the product according to directions for hot and cold pack.

1. Place the filled jars on the rack in the canner far enough apart to allow the free circulation of water around them. The water should cover the jars at least one inch over the top. Start counting processing time as soon as water surrounding the jars begins to boil. Keep the water boiling for entire processing period. If water boils down, add sufficient boiling water to keep it at the required height.

2. Process the required length of time (see timetables).

3. As soon as the processing period is up, remove jars from the canner. Set jars on several thicknesses of cloth and allow to cool. Do not set hot jars in a draft.

4. Test for seal.

Steam Cooker

Start counting processing time when cooker is well filled with steam. Follow water-bath timetables.

Canning Timetable

VEGETABLES (see notes at end of timetable)	Hot-Water Bath—Time in minutes	Pressure Cooker	
		Minutes	Pounds
Artichokes	Wash, trim. Precook 5 minutes in water with a little vinegar. Pack.	180	40	10
Asparagus	Wash, precook 3 minutes. Pack.	180	40	10
Beans (string or wax)	Wash, string, cut or leave whole, precook 3 minutes. Pack.	180	40	10
Beans (lima)	Shell, grade, precook 3 minutes. Pack loosely to within 1 inch of top of jar.	180	55	10
Beets	Wash, leave roots and stems long, precook 15 minutes, slip skins, pack.	120	40	10
Brussels sprouts or cabbage	Remove outer leaves, wash, precook 5 minutes. Pack.	120	35	10
Carrots, Kohlrabi	Wash, peel, precook 5 minutes. Pack.	120	35	10
Cauliflower or Broccoli	Remove outside leaves, wash, precook 4 minutes. Pack.	150	35	10

Corn on cob	Remove husks, precook 3 to 5 minutes. Pack.	210	80	10
Corn	Remove husks. Cut from cob. Precook 3 to 5 minutes. Pack loosely to within 1 inch of top of jar.	210	80	10
Eggplant	Peel, cut in slices or strips, precook 5 minutes. Pack.	120	40	10
Greens (all kinds)	Wash thoroughly. Steam or precook, to wilt. Pack loosely.	180	60	10
Mushrooms	Clean, wash, cut large ones, precook 3 minutes. Pack loosely.	180	60	10
Okra	Wash, precook 3 minutes, pack.	180	40	10
Onions	Peel, wash, precook 5 minutes. Pack.	180	40	10
Parsnips, Turnips, or Rutabagas	Wash, pare, precook 5 minutes. Pack.	90	35	10
Peas	Shell, grade, using only young fresh peas, precook 3 to 7 minutes. Pack loosely to within 1 inch of top of jar.	180	60	10
Peppers (green, sweet)	Wash, remove seed pod, precook 3 minutes. Pack.	120	35	5

Canning Timetable (*continued*)

VEGETABLES (*see notes at end of timetable*)	Hot-Water Bath—Time in minutes	Pressure Cooker	
		Minutes	Pounds
(*continued*)			
Peppers (pimiento) — Place in moderate oven 6 to 8 minutes or 1 to 2 minutes in hot oil or 12 to 15 minutes in boiling water. Peel, stem, cut out seeds, flatten. Pack.	40	10	5
Pumpkin — Cut in pieces. Remove peel. Steam, boil, or bake tender. Pack.	180	60	10
Sauerkraut — Pack, add kraut juice.	15	—	—
Soybeans — Pack hot after blanching the shelled beans for 3 minutes in boiling water. Pack to within ½ inch of top of jar.	210	80	10
Spinach — Wash thoroughly. Steam or precook to wilt. Pack loosely.	180	60	10
Squash (summer, Chayote or Zucchini) — Precook 3 to 5 minutes. Pack.	180	40	10

Squash (crookneck, Hubbard, or banana)	Cut in pieces, steam or bake tender. Remove pulp from shell. Pack.	180	60	10
Sweet Potatoes	Wash, boil, or steam 20 minutes, remove skins. Pack.	180	60	10
Tomatoes	(See under Fruits.)			—
Tomato juice	Wash, peel, cut in sections. Simmer until soft, press through fine sieve. Bring to boiling. Pour at once into sterilized Kerr jars.	5	—	
Vegetable Mixtures	Prepare vegetables, precook separately, combine, process length of time necessary for vegetable requiring longest processing.	—	—	

FRUITS (see notes at end of timetable)	Hot-Water Bath—Time in minutes	Pressure-Cooker 5 lbs. Time in minutes
Apples	Wash, pare, core, cut in pieces. Drop in slightly salted water. Pack. Add syrup. Or boil 3 to 5 minutes in syrup. Pack. Add syrup.	25	10
Apricots	Wash, halve, and pit. Pack. Add syrup.	20	10

Canning Timetable (*continued*)

FRUITS (*see notes at end of timetable*)	Hot-Water Bath—Time in minutes	Pressure-Cooker 5 lbs. Time in minutes
(*continued*)		
Berries (except Strawberries and Cranberries)		
Wash, stem, pack. Add syrup or water.	20	8
Cherries		
Wash, stem, pit, pack. Add syrup.	20	10
Cranberries		
Wash, remove stems. Boil 3 minutes in No. 3 syrup. Pack.	10	—
Currants		
Wash, stem, pack. Add syrup or water.	20	10
Figs		
Cover with fresh water, boil 2 minutes. Drain and use this water to make syrup. Precook 5 minutes in syrup. Pack, add syrup.	30	10
Fruit Juices		
Crush fruit, heat slowly, strain. Pour into jars. Process in water bath.	20 (180°—simmering)	
Grapes		
Wash, stem, pack. Add syrup or water.	20	8
Peaches		
Peel, pack, add syrup, or precook 3 minutes in syrup. Pack, add syrup.	20	10

Pears	Select not overripe pears, pare, halve, precook 3 to 5 minutes in syrup. Pack. Add syrup.	25	10
Pineapple	Peel, remove eyes, cut or slice. Precook in No. 2 syrup 5 to 10 minutes. Pack. Add syrup.	30	15
Plums	Wash, prick skins. Pack. Add syrup.	20	10
Preserves	Prepare as per recipe. Cook until thick. Pack. Process in water bath.	20 (180°—simmering)	
Quinces	Wash, pare, cut in pieces. Precook 3 minutes in syrup. Pack, add syrup.	35	15
Rhubarb	Wash, cut into pieces without removing skin. Pack. Add syrup.	10	5
Strawberries	Wash, stem, precook gently for 3 minutes in syrup. Cover the kettle and let stand for several hours. Pack.	15	—
Tomatoes	Scald ½ minute, cold dip 1 minute, peel, core, quarter. Pack.	35	10
Tomatoes for salad	Scald ½ minute, cold dip 1 minute, peel, core. Pack. Cover with tomato juice.	35	10
Tomato purée	Irregular or undersized tomatoes may be used. Cook all ingredients until soft. Press through sieve. Pack.	35	10

Canning Timetable (continued)

FRUITS (see notes at end of timetable)

	Hot-Water Bath—Time in minutes	Pressure Cooker 5 lbs. Time in minutes
(continued)		
Walnuts	Pack into jar. Process in oven at 225° F. for 45 minutes.	—	—

MEATS (see notes at end of timetable)

		Hot-Water Bath—Time in minutes	Pressure Cooker 15 lbs. Time in minutes
Meats packed raw do not require the addition of liquid. Pack meats loosely and only to within 1 inch of top of jar.			
Meat or chicken stock	Pour prepared stock in jars.	180	45
Lamb, Veal, Beef, Steak	Bleed well and cool thoroughly. Precook, pack, add 3 to 4 tablespoons liquid. Or pack raw. Then process.	180	60
Pork	Bleed well and cool thoroughly. Precook, pack, add 3 to 4 tablespoons liquid. Or pack raw. Then process.	180	60

Chicken, Rabbit, Duck, Turkey	Bleed well and cool thoroughly. Precook, pack, add 3 to 4 tablespoons liquid. Or pack raw. Then process.	180	60 min. at 15 lbs. or 90 min. at 10 lbs.
Deer, wild birds, Geese	Bleed well, cool thoroughly, soak in brine 30 minutes or parboil. Precook, pack, add 3 to 4 tablespoons liquid. Or pack raw. Then process.	180	60
Fish, all kinds	Use only firm, fresh fish. Bleed well. Wash. Precook. Pack. Or pack raw. Then process.	240	90

NOTE: The time given in these tables applies to both pint and quart jars. If canning fruit in water bath with half-gallon jars, add ten minutes to time given; for pressure cooker, add five minutes to time given. When canning vegetables and meats for half gallons in pressure cooker or water bath, increase time 20%.

LIQUIDS: All foods (except meats) are packed in water or syrup except where instructions state otherwise. When using water add enough to fill jar only to within ½ inch of top. When using syrup on fruits packed cold, add syrup to within 1½ inches of top of jar. Or syrup to within ½ inch of top when fruits are packed hot.

TIME FOR DIFFERENT ALTITUDES: The time given in the timetables in this book is based on the one-pint or one-quart pack (except as per note above) and on fresh products at altitudes up to 1,000 feet. For higher altitudes increase the time 10% for each additional 500 feet, except for pressure-cooker canning. For elevation up to 2,000 feet, use pressure given in timetable. After the first 2,000 feet, one pound of pressure should be added for each additional 2,000 feet of elevation.

NOTE: ALL VEGETABLES EXCEPT TOMATOES, ALSO ALL MEATS, POULTRY, AND FISH CANNED AT HOME MUST BE BOILED IN AN OPEN VESSEL TEN TO FIFTEEN MINUTES BEFORE TASTING OR USING.

CANNED FRUITS

Honey Syrup for Canning Fruits

To make syrup wholly from honey, use the following measures in an oiled cup to prevent sticking. You may use smaller amounts of barley malt or brown rice syrups, or concentrated fruit juices instead of honey.

THIN : 3 cups water or fruit juice, 1 cup honey. Bring to boil.
MEDIUM : 2 cups water or fruit juice, 1 cup honey. Bring to boil.
HEAVY : 1 cup water or fruit juice, 1 cup honey. Bring to boil.

Apples (hot pack)

Select healthy, unsprayed organically grown apples. Wash, core and peel if desired. Cut to desired size. If fruit is to stand several minutes before packing, drop it into lemon water to prevent discoloration. Drain. Boil 3 to 5 minutes in light syrup. Pack in clean jars and fill to within 1-1/2 inches of top with syrup. Process according to timetable.

Apricots (cold pack)

Select firm, ripe fruit. Wash, halve and pit. (Save the pit kernal–it's rich in B-17.) Pack in clean jars filled within 1-1/2 inches of top with light syrup. Process according to timetable. If water pack or fruit-juice pack used instead of syrup, fill to within 1/2 inch of top.

Berries (cold pack)

(For all berries except strawberries.) Wash and stem berries. Pack into clean jars. Fill to within 1-1/2 inches of top with light syrup. Process according to timetable. If water pack or fruit-juice pack is used, fill to within 1/2 inch of top.

Cherries (cold pack)

Wash, stem, pit if desired. Pack into clean jars to within 1-1/2 inches of top with medium or light syrup, depending on the cherries' sweetness. If water pack or fruit-juice pack is desired, pack to within 1/2 inch of top. Process according to timetable.

Fresh Figs (hot pack)

Figs should not be over-ripe. Leave the stems on. Wash thoroughly. Cover with fresh water and boil for two minutes. Drain and use this water to make a thin syrup. Precook figs five minutes in syrup. Pack in clean jars, filling to within ½ inch of top. Process according to timetable. If a sweeter product is desired, make a heavy syrup. Add a few slices of lemon to the syrup and precook the figs for five minutes before packing. Adjust jar caps and process.

Fruit Salad (cold pack)

A combination of all kinds of raw fruits. Pack cold in clean jars; fill with medium syrup to 1½ inches of top, or pour water or fruit-juice pack to within ½ inch of top. Process length of time necessary for fruit requiring longest processing.

Grapes (cold pack)

Prepare grapes and pack tightly in clean jars without crushing. Fill to within 1½ inches of the top with medium syrup, or to within ½ inch of top with fruit juice or water. Consult timetable.

Guavas (open kettle)

Pare the fruit, cut into half, and remove seeds. Cook in boiling syrup for 30 minutes, pack boiling-hot into sterilized jars, and seal.

Nectarines (open kettle)

Select firm fruit, not too ripe; wash but do not peel. Simmer in a medium syrup 10 to 15 minutes, then bring to a full boil. Pack boiling-hot into sterilized jars, and seal. If hot- or cold-pack method is used, follow recipe for peaches as to time and handling.

Peaches (cold pack)

Select ripe, firm peaches. Remove peel and pit. If peeled fruit is to stand several minutes before packing, drop it into slightly salted water to prevent discoloration. Drain. Pack, halved or sliced, into clean jars. Fill to within 1½ inches of the top with medium syrup, or if water pack or fruit is used, to within ½ inch of top. Consult timetable. Peaches may also be canned without removing the peel. Wash thoroughly; halve; pack; add syrup. Process the same as peeled peaches.

Pears (hot pack)

Wash, pare, core the fruit. Precook 3 to 5 minutes in a thin or medium syrup. Pack in clean jars filled with syrup to within ½ inch of top. If pears are ripe enough to be quite soft, they may be packed without precooking. Consult timetable.

Plums (cold pack)

Select plums not too ripe; wash and prick the skin with needle to prevent bursting. Pack in clean jars and fill to within 1½ inches of the top with medium or heavy syrup. If water or fruit-juice pack is preferred, fill to within ½ inch of top. Consult timetable.

Strawberries (open kettle)

Select only firm, highly colored berries. Wash, stem and measure. For each quart of berries, allow 1/2 cup sweetener such as honey or brown rice syrup. Cover berries with sweetener of choice and let stand several hours — overnight if possible. Then place on stove and bring to boil. Boil rapidly for 10 minutes, removing scum as it forms. Pack boiling-hot into sterilized jars and seal.

CANNED VEGETABLES

Precooking

To precook vegetables, cover them with boiling water and boil for the time suggested in the recipe. In filling jars, pack the product to not more than ½ inch from the top of the jar. The exceptions are corn, peas, lima beans and such products, and they should be packed to only within 1 inch of the top. For all packs, add water in which vegetables were precooked, or boiling water, to within ½ inch of the top of the jar.

Flavoring Mixture

If desired, a flavoring mixture may be used to season such vegetables as corn, peas, beets, and tomatoes. This can be made by mixing two parts of honey and adding two teaspoons of the mixture to each quart jar.

Asparagus

Remove scales from stalk. Wash thoroughly to remove all sand. Cut in jar lengths. Tie in bundle. Place, tips up, in boiling water to cover lowest portions. Cover vessel tightly. Precook 3 minutes. Drain, pack in clean pint jars, tips up. Fill jar to within ½ inch of top with water in which vegetable was precooked, or boiling water. Cap and consult timetable.

Lima Beans

Wash, shell, and place in pan with boiling water to cover. Precook 3 minutes. Pack loosely to within 1 inch of top in clean jars. Fill to within ½ inch of top with water in which vegetable within ½ inch of top with water in which vegetable was precooked, or boiling water. Cap and consult timetable.

String Beans

Wash, string, and cut in convenient lengths, or leave whole. Precook for 3 minutes. Pack to within ½ inch of the top of the jars. Fill to within ½ inch of top with water in which vegetable within ½ inch of top with water in which vegetable was precooked, or boiling water. Cap tight, process according to timetable.

Beets

Use small, uniform beets. Wash carefully; leave roots and stems long. Boil 15 minutes. Plunge into cold water. Remove skins. Pack in clean jars. Add 2 teaspoons of flavoring mixture described above to each quart jar, if desired. Fill to within ½ inch of top with boiling water. Screw on cap; consult timetable.

Black-eyed or Field peas

Follow recipe for lima beans.

Broccoli

Remove the largest leaves or stems. Wash through several waters and precook 4 minutes. Pack in jars. Fill jar to within ½ inch of top with water in which vegetable was precooked, or boiling water Screw cap tight; consult timetable.

Cabbage or Brussels Sprouts

Wash, remove outside leaves, cut into desired pieces, and precook for 5 minutes. Pack in clean jars, fill to within ½ inch of top with water in which vegetable was precooked, or boiling water. Screw cap tight; consult timetable.

Carrots

Wash thoroughly, scrubbing dark parts well, but do not remove skin. Precook 5 minutes. Pack in clean jars. Fill to within ½ inch of top with water in which vegetable was precooked, or boiling water. Screw cap tight; consult timetable.

Cauliflower

Remove all outside green leaves. Wash and break the head into small or medium-sized flowerets. Soak for 20 minutes in 1 quart of water to which 1 tablespoon of salt has been added. This will draw out small insects. Rinse thoroughly in clear water. Precook 4 minutes. Pack in clean jars and fill to within ½ inch of top with water in which vegetable was precooked, or boiling water. Screw cap tight and process according to timetable.

Corn

Use only absolutely fresh corn that is tender and juicy. Husk; cut from cob, place in pan with enough boiling water to cover. Precook 3 to 5 minutes. Pack loosely to within one inch of top in clean jars and fill with water in which vegetable was precooked, or boiling water, to within ½ inch of top. Add 1 teaspoon of seasoning mixture to each pint jar. Screw cap tightly; consult timetable. Corn may be canned on the cob by following this recipe. The flavor of the corn on the cob will be improved if no liquid is added to the jar. Jars without liquid must be processed in the pressure cooker.

Sliced Eggplant

Peel, cut in slices, and precook for 5 minutes. Pack in clean jars, fill to within ½ inch of top with water in which vegetable was precooked, or boiling water. Screw cap tightly; process according to timetable.

Jerusalem Artichokes

Follow recipe for parsnips. Process in pressure cooker 40 minutes at 10 pounds, or in water bath for 180 minutes.

Kohlrabi

Follow recipe for carrots.

Mushrooms

Wash; leave small ones whole, cut large ones, and precook 3 minutes. Pack in clean jars. Fill jars to within ½ inch of top with water in which vegetable was precooked, or boiling water. Screw cap tight; consult timetable.

Okra

Select young, tender pods. Wash well and remove stem end without cutting the seed section. Precook 3 minutes. Drain thoroughly and pack quickly in clean jars. . . . and fill to within ½ inch of top with boiling water . . . Screw cap tight; process according to timetable.

Parsnips

Grade for size. Wash thoroughly. Scrape clean. Precook 5 minutes. Pack in clean jars filled to within ½ inch of top with water in which vegetable was precooked, or boiling water. . . . Screw cap tight; process according to timetable.

Peas

Use only young, tender freshly gathered peas. Shell; wash and sort according to size. Precook 3 to 7 minutes, depending upon the age and size of the peas. Pack loosely to within 1 inch of the top of jar. Fill to ½ inch of top with water in which vegetable was precooked, or boiling water. Add 1 teaspoon seasoning mixture to each pint jar. Screw cap tight; process according to timetable.

Rutabagas

Follow recipe for parsnips.

Soybeans

Green soybeans, varieties suitable for table use, may be canned. Follow recipe for lima beans, except process soybeans in pressure cooker 80 minutes at 10 pounds, or 210 minutes in water bath.

Spinach or Greens of all kinds

Wash carefully and precook in live steam, or place in kettle with just the water clinging to the leaves after the last washing, and precook until wilted. Pack at once in clean jars, being careful not to press too tightly.   fill within ½ inch of top with boiling water. Screw cap tight; process according to timetable.

Tomatoes

Wash tomatoes in clear water. Then scald in boiling water only long enough to remove peel (about ½ minute). Plunge in cold water if necessary, peel, core, quarter, and pack in clean jars. Add no water. . . . . . If desired, fill jars to within ½ inch of top with tomato juice.   Screw cap tight; process according to timetable.

There is much false economy: those who are too poor to have seasonable fruits and vegetables, will yet have pie and pickles all the year. They cannot afford oranges, yet can afford tea and coffee daily.   — Health Calendar

Hearty foods are those in which there is an abundance of potential energy.

Tomato Juice

Select firm, ripe tomatoes. Wash well; peel and drain. Cut in sections. Simmer until softened. Stir occasionally to prevent burning. Put through sieve fine enough to remove seeds. Bring juice to boiling and pour immediately into sterilized jars, filling to within ½ inch of top. Screw cap tight and process in water bath 5 minutes.

Turnips

Follow recipe for parsnips.

CANNED MEATS

Only recipes for venison or game are included here, as most meats are easily obtainable all the year round in the markets. However, for other recipes, consult the timetable.

Meats should not be canned until all animal heat has left them, which is usually from 6 to 24 hours after killing. Meat may be precooked or packed raw. In filling jars, pack the meat to not more than 1 inch from top of jar. For precooked meats, add 3 or 4 tablespoons of liquid. Meats packed raw do not require the addition of the liquid. Important: Wipe the top of the jar free from all grease or meat particles.

Venison

If roasting, cook slowly in moderate oven about 15 minutes for each pound of venison. Season well. Slice. Pack in clean jars to within 1 inch of the top. Add 4 tablespoons basting broth used for roast. Onion may be added if desired. Seal for cooking and process in pressure cooker 60 minutes at 15 pounds.

Chicken and Game Birds

1. Dress fowl and allow to cool; cut into convenient pieces. Boil until meat can be removed from bone. Pack meat in clean jars to within 1 inch of top. . . Add 4 tablespoons of the hot liquid after

it has been concentrated one half. Seal for cooking; process according to timetable.

2. Dress fowl and allow to cool. Wash in cold water. Cut into pieces or pack whole in clean jars to within 1 inch of top without precooking.

Cap; process according to timetable.

Canning Stock

Pour prepared stock (see recipes on pages 30 and 31) into clean jars. Seal for cooking. Process according to timetable.

Holiday Mincemeat

2½ *lbs. cooked lean meat*
½ *cup oil*
3¾ *quarts sour apples*
3¾ *lbs. seeded raisins*
2½ *lbs. currants*
4 *oranges*
4 *lemons*
1 *cup honey*
1¼ *cups unsulphured molasses*

2½ *tablespoons cinnamon*
2½ *teaspoons nutmeg*
2½ *teaspoons mace*
2½ *teaspoons powdered clove*
1¼ *teaspoons allspice*
1¼ *quarts meat broth*
3¾ *cups boiled apple juice*

Grind cooked meat, and apples in food-chopper.....or chop in wooden bowl. Add raisins, and currants. Add oranges and lemons that have been washed and grated. Add rest of ingredients and simmer for 2 hours. Pack in clean, hot jars and process 15 minutes in hot-water bath. Makes about 11 pints.

ટે

JAMS AND JELLIES

California Fig Jam

5 *cups unpeeled purple figs*
   (*quartered*)
2¼ *cups honey*
1 *lemon, sliced very thin*

Boil fruit, lemon, and 1 cup honey exactly 5 minutes.... Add 1 cup honey and boil again for 5 minutes. (Should be timed after boiling-point is reached.) Add last of sweetening and boil again for 3 to 5 minutes. Bottle hot and seal.

Quick Grape Jelly

3 cups unsweetened grape juice
1½ cups water

1½ pkgs. powdered pectin
2 cups honey

Combine grape juice and water; stir in pectin. Heat to the boiling-point and add sweetening . . . . Bring to full rolling boil, and boil exactly two minutes. Remove from stove, skim, and pour into sterilized glasses. Seal.

Apricot Butter

6 lbs. apricots
1 lb honey

juice and grated rind of one orange

Pit apricots, cut into small pieces. . . . . . . Add sweetening, orange juice and rind. Bring to boil and cook, stirring frequently until of desired consistency, usually thick. Watch carefully to prevent burning. If spices are desired, tie stick cinnamon and whole cloves in a cheesecloth bag and add to mixture while cooking. Remove before pouring into jars. Pour into hot sterilized jars, fill to top, and seal.

Tomato Preserves

5 to 10 lbs. tomatoes
1 lemon, sliced thin

1 cup honey

Dip tomatoes in boiling water for a few minutes, plunge into cold water, and peel. Gently squeeze what juice can be removed without breaking the fruit. Cut in quarters, cook gently about 20 minutes. Measure tomatoes and add the sweetening . . . . and the sliced lemon . . . . Simmer until thick, about 20 minutes, stirring frequently to prevent burning. Pour into hot sterilized jars and seal.

Youngberry or Raspberry Jelly

6 cups berry juice
1½ cups liquid pectin

3 tablespoons lemon juice
2 cups honey

To prepare juice, wash berries, crush. Place in jelly bag; squeeze out juice. Mix juice, lemon juice, and honey in large saucepan. Bring to boil as quickly as possible and add pectin at once, stirring constantly. Bring to full rolling boil and boil hard exactly ½ minute. Remove from heat; skim and pour into hot sterilized jars. Seal at once.

Strawberry and Rhubarb Jelly

3 *cups strawberry and rhubarb juice*
1½ *cups honey*

6 *oz. liquid pectin* (¾ *of 8-oz. bottle*)

To prepare fruit, cut about ¾ lb. fully ripe rhubarb in 1-inch pieces and put through food-chopper, using medium blade. Thoroughly crush about 1½ quarts fully ripe washed strawberries. Combine fruits, place in jelly cloth spread over a colander, and squeeze out juice. Measure sweetening . . . . and juice into large saucepan and mix. Bring to a boil over high heat, and at once add the liquid pectin, stirring constantly. Then bring to a full rolling boil, and boil hard ½ minute. Remove from heat, skim, and pour quickly into clean, freshly sterilized jelly glasses to within ½ inch of top. Cool and cover with a ⅛-inch layer of hot paraffin. Makes 6 6-ounce glasses.

Whole Strawberry Jam

3 *cups honey*
3 *tablespoons lemon juice*

6 *cups* (3 *lbs.*) *prepared fruit*
6 *ounces liquid pectin* (¾ *of 8-oz. bottle*)

To prepare fruit, use about 3 quarts small, fully ripe strawberries. Spread ¼ of berries at a time in a single layer, and with bottom of tumbler press gently to a thickness of ½ inch. This crushes centers of berries without breaking skins. Measure honey and fruit into separate dishes. Put layer of pressed berries into large kettle and cover with layer of honey. Continue to alternate layers of pressed berries and honey until all have been used, having honey on top. Add lemon juice. Let stand overnight or for at least 5 hours. Mix well and bring to a full, rolling boil over high heat. Stir constantly before and while boiling. Boil hard 1 minute. Remove from heat and stir in liquid pectin. Ladle off a few glasses of hot, clear syrup for jelly. (To separate syrup from fruit, press a sieve into jam.) Then stir and skim jam by turns for just 5 minutes; cool slightly to prevent floating fruit. Pour quickly into clean, freshly sterilized jelly glasses to within ½ inch of top. Cool and cover with melted paraffin. Makes 8 6-ounce glasses of jam.

Strawberry Relish

3 quarts ripe strawberries
½ teaspoon allspice
¾ teaspoon cinnamon
½ teaspoon powdered cloves

1½ cups honey
3 tablespoons lemon juice
6 ounces liquid pectin (¾ of 8-oz. bottle)

Wash and stem strawberries. Crush or put through food-chopper, using coarse blade. In a large kettle combine crushed berries—there should be 6 cups—spices (adjust amount to suit taste), honey, and lemon juice; mix well. Bring to a full rolling boil over high heat; boil 3 minutes, stirring constantly. Remove from heat; stir in liquid pectin. Then stir and skim by turns for 5 minutes. Cool slightly to prevent floating fruit. Pour into clean, freshly sterilized jelly glasses to within ½ inch of top. Cool and cover with melted paraffin. Makes about 10 6-ounce glasses.

Rhubarb Conserve

10 lbs. rhubarb
2 cans crushed pineapple
6 ounces liquid pectin

6 small whole oranges, diced
1 cup broken walnuts
2 cups honey

Wash rhubarb; cut into ½ inch pieces. Combine with remaining ingredients in kettle; bring to a boil, stirring constantly. Reduce heat; simmer, uncovered, over low heat about 1½ hours, or until a conserve in consistency. Stir occasionally the first hour and more often during last half hour. Remove from heat; stir in liquid pectin pour immediately into clean, freshly sterilized pint preserve jars. Seal. Makes about 8 pint jars.

Green-Tomato Marmalade

8 lbs. green tomatoes (about 12 medium tomatoes)
8 lemons

1½ cups honey
2 cups water
2 teaspoons powdered ginger

Slice green tomatoes in ½-inch crosswise slices; slice lemons paper thin. Bring the honey, water, and ginger to a boil. Add the tomato and lemon slices. Bring to a boil and simmer, uncovered, for 15 minutes. Then with a skimmer carefully remove the fruit. Boil the liquid down until it measures 6 cups. Boil it slowly so as not to scorch it. Replace fruit in liquid and bring to boil. Immediately place in clean, hot preserve jars. Adjust covers as directed by manufacturer. Set on wire rack in covered, deep kettle with boiling water to cover top 1 inch. Process 30 minutes, counting time from moment active boiling resumes. Remove; immediately adjust seal according to manufacturer's directions. Makes about 4 pints. Serve this as a spread for bread, as well as a garnish for meat or poultry.

Sliced Orange Marmalade

3 *cups orange slices,* ⅛ *in.*
  thick
2½ *cups water*
2 *cups honey*

⅜ *cup lemon juice*
12 *oz. liquid pectin* (1½
  8-ounce bottles)

Cut unpeeled orange slices in halves or quarters or leave whole, as preferred. Remove seeds. Put in saucepan with water, 1½ cups honey or raw sugar, and lemon juice . . . . .Cover; bring to a boil; then reduce heat and simmer 30 minutes. Next measure fruit and liquid into a large kettle, using additional water as necessary to make 5¼ cups . . . . Add remaining honey. Mix well and bring to a full rolling boil over hottest heat, stirring constantly. Boil hard for 1 minute. Remove from heat and stir in liquid pectin. Stir and skim by turns for 5 minutes. Pour quickly into clean, hot, sterilized jelly glasses to within ½ inch of top. Cool and cover with melted paraffin. Makes 10 6-ounce glasses.

California Tangerine Marmalade

6 *medium tangerines*
1½ *cups lemons sliced very thin*
water

honey
3 *tablespoons lemon juice*

Separate peeled tangerines into sections and cut into small pieces— there should be about 3 cups. Remove seeds. Cut peel into very thin slices. Measure tangerine pieces and lemons into saucepan. Add four times as much water. Add peel. Bring to boil; cook until tender, uncovered, 30 to 35 minutes. Measure 3 cups of this mixture into a saucepan; add 1½ cups honey or raw sugar. Boil vigorously, uncovered, stirring constantly for about 10 minutes, or until syrup reaches jelly stage. To test for jelly stage, dip large spoon into boiling mixture, then lift spoon so syrup runs off side. When syrup no longer runs off spoon in a steady stream, but separates into 2 distinct lines of drops that cling together, stop cooking. Add lemon juice; boil about 1 minute or until syrup again reaches jelly stage. Pour into clean, hot, sterilized jelly glasses; paraffin, and cover.

Cranberry-Orange Marmalade

4 whole medium oranges, quartered and seeded
4 cups fresh, washed cranberries

4½ cups water
3 cups honey

Put oranges and cranberries through medium blade of food-chopper, catching juice in bowl—there should be about 6 cups ground fruit. Combine fruit, juice, water, and honey in saucepan. Cook, uncovered, until thick—about 30 minutes, stirring frequently. Pour into clean, hot, sterilized jelly glasses. Paraffin, and cover. Makes about 10 6-ounce glasses.

Peach Butter

6 lbs. peaches
3 cups water
honey
3 teaspoons cinnamon

1½ teaspoons cloves
¾ teaspoon allspice
juice and rind of lemon

Wash, peel, and quarter peaches. Cook in water very slowly until soft. Put the fruit through a strainer. To each cup fruit pulp add two-thirds cup honey or raw sugar. Add cinnamon, cloves, allspice, juice, and grated rind of a lemon. Cook the butter slowly until it is thick and clear. Pour into sterilized glasses and seal.

Grape Conserve

6 lbs. Concord grapes
1 large orange
2 cups honey
6 ounces liquid pectin

1½ cups raisins
1⅛ cups chopped nut meats

Wash, drain, and stem Concord grapes. Slip skins and reserve to use later. Place pulp in kettle, bring to boiling, and cook slowly about 10 minutes. Press through strainer to remove seeds. Put orange through the food-chopper. Combine grape pulp and orange in large kettle, then add sweetening........and raisins. Cook rapidly until mixture thickens, add chopped grape skins, and cook 15 minutes more, stirring constantly. Stir in nut meats. Pour into hot sterilized glasses and seal.

Pineapple-Strawberry Spread

6 *cups strawberries*   3 *cups honey*
6 *cups shredded pineapple*

Put half the honey over the pineapple and half over the strawberries and let stand for four hours. It can stand overnight without too much juice forming. Put all together in a large kettle, mix well, and cook 25 minutes after rolling boil is reached. Put in glass jars and seal.

Date and Nut Spread

⅓ *cup chopped walnuts*   1¼ *tablespoons orange juice*
¾ *cup chopped dates*   ¾ *cup pineapple juice*

Mix all ingredients in saucepan and cook together until mixture thickens slightly (about 5 minutes). Cook and serve on whole-wheat bread or wafers.

TIME

I have just a little minute,
Only sixty seconds in it,
Just a tiny little minute,
Give account if I abuse it;
Forced upon me; can't refuse it.
Didn't seek it, didn't choose it,
But it's up to me to use it.
I must suffer if I lose it;
But eternity is in it.—Unknown

Important—Special Health Insert we want to share with you.

HEALTHY HEART HABITS FOR A LONG, VITAL LIFE

Remember, live foods make live people, and you are what you eat, drink and do so eat a low-fat, low-sugar, high-fiber diet of natural whole grains and starches, sprouts, fresh salad greens, vegetables, fruits, raw seeds, nuts, pure juices and chemical free distilled water.

Earn your food with daily exercise, for regular exercise improves your health, stamina, flexibility, endurance and helps open the cardiovascular system. Only 45 minutes a day can do miracles for your mind and body. You become revitalized with new zest for living.

We are made of tubes: to help keep them clean and open, make a mixture using 2/3 raw oat bran and 1/3 psyllium husk powder and add 2-3 tablespoons daily to juices, pep drinks, herbal teas, soups, hot cereals, foods, etc. Be sure it's wet and expanded for 2 minutes.

Niacin (B-3) helps also to cleanse and open the cardiovascular system. Take regular-released Niacin (100 mg) with one meal daily. Some skin flushing occurs sometimes, nothing to worry about as it shows it's working! After cholesterol level reaches 180 or lower, you can take Niacin once or twice weekly.

Remember, your heart needs a good balance of nutrients, so take a natural vitamin-mineral food supplement with extra vitamin E (mixed Tocopherols), the new Ester-C, Magnesium and Beta Carotene, for these are your heart's super helpers!

Also use this amazing enzyme SOD (super oxide dismutase) for it helps flush out dangerous free radicals that can cause havoc with your cardiovascular pipes and general health. Latest research shows extra benefits . . . promotes longevity, slows aging, fights arthritis and its stiffness, swelling and pain, helps prevent jet lag and exhaustion.

Count your blessings daily while you do your brisk walking and exercises with these affirmations—"health! strength! youth! vitality! peace! laughter! humbleness! energy! understanding! forgiveness! joy! and love for eternity!"— and soon all these qualities will come flooding and bouncing into your life. With blessings of health, peace and love to you, our dear friends and readers.   - Patricia Bragg

RECOMMENDED BLOOD CHEMISTRY VALUES

- Total Cholesterol: 180 mg/dl or less, 150 mg/dl or less (optimal)
- Total Cholesterol Childhood Years: 140 mg/dl or less
- HDL Cholesterol: Men: 46 mg/dl or more, Women: 56 mg/dl or more
- HDL Cholesterol Ratio 3.2 or less   •Glucose 80-100 md/dl
- Triglycerides 100 mg/dl or less   •LDL Cholesterol: 120 or less

BENEFITS FROM THE JOYS OF FASTING

Fasting is easier than any diet. • Fasting is quickest way to lose weight.

Fasting is adaptable to busy life. • Fasting gives body a physiological rest.
Fasting is used successfully in the treatment of many physical ills.
Fasting can yield weight losses up to 10 pounds or more in first week.
Fasting lowers & normalizes cholesterol & blood pressure levels.
Fasting is a calming experience, often relieving tension and insomnia.
Fasting improves dietary habits. • Fasting increases eating pleasure.
Fasting frequently induces feelings of euphoria, a natural "high".
Fasting is a rejuvenator, slowing the aging process.
Fasting is an energizer, not a debilitator. • Fasting aids elimination process.
Fasting often results in a more vigorous sex life.
Fasting can eliminate or modify smoking, drug, & drinking addictions.
Fasting is a regulator, educating the body to consume food only as needed.
Fasting saves all time spent marketing, preparing & eating.
Fasting rids the body of toxins, giving it an "internal shower" & cleansing.
Fasting does not deprive the body of essential nutrients.
Fasting can be used to uncover the sources of food allergies.
Fasting is used effectively in schizophrenia treatment & other mental ills.
Fasting under proper supervision can be tolerated easily up to 4 weeks.
Fasting does not accumulate appetite; hunger "pangs" disappear in 1-2 days.
Fasting is routine for the animal kingdom.
Fasting has been a commonplace experience since existence for man.
Fasting is a rite in all religions; the Bible alone has 74 references to it.
Fasting under proper conditions is absolutely safe.
Fasting is not starving, it is nature's cure Jesus has given us. - Patricia Bragg
Allan Cott, M.D. "Fasting As A Way Of Life"

Spiritual Reasons Why We Should Fast For
A Healthier, Happier, Longer Walk with the Lord

3 John 2	Deut. 11:7-15, 21	Luke 9:11	Matt. 9:9-15
Gen. 6:3	Gal. 5:13-26	Mark 2:16-20	Neh. 9:1,20-24
I Cor. 7:5	Isaiah 58	Matthew 4:1-4	Psalm 35:13
II Cor. 6	James 5:10-20	Matthew 6:6-18	Romans 16:16-20
Deut. 8:7-8	John 15	Matthew 7	Zechariah 8:19

Dear Health Friend,

This is a gentle reminder of the great benefits from "The Miracle of Fasting" that you will enjoy once you get started on your weekly 24-hour Bragg Fasting Program for Super Health! I fast every Monday and the first 3 days of each month; it's a precious time of body-mind-soul cleansing and renewal. On "fast" days I drink daily 7-9 glasses of pure distilled water or you can have some herb teas or diluted juices. You may add 1 tablespoon of this mixture (2/3 oat bran and 1/3 psyllium husk powder) to these liquids twice a day. Soak mixture two minutes before drinking! It's an extra cleanser and helps normalize weight, cholesterol, blood pressures and helps maintain healthy elimination. Fasting is the oldest, most effective healing method known to man. Fasting offers many Great and Miraculous Blessings from Mother Nature and Jesus.

My father and I wrote the book "Miracle of Fasting" to share with you the health miracles it can perform in your life and it's all so easy-to-do — it's part of the Bragg Healthy Lifestyle.

Patricia Bragg

◇◇

Section Three: Special-Purpose Diets

◇◇

Chapter 25

Reducing

If you are overweight, don't start reducing today! Peculiar advice? No, just a lesson learned from my experience with many thousand would-be yo-yo reducers. Don't start your reducing program today. Think about it for three days. If you are still determined to do it, then by all means begin. If you have weakened in this length of time, you would have weakened anyway and nothing is lost. But if you are really determined and mean business to gain better Health and desire a greater capacity for enjoying a long fit life . . . you will be more likely to carry through with your reducing program, if you have planned it carefully than if you proceed impulsively.

The erratic reducer cannot be blamed. It is hard for the normal person to realize the real difficulty that confronts those overweight. Superhuman will-power is needed to control the appetite and this is nearly always required at a time when the reducer is not feeling well, because no abnormally overweight person can feel completely well! So we require the greatest exhibition of strong character at a period of low vitality and often poor physical health. We pamper our invalids when they are bedridden, but the poor overweight person is no less an invalid because they are walking around. They receive no pampering and very little sympathy.

Whatever you do, don't try to reach normal weight within one week, or even one month. Reducing healthfully must be done gradually with daily persistence, patience, and a sensible, consistent diet and exercise program ... this is the only sure and safe way. Pills, powders, "magic potions," diets, over-strenuous exercise programs . . . these can be potentially dangerous.

If you have indulged in over-eating . . . it's now time to repent and get busy cleansing and reducing the excesses off and out of your body. Remember, following the Bragg Healthy Lifestyle helped millions balance and normalize their weight and their life.

Counting calories can be very dull. Eating flat, tasteless foods is unpleasant and an ordeal! If the food the reducer eats is attractive, delicious, digestible, he will be much more inclined to be satisfied and happy with his diet and more determined to stick to it. Yes, and less inclined to cheat until the ideal, normal weight is achieved! For that reason these menus have been carefully worked out to take into consideration lowered calorie intake and your taste satisfaction.

A great mistake made by many on reducing programs is the elimination of *all* fats and starches. It is true, these are the weight-builders, but the human body is so constituted that it requires some of these food factors. Natural fats, starches and natural sugars should be limited but not eliminated completely. The reducer should have ample vitamins and minerals while on a lowered food intake. We suggest natural vitamin and mineral supplements and you may add green barley or spirulina powder to juices or pep drinks on food days, but on fast days take no supplements.

The World Health Organization sets protein requirements at 4.5% of total food intake for men and women. The U.S. Food and Nutrition Board of the National Academy of Science sets protein requirements at 4.8% but adds an extra 20% for safety. Health professionals feel 20% of the total food intake is a healthier amount of protein from animal or vegetable sources.

They who provide food for the world decide the health of the world. You have only to see the meals served in restaurants, hotels and homes in America, Britain and around the world to appreciate the fact that a vast multitude of the human race is slaughtered by incompetent health-destroying cookery. Though a young woman may have taken lessons in music, painting, astronomy, etc., she is not well educated unless she has taken basic lessons in preparing healthy meals. Women can either prepare health or sickness with their two hands. Proper nutritional planning is a must! The right fuel (foods) produces good performance of the human (machine) body.

Dick Gregory, Famous Comedian and Author, weighed 320 pounds and his inspiration was the Bragg Book . . . Miracle of Fasting that guided him to fasting and healthy lifestyle living. He traded his bad habits — dead, processed foods, drinking, drugs, smoking, etc. for healthy habits! He now weighs a trim 150 pounds and has been in eight Boston Marathons. He is now guiding others to reduce and enjoy healthy, live foods. Dick also praises the Bragg Book . . . Building Powerful Nerve Force and says he now has nerves of steel, thanks to the Bragg teachings in that mighty book . . . See back pages for information on book ordering.

One-Day Juice Diet

The weekly one-day juice diet is a super cleanser of body toxins. For more cleansing and reducing follow with a one-day water fast.

Two 8-oz glasses orange juice, freshly squeezed
Two 8-oz glasses grapefruit juice, freshly squeezed

Two 8-oz glasses pineapple juice, unsweetened
Two 8-oz glasses tomato juice, salt-free
Eight 8-oz glasses of the following juice of 8 lemons, 2 to 3 tablespoons honey, with enough distilled water to make 8 glasses

This makes a total of 16 glasses of liquid, 2 to be taken each hour. The quantities of the above liquids may be varied; that is, you may use four of orange juice and none of pineapple, etc., but the total liquid should be one gallon during the day. The results are amazing, you feel light and good — so continue on juice or water another day if desired. Suggest you have daily the mixture on page 346 (2/3 oat bran and 1/3 psyllium husk powder—a bulk, no-calorie lubricant). Use 1 tablespoon am and pm in your liquids on juice and fasting days and also good for regular eating days.

Healthy, Organic, Live Fruits and Vegetables

Fresh organically grown fruits and vegetables are best for reducing as these will give you full nutritional value and none of the harmful pesticides, etc., used on commercial fruits and vegetables.

Low-Calorie Menu for Reducers

Eight full glasses of liquid must be taken daily. (All items on menus preceded by an asterisk [*] are recipes listed in the index).

Upon Rising
(Use any of the following)

An 8-oz glass, citrus juice, fresh orange or grapefruit
An 8-oz glass hot herb or mint tea with lemon juice

An 8-oz glass hot or cold water (distilled) with lemon juice or tsp apple cider vinegar with 1/2 tsp honey

For two inspiring Bragg Books on reducing, read "The Natural Way To Reduce" and learn the incredible health benefits of fasting in "Miracle of Fasting" — See back pages for ordering information.

Breakfast
(Choice of any one)

1 *serving fresh fruit*
1 *(8-oz.) glass of fruit juice*
1 *serving canned fruit*
  (*water pack)

1 *serving dried fruit, cooked*
  with honey

(Choice of any one)

*1 *soft-boiled egg*
1 *slice whole-grain toast*
(NOTE: This means toast *only*
—not the other foods listed
plus toast.)
*1 *poached egg*

*1 *scrambled egg with tomato*
*1 *scrambled egg with capers*
*2 *oz. cooked whole-grain*
  cereal with ½ teaspoon
  honey and ¼ cup milk

(Choice of any one)

1 *(8-oz.) glass of fruit juice*
1 *(8-oz.) glass of herb or mint*
  tea

1 *(8-oz.) glass of water with*
  lemon juice

Lunch
(Choice of one of the following)

1 (8-oz.) bowl of any of the following soups:

Consommé
California clam chowder
Chinese cabbage soup

Chicken gumbo
Iced orange bouillon

(Choice of one)

A medium-sized salad serving of any of the following salads:

Nasturtium salad
Purslane salad
Tarragon salad
Escarole salad
Lamb's lettuce salad
Spring salad bowl
Skin-beautiful salad
Famous vegetable salad

Cabbage salad bowl
Grand-slam salad
Papaya salad
Concord bouquet salad
Cottage cheese and onion
  salad
Cottage cheese with pimiento
  salad

◇◇

(With any salad on the reducing program, fresh lemon or orange juice is delicious, or use dressings on pages 352-354.)

(Choice of any one of the following)

1 slice whole-wheat toast *3 whole-grain wafers*
1 slice any whole-grain toast

Dinner
(Choice of any one of the following)

1 medium salad serving of any of the following salads:

* *Dandelion salad*   * *Summer herb salad*
* *Gourmet mixed-green salad* * *Famous vegetable salad*
* *Spring herb salad*   * *Sprouted soybean salad*
 Buckwheat salad   * *Tropical delight*

(Choice of one)

)-oz.) serving of any one of the following soups:

* *Jellied tomato soup*   * *Spring broth*
* *Meatless vegetable soup* * *French onion soup*

(Choice of one)

1 medium serving of any of the following:

* *Broiled steak*   * *Eggplant roast*
* *Broiled lamb chop*   * *Vegetarian loaf*
 Savory beef roast   * *Lima-bean loaf*
 Steak with herbs   * *Lentil loaf*
 Roast beef   * *Baked lima beans*
 Roast leg of lamb   * *Broiled mushrooms*
 Broiled liver   * *Hawaiian chicken*
* *Basic broiled fish*   * *Broiled chicken*
* *Steamed clams*   * *Poached eggs & mushrooms*
* *Broiled crab or lobster* * *Scrambled eggs with*
* *Fish with herbs*   *mushrooms*

(Choice of small servings of two
of the following)

Artichokes with garlic
Lemon beets pickled
7-minute cabbage
Carrots and celery
*Any of the basic greens recipes
(Nos. 1 to 6)*
Onions and apples

Peas with thyme
Green beans with mint
Sauerkraut
Broiled tomatoes
Spinach tomatoes
Zucchini with herbs

(Choice of any one of the following,
thoroughly toasted)

*1 slice of 100% whole-wheat
bread*
1 slice of Dutch rye bread

1 slice of barley bread
1 slice of rice bread
1 pat butter

(Choice of any one of the following,
for dessert)

Broiled grapefruit
*Lemon ice or grape-juice
sherbet*
Apple sauce

*Any combination listed under
Fruit compote
1 serving any dried fruit
cooked with honey
any fresh fruit*

Between Meals

To make up part of the 8 glasses of liquid per day, two glasses of fruit or vegetable juices may be taken. Use any of the combinations or *Tomato-herb drinks or other combinations listed under the chapter "Drink Health the New Way." Hot bouillons of any kind are excellent.

Here are some special salad dressings for those on reducing diets:

Tomato-Basil Dressing for Reducers

⅓ cup lemon juice
1 tablespoon honey
½ tablespoon Bragg Aminos
½ teaspoon rosemary

½ cup yogurt
1 cup tomato juice
1 clove garlic
½ teaspoon sweet basil

Blend well. Allow to stand 12 hours before using. Remove garlic before serving.

Tomato Dressing with Onion Juice
for Reducers

½ *cup tomato juice*
¼ *cup lemon juice*
⅓ *teaspoon Bragg Aminos*

½ *teaspoon onion juice*
½ *teaspoon chives*

Blend ingredients. Beat vigorously and let stand 1 hour before serving.

Grapefruit French Dressing
for Reducers

2 *tablespoons yogurt*
3 *tablespoons grapefruit juice*
½ *tablespoon lemon juice*
½ *teaspoon honey*

¼ *teaspoon paprika*
1 *teaspoon Roquefort cheese, crumbled fine*

Blend ingredients. Beat vigorously. Allow to stand 2 hours before serving.

Lime Dressing for Reducers

3 *tablespoons yogurt*
4 *tablespoons fresh lime juice*
2 *teaspoons honey*
1 *teaspoon oregano*

⅛ *teaspoon Bragg Aminos*
1 *teaspoon celery seed*

Blend ingredients. Beat vigorously and allow to stand 1 hour before serving.

Mustard Dressing for Reducers

⅓ *cup lemon juice*
½ *cup yogurt*
1 *teaspoon honey*

1 *teaspoon mustard*
½ *teaspoon Bragg Aminos*

Blend all ingredients and allow to stand 1 hour before serving.

Lemon or Orange Fresh Squeeze Squirter

Great for reducers . . . roll a lemon or orange on kitchen counter to break down the cells for more juice. Poke a small hole in the end with a toothpick or knife. Now you have a super lemon squirter for distilled water on fasting days at work or home & it is great for salads, vegetables, fish dishes & even herb teas.

Walking is Important

No reducing program is complete without a program of systematic walking. The day you start your diet is the day you should start stretching, deep breathing & walking. Begin with a short, brisk walk every day for a week, then each week increase the distance until you walk 2 to 5 miles. For a busy person, brisk walking is the king of exercise and, in conjunction with the diet, is absolutely necessary for successful reducing.

Paul Bragg enjoying a cross country run — which demands the 100% physical fitness provided by his 100% natural diet.

Chapter 26

Gaining

No person who is underweight can enjoy the exuberance of positive Health. Excessive thinness brings on a general run-down condition and a depleted nervous system. It is unfortunate that, unlike most overweight persons, the majority of the underweight cannot regulate their size entirely by the intake of food. It has been popular belief that gaining is simply a matter of stuffing food into the body. That is not true. I have seen thin people gorge for years and never gain a pound, but often stuff themselves on foods low in calories. The thin person who has nothing organically wrong with him may find the basic weight-gaining menus given below a source of the foods he needs.

Rest and Exercise

Rest and exercise are important. The ordinary person requires eight hours' sleep a night, but the thin person should have a minimum of nine, and ten hours are preferable. By ten hours' sleep I mean actual sleeping time. If it takes you half an hour to relax and go to sleep after you hit the bed, that time is well spent, but it is not sleeping time.

The Richness of Whole Grains

The whole grains are nature's richest offering among all her tremendous stores of bounty. The cereals, breads, and other baked foods made from 100% whole grain offer the person who is trying to gain weight not only delicious flavors but the protective value of the little golden flakes of germs found in the grains. This germ contains oily substances that add flavor and nutrition to the diet. Be sure to get whole grains in wide varieties. When you use only one grain (such as whole wheat), even though it may be one of nature's finest foods, you are not getting the benefit of all the wide variety of nutritional forces found in the various whole grains. Vary your whole grain diet by using the wide variety of whole-grains listed throughout this book. Many grains can be blended into one delicious cereal, and variety an be obtained each day by using this selection.

A complete set of weight-gaining menus is given below, but there are a few important points to remember. The underweight person can use a great variety of dried legumes, lentils, peas, lima beans, garbanzos, and soybeans. These can be enjoyed throughout the week in soups, casseroles, entrees and cold in salads.

Brown rice is one of our main staples. It is high in nutrition, is non-allergenic and gluten-free as well as easy to digest for sensitive stomachs and great blended for babies. It should be eaten 4-6 times per week and is ideal as an entree or side dish.

Tofu from soy beans is one of the best protein foods, ideal for normalizing and building strong bodies. Broiled, baked or blended, tofu is great - you can even have tofu ice-cream! The organs of the animal, the liver, sweetbreads, kidney and brains are some of the finest forms of weight-builders. They contain rich minerals and vitamins and are excellent forms of protein. Unsulphured dried fruits, blackstrap unsulphured molasses, raw nuts & seeds, honey and fresh fruits — bananas, apples, pears and avocado, as well as olive, safflower and soy oils are wonderful additions to help normalize the body.

Healthy Foods to Normalize Weight

The average underweight person whose thinness is due to malnutrition and not organic disturbance, does not have enough of the right wholesome foods. They may have even more total food intake per day than their overweight neighbor but it may not be food designed to give them healthful weight. Here is a set of healthful menus, easy to follow.

Menus for Weight-Building

8-10 full glasses of healthful liquid must be taken daily — distilled water, fresh juices, herbal teas or hot cup distilled water with 1-2 tbs blackstrap molasses or herbal tea or fresh squeezed juice. See pages 300, 301 for juices and page 304 for Pep Drink. (Recipes indicated with asterisk [*] are listed in the index.)

Upon Rising

Do some stretching, deep breathing & exercise. Then have an 8 oz glass of distilled water with 1 tsp apple cider vinegar and 1/2 tsp raw honey.

Breakfast — for Gaining

Remember to earn your breakfast first with exercise and activity.

Remember, take vitamin / mineral supplements with a multiple enzyme with your meals. The Bragg Health Pep Drink, can be substitued for breakfast. See recipe on page 304.

Choice of 1 large portion of any of the following:

*Fresh fruit in season
*Any dried, unsulphured, cooked or soaked fruit
*A combination of dried figs, apricots, peaches and pears

Choice of 1 large portion of any of the following:
[Health Meal Recipe on page 188]

*Meal with sliced figs, pecans, honey and soy cream
*Meal with fresh fruit, honey and soy cream
*Meal with dried or soaked apricots, chopped walnuts, honey
  and soy cream.

Choice of 1 portion of any of the following:

*2 poached eggs Vienna   *Scrambled eggs with cheese
*2 poached eggs with   *Filled omelet
  mushrooms   *Whole-wheat pancakes
*2 poached eggs with   *Soybean waffles
  chicken livers   *Waffle King buckwheat
*Scrambled eggs with   waffles
  mushrooms   *Fresh-fruit waffles

Choice of one 8-oz glass or cup of any of the following:

*Any herbal tea
*Grain coffee substitute

Choice of one of the following:

*2 slices whole-grain toast
* breakfast muffin or breakfast roll
  (optional — 2 pats butter, honey or fruit spread if desired)

At 10.00 a.m.

(Choice of one 8-oz. glass of any of the following)

Citrus-fruit juice   Grape or berry juice
Pineapple juice

Lunch

(Choice of one)

1 large serving of any of the following:

*Fresh mushroom salad   *Crab salad
*Avocado tomato salad bowl   *Lobster salad
*Stuffed artichoke salad   *Artichoke-chicken salad
*Famous vegetable salad   *Duck and orange salad
*Pear and grape salad   *Pear and Camembert salad
*Cranberry specialty salad   *Gorgonzola-pineapple salad
*Ambrosia   *Cottage-cheese and onion salad
*Avocado filled with salmon   *Cottage-cheese and endive salad
*Tuna-fish salad

(Choice of one)

medium portion of any of the following:

*Cream of lettuce soup   *Peanut-butter soup
*Marrow balls with consommé   *Cream of carrot soup
*Onion and pea soup   *Sweet-potato soup
*Oyster stew   *Tasty cheese soup
*Black soybean soup   *Golden banana soup
*Sour-cream bean soup   *Smooth avocado soup
*Lentil soup

(Choice of one)

1 medium-sized serving of any of the following:

*Asparagus hollandaise   *Cheese in onion butter sauce
*Sour-cream asparagus   *Cheese with thyme
*Stuffed artichokes   *Green beans with mint
*Beet greens   *Green beans with herbs
*Broccoli with cheese   *Sauerkraut-stuffed peppers
*Green buttered cabbage   *Spinach with pepper
*Any of the basic greens recipes *Spinach tomatoes
   (Nos. 1 to 6)   *Zucchini with herbs
*Leeks au gratin

(Choice of one)

1 medium serving of the following:

*Sour-cream beets
*Orange beets
*Carrots en casserole
*Caramelized carrots
*Glazed carrots with honey
*Cauliflower
*Braised celery
*Corn

*Eggplant with herbs and cheese
*Eggplant in okra
*Tomato okra
*Onions with cheese
*Parsnip patties
*Squash and limas
*Onion baked tomatoes

NOTE: The entree should be balanced with the salad for this meal. If you have a filling salad, such as fish or meat salads, choose a lighter entree.

(Choice of one)

1 large serving of any of the following:

*Mushroomed oysters
*Broiled mushrooms
*Baked lima beans
*Lima beans with cheese
*Baby limas marjoram
*Sprouted soybean omelet
*Sweetbread tomatoes
*Fluffy salmon loaf
*Crabs à la rice
*Fish pudding
*Tuna fish à la rice and cheese
*Baked halibut with herb sauce
*Cioppino
*Lentil loaf

*Lima-bean loaf
*Lentils with wild rice
*Vegetable and soybean stew
*Soy vegetable roast
*Vegetarian loaf
*Vegetarian sausages
*Eggplant roast
*Cincinnati mock turkey
*Chestnut croquettes
*Cheese and nut roast
*Cheese soufflé
* Baked eggs on Spanish rice
*Spanish omelet

(Choice of one)

1 slice of any of the following:

*Whole-wheat bread
*Dutch rye bread
*Barley bread

*Rice bread
*Oatmeal bread

2 of any of the following:

Corn bread   *Dinner rolls*
Whole-wheat rolls   *Speedy pan rolls*
Fluff rolls

3 of any of the following:

Buttermilk biscuits
Cheese-lemon buns
2 pats butter   *Rye muffins*

(Choice of any of the following)

1 (8-oz.) cup or glass of

Mint
Herb tea

(Choice of one)

Fresh fruit with inch square of *Favorite custard*
   cheese   *Rice and raisin pudding*
Fresh strawberry sponge   *Carob custard*
Raisin pudding

At 3.00 p.m.

1 (8-oz.) glass of any of the following:

Tomato juice with herbs
Tomato juice with celery juice

Dinner
(Choice of one)

1 large portion of any of the following:

Nasturtium salad   *Spring herb salad*
Dandelion salad   *Escarole salad*
Purslane salad   *Romaine with garlic bread*
Gourmet mixed-green salad   *Grand-slam salad*
Tarragon salad

<<<<<<<<<<<<<<<<<<<<<<<<<<<<<<<<<<<<<<<<<<<<<<<<<<>

(Choice of one)

1 medium serving of any of the following:

Consommé
Marrow balls with consommé
Chinese cabbage soup
Ripe-olive soup
Chicken gumbo

Jellied tomato soup
Meatless vegetable soup
Creole consommé
Spring broth

(Choice of one)

Choose any vegetable in the first Luncheon Vegetable section that you did not use on your luncheon menu.

(Choice of one)

Choose any vegetable in your Luncheon Vegetable section No. 2 that you did not use on your luncheon menu.

(Choice of one)

Choose any item on the Luncheon Entree section that you did not use for lunch, or any large portion of the following:

Beef stew with herbs
Savory Swiss steak
Sour-cream Swiss steak
Syrian beef stew
Hungarian goulash
Steak rolls and noodles
Italian spaghetti
Stuffed peppers
Stuffed breast of lamb
Lamb casserole with eggplant
Veal scallopine
Veal garden stew
Spanish roast loin of pork

Scrambled brains in cereal
Broiled liver
Stuffed calves' heart
Liver a la bourgeoise
Kidney stew
*Turkey with chestnut herb
   dressing*
*Roast chicken with walnut
   stuffing*
Hawaiian chicken
Roast duck
Roast goose

(Choice of one)

1 large serving of any of the following:

Baked potato
Potatoes au gratin

Thrifty potato casserole
Cheese-stuffed potatoes

(Choice of one)

Choice of any of the breads listed in the Luncheon Bread section.
2 pats butter

(Choice of one)

Choice of any of the desserts listed in the Luncheon Dessert section that have not been used for lunch *or* 1 serving of any of the following:

Upside-down cake
Date shortcake
Blueberry squares
Fruited spice cake
California cheesecake
Banana cupcakes
Banana gingerbread
Strawberry shortcake

Pittsburgh pumpkin pie
Pecan pie
Banana cream pie supreme
Glazed apricot pie
Cream pie
Custard strawberries
Baked bananas
Sweet-potato pudding

(Choice of one)

1 (8-oz.) glass or cup of any of the following:

Mint or other herb tea   *Fruit or vegetable juice*

Patricia's Delicious Health Popcorn
For more healthy fiber in your diet!

Use fresh home-popped popcorn (my favorite method is the air (non-oil) popper). Melt desired amount of salt-free butter or oil (olive, soy, canola or safflower) or blend oil with butter, add 3-5 fresh crushed garlic cloves and several sprays or dashes of Bragg Liquid Aminos to mixture & pour over popcorn. Then sprinkle with Brewer's yeast flakes or grated Parmesan cheese. For variety, add a pinch of Italian herbs or cayenne pepper to liquid mixture. This is a delicious bread substitute served with soups, salads and almost any meal. Keep warm in oven until serving.

Chapter 27

Food Allergies

Most Common Food Allergens

CEREALS: Wheat, Corn, Oats, Rye, Buckwheat
MILK: Cheese, Ice Cream, Butter, etc.
EGGS: Cakes, Noodles, Dressings, Custards, Mayonnaise
FISH: Shellfish, Crabs, lobster, Shrimp, Shad roe
MEATS: Pork, Bacon, Sausage, Veal, Chicken
FRUITS: Strawberries, Citrus Fruits, Melons
VEGETABLES: Cauliflower, Brussels sprouts, Onions,
Celery, Spinach, Legumes. As well as Tomatoes, Potatoes,
Eggplant and others of the nightshade family.
NUTS: Peanuts, Walnuts, Pecans
MISCELLANEOUS: Chocolate, Cocoa, Coffee, China Tea,
Spices, Salt, MSG, Cottonseed Oil, Palm Oil , Honey

Foods Rarely Causing Allergies
Often Used in "Elimination" Diets

Every known food may cause some allergic reaction at times. Thus, the foods used in "elimination" diets may cause allergic reactions in some individuals and a few are listed among the "Most Common Food Allergens". Since the incidence of reaction to these foods is generally low, they are widely used in making test diets. By keeping your own food journal you will soon know your "problem" foods that must be eliminated from the diet.

Apricots	Corn	Olive-Oil	Rice
Asparagus	Corn-Oil	Pears	Rye
Beets	Grapefruit	Peas	Soybeans
Carrots	Green Beans	Pineapple	Squash

Food Allergies and Their Reactions

After eating some particular type of food and especially if it happens each time you eat that food, your body has a reaction, the chances are you may have an allergy. Here are some of the allergic reactions and they can happen very quickly! If you wheeze, sneeze, develop a stuffy nose, nasal drip or mucus, dark circles or waterbags under your eyes, headaches, feel light-headed or dizzy, stomach and chest pains, diarrhea, extreme thirst, break out in a rash or have a swelling of the tissues, either externally or internally (ankles, feet, hands or stomach bloating, etc.).

If you know what your allergy is, you are lucky; if you don't, you had better find out as fast as possible and eliminate all irritating foods from your diet. To re-evaluate your daily life, as a guide to your future start a daily journal (8.5x11 notebook) of foods eaten and your reactions, moods, energy levels, weight, elimination and sleep patterns. You will discover in a short time the foods and situations causing your problems. By charting your activities you will be amazed at the swings following eating certain foods. My father, Paul C. Bragg faithfully kept his journal for over 70 years.

If you are hypersensitive to certain foods, you must reject them from your diet! There are hundreds of allergies and of course it is impossible here to take up each one. Many who suffer from this unpleasant affliction have allergies to wheat, milk or eggs, while some persons are allergic to all grains. Fruit allergies have been purposely omitted here, not because they are not so important as the wheat, but because it is easier to secure a variety of substitute fruits than substitute grain foods. It is for this latter type of allergy that most of the recipes have been planned.

 ## Some General Tips for Allergics

Milk. Milk and its by-products are the #1 allergy culprits by clogging the respiratory and arterial systems. Since pasteurization and homogenization, heart and respiratory ailments in America have climbed rapidly! The non-dairy products are healthiest to use: Soy, Rice, Nut-Milks, and their products (cheeses, creams, butters, yogurts, spreads, etc.) are delicious. Those who insist on using Cows and Goat Milk should take the enzyme lactase (available in Health Stores) to better tolerate milk.

Wheat. There are many wonderful, healthy substitutes for this grain. Health Food Stores carry a wide variety of wheat-less flours; Rye, Corn, Brown Rice, Millet, Barley, Oat, Soybean, Lima-Bean, Potato flour, etc. You can use them alone or blended.

Eggs. Fertile eggs from healthy free-range chickens are best. Health Stores have egg replacer (cholesterol-free) and tofu products. For thickening in baking use Arrowroot, Instant Tapioca, Agar Agar. Use Potato Flour for gravies, soups, stews, casseroles, vegetable pies, etc.

◇◇

Oil. Cottonseed, Coconut, Palm and Palm Kernel oils should never be used as they cause clogging of the arteries and other health problems, especially for the allergic person. You can often consume these oils without knowing it, as many shortenings, candies, dressings and commercially baked products use these cheap oils. Read labels carefully to know what you are eating.

Raw Foods. Many persons suffering from allergies discover they can tolerate cooked foods better than raw and fresh foods. After following the "Bragg Healthy Lifestyle" people can tolerate more raw fruits and vegetables and their health begins to thrive.

Special Products. Health Food Stores have wheat-less mixes, non-dairy products, cold (expeller) pressed vegetable oils, eggless-salt-free mayonnaises and many other products for allergic people.

Food Preparation. It is especially important that the allergic understand the preparation of food. Many foods you can tolerate successfully become definitely irritating if prepared with an ingredient to which you are allergic. If you are allergic to egg and milk, a baked crust over a meat dish or a stuffing in it may make a perfectly harmless serving of meat irritating. Take care not to be misled by creamed dishes, sauces or foods containing fillings, seasonings and additives that you may not be able to tolerate. But with a knowledge of food-preparation, the health menu of the allergic may be every bit as appetizing, attractive and varied as that of the unrestricted person.

RECIPES

Bread, muffins, etc., baked without wheat flour are not as light and fine in texture, but can be just as delicious and nutritious. Experiment and at first make a smaller version of the recipe and remember that wheat-less mixtures often require longer and slower baking times. Sift flours well and thoroughly beat the mixtures, as the enclosed air helps lighten the batter.

Apricot Rye Bread

1 teaspoon dry yeast
4 tablespoons lukewarm
  distilled water
4 teaspoons raw honey

2 tablespoons cold-pressed oil
2 cups cooked pureed apricots
5-1/2 cups 100% rye pastry flour
  or flour of choice

Dissolve the yeast in lukewarm water; beat in half the flour, add sweetening, oil and pureed (sundried, unsulphured) apricots.

Blend well; add the other half of the flour slowly. Mix again, flour board and hands and knead well. Cover, let rise in a warm place until double in bulk. Flour board, shape into loaves and knead again for several minutes. Place in oiled pan (liquid lecithin is great). Let rise until light. Bake in a hot oven (375° to 400°F.) for 20 minutes. Reduce heat to moderate oven (about 350°F.). Bake 40 to 50 minutes longer. This makes 2 large loaves.

Rye Bread

3 cups 100% rye pastry flour
1 teaspoon dry yeast
1 tablespoon raw honey

1-3/4 cups lukewarm
distilled water
1 tbs cold-pressed oil

Dissolve yeast in lukewarm water; add oil, honey (to prevent sticking, oil measuring cup or spoon) and then the rye flour. Mix and knead to a dough on rye-floured board. While kneading, add several caraway, chia or sesame seeds if desired. Optional - 2 tbs drained sauerkraut. Cover and let rise in a warm place until double in bulk. Shape into loaves. Place in oiled bread pan; let rise again and bake in hot oven (375° to 400°F.) for 20 minutes. Reduce heat to moderate oven (about 350°F.). Continue to bake 40 to 50 minutes. Makes 2 loaves.

100% Corn Bread

2 cups corn meal, stone ground
2 eggs (or egg replacer)
2 tablespoons raw honey
1/2 cup soy or nut milk

Scald cornmeal with all the hot distilled water it will absorb. Add milk and honey. Mix well. Add eggs or substitute and mix batter well. For variety add one or more of grated zucchini, carrots, raisins, currants, sunflower seeds, fresh garlic or pinch of Italian herbs. Bake in shallow, oiled pan (use liquid lecithin to prevent sticking) in moderate oven for 35 minutes. Serves 8.

Four-Flour Bread

1-1/2 cups soy flour
1-1/2 cups lima-bean flour
1-1/4 cups brown rice flour
1-1/4 cups oat flour
2 teaspoons dry yeast

3 cups lukewarm distilled
water or soy milk
2 tbs cold-pressed oil
2 tbs raw honey or barley malt
or brown rice syrup

◇◇◇

Dissolve yeast in 1 cup lukewarm water or soy milk. Scald milk; cool to lukewarm. Add oil, sweetener, yeast and flours. Flour board and hands with one of the flours used in the recipe and knead to a stiff dough. Cover and let rise in a warm place until double in bulk. Shape into loaves. Placed in oiled bread pan and let rise again. Bake in a hot oven (about 375°F. to 400°F.) for 20 minutes. Reduce heat to moderate oven (350°F.) and continue to bake 40 or 50 minutes longer. Makes 2 large loaves.

Brown Rice and Lima Bean Flour Bread

1 cup brown rice flour
3/4 cup soy or oat flour
1/4 cup lima-bean flour
1/8 cup warm water or
  warm soybean milk

1 teaspoon dry yeast
1 teaspoon raw honey
2 teaspoons cold-pressed oil
1-1/2 cups distilled water

Dissolve the yeast in warm soybean milk; blend well with oil and honey and allow to stand. Sift all dry ingredients several times. Stir water into dry ingredients; add yeast and honey mixture and blend thoroughly. Let rise in a warm place until doubled in bulk. Flour board and hands with soy flour. Knead well, shape into loaves, place in pan coated with liquid lecithin and let rise again. Place in moderate oven (about 300°F.) for 12 minutes. Increase heat to moderately hot oven (375°F.) and continue baking 40 to 50 minutes longer. Makes 2 small loaves.

Rye Rolls

2 cups skim or soy milk
2 tablespoons cold-pressed oil
2 tablespoons raw honey

1 teaspoon dry yeast
4 or 5 cups rye pastry flour
or mixed flours as desired

Dissolve yeast in 1/2 cup warm milk. Heat 1-1/2 cups milk, add honey and oil then cool. Combine liquids then add flour, unsifted. Mix well and set aside to double in bulk. Make into rolls or loaf. Set aside again until bulk is doubled and bake 30 minutes in a very hot oven (425°F.). The first setting of the dough will be very soft, but will be easy to handle. Add if desired 1 tablespoon caraway, sesame or chia seeds. Makes 4 dozen rolls.

Whole grains are rich in complex carbohydrates, protein, vitamins, minerals, polyunsaturated fatty acids and fiber.

Brown rice is non-allergenic and gluten free.
It is easy to digest for sensitive stomachs and is great blended for babies from eight months on.

Rye Muffins

See recipe for Rye Muffins on page 208.

Rye Fruit Muffins

See recipe for Rye Fruit Muffins on page 208.

Rye Biscuits

    2 *cups rye flour*
    2 *tablespoons butter or soy oil*   ¾ *cup milk or soy milk*
    3 *teaspoons baking powder*

Sift flour, and baking powder. Cut in butter . . . . and mix to light dough with milk. Roll out on a board floured with rye flour. Cut into biscuits and bake in hot oven (400°F.) for 15 minutes. Makes 1 dozen biscuits.

Wheatless Pancakes

    1 *cup potato flour*
    1 *cup rice flour*   1½ *cups milk*
    2¼ *teaspoons baking powder*   2 *eggs*
    4½ *tablespoons honey*   4½ *teaspoons melted butter or
                                         soy oil*

Combine and sift dry ingredients three or four times. Beat eggs light. Add melted butter or oil slowly while beating eggs. Add milk and beat again. Add dry ingredients. Beat and bake on hot griddle iron. Makes 8 to 10 pancakes.

Cornmeal Waffles

    2 *cups cornmeal*   3 *eggs*
    4 *teaspoons baking powder*   1½ *cups milk*
                                   ⅓ *cup melted butter or soy oil*
    2 *tablespoons honey*

Sift cornmeal, baking powder, and honey together.   Beat egg yolks. Add melted shortening and milk. Combine with dry ingredients, stirring until smooth. Fold in egg whites, beaten stiff. Bake in hot waffle iron. Makes 6 waffles.

Wheatless Waffles

1 *cup rice flour*
½ *cup yellow cornmeal*
½ *cup potato flour*
2 *tablespoons cornstarch*
2 *tablespoons arrowroot*
3 *teaspoons baking powder*

2 *tablespoons honey*

2 *eggs*
1 *cup milk or soy milk*
6 *tablespoons melted butter or soy oil*

Sift flours twice before measuring. Then mix and sift all dry ingredients several times. Beat eggs; add butter or oil and beat again. Add milk. Beat again. Add dry ingredients and mix until smooth. Bake in hot waffle iron. Makes 6 waffles.

Soybean Waffles

See recipe for Soybean Waffles on page 212. Substitute ¼ cup coarse rye and oatmeal for ¼ cup wheat germ called for in that recipe.

Fresh Fruit Waffles

Add ½ cup mashed strawberries, raspberries, or other fresh fruits to recipe for Soybean Waffles.

Rice-Flour Sponge Cake

½ *cup rice flour*
1 *scant cup honey*
4 *eggs*

1 *teaspoon baking powder*
½ *teaspoon vanilla*

Separate eggs. Beat yolks thoroughly. Add half the honey; beat until well blended and thick. Add rice flour to egg-yolk mixture, mixing it lightly. Beat egg whites; add baking powder. . .and remaining honey. Add vanilla. Add all to egg-yolk and flour mixture. Continue to mix lightly; do not beat hard. Bake in ungreased pan in moderate oven (about 325°F.) for one hour. Turn onto cake rack and allow to cool at room temperature. Serves 6.

Peanut-Butter Cupcakes

See recipe for Peanut Butter Cupcakes on page 234. Substitute 1 cup rice flour and ½ cup potato flour for the 1½ cups whole-wheat flour called for in that recipe.

Banana Cupcakes

See recipe for Banana Cupcakes on page 234. Substitute ⅔ cup rice flour and ⅓ cup soy flour and ½ cup potato flour for 1½ cups whole-wheat flour called for in that recipe.

Banana Gingerbread

See recipe for Banana Gingerbread on page 235. Substitute ⅔ cup rice flour and ⅔ cup rye flour for 1⅓ cups whole-wheat flour called for in that recipe.

Apple Sauce Cake

See recipe for Apple Sauce Cake on page 235. Substitute 1 cup rice flour, 1 cup potato flour for the two cups whole-wheat flour called for in that recipe.

Molasses Fruit Bars

See recipe for Molasses Fruit Bars on page 240. Substitute ¾ cup rye pastry flour, ¾ cup rice flour for 1½ cups whole-wheat flour called for in that recipe. Substitute ½ cup soybean milk for ½ cup milk called for in that recipe.

Lemon Oatmeal Cookies

See recipe for Lemon Oatmeal Cookies on page 242. Substitute ¾ cup rice flour for ¾ cup whole-wheat flour called for in that recipe.

Oat Macaroons

See recipe for Bran Macaroons on page 242. Substitute 2 tablespoons potato flour for 2 tablespoons whole-wheat flour called for in that recipe. Substitute 1½ cups rolled oats for 1½ cups wheat bran called for in that recipe.

Gravies

Use any good gravy recipe, substituting potato flour for whole-wheat flour in equal amounts.

Soy Milk

See recipe for Soy Milk on page 95.

Soybean Cheese

See recipe for Soybean Cheese on page 95.

Cornmeal Pie Crust
(This is ideal for pumpkin pie.)

Grease a pie pan very generously with butter. Grease it with twice as much butter as you would ordinarily use for greasing a pan. Pack yellow cornmeal into the pan, using about ¼ cup. Cover pan entirely with yellow cornmeal. Shake off any excess very gently so as not to disturb that which clings to the sides of the pan. Pour in pumpkin-pie filling carefully and fill pan as full as possible. Bake as for any pumpkin pie.

Wheatless Pie Crust

1 *cup rye pastry flour*
1 *cup potato flour*
½ *cup butter or soy oil*

½ *teaspoon baking powder*
ice water

Mix and sift dry ingredients. Cut in shortening. Add as much ice water as needed to form a soft dough. Wrap with wax paper and put in refrigerator for about 2 hours.

Filling for Pies

Use any fillings under section of "Pies and Fillings" that contain ingredients to which you are not allergic. Or fill with fresh fruit filling sweetened with honey to taste.

Fruit Filling

1 *quart desired fruit*
⅓ *cup honey*

¼ *cup fruit juice*
2 *teaspoons butter*

Blend ingredients and fill pie.

Gentle and Transition Diets

Not everyone is fortunate enough to get off to a flying start in eating the Health Way. Those with ulcers, colon problems, colitis, recent stomach surgery, etc. to those who are just recovering from surgery or illness require a more gentle diet. A diet composed of these foods is not, of course always perfect nutritionally. But during the brief transition back to health, compromises are often needed.

Slowly introduce the healthy fiber plant foods into your diet . . . grated and minced salads, fresh sprouts, fresh fruits and the whole grains, especially the oat bran and psyllium husk powder mixture. See page 345.

These recipes are created not to outline a complete diet but to make the gentle diet more interesting, appetizing and as nutritionally correct as possible. People on recovering diets must have ample vitamin-mineral supplements, especially vitamin C, green barley, spirulina powders and live juices. See pages 300/301. For stomach, ulcer and colon problems . . . 3 times a day drink this healing combination—freshly squeezed 2/3 cabbage juice, 1/3 fresh celery and apple juice (remove seeds).

The old idea of dull, blah foods for invalids is outmoded. Unusual flavors may be introduced without harm in the gentle diet, but keep in mind that although the invalid's appetite may be tempted, foods with strong or harsh flavors can be distasteful to those in poor health. Judgment should be used in adapting the seasonings in these recipes to the individual. Very often seasonings of any kind are not allowed and must be eliminated from these recipes. This may also be true of other foods. Obviously these are general diets adaptable to many persons and may need to be individualized according to their possible allergies and immediate health requirements. Your daily journal helps monitor food reactions. See page 364.

Pureed and Juiced Foods

Many foods that ordinarily could not be used in gentle diets can be adapted by juicing, pureeing, blending or straining the foods. Pureeing is easily done with blenders, strainers, food processors or juicers.

Liquefied and Fresh Juiced Foods

The juicer, food processor and blender are great for preparing foods for gentle or bland diets and baby foods. Fibers of fresh fruits and vegetables juiced can be tolerated on most gentle diets. Any raw or cooked fruit or vegetable can be liquefied and added to skim milk or non-dairy (nut, rice or soy) milks, broth or soups. Live fresh juices super charge your energy level and immune system, and maximize your body's health power. You may fortify your liquid meal with green barley or spirulina powder for extra nutrition.

Suggestions for Bland and Gentle Diets

There are many recipes throughout this book that can be either used as they are or adapted to the bland, gentle diet. Also, most of the recipes for fruit and vegetable juices under the section "Drink Health The Live Juice Way" are excellent for anyone on a bland, gentle diet.

Bragg Healthy Lifestyle Promotes Super-Health

Bragg Healthy Lifestyle living consists of eating 70-80% of your diet from fresh live organically grown foods, raw vegetables, salads, fresh fruits and juices, sprouts, raw seeds, nuts and the all-natural 100% whole-grained breads, pastas & cereals and the nutritious beans and legumes — and these are the no-cholesterol, no-fat, no-salt, just "live foods" body fuel for more health that make live people. This is the reason people become revitalized and reborn into a fresh new life filled with Joy, Health, Vitality, Youthfulness, and Longevity! There are millions of Healthy Bragg Followers around the world proving this works!

Pure Water is Important for Health

To the days of the aged it addeth length;
To the might of the strong it added strength;
It freshens the heart, it brings the sight;
'Tis like quaffing a goblet of morning light;

The body is 65% water and pure, steam distilled (chemical-free) water is important for total health. 7-9 glasses of pure liquids a day are best. See back pages for ordering the Bragg Book "Shocking Truth about Water".

Beef Broth

2 lbs round steak,	*1 onion, sliced*
cut in squares	*1 teaspoon Bragg Aminos*
1/4 cup celery, chopped	*pinch Italian herbs*

Sautee meat, onion and seasonings in saucepan. Add ample distilled water to cover meat, then add celery. Simmer slowly 1 to 2 hours, adding more water if necessary. Strain, cool and skim off fat.

Beef-Vegetable Broth

1 lb lean beef or 2 small	*3 celery stalks, chopped*
soup bones and meat	*2 sprigs parsley*
1 teaspoon Bragg Aminos	*pinch Italian herbs*
1 cup distilled water	*vegetables of choice*

Remove fat from meat and place in pressure cooker with vegetables, celery, seasonings and water. Cook 20 to 25 minutes. Strain. Cool and skim off fat. Any excess, freeze in ice-cube trays to use as needed.

Pureed Vegetable Soup in 8 Minutes !

Pureed soups provide an excellent means of introducing vegetables into the restricted diet. Use one or more vegetables of choice; sliced carrots, onions, potatoes, zucchini, etc. Steam 8 minutes in steamer basket using distilled water. For seasoning variety add as desired to water (fresh garlic, Italian or salad herbs, Bragg Liquid Aminos, frozen stock cubes, etc.). Blend steamed vegetables and liquid in blender. Add more distilled water if needed, serve. Garnish with crumbled tofu, minced parsley and a sprinkle of Brewers yeast flakes.

Cream of Mushroom Soup

1/2 lb mushrooms and stems	*3 tbs tofu (optional)*
2 cups distilled water	*1/2 cup soy or skim milk*
3 tablespoons potato flour	*1/2 teaspoon Bragg Aminos*
2 tablespoons olive oil	*pinch Italian herbs*

Slice mushrooms, sautee in oil. Puree blend, add flour and tofu to milk and water, mix all ingredients to smoothness. Heat again, stirring until heated. Garnish with lowfat yogurt. Serves 4.

Cream of Celery Soup

1-1/2 cups evaporated milk
1 cup boiling water
1 cup meat or veg stock
1 tbs whole-wheat or potato flour
1 tablespoon olive oil

2 cups chopped celery
1 sliced onion
1 tablespoon minced chives
1 tablespoon salt free butter
1/2 teaspoon Bragg Aminos

Steam or boil celery and onion in water until just tender. Blend or puree and add to chicken, meat or vegetable stock (made from fresh stock or frozen stock cubes). Add milk (or non-dairy) and seasoning. Melt butter, blend with whole wheat or potato flour and olive oil and stir into soup. Heat and serve. Serves 4.

Cream of Spinach Soup

Use above recipe for Cream of Celery Soup, replacing celery with 3/4 cup cooked spinach and stems. Variation: Any fresh vegetable of your choice can make a creamed soup.

Jellied Consomme

1 quart consomme
(see recipe on page 62)

3 tablespoons unflavored gelatin
or arrowroot powder

Mix gelatin or arrowroot powder with consomme. Allow to cool in shallow bowl. When cool, place in refrigerator; allow to chill. Cut into cubes and stir. Garnish with finely minced parsley, watercress and green onions.

PUREED VEGETABLES

Puree of Asparagus

2-1/2 lbs asparagus
pinch salad herbs
4 tablespoons butter

1 egg yolk
1/3 teaspoon Bragg Aminos
1/2 cup soy cream or milk

Steam asparagus with seasonings until tender. Cut off any stem ends that are not completely tender after cooking. Puree blend in blender or food processor cooked asparagus with butter, cream and beaten egg yolk. Warm and serve plain or on whole-grain toast. Garnish with grated Parmesan or Romano cheese and Brewers yeast flakes. Serves 4.

Puree of String Beans

2 lbs string beans
1 teaspoon minced onion
1 cup chicken stock or
   1 chicken bouillon cube
   in 1 cup distilled water

pinch Italian herbs
1 cup distilled water
1 teaspoon Bragg Aminos
pinch Parmesan cheese

Remove strings from beans and slice into small pieces. Steam beans 8-10 minutes in steamer basket with distilled water, stock, minced onions and seasonings. Puree beans and liquid in blender and serve. Optional - top with lowfat yogurt or grated Parmesan cheese. Serves 6-8.

Puree of Minted Carrots

2 cups sliced carrots
1 tablespoon mint leaves,
   minced

1 teaspoon raw honey
2 tablespoons butter or
   olive oil

Steam carrots in steamer basket until lightly done. Puree carrots, liquid, oil and honey in blender. Garnish with minced fresh mint leaves. Serves 2-4.

Pureed Okra and Tomatoes

2 cups okra, sliced
2 cups tomatoes, diced
1 teaspoon parsley, minced
pinch Italian herbs

1 tablespoon olive oil
1 teaspoon Bragg Aminos
1 teaspoon chives

Cook okra in small amount of water until tender, then add tomatoes, parsley, chives, seasonings and simmer 10 minutes. Puree in blender and serve. Optional — garnish with grated Parmesan cheese or Brewers yeast flakes. Serves 4-6.

Pureed Celery Root and Eggplant

2 cups celery root, sliced
2 cups eggplant (unpeeled),
   diced

1 teaspoon onion, minced
1 tablespoon olive oil
1 teaspoon Bragg Aminos

Cook celery root (unpeeled) until tender, then peel and slice celery root and add to eggplant, onions and seasonings, then simmer 15 minutes in small amount of distilled water. Puree in blender and serve. Garnish with grated Parmesan cheese and Brewers yeast flakes. Serves 4.

Puree of Squash

2 cups summer or winter
   squash, sliced
pinch Italian herbs

1 tablespoon olive oil
1/2 teaspoon Bragg Aminos

Slice summer or winter squash, remove seeds and pulp and steam until tender in distilled water adding seasonings desired. Puree steamed squash and liquid in blender with olive oil and Bragg Aminos. Reheat and serve. Garnish with grated Parmesan cheese and Brewers yeast flakes. Serves 4.

Puree of Beets with Yogurt

2 lbs. beets
4 tablespoons lowfat yogurt

1 tablespoon olive oil
1/3 teaspoon Bragg Aminos

Cook or steam beets with skins until tender in distilled water. Puree cooked beets with liquid, add olive oil and Bragg Aminos. This is delicious hot or cold. Top with lowfat yogurt or sour cream. Serves 6.

Puree of Peas

2 cups shelled peas
1/2 tsp. onion, minced

1/2 teaspoon Bragg Aminos
2 tablespoons butter, salt-free

Cook peas and onion until tender. Puree peas, adding butter and Bragg Liquid Aminos and serve. Garnish with grated Parmesan cheese or lowfat yogurt. Serves 2 to 3.

Healthy, healing dietary fibers are fresh vegetables, fresh fruits, salads and whole grains and their products. These health builders help normalize blood pressures, cholesterol and promote healthy elimination.

Puree of Celery with Mushrooms

2 cups cut celery
1/2 cup mushrooms
button or shiitake

1 tbs virgin olive oil
pinch salad herbs
pinch Brewers yeast flakes

Cook celery, mushrooms and seasonings together until tender. Puree in blender with olive oil and seasonings. If desired as soup, add more distilled water and 1 tablespoon potato flour while cooking. Serves 3.

FRUIT COMPOTES

Prune-Plum Compote

1 cup prunes
6 Satsuma plums
1 tablespoon raw honey

1/4 teaspoon cinnamon
3 tbs soy or nut cream

Add cinnamon to prunes and plums and cook in distilled water until tender. Pit. Puree blend with honey. Top with soy or nut cream or low-fat cottage cheese. Serves 2.

Pureed Pears

4 pears, halved, seeded
1 clove

1 cup pineapple juice,
unsweetened

Cook pears in pineapple juice with clove for 10 minutes. Remove clove. Puree blend pears with liquid. Serve plain or top with soy or nut cream or low-fat cottage cheese. Serves 2 to 3.

Puree of Apricots

1 dozen apricots
fresh or dried

1 teaspoon grated orange rind
1 tablespoon raw honey

Cook ingredients in small amount of distilled water until tender. Puree blend. Serve plain or with soy or nut cream. Serves 4.

Puree of Minted Apples

2 cups apples, cored,   4 tablespoons mint leaves,
    quartered, peeled-optional   minced
1 tablespoon honey   3 tbs distilled water

Cook apples until tender. Add mint and raisins if desired during last 5 minutes of cooking. Puree in blender with liquid, add honey if desired. Top with soy or nut cream. Serves 3.

Apricot and Banana Compote

1 dozen apricots fresh or dried   1 tbs raw honey
2 ripe bananas   soy or nut cream

Cook apricots until tender in small amount of distilled water. Puree blend with honey, then cool. Before serving add bananas (or fresh fruit of choice) and blend with apricot puree. Top with soy or nut cream or low-fat cottage cheese. Serves 3.

Souffle Base

Many delicious souffles can be prepared for the gentle diet using this recipe as a base and adding suggested ingredients listed below or using other variations as desired.

1 tbs virgin olive oil   2 eggs fertile, free-range
2 tbs potato flour   1 cup soy or skim milk
1 tsp Bragg Liquid Aminos

Mix flour and oil in pan, stirring slowly add milk and boil for 2 minutes, reduce heat and simmer for 8-12 minutes, stirring frequently. Allow to cool to room temperature. Stir in beaten eggs, Bragg Aminos and seasonings desired. Add one or more of the ingredients listed below, making sure they are as dry as possible. If using a vegetable puree, make them thick, never thin or watery.

- One cup pureed kale, mustard or dandelion greens.
- 1-1/2 cups pureed asparagus or zucchini.
- 1 cup pureed celery or steamed pureed spinach.
- Combination of 1 cup pureed peas and 1 cup pureed carrots that have been lightly cooked with a little onion.

After adding one or more of above cooked ingredients to the souffle base, turn into oiled baking dish, bake at 300°F. for 25 minutes. Last 5 minutes garnish with parmesan or soy cheese.

FOOD FOR THOUGHT

Thomson, in his poem, "The Seasons," written two hundred and twenty-four years ago, pays the following tribute to a diet composed of seeds and vegetable products: —

"With such a liberal hand has Nature flung
These seeds abroad, blown them about in winds —
But who their virtues can declare? who pierce,
With vision pure, into those secret stores
Of health and life and joy — the food of man,
While yet he lived in innocence and told
A length of golden years, unfleshed in blood?
A stranger to the savage arts of life —
Death, rapine, carnage, surfeit, and disease —
The lord, and not the tyrant of the world."

Most assuredly I do believe that body and mind are much influenced by the kind of food habitually depended upon. I can never stray among the village people of our windy capes without now and then coming upon a human being who looks as if he had been split, salted, and dried, like the salt fish which has built up his arid organism. If the body is modified by the food which nourishes it, the mind and character very certainly will be modified by it also. We know enough of their close connection with each other to be sure of that without any statistical observation to prove it.

— Oliver Wendell Holmes

The word "vegetarian" is not derived from "vegetable," but from the Latin, homo vegetus, meaning among the Romans a strong, robust, thoroughly healthy man.

An intellectual feast — Professor Louis Agassiz in his early manhood visited Germany to consult Oken, the transcendentalist in zoological classification. "After I had delivered to him my letter of introduction," he once said to a friend, "Oken asked me to dine with him, and you may suppose with what joy I accepted the invitation. The dinner consisted only of potatoes, boiled and roasted; but it was the best dinner I ever ate; for there was Oken. Never before were such potatoes grown on this planet; for the mind of the man seemed to enter into what we ate sociably together, and I devoured his intellect while munching his potatoes."

APPENDIX

ENJOY THE BRAGG HEALTHY LIFESTYLE FOR A LIFETIME OF SUPER HEALTH

In a broad sense, "Bragg Healthy Lifestyle for the Total Person" is a combination of physical, mental, emotional, social and the spiritual components. The ability of the individual to function effectively in his environment depends on how smoothly these components function as a whole. Of all the qualities that comprise an integrated personality, a totally healthy, fit body is one of the most desirable. . . so start today for achieving your health goals!

A person may be said to be totally physically fit if he functions as a total personality with efficiency and without pain or discomfort of any kind. This is to have a Painless, Tireless, Ageless Body, possessing sufficient muscular strength and endurance to maintain a healthy posture and successfully carry on the duties imposed by life and the environment, to meet emergencies satisfactorily and have enough energy for recreation and social obligations after the "work day" has ended. It is to meet the requirements for his environment through possessing the resilience to recover rapidly from fatigue, tension, stress and strain of daily living without the aid of stimulants, drugs or alcohol, and enjoy natural recharging sleep at night and awaken fit and alert in the morning for the challenges of the new fresh day ahead.

Keeping the body totally healthy and fit is not a job for the uninformed or the careless person. It requires an understanding of the body and of a healthy lifestyle and then following that lifestyle for a long, happy life. The results of the "Bragg Healthy Lifestyle" is to wake up the possibilities within you, rejuvenate your body, mind and soul to total balanced health . . . It's within your reach, so don't procrastinate, start today! Our hearts go out to touch your heart with nourishing, caring love for your total health.

Patricia Bragg and Paul C. Bragg

Dear friend, I wish above all things that thou may prosper and be in health even as the soul prospers. - 3 John 2

Chart for "Sweet" Herbs,

	Soups	Salads	Cheese and Eggs	Fish	Meat
ALLSPICE					
ANISE LEAF					
ANISEED					
BASIL	Pot-herb in soups. In tomato, bean, or turtle soups	With tomatoes, celery, or celery root	With shirred, scrambled, creamed eggs, omelet, or cheese soufflés	With butter sauce, particularly with mackerel	In stews, or with chopped meat. Pot-herb in stews
BAY LEAF	Alone in any soup or mixed with other herbs			In boiled fish	In kidney stews and with other meats. Particularly good with beef. With tomato sauce for meats
BURNET	Blended with other herbs	Blended with other herbs			
CARDAMOM SEED					

Herb Seeds, and Spices

	Poultry	Fruits and Vegetables	Breads, Cakes, and Sweets	
(continued)				
(allspice)			In puddings, cakes, relishes, frostings, jellies, sweet sauce	It resembles a mixture of cinnamon, nutmeg, and cloves—therefore called "allspice." Actually it is one fruit.
(anise leaf)			In cake	
(aniseed)			In puddings, custards, pastries, frostings, cookies	
(basil)	In fricassees or with any fowl with tomato sauce	With stewed or broiled tomatoes, with peas, with celery root, with onions, with new potatoes		Flavor is a blend of licorice and anise and sometimes can be used as seasoning in place of pepper. Flavor also resembles cloves. A highly aromatic, sweet herb.
(bay leaf)	Mixed with other herbs in fricassees	In stewed tomatoes or zucchini		Very strong—use in moderation. Remove from soups or stews before serving. In chopped meats, chop very fine and blend well with other spices.
(burnet)				Suggests cucumber flavor.
(cardamom seed)			Breads, rolls, & pastries, especially Swedish	One seed often used in hot beverages for flavor, such as in mint tea or other herb teas.

Chart for "Sweet" Herbs, Herb

	Soups	Salads	Cheese and Eggs	Fish	Meat
CARAWAY LEAF	Blended with other herbs	Alone or with other herbs			In stews
CARAWAY SEED			With sharp cheeses	Sauce for fish	Pork, liver, kidneys
CAYENNE				All fish sparingly	All meats sparingly
CELERY SEED	Alone or blended	Alone or blended	Alone or blended	Alone or blended	Alone or blended
CHERVIL	In spinach soup	In French dressing	Alone or blended with other herbs in egg dishes	In butter sauce for fish	Sauce for veal cutlets or in sauces for beef
CHILI			Mexican type egg and cheese dishes	Cocktail sauces for oysters, shellfish	Chili con carne
CHIVES	Alone or blended	Alone or blended	In omelets or eggs of any kind. Mixed with cottage cheese	Sauce for filet of sole. With crab	Alone or blended for stews, or roasts, or chopped as garnishing
CINNA-MON					
CLOVE					With pork

Seeds, and Spices (*continued*)

	Poultry	Fruits and Vegetables	Breads, Cakes, and Sweets
(*continued*)			
(caraway leaf)			The roots of the caraway plant, when they are young, make a delicious vegetable.
(caraway seed)		Sauerkraut	Rye bread & crackers
(cayenne)			Sometimes combined with spicy sweet foods such as cookies, beverages, etc. A very strong spice, to be used cautiously.
(celery seed)	Stuffing and cooking fowl	Alone or blended	Use wherever the flavor of celery is desired.
(chervil)	In sauce for broiled chicken		Resembles parsley.
(chili)	Chicken tamale		In many types of Mexican dishes and in Italian sauces for spaghetti, etc.
(chives)	With sauce for roast chicken or for basting liquor	With mushrooms, tomatoes	Very mild, delicate, onion-like flavor.
(cinnamon)		Applesauce, stewed or baked fruit	Cakes, puddings, preserving
(clove)		Baked fruit	Puddings, syrups, jellies

Chart for "Sweet" Herbs, Herb

	Soups	Salads	Cheese and Eggs	Fish	Meat
CORI- ANDER	In Mexican soups				Pork
CURRY			With cream sauces	With shell- fish	
CUMIN	Alone or blended		In cheese		
DILL		Blended		In fish sauce	In stews
FENNEL		Used fresh in salads		With cook- ing fish & fish sauces	
FILE	Used in Creole dishes—to thicken gumbo				In tomato sauces for meats
GINGER					
LAVEN- DER					

Seeds, and Spices (*continued*)

	Poultry	*Fruits and Vegetables*	*Breads, Cakes, and Sweets*	
(*continued*)				
(coriander)			Rolls & pastries	One seed sometimes used in hot teas such as mint tea.
(curry)	In sauce for fowl	With rice		A strong blend that is a mixture of coriander, fenugreek turmeric, cumin, celery, bay leaves, black pepper, cardamom, savory, cayenne, orange peel, clove, and nutmeg.
(cumin)			In pastries	
(dill)		Sauerkraut, potatoes		A combination of the flavor of fennel and mint, sometimes preferred to both herbs because of blended flavor.
(fennel)		Blended, especially with peas	Pastries	
(filé)		In vegetable casseroles		
(ginger)			In baked goods, preserves	Used in beverages— ginger tea.
(lavender)			In candies, for flavoring jellies	Used as a pot-herb in old times. Now popular only in sweets, but the adventuresome cook will try it sparingly in stews and casserole dishes.

Chart for "Sweet" Herbs, Herb

	Soups	Salads	Cheese and Eggs	Fish	Meat
LEMON BALM		In fruit salads		With broiled or baked fish or fish sauces	In sauces for meats
MACE	In bouillons, pea soup			With fish & fish sauces; dash in oyster stew	
MAR-JORAM	Blended with other herbs		Blended with other herbs for ramekins both cheese & eggs	In butter sauce for white fish	With lamb, pork, or beef. In chopped meat. With steak & chops
MINT	In cream soups. In split or fresh pea soup	With fruit salads, or raw cabbage		With mackerel	With roast lamb
MUSTARD			Dash in cheese dishes	Fish sauces	Pork and meat sauces
NASTUR-TIUM		In fruit & vegetable salads	Chopped stems in scrambled eggs		

Seeds, and Spices (*continued*)

	Poultry	Fruits and Vegetables	Breads, Cakes, and Sweets
(*continued*)			
(lemon balm)			A delicate combination of mint and lemon flavors.
(mace)		In stewed cherries	In preserving cakes	Closely resembles nutmeg—to many more pleasing.
(marjoram)	In stuffing. Over roasted goose or with game	With spinach, tomato, or mushroom. With vegetable sauces		There are several varieties. The "sweet" is most desirable.
(mint)		With peas, potatoes, carrots, spinach	In candies, ice cream, puddings, jellies	The choice mint is the "black" or "bluestem mint." One of the most popular herb beverages.
(mustard)				Use only the dry powdered mustard. Do not use the commercial paste varieties as they are mixed with vinegar. If paste is desired, mix with water for strong flavor, with oils or cream for milder flavor.
(nasturtium)				The whole plant can be used—leaves, shoots, flower buds, and seed pods. The last can be substituted for capers.

Chart for "Sweet" Herbs, Herb

	Soups	Salads	Cheese and Eggs	Fish	Meat
NASTUR-TIUM SEEDS		Alone	Alone in eggs	In fish sauces	
NUTMEG	Lettuce soup		Egg nogs	Baked shad	
OREGANO					In lamb and pork dishes
PAPRIKA	Coloring for soups	In salad dressings, toppings		With fish sauce, shellfish, & all fish	Coloring for sauces
PARSLEY	Alone or blended	Alone or blended	Alone or blended	Alone or blended	Alone or blended
PEPPER-CORN	Alone or blended	Alone or blended	Alone or blended	Alone or blended	
ROSE-MARY	Alone or blended		Blended in egg dishes		Over roasting beef. With veal stew. With roast pork. In sauces for meats or spaghetti
RUE		For bitter effect in salads			
SAFFRON				In fish sauces	
SAGE	Blended		Blended with cheese		Over roasting pork

Seeds, and Spices (*continued*)

	Poultry	Fruits and Vegetables	Breads, Cakes, and Sweets	
(*continued*)				
(nasturtium seeds)		Alone		
(nutmeg)		With cauli-flower, spinach, spiced fruit	In baked foods, sauces, puddings	Always use whole nutmeg, grating a little as needed. Ready-powdered nutmeg will not retain the flavor.
(oregano)				
(paprika)		On sweet corn on cob, baked potatoes		
(parsley)	Alone or blended			
(pepper-corn)		In vegetables		
(rose-mary)	Blended for fricassees. With chicken or rabbit	With peas		Very popular in Italian cooking for spaghetti, etc. Fresh sprigs are a delightful garnish.
(rue)				Not a popular herb, but sometimes effective for a bitter touch in salads.
(saffron)		In rice	In cakes, confections, breads	For coloring as well as flavoring.
(sage)	In stuffing for goose or duck and all poultry	Stewed tomatoes or string beans		

Chart for "Sweet" Herbs, Herb

	Soups	Salads	Cheese and Eggs	Fish	Meat
SASSA-FRAS	For thickening soups such as gumbos				
SAVORY	Alone or blended in pea soup		Blended	With trout	Over roasting pork. With veal, roasting lamb, meat sauces. In meat stuffings
TARRA-GON	In tomato juice (hot or cold)	Alone or mixed with chervil	Alone	In butter sauce for lobster. Minced on fish	In Béarnaise sauce, for meats. Minced on steak or chops
THYME	In onion soup. Blended with other herbs in vegetable or oyster soups. In chowders		Blended	Alone or blended. With oysters	Alone or blended. For stuffing
TUR-MERIC	Adds flavor and color. Use sparingly			Dash with mustard	
WATER-CRESS	In cream soups	Alone or blended	Sparingly in egg dishes	Alone or blended, added to cream sauce for fish	Garnishing. Over roasting or broiling meats & game

Seeds, and Spices (*continued*)

	Poultry	Fruits and Vegetables	Breads, Cakes, and Sweets
(*continued*)			
(sassafras)			
(savory)		In string beans, peas	Very mild sagelike flavor. Summer savory is best flavoring variety.
(tarragon)	Alone	With mushrooms	
(thyme)	Blended	With peas, carrots, onions	Very pungent and powerful. Use sparingly.
(turmeric)			Mixes well with mustard and other spices.
(water- cress)	Sparingly	Boiled with greens	

How to Grow a Savory Herb Garden

SAVORY herbs obtain a special flavoring quality from their characteristic essential oils, in either their seeds or their leaves. These are at their best when fresh, but they can be quite satisfactory when dried.

The cultivation of the savory herbs is not difficult, and even the novice can be successful in growing a very satisfactory herb garden by following a few simple directions. Many of the savory herbs can be grown in cold frames during the winter in mild climates; in the warm southern sections of the country, quite a few of them can be grown in the open all the year round. In the more northern sections of this country they must be protected carefully. Some, of course, will not stand extreme heat or direct exposure to the sun, and these, when grown in the warmer parts of the country, require shade and plenty of moisture.

It may not be practical for every gardener in every section of the country to grow a large, complete list of herbs for his kitchen, and yet even a limited number of herbs can contribute greatly to the enjoyment of creating really fine foods.

Set aside a small section of the garden where the biennial and perennial herbs may be grown year after year without disturbing the pollen and cultivation of other parts of the garden. The location of the herb garden should be convenient for frequent watering during dry periods. The ideal location is close to the kitchen, where small quantities of fresh herbs can be gathered almost at the moment they are wanted during the preparation of the meal. A garden about 10 feet by 10 feet, or, at the most, 10 feet by 18 feet, will supply about all the herbs the average family can use.

It is wise to plan your herb garden carefully, because certain of the herbs are annual and these must be started from seeds each year, while the biennials and perennials can remain in their allotted space more than one season. Order and neatness can be maintained in the herb garden by locating all of the biennials and perennials at one side of the plot of ground.

Because many of your plants will remain in the ground for more than one year, it is extremely important that the soil be well fertilized before the plants are started. Plow or spade the ground to a depth of 15 inches. Bone meal, cottonseed meal, and well-rotted manure can be worked into the soil down to the full depth of plowing. For each 100 square feet, use at least 5 pounds of bone meal, 5 pounds of cottonseed meal, and one bag of rich steer manure. It is of the utmost importance to mix in the fertilizer thoroughly with the soil to the full depth that the soil is broken. All lumps of soil should be broken so that it is pulverized and blended with the fertilizer. The soil must be kept well cultivated and free from weeds, and be watered frequently.

Many of the herbs can be started by sowing the seeds where the plants are to be, then thinning them to their proper spacing after they have become established. Other plants do best when started in a cold frame, in the house, or in a hotbed, and transplanted later when soil and weather conditions are favorable.

The culture of the various savory herbs does not differ greatly, but there are a few requirements that make for the better development of certain herbs.

Anise

Anise is an annual and can easily be grown from seed sown in the garden. Only very fresh seed should be used, as this plant does not develop well from older seed. The seeds should be planted in rows about 3 feet apart, with the plants 12 to 18 inches apart in the row, and about ¾ to 1 inch deep in mellow soil; if the soil is heavier, plant not quite so deep. Half a dozen plants will usually produce all of the seeds required for your kitchen.

Basil

Basil is an annual and the seeds can be started by sowing in the open ground where the plants are to remain. Sow the seeds in a drill, cover about ¾ of an inch, and then thin the plants so that they will be 12 to 14 inches apart. A very few plants are all that are needed for kitchen use for the average family.

Caraway

Caraway grows best as a biennial. In cold climates the plants need protection during the winter. Normally, caraway produces its seed after the second season. If the seed is sown during the spring and the plants carried through the winter with protection, they will produce a crop of seeds early the following season. The seeds are saved by cutting off the seed heads before the ripening seeds begin to shatter and spreading them on cloth in the shade to dry. When they are reasonably dry, they can be rubbed or shaken out of the heads, after which they should be thoroughly dried, and not washed until just before using for flavoring. But do not disregard the young shoots of tender leaves for use in salads. A dozen plants grown a foot apart in rows 3 feet apart will furnish a supply for the average kitchen.

Chives

The clumps or bunches of bulbs should be divided either in the fall or in the spring and set in the soil. They should be redivided at least once every 3 years. Aside from a fair amount of moisture and being kept free of weeds, they demand very little cultivation.

Coriander

Coriander is an annual. Plant a few seeds early in the spring, but do not allow them to become scattered or they will be a weed pest. They should be grown in 3-foot rows with the plants about 18 inches apart in the row. The seeds should be gathered when they are nearly ripe. Cut the seed heads off and spread on a tray to dry. After they are dry, they may be shaken out and cleaned.

Dill

Normally, dill does not produce seeds until the second season. But it is possible, if plants are started very early, to grow them as an annual and mature the seeds the first season. If this is desired, plants should be started indoors and transplanted later to the garden. If you wish them to grow as a biennial, sow the seed in the ground in rows 3 feet apart, with the plants 12 to 15 inches apart in the row. They require a rich soil and plenty of moisture.

Sweet Marjoram

Sweet marjoram is a perennial and requires about 2 years to ripen into seed. It can be grown as an annual and this is desirable in cold climates, because the plants require very thorough protection in the winter. The seeds are difficult to start, so either they should be grown from cuttings, or the seeds grown indoors in the early spring. This is possible as sweet marjoram can very easily be grown in flowerpots in the house.

Mint

Both peppermint and spearmint are easy to grow; in fact, they spread wildly. But the true flavoring mints are not easy to grow and must be cultivated constantly and kept within bounds. 5 or 6 plants of mint occupying a space not more than 3 by 3 feet will provide plenty of flavoring for the average family. The mint bed should be constantly cut and very frequently watered. The plants should not be allowed to grow too high if you are to have good flavoring plants.

Nasturtiums

Although the nasturtium is ordinarily considered a flower, it is excellent to include with the savory herbs. Use plants of the dwarf nasturtium and thin them to stand 6 or 8 inches apart. They require a rich soil and plenty of moisture. The first planting should be made as soon as the ground is warm in the spring, and other plantings should follow at intervals of 5 and 6 weeks.

Parsley

The moss-curled parsley is the best variety to grow for flavoring purposes. A half dozen plants are sufficient for the average family. The seeds should be very fresh, for they soon lose their vitality. They can be sown in a box in the house and the plants transplanted to a cold frame and then to the garden. They should be thinned to stand 6 to 8 inches apart. The plants will continue to produce fresh growth if the leaves are kept closely cut.

Sage

Sage plants can be grown from seed and should stand about 2 feet apart. One or two plants will supply enough seasoning. For the best dried sage, the leaves should be picked before the blooming stage. The sage can be dried in the oven, but should be thoroughly dried before placing in airtight containers.

Savory

Summer savory is an annual. Sow the seeds in open ground in the early spring, thin the plants to stand 6 to 8 inches apart. The rows need not be more than 18 inches apart.

◇◇

Tarragon

Tarragon is a perennial. Cuttings should be rooted in a propagating bed and the roots divided. Whenever the flower stems appear, they should be cut out. The plants should be set about 1 foot apart. They require a moist, but not wet soil. Tarragon plants are not very hardy, and in winter the stems should be cut down and the plants well covered with leaves. The tarragon bed should be relocated every three or four years to avoid disease.

Thyme

Thyme can be grown from seed, and new plants should be started every two or three years or they will not produce a good grade of tender leaves. They should be set about 18 inches apart, in rows wide enough to cultivate. They require a rich soil and plenty of moisture.

Watercress

Watercress is the only herb mentioned here that will not grow practically in the herb garden. It grows best in shallow ponds of water, especially in localities where limestone springs occur. It can, however, be grown successfully on beds of rich soil if provided with an abundance of lime and kept moist. The watercress grown in this manner should be in a cold frame, or in a special framework of boards for protection, and it also requires considerable shade in hot weather. Either the seeds or the tips of the stems will root quite readily if placed in water fortified by lime. The soil should be specially prepared for watercress, working it over and screening it and then adding enough lime to make the surface white. The lime must be worked thoroughly into the soil and then moistened. The plants should be set 6 inches apart in each direction. Plants will not stand freezing nor exposure to extreme heat.

The Window-Box Herb Garden

It is not always possible to have your own herb garden although it is very desirable both from the standpoint of variety and the quantities of herbs you can grow, and because an herb garden is a delightful hobby. But if you cannot have your outdoor garden, you need not be without a small indoor garden.

In the fall, before the freezing weather begins, such savory herbs as parsley, basil, sweet marjoram, and chives may be placed in flowerpots or in a window box, and often the window box can be kept in a south window during the winter.

In the southern sections of the United States these plants can be kept in good condition all winter long. In the window box good soil is even more important, if possible, than in the garden plot. Here is a good mixture:

1 *part sharp sand*
1 *part well-rotted cow manure*
2 *or* 3 *parts of good garden loam*

Well-rotted sods contribute to a rich foundation, and then the rotted cow manure, sand, and a small quantity of bone meal can be added. The soil should be very thoroughly mixed and screened through a coarse screen.

The window box can be any size, provided it is at least 8 inches deep. Place a layer of broken stones about an inch in thickness at the bottom of the box to provide for efficient drainage, and be sure there are several holes in the bottom of the box to allow excess water to drain off. Do not crowd the plants. They should be watered frequently, or as often as the soil becomes dry.

By painting a window box in gay colors you have a lovely flower decoration for your window, as well as herbs for your kitchen.

Organic Gardening
Good Nutrition Starts in the Ground

A chapter on gardening in a cookbook is not so strange as it might appear at first glance. Food, no matter how cleverly or artfully cooked, is no better than the original ingredients from which it is prepared.

This is a sad day for all of civilization because man is slowly losing the great vital Health he could possess. Look at China and India with their thousands upon thousands suffering with every form of vicious and fatal malnutrition. History tells us these were happy countries at one time, where people had an abundance to eat, and lived long, happy lives. But somewhere in their culture of the land they lost the art of fertilizing—they took out crops in abundance, but they failed to put back the necessary minerals to produce nutritionally strong foods. This went on for years and years and finally they "mined out" their soil. The foods that the land produced were meager and failed to nourish and sustain the human body.

Beautiful, bountiful farms that once used to produce crops high in nutritional value, which in turn produced healthy vigorous people, animals, and fowl became barren, bare, desolate ground. Finally, with nothing growing on it to protect it from rain and wind, all the top soil that was left was blown away. This happened in our own dust bowl in the last few years. That is the reason today that great areas of India and China are deserts or barren wastes in which nothing will grow. The reason? The top soil—the life-producing top soil—either is minerally dead or has disappeared.

When our forefathers arrived on that part of the North American continent which is now the U.S.A., they found a most priceless treasure—a wonderfully rich 9-inch top soil, which it had taken nature millions of years to prepare. For millions of years the leaves, falling from the trees, had rotted and made a rich, minerally powerful top soil. Grass crops, wild weeds, wild grains, droppings of thousands of birds and animals produced a rich, fertile soil. It was an agricultural paradise in which the first American produced his crops.

Today Thanksgiving Day commemorates the abundance produced by our Pilgrim forefathers. The soil was so rich with Health and life-giving minerals that one of the most hearty and sturdy races of men and women prospered. The rich land produced the people who fought the Revolutionary War, won our freedom, and gave birth to these United States of America. It produced the pioneers who blazed a trail from the Atlantic to the Pacific Ocean —men and women with physical endurance that has never been equaled in the world's history—men and women who could fight and win when the greatest of odds were against them: forests full of blood-hungry, wild Indians, uncharted wildernesses, intense cold, burning deserts. These makers of our republic were products of a hearty land—they were no weaklings. They were tough, vigorous pioneers who knew no fear and won a new country by their great physical strength.

Look at the physical record of our country today. When we were attacked at Pearl Harbor on December 7, 1941, we declared war on Japan and Germany and started to raise an Army, a Navy, and a Marine Corps to defend ourselves. The flower of our youth applied for enlistment.

Then the shock came—we found that an amazingly large percentage of our young men between the ages of eighteen and thirty-five were totally unfit for any type of military service, and a lot of these young men, the cream of the crop, were suffering from bad teeth, weak, misshapen bones, broken-down flat feet, night blindness and hundreds of crippling diseases produced by nutritional, mineral, and vitamin deficiency. The same sad facts repeated themselves during Korea, Vietnam and recently Desert Storm.

Today, there are millions of people in our hospitals and nursing homes, which are crowded to capacity. Outside their walls we have millions more crippled with arthritis, heart disease, cancer, diabetes, osteoporosis, Alzheimer's, Parkinson's, etc. (American nationwide health care costs soared to $700 billion in 1991 and this is expected to more than double by the year 2000.)

In this short period of history we "mined" our soil instead of using "organic farming." Then we took our nutritionally poor food and refined it, further destroying most of the remaining minerals and vitamins. Many people still believe that all lettuce, for example, has the same vitamin and mineral content. This is not true. One head of lettuce can be high in vitamin and mineral content, and another may have hardly any nutritional value. This is because the mineral and, to a large extent, the vitamin content of any vegetable is determined by the mineral content of the soil on which it is grown. As the soil varies so does the health of the plant.

Healthy citizens cannot be produced from eroded, dead, depleted, chemicalized soils (Millions of pounds of petrochemicals are dumped on American farm land each year!) that have no earthworms, natural humus and organic compost. Farmers take big, bountiful crops out of the soil and put little or nothing back. Some of our soil is completely worn out; and today all over the United States there are millions of acres of farm land that have been completely "mined out" — the minerals are not in the soil —it is depleted, dead.

In thousand of instances the top soil has been so mistreated that it has been either washed away by rain or blown away by wind, and you see the naked subsoil, which will only support some rank, useless weed. Few people realize that this country is slowly but surely moving to the same agriculture tragedy that India, Africa and other countries are now suffering. When the little good top soil is gone, we shall be one of the impoverished nations.

There is a way you personally can remedy this sad tragedy. Begin with your family organic garden and / or help organize a community organic, mineralized, vegetable garden where you can eat not only delicious, but highly mineralized foods. With a little space in your back yard, you can have a mineralized garden —a Health garden.

How to Make a Compost Pile

It is very simple to make a compost pile. Just set aside a special space where you can keep all the dead leaves that fall from trees. What a crime it is to burn this rich material! Place on this pile all the peelings from fruits and vegetables, which are ordinarily thrown away, all the fish and chicken bones, and cuttings from your lawn—grass or any other green shrubbery.

Make a square 6 feet by 6 feet. Cover with a layer of 6 inches of dead leaves, grass cuttings, vegetable and fruit leavings. On top of this place a layer of 2 inches of manure. Over that put a thin sprinkling of earth and ground limestone. In 3 to 4 months it will become real, rich compost to be worked into the soil of your vegetable garden. At times when the compost pile is working, the inside temperature of the pile will be from 140° to 145°F.

Put these rich organic materials back into the soil. Give nature a chance to work her amazing miracle of transferring them, through growing food, to your body. Reclaim your true heritage of Health and well-being from the soil and the food you eat.

Our sincere blessings to you dear friends, who make our lives so worthwhile and fulfilled by reading our teachings on natural living as our Creator laid down for us all to follow . . . Yes—he wants us all to follow the simple path of natural living and this is what we teach in our books and health crusades world-wide. Our prayers reach out to you for the best in health and happiness for you and your loved ones. This is the birthright He gives us all . . . but we must follow the laws He has laid down for us, so we can reap this precious health, physically, mentally and spiritually!

Paul C. Bragg   *Patricia Bragg*

"Teach me Thy way, O Lord;
and lead me in a plain path . . ."
Psalms 97:11

INDEX

◇◇

PLEASE REMEMBER
YOUR HEALTH IS YOUR WEALTH

Open thou mine eyes, that I may behold wondrous things out of thy law. —Psalm 119:18

Of all the knowledge, that most worth having is knowledge about health. The first requisite of a good life is to be a healthy person. —Herbert Spencer

---

When you have been stricken by illness, your new car, your new home, your new big bank balance—all these fade into unimportance until you have regained your vigor and zest for living again.
—Peter J. Steincrohn, M.D.

If your food is devitalized, the important elements of nourishment have been removed, or if its value has been diminished by wrong cooking processes—you can then starve to death on a full stomach.

The unexamined life is not worth living. It is a time to re-evaluate your past as a guide to your future. —Socrates

---

Morning Resolve

I will this day live a simple, sincere and serene life, repelling promptly every thought of impurity, discontent, anxiety, discouragement and self-seeking. I will cultivate cheerfulness, happiness, charity and the love of brotherhood; exercising economy in expenditure, generosity in giving, carefulness in conversation and diligence in appointed service. I pledge fidelity to every trust and a childlike faith in God, in particular, I will be faithful in those habits of prayer, study, work, physical exercise, deep breathing and good posture. I shall fast one 24 hour period each week, eat only natural foods and get sufficient sleep each night. I will make every effort to improve myself physically, mentally and spiritually every day.

Morning prayer used by Paul C. Bragg and Patricia Bragg

SEND FOR IMPORTANT FREE HEALTH BULLETINS

Let Patricia Bragg send you, your relatives and friends the latest News Bulletins on Health and Nutrition Discoveries. These are sent periodically. Please enclose two stamps for each U.S.A. name listed. Foreign listings send international postal reply coupons. Please print or type addresses, thank you.

HEALTH SCIENCE Box 7, Santa Barbara, California 93102 U.S.A.

●
_____
Name

_____ (___) _____
Address   Phone

_____
City   State   Zip Code

●
_____
Name

_____ (___) _____
Address   Phone

_____
City   State   Zip Code

●
_____
Name

_____ (___) _____
Address   Phone

_____
City   State   Zip Code

●
_____
Name

_____ (___) _____
Address   Phone

_____
City   State   Zip Code

●
_____
Name

_____ (___) _____
Address   Phone

_____
City   State   Zip Code

BRAGG ALL NATURAL LIQUID AMINOS
Order Form

Delicious, Healthy Alternative to Tamari-Soy Sauce

BRAGG LIQUID AMINOS — Nutrition you need...taste you will love...a family favorite for over 75 years. A delicious source of nutritious life-renewing protein from soybeans only. Add to or spray over casseroles, soups, sauces, gravies, potatoes, popcorn, and vegetables. An ideal "pick-me-up" broth at work, home or the gym. Gourmet health replacement for Tamari & Soy Sauce. Start today and add more Amino Acids for healthy living to your daily diet — the easy BRAGG LIQUID AMINOS Way!

DASH or SPRAY for NEW TASTE DELIGHTS! PROVEN & ENJOYED BY MILLIONS.

DELICIOUS, NUTRITIOUS, FAMILY FAVORITE FOR OVER 75 YEARS!

Dash of Bragg Aminos Brings New Taste Delights to Season:
- Salads
- Dressings
- Soups
- Vegies
- Rice/Beans
- Tofu
- Tempeh
- Wok foods
- Stir-frys
- Casseroles & Potatoes
- Meats
- Poultry
- Fish
- Popcorn
- Gravies
- Sauces
- Macrobiotics

Pure Soybeans and Pure Water Only
- No Added Sodium
- No Coloring Agents
- No Preservatives
- Not Fermented
- No Chemicals
- No Additives
- No MSG

BRAGG LIQUID AMINOS

SIZE	PRICE	SHIPPING	AMT.	TOTAL $
16 oz.	$ 3.95 ea.	Please add $3.00 for 1st bottle/$1.50 for each additional bottle		
32 oz.	$ 6.45 ea.	Please add $3.90 for 1st bottle/$1.90 for each additional bottle		
16 oz.	$ 47.40 ea.	Case/12 bottles add $9.00 per case		
32 oz.	$ 77.40 ea.	Case/12 bottles add $14.00 per case		

Bragg Aminos is a food & not taxable

Total Aminos	$
Shipping & Handling	
Total Enclosed	$

Please Specify: (U.S. Funds Only)

☐ Check ☐ Money Order ☐ Cash ☐ Credit Card

Charge My Order To: ☐ Visa ☐ MasterCard

Credit Card Number: _ _ _ _ — _ _ _ _ — _ _ _ _ — _ _ _ _   Card Expires: Month | Year _ _ | _ _

MasterCard VISA Signature: _____

CREDIT CARD CUSTOMERS ONLY USE OUR FAST PHONE SERVICE: (800) 446-1990

In a hurry? Call (805) 968-1028. We can accept MasterCard & VISA phone orders only. Please prepare your order using this order form. It will speed your call & serve as your order record. Hours: 9 to 4 pm Pacific Time, Monday to Thursday ... or you can fax your order to: FAX (805) 968-1001.

Mail to: **HEALTH SCIENCE, Box 7, Santa Barbara, CA 93102 USA**

Please Print or Type – Be sure to give street & house number to facilitate delivery

A-BOF-9201

Name _____

Address _____ Apt. No. _____

City _____ State _____

( ) _____ Zip _ _ _ _ _
Phone

Bragg Aminos ---Taste You Love, Nutrition You Need

PATRICIA BRAGG N.D., Ph.D.
Angel of Health & Healing
Lecturer, Author, Nutritionist, Health Educator & Fitness Advisor to World Leaders, Glamorous Hollywood Stars, Singers, Dancers & Athletes.

Daughter of the world renowned health authority, Paul C. Bragg, Patricia Bragg has won international fame on her own in this field. She conducts Health and Fitness Seminars for Women's, Men's, Youth and Church Groups throughout the world... and promotes Bragg "How-To, Self-Health" Books in Lectures, on Radio and Television Talk Shows throughout the English-speaking world. Consultants to Presidents and Royalty, to the Stars of Stage, Screen and TV and to Champion Athletes, Patricia Bragg and her father are Co-Authors of the Bragg Health Library of Instructive, Inspiring Books that promote a healthy lifestyle for a long, vital, active life!

Patricia herself is the symbol of perpetual youth and super energy. She is a living and sparkling example of her and her father's healthy lifestyle precepts and this she shares world-wide.

A fifth generation Californian on her mother's side, Patricia was reared by the Natural Health Method from infancy. In school, she not only excelled in athletics but also won high honors in her studies and her counseling. She is an accomplished musician and dancer... as well as tennis player, swimmer and mountain climber... and the youngest woman ever to be granted a U.S. Patent. Patricia is a popular gifted Health Teacher and a dynamic, in-demand Talk Show Guest where she spreads simple, easy-to-follow health teachings for everyone.

Man's body is the Temple of the Holy Spirit, and our creator wants us filled with Joy and Health for a long walk with Him for Eternity. The Bragg Crusade of Health and Fitness (3 John 2) has carried her around the world... spreading physical, spiritual, emotional and mental health and joy. Health is our birthright and Patricia teaches how to prevent the destruction of our health from man-made wrong habits of living.

Patricia's been Health Consultant to American Presidents and to the British Royal Family, to Betty Cuthbert, Australia's "Golden Girl" who holds 16 world records and four Olympic gold medals in women's track and to New Zealand's Olympic Track Star Allison Roe. Among those who come to her for advice are some of Hollywood's top stars from Clint Eastwood to the ever youthful singing group The Beach Boys and their families, singing stars of the Metropolitan Opera and top ballet stars. Patricia's message is of world-wide appeal to the people of all ages, nationalities and walks-of-life. Those who follow the Bragg Health Books & attend the Bragg Crusades are living testimonials like Super Athlete, Ageless - Jack LaLanne—at age 14 he went from sickness to health.

Patricia Bragg inspires you to Renew, Rejuvenate & Revitalize your life with the "Bragg Healthy Lifestyle" Seminars and Lectures world-wide. These are life-changing and millions have benefited with a longer, healthier life! She would love to share her Crusade with your organizations, businesses, churches, etc. Also, she is a perfect radio and T.V. talk show guest to spread the message of health and fitness in your area.

Write or call for requests and information:
HEALTH SCIENCE, BOX 7, SANTA BARBARA, CA 93102 1-805-968-1028